Christians in the Movies

A Century of Saints and Sinners

Peter E. Dans

A SHEED & WARD BOOK

ROWMAN & LITTLEFIELD PUBLISHERS, INC.
Lanham • Boulder • New York • Toronto • Plymouth, UK

All photos: Photofest New York

Cover photos:

Top: In *Doubt*, Sister Aloysius (Meryl Streep) suspects Father Flynn (Philip Seymour Hoffman) of having an inappropriate relationship with an 8th grader.

Bottom left: In *Elmer Gantry*, itinerant preacher and con man Elmer Gantry (Burt Lancaster) stirs up his listeners with fire and brimstone oratory.

Bottom right: Joan (Renee Maria Falconetti) in ecstasy in *The Passion of Joan of Arc*.

A SHEED & WARD BOOK

ROWMAN & LITTLEFIELD PUBLISHERS, INC.

Published in the United States of America
by Rowman & Littlefield Publishers, Inc.
A wholly owned subsidary of
The Rowman & Littlefield Publishing Group, Inc.
4501 Forbes Boulevard, Suite 200, Lanham, Maryland 20706
www.rowmanlittlefield.com

Estover Road
Plymouth PL6 7PY
United Kingdom

British Library Cataloguing in Publication Information Available

Library of Congress Cataloging-in-Publication Data

Dans, Peter E.
  Christians in the movies / Peter E. Dans.
    p. cm.
  "A Sheed & Ward book."
  Includes bibliographical references and index.
  ISBN 978-0-7425-7030-6 (cloth : alk. paper) — ISBN 978-0-7425-7032-0 (electronic)
  1. Christians in motion pictures. 2. Christianity in motion pictures. I. Title.

PN1995.9.C49D36 2009
  793.43'652827—dc22   2008055812

Printed in the United States of America

For Colette

4321

121199

CONTENTS

CONTENTS

CONTENTS

CONTENTS

FOREWORD

You'd think movies would be the most ethereal of arts: luminous, mystical, sacred. I mean, it's only light—pure, sweet, holy light—that shines in the darkness of the theater's hushed and confessional darkness, playing across the snow-white screen. How else could the numinous be displayed? How else the supernatural? How else the consecrated?

Of course, it didn't quite turn out that way. You want pornography—really effective, filthy, eye-popping smut—you watch a movie. You want God, you read the Bible. Or put on some Bach. Or recite "Ash Wednesday." Or go look at Renaissance paintings. Any art, *every* art, except film. The lightest of arts, in theory, turns out to be the earthiest, in practice; the most ethereal turns out to focus on the nearly perfect human bodies of its nearly perfect stars—not *the Savior, the Lord Jesus Christ, who shall change our vile body, that it may be fashioned like unto his glorious body*, but the celebrity bodies of the matinee idols: Clara Bow, and Rudolph Valentino, and Claudette Colbert, and Clark Gable, and Grace Kelly, and on and on among the beautiful people.

We could probably construct a philosophical account of why film, the art that is most about insubstantial light, should prove the art most fascinated by the substance of the human body: the angles of the face, the swish of walking legs, the cock of an eyebrow, the anger of arms set akimbo. It might have something to do with the simultaneous mysticism and physicality that the great philosopher of light, the 13th-century Robert Grosseteste, captured. And it might have something to do with the inherently eye-capturing quality of the face, the human necessity to see the face of others, that the great 20th-century anti-mystical mystic Emmanuel Levinas observed.

The funny thing is that we don't actually have to build a high, intellectual explanation of the tension down at the root of film. We can go out and see it, anytime we want, down at the theater or home with a DVD. Movies themselves always know—at some level, regardless of how conscious it may be in the actors and the crew—that film is a divided art. It wants to be spiritual even while it ties itself to be earthly. It wants to make the divine comedy even while filming the human comedy. Why should this surprise us? Like everything else, even movies come under the rule of creation, *according to the working whereby he is able even to subdue all things unto himself.*

Sometimes, when I see Claudette Colbert and Clark Gable in the 1934 *It Happened One Night*—a movie about, in essence, the lengths to which an impossibly beautiful and highly aroused couple will go *not* to sleep together before they're married—I think the worst thing that ever happened to Hollywood was the death of the old Hays Code and the Legion of Decency. Censorship (if that's what it was) proved good for film: Naked breasts are eye-catching, and well-sculpted nudes don't need much dialogue. So what happens when you can't show them? Turns out, you have to tell a story instead.

Whole genres of movies depended on the Legion of Decency for their success. The screwball comedy, for instance, which gets all of its drive from its lack of sex. Why wouldn't two people, arguing as much as Katharine Hepburn and Cary Grant are in the 1938 *Bringing Up Baby*, simply walk away from each other? Because the sexual attraction between them is so high. Get rid of the code, and the pair sleep together in the first few minutes, and then what does a poor director do for the rest of the film? The Legion of Decency may have been the Catholics' greatest contribution to the golden age of Hollywood.

Of course, it wasn't their only contribution—and the real success of this book, an account of Christians in the movies, is the way Peter Dans makes us realize that movies are, in their origin, about faith: *Origin* in the sense of beginning, and *origin* in the sense of philosophical root. There is something religious that movies began by doing, something that the art form itself wants to do, and it is a sign of the weakness of our age—the weakness of our age in filmmaking and the weakness of our age in culture—that movies seem no longer able to do it.

Peter Dans seems to have spent countless hours looking at movies, and in his marvelously encyclopedic way, he begins by walking the reader through the great religious silent films, from the 1905 *Life and Passion of Jesus Christ* to the 1928 *The Passion of Joan of Arc*. He knows the early 1930s talkies that set in place all the golden-age conventions, from the 1931 *Miracle Woman* on.

What he demonstrates, as well, is the importance of 1938—the moment when, with the release of *Angels with Dirty Faces* and *Boys Town*, Hollywood decided to take seriously the faith of Catholics. Well, maybe *seriously* is too strong a word. How profound, really, can any movie be, when it stars the Dead End Kids or Mickey Rooney? But think of it this way: One solution to the religious problem of film is the great, and very Protestant, Cecil B. DeMille–style epic—the spectacle and extravaganza, the biblical block-buster—that dominated the movies of the 1920s and early 1930s and would return in the 1950s and early 1960s. And yet, that style of Christian film-making brackets the late 1930s and the 1940s, when the human story was thought to be the vehicle for talking about faith and redemption.

This is the era of *Song of Bernadette* (1943), and *The Keys of the Kingdom* (1944), and *Going My Way* (1944), and *The Bishop's Wife* (1947), and *Come to the Stable* (1949). This is the time of *Brother Orchid* (1940), and *One Foot in Heaven* (1941), and *God Is My Co-Pilot* (1945), and *3 Godfathers* (1948), and *The Miracle of the Bells* (1948).

What's curious about these films is that they are rarely weighty reflec-tions on the divine. Who ever found Jesus by watching *The Bells of St. Mary's*? Who ever heard the altar call in *Black Narcissus* (1946)? But the films all somehow assume a Christian culture. They live in a world in which Catholic nuns and Protestant ministers walk the street without self-consciousness. These movies rely on the reality of faith as the background against which their stories play out.

Some of that was still present in the 1950s, with movies like *High Noon* (1952) and *On the Waterfront* (1954) and *Heaven Knows, Mr. Allison* (1957). But such films as *The Night of the Hunter* (1955) showed that something new, and vastly unpleasant, was coming down the pike. The 1960s opened with *Elmer Gantry* (1960) and *Inherit the Wind* (1960), and by 1970, the America shown in those 1940s films was gone—not the real America of believers, of course, but the willingness of moviemakers to portray it. Protestants became almost exclusively Bible-thumping idiots. Catholic priests became figures of menace. And God—ah, well, God disappeared.

Perhaps that's too strong. Personally, I'd rather drown myself in a vat of viscous and syrupy goo—cheaper and easier on the stomach, in the long run—than sit through 1973's *Jesus Christ Superstar* and *Godspell* again. But that same year saw *The Exorcist*, which, in its stomach-churning way, still re-lied on the old conventions—as did, for that matter, *Chariots of Fire* (1981), *Tender Mercies* (1983), *Shadowlands* (1993), and *Amazing Grace* (2007).

Still, from *Monty Python's Life of Brian* (1979) on, movies had basically lost the religious background that made them work in their golden age. This is something more than merely the great turn against Christianity that movies made at the time. Certainly there were lots of anti-Christian and anti-Catholic films. But that was all moved to the foreground; it's what those movies were *about*. And movies that weren't *about* that had no Christianity in them at all. God and Christian faith became like a set on the MGM backlot that no directors needed to use anymore when they filmed their stories.

And that's the part that's most unreal. It's true that movies are only light, the beam of a lantern through a piece of celluloid film. And thus the lightest of arts turns out to be the earthiest; the ethereal turns out to focus on the bodily. But what Peter Dans advocates in *Christians in the Movies* is that movies begin by *accepting* that tension. People really do believe, God is not mocked, and how are movies to show that? By matching the actual life of actual believers. It's down in the very root of film, and by having seen nearly *every* movie, Peter Dans is uniquely able to show us how.

Joseph Bottum
Editor, *First Things*
New York, New York

PREFACE

ovies have played an important part in my life since growing up in
the 1940s in a cold-water flat on Manhattan's Lower East Side.
Trips to the now-defunct Tribune Theater near City Hall allowed
me to escape into other worlds and other cultures. That cinematic passion
remained after I became a doctor in 1961, but as a practicing physician and
father of four, I had little time to go to the movies. That changed in 1990,
when I agreed to write the "Physician at the Movies" column for *Pharos*, the
quarterly journal of the Alpha Omega Alpha honor medical society and began to see many more movies. In doing so, it was hard to miss the profound
changes that had occurred while I had been away. Most notable were the
recurrent bashing and negative portrayal of institutions like government and
corporations as well as the profession of medicine. As one who considers
medicine a noble profession and has found its practitioners to be generally
compassionate public servants, I decided to write *Doctors in the Movies: Boil
the Water and Just Say Aah*, a book about how Hollywood portrayed doctors
from 1931 to 2000 and was buoyed by its very positive reception.

As a practicing Catholic, I was also struck by the ridicule of organized
religion, especially Christianity. The movie clergymen of my youth were
tough-yet-good-hearted priests, often portrayed by big stars like Spencer
Tracy, Pat O'Brien, and Bing Crosby. Now it appeared that all orthodox
clergy and believers were either vicious predators or narrow-minded, mean-
spirited Pharisees. The "Christian" characters in such films as *The Godfather
Part III* and *The Da Vinci Code* come to mind. The "good" Christians were
those who were fighting the Church hierarchy and hypocritical Christian
leaders. These portraits bore little resemblance to my experience or that of
my family and friends.

One of the most perceptive commentators on this phenomenon was
film critic Michael Medved, himself an Orthodox Jew. In his 1992 book
Hollywood vs. America: Popular Culture and the War on Traditional Values,
Medved described what he called "Hollywood's war against religion." Un-
der the headings "Kicking the Catholics," "Bashing the Born-Agains," and
"Jabbing the Jews" he cited films that ridiculed Catholics, Fundamentalist

Protestants, and, to a lesser extent, Jews. He went on to say that "whenever someone turns up in a contemporary film with the title 'Reverend,' 'Father,' or 'Rabbi' in front of his name, you can count on the fact that he will be corrupt, crazy—or probably both." Since then, there have been many more examples of films featuring killers, low-lifes, sadists, and hypocrites who profess Catholicism and Pentecostal Christianity.

By contrast, the only unalloyed encomiums Hollywood has recently bestowed on believers seem to be reserved for those who practice Eastern religions like Buddhism, as in the 1997 films *Kundun* and *Seven Years in Tibet* or forms of New Age spirituality as in the 1996 film *Phenomenon* and the numerous "angel" films. The major distinction here is that unlike Christianity and Orthodox Judaism, they are more personal in nature and can be embraced without requiring any commitment to specific dogmas, especially those related to sexual and reproductive matters. This disdain for dogma was best articulated in a 1999 film appropriately titled *Dogma*. Rufus, the 13th apostle, who was presumably left out of the Bible because he was black, tells Bethany, a descendant of Mary and Joseph who works in an abortion clinic, that having "beliefs" is bad, in contrast to having "ideas" which can be changed. He goes on to say that "Life should be malleable and progressive. Working from idea to idea permits that. Beliefs anchor you to certain points and limit growth" with the result that life becomes "stagnant." Serendipity, the 14th apostle, a stripper who was also left out of the Bible "because she was a woman," agrees, "It doesn't matter what you have faith in, just that you have faith."

Interestingly, not too long ago, Muslims, whose belief system is not only rigidly defined, but in some cases extreme as in the status of women and the encouragement to wage Jihad, were portrayed as villains (*True Lies* [1994], *Executive Decision* [1996], and *The Siege* [1998] are good examples). They are no longer vilified by Hollywood, and it's unclear why. Perhaps, it is because of concern about accusations of profiling by powerful Muslim advocacy groups following the 9/11 Muslim terrorist attacks on the United States or because of the fear of violent retribution, as happened following the publication of the Danish newspaper cartoons portraying Mohammed. Christians, who are taught to turn the other cheek, may be easier and safer targets.

I couldn't help but wonder what had happened to create such an extreme pendulum swing in attitudes. Why had Christians gone from being portrayed as saints in the early and mid-century films to sinners in later ones? I decided to begin looking at older films that featured priests, nuns, ministers, saints, and other Christian believers to see if they indeed were portrayed in the laudatory ways that I remembered. Although the "project" began casually, it didn't take long before I realized that hundreds of movies had been produced over the past century featuring Christians. These included not only films about priests, ministers, nuns, and saints (*Going My Way, A Man Called Peter, The Nun's Story, The Passion of Joan of Arc*), but a wide range of films from classic biblical themes (*Quo Vadis, King of Kings, The Passion of the Christ*) to those that dealt with struggles of orthodox believers (*Sergeant York, Friendly Persuasion,* and *Chariots of Fire*).

After watching or rewatching over 200 Christian-themed films produced from 1905 through 2008, I arranged the analyses of the films chronologically by decade. Doing so vividly demonstrated the arc of the portrayal of Christians as "saints" or favorably in the early decades and progressively less favorably as the millennium approached. I thought it would be interesting to delineate this arc providing a brief historical overview for each period or decade, followed by the films that most closely represented the portrayal of Christians and Christianity in that era. Approximately 200 films are discussed, some in depth. Many I like very much and I believe are worth seeing; others, most critics and I believe to be terrible but are included to reinforce the book's thesis. Sprinkled throughout the text are also a number of "Backstories," or brief snippets of history and film biography that, I hope, will help enhance the understanding of the films and their subjects. Also included are an extensive filmography and a bibliography.

Unlike many of the books about religion and film, I make no attempt to analyze any given film's faithfulness to biblical texts or as a guide to meditation or theological discussion. Instead, my wish is that this book will be read primarily for pleasure and will stimulate readers to take another look at films that they once enjoyed or to discover hidden gems that they have never seen before. I also hope it will encourage orthodox Christian believers who have stopped going to movies to get more involved in helping to reshape this important industry, which all agree has badly lost its way.

This book is dedicated to Colette, my beloved wife of over 38 years, who, in the midst of her difficult struggle with breast cancer, was an enthusiastic companion on this quixotic journey and whose insights will be noted along the way. I also dedicate the book to our four children and their families. I also must acknowledge my great debt to my parents who supported me on our journey from a cold-water flat on New York's Lower East Side to a tenement, a housing project, and a rented apartment, foregoing owning a home of their own until I graduated from medical school, in order to provide me opportunities that were closed to them.

I am grateful to those who encouraged me when this venture seemed truly to be an impossible dream, including Charles Perdue, Alex Hoyt, Janet Worthington, Joseph Bottum, Ross Miller, and Peter Malone, as well as Turner Classic Movies and Video American in Baltimore as sources of hard-to-find films. I am especially indebted to Pam Thomas, who helped me shape, clarify, and prune what sometimes seemed to be incoherent ramblings into a book and to Stephen Ryan for his careful editing, fact checking, and development of the filmography. I also thank Sarah Stanton, Melissa McNitt, and Lee Y. Miao for their help in the editing and production process. Any remaining errors are my responsibility alone. I thank also Ron Mandelbaum and Buddy Weiss at Photofest for their gracious assistance in selecting the photos.

I also am grateful to the nuns, brothers, and lay teachers at St. John's Villa Academy, Transfiguration School in Chinatown, La Salle Military Academy, and Manhattan College for helping me gain a strong foundation in my faith and instilling in a future scientist, a love of literature and careful writing. Finally, I must acknowledge a profound debt to film critic Michael Medved who first laid out the book's thesis in *Hollywood vs. America*, and to the late A. M. Rosenthal, executive editor of the *New York Times*, who was often a lone voice in calling attention to the atrocities being perpetrated on Christians throughout the world.

CHAPTER ONE
PORTRAYING CHRISTIANS IN FILM

The portrayal of Christians and Christianity in film has undergone tremendous change since the release of the French film *The Passion of Jesus Christ* in 1905. Much of this shift is related to the enormous societal changes that have taken place as well as the advances in the technology of film. Despite the influx of Catholic immigrants, the American social fabric and its institutions, at the birth of the movies and well into the 1940s, were still predominantly Anglo-Saxon Protestant. The Bible was widely read and memorized in homes, churches, and meeting houses—even by those who had little schooling and were hardly literate. Not surprisingly, early filmmakers turned to the Bible, which was filled with memorable stories and provided a rich and free source material for dramatic screenplays. As Donnelly notes in *Fade to Black*, when asked why he made so many biblical films, Cecil B. DeMille, whose epics are his enduring legacy, responded, "Why let two thousand years of publicity go to waste?"

That the societal reverence for religion and the "good book" was not restricted to rural areas is borne out by the program of my mother's eighth grade graduation in 1931 from Public School 1 on Manhattan's impoverished Lower East Side. Except for the awards and diploma ceremony, it consisted mainly of scripture readings and patriotic songs like "In God We Trust," "The Battle Hymn of the Republic," "America," and "Columbus." This mix of religious and patriotic fervor was common in public school assemblies and graduation ceremonies until the early 1960s, when Supreme Court decisions began barring organized prayer in school.

As noted, the early films about Christians evolved as the technology improved from a series of static tableaux to the addition of a narrative thread and continuity of action through the use of mobile cameras and finally with the advent of sound and Technicolor. There was one constant, however, and that was the generally respectful attitude toward religion and Christianity. For a country that had suffered through World War I, the Depression, and profound social change, religion provided comfort and stability, which early filmmakers understood. Like their audience, many were also recent immigrants and were proud and grateful to be Americans. Like them too, many served in the armed forces and could relate to the sacrifices of those who fought and died for our country in World War II. It's hard today to fathom that in the Battle of Iwo Jima alone America suffered over twice as many deaths in 35 days as in the Iraq war from 2003 through 2007, and yet maintained its resolve. In short, the movies of my youth—those that made me a lifelong movie maven—were suffused with love of country and a strong belief in God.

The victory in World War II, along with increasing affluence and relative peace created an era of good feeling and optimism. However, by the late 1940s, below the surface, changes were taking place that would alter Hollywood's reverential approach to how religion was portrayed in film. The advent of television and the Supreme Court decision forbidding movie studios from owning chains of theaters eroded the industry's economic and entertainment dominance. At the same time, producers like Howard Hughes and Otto Preminger began to challenge the strictures of the Motion Picture Production Code, established in 1930, which had been used to regulate film content with regard to the handling of sensitive subjects like religion, sexuality, and violence. The importation of widely acclaimed, more sexually explicit foreign films, which were not subject to the Code, added further pressure to modify or do away with the Code.

Nonetheless, films respectful of Christianity, such as *Lilies of the Field*, *The Greatest Story Ever Told*, *The Sound of Music*, and *A Man for All Seasons* continued to be made well into the 1960s. However, that decade ended up being one of the most tumultuous in American history—with the assassinations of the Kennedys and Martin Luther King, Jr., the protests against the Vietnam War, the intensification of the Civil Rights Movement, the attendant Black Power movement and rioting in many cities as well as the Berkeley Free Speech Movement. Along with the sexual revolution and its accompanying hippie lifestyle, which earned the era its sobriquet "Sex, Drugs, and Rock and Roll," the 1960s was a watershed period bringing social changes that continue to affect our society.

Early on, the editors of *Time* sensed the rumblings of moral and religious change and ran a famous cover story on April 8, 1966, asking, "Is God Dead?" The tenor of the time, "Do your own thing," was best captured in the very popular book *I'm OK, You're OK*, which advocated practicing a live-and-let-live approach to diametrically opposite moral stances and behaviors. In the 1970s, at the University of Colorado venereal disease clinic I directed, where many patients returned reinfected and having infected others with gonorrhea, herpes, trichomoniasis, human papillomavirus and the like, it was common to hear calls for "nonjudgmentalism." This was predicated on the deepening disagreement about "right and wrong" and the rise in the affirmation of personal autonomy rights that held that individual lifestyle choices, regardless of their consequences on that person or others, should be respected. This attitude led the noted psychiatrist Karl Menninger to title his 1973 book *Whatever Became of Sin?* That year, the Supreme Court handed down the *Roe v. Wade* decision overriding state laws forbidding abortion, which further polarized the population.

Another major social change in the mid-1960s occurred within the Catholic Church, which had been very influential in affecting film content through the Legion of Decency, a rating system instituted in 1933 (see p. 6). The decrees of the Vatican II Church Council, which closed on December 8, 1965, led to sweeping changes in practices that had been seen as epitomizing Catholic beliefs and were often used as convenient shorthand for depicting Catholicism in films. These included the abandonment of the proscription against eating meat on Friday, the need to fast overnight before receiving Communion, the requirement that nuns wear distinctive habits, and the use of Latin in the Mass. These changes sent shock waves through Catholic circles, polarizing many believers. The next few decades saw a sharp drop in vocations to the religious life, the release of many priests and nuns from their vows, a decrease in attendance at Sunday mass, and the marked diminution of regular confessions, which had also been a favorite staple in movies with Catholic themes.

Protestant and Jewish denominations attempting to hold on to orthodox dogma that codified right and wrong with regard to abortion, premarital sex, and later, homosexuality, also saw declines in membership starting in the 1960s. By the 1970s, the so-called Me Generation began to turn more inward, placing more emphasis on self-actualization and self-fulfillment. As Americans became more affluent and secure, there seemed to be less of a need for regular church attendance and practicing a faith whose God demanded behaviors that restricted lifestyle choices. This was replaced by widespread attitudes of cultural relativism and the philosophy of secular humanism, which had gained currency as early as 1933 with the publication of the "Humanist Manifesto" whose signatories included famed educator John Dewey.

This philosophy had been reinforced by Supreme Court rulings beginning in the 1940s regarding various "church-state" issues. The most famous of these occurred in the 1947 case *Everson v. Board of Education* upholding New Jersey's right to give funds to Catholic schools for textbooks and activities unrelated to religious promulgation. In writing the majority opinion, Supreme Court Justice and ex–Ku Klux Klanner Hugo Black cited Jefferson's 1802 letter to the Danbury Baptists about the existence of "a wall of separation" between church and state. Since then, this phrase has been regularly cited in the press and in court opinions such that many believe it to be in the Bill of Rights, whereas the First Amendment only affirms the freedom to worship as one pleases and the prevention of the establishment of a state-sponsored religion which was common in the colonies.

In his 1993 book *The Culture of Disbelief: How American Law and Politics Trivialize Religious Devotion*, Yale law professor Stephen L. Carter pointed out that "In our sensible zeal to keep religion from dominating our politics," a wall of separation has been erected such that believers are encouraged "to act publicly, and sometimes privately as well, as though their faith doesn't matter." In the past three decades, the courts have increasingly become the principal venues for adjudicating contentious and complex moral issues. This has led to an escalation in the conflict between the orthodoxy of religious believers and that of secular nonbelievers as Robert George, holder of the McCormick Chair of Jurisprudence at Princeton University, pointed out in his 2002 book *The Clash of Orthodoxies*. In contrast to those who held secular laissez-faire views, he argued that private morals do have public consequences.

That such a gulf in orthodoxies exists between current filmmakers and many in their audience was best seen in a 1998 University of Texas survey of a representative sample of Hollywood writers, actors, producers, and executives. It showed that only 2 to 3 percent attended religious services weekly compared to about 41 percent of the public at that time. The ascendance of this cultural disconnect and its reflection in movies was accelerated by two important cinematic changes in the sixties. One was the abolition of the Motion Picture Production Code and its replacement by the Motion Picture Association of America's Rating System in 1968. The other was the replacement in 1965 of the very hands-on Legion of Decency rating system by the less obtrusive rating system of the National Catholic Office of Motion Pictures which did not require Catholics to follow its dictates. Both deserve expanded treatment.

The Motion Picture Production Code

In 1922, the Motion Picture Producers and Distributors of America (MP-PDA) association was established and headed by ex–Postmaster General Will Hays, a Presbyterian. These early filmmakers were reacting in part to complaints by predominantly Protestant groups about a plethora of Hollywood sex and drug scandals, but mostly to the development of movie censorship boards in many states and municipalities concerned about the cultural impact of film. Hays worked informally to reconcile the censors' concerns and to amalgamate the disparate censorship criteria of different jurisdictions and religious groups. This led in 1930 to the promulgation of the Motion Picture Production Code aimed at maintaining good taste, especially when filming scenes that involved sex, violence, religion, and other sensitive subjects. The twelve sections of the Code outlined the areas to be regulated: crimes against the law, sex, vulgarity, obscenity, profanity, costume, dances, religion, locations, national feelings, titles, and repellent subjects.

The Code required that "no picture should be produced which will lower the standards of those who see it. Hence the sympathy of the audience should never be thrown on the side of crime, wrongdoing, evil, or sin. The sanctity of the institution of marriage and the home should be upheld." The Code also stated that "No film or episode should throw ridicule on any religious faith. Ministers of religion in their character as ministers of religion should not be used as comic characters or as villains. Ceremonies of any definite religion should be carefully and respectfully handled."

Many myths have arisen about the Code and its enforcement. One is that the Code mandated separate beds for married couples or that each partner had to have one foot on the floor if they were in the same bed. As film historian Richard Maltby notes in his article "More Sinned Against Than Sinning: The Fabrications of Pre-Code Cinema," the Code simply said that "the treatment of bedrooms must be governed by good taste and delicacy." In fact, the use of separate beds by married couples in films met a requirement of the "British Board of Film Censors," bringing to mind the title of the play *No Sex Please, We're British*.

Another myth relates to the labeling of certain films made during the Code's early days (between 1931 and 1934) as "Pre-Code" films. The films in question include such classics as *Little Caesar, Public Enemy, Red-Headed Woman, Baby Face, The Sign of the Cross*, and several Mae West films. As Maltby points out, the Code was already being imposed on the vast majority of films, but the producers of these films chose to flout the code. The public backlash to these films is widely credited for the decision of producers to enforce the Code; however, the economic downturn may have been just as important in pushing Hollywood filmmakers to be even more serious about enforcement. With the onset of the Depression, average weekly movie attendance dropped from 90 million in 1930 to 70 million in 1931 and to 60 million in 1932 and 1933. Studios like Paramount, Warner Bros., and RKO which owned the most theaters, suffered financially and tried to spur attendance by promoting dish-giveaway nights and double features. At the same time, with the end of the Roaring Twenties, the nation became more culturally conservative, and the large wave of immigrants who had arrived between 1890 and 1930 from predominantly Catholic countries became more influential.

The National Legion of Decency

The concerns about the impact of film also led the American Catholic bishops to establish the Catholic Legion of Decency in 1933. Because the organization included many Protestant and Jewish clergymen, the name was changed to National Legion of Decency in 1934. The Legion rated films as A (morally unobjectionable)—later subdivided into 4 categories by age group; B (morally objectionable in part); and C (condemned). For Catholics, attendance at condemned films was forbidden under pain of sin, and they were asked to take a pledge annually (usually on December 8th, the feast of the Immaculate Conception) to avoid morally objectionable films and places that showed them as a matter of policy. The Legion wielded great influence over the next three decades, mainly because the economic clout of the large Catholic population could be harnessed through the extensive network of Catholic schools and churches. Thomas Doherty's *Hollywood's Censor* shows in great detail how the devout Catholic Joseph I. Breen, who was hired by the aforementioned Will Hays, became the face of the Production Code Administration Office to the industry, such that it was nicknamed the "Breen Office." He developed a synergistic partnership with Martin Quigley at the Legion of Decency that fostered their joint role as arbiters of film content and enforcers of stricter adherence to the Motion Picture Production Code. They were consulted about scripts and often wielded power over final cuts. The annual pledge by Catholics was abandoned after Pope Pius XII's 1957 encyclical on motion pictures, radio, and television titled *Miranda Prorsus* ("The Remarkable Inventions") emphasized encouraging good movies rather than condemning bad ones. By 1965, the Legion of Decency had become widely ignored by Catholics.

Father Gene Phillips, a professor of film studies at Loyola University in Chicago and a consultant to the National Catholic Office of Motion Pictures, the organization that replaced the Legion of Decency in 1966, answered the many critics who have attacked the Catholic Church as being a censor imposing its views on Americans at large as follows:

> When the American bishops instituted [the Legion of Decency], it was aimed at determining the moral suitability of films for its Roman Catholic constituency. Nevertheless, in the absence of an industry rating system, which was not inaugurated until 1968, many non-Catholics followed the Legion's ratings. The studio bosses tended to do the Legion's bidding in order to avoid an objectionable rating which could damage the film's chances at the box office. . . . So, the Catholic Church was allowed to affect the moral content of Hollywood films for more than three decades, something that was never envisioned at the outset.

As Paula M. Kane points out in her contribution to *Catholics in the Movies*, "Jews and Catholics Converge," early on there was, in addition to Protestant support, "grassroots Jewish support for the Legion of Decency pledge."

The official end of the Hays Code came in response to a case involving a challenge to the city of Dallas for forbidding the showing of a French movie, *Viva Maria!*, starring Brigitte Bardot and Jeanne Moreau. In April 1968, in *Interstate Circuit v. Dallas*, the Supreme Court upheld the First Amendment rights of filmmakers to show their films, but because of licensure requirements, it ordered the Motion Picture Association of America to come up promptly with its own rating system to replace the vague and disparate criteria applied by various licensing boards. Jack Valenti, a Catholic and close aide of then-president Lyndon B. Johnson, was hired as director of the Motion Picture Association of America (MPAA) and charged with developing the system.

By the end of 1968, Hollywood debuted a self-policing system, which has come to be geared to restrictions by age. After several revisions, the MPAA now classifies movies as G (all ages admitted); PG (parental guidance suggested); PG-13 (parental guidance, and no one under the age of 13 is admitted without a parent); R (restricted, no one age 17 and under is admitted without a parent); NC-17 (no one age 17 and under is admitted). The latter replaced the X, or condemned, rating in 1990. Films can still be released if they get an NC-17 rating, but they will not receive distribution in most theaters.

For a variety of reasons, the rating system has come under attack by critics from every point on the political spectrum. The criteria used to arrive at the individual ratings are not publicly stated and are applied by a group of people whose identities are kept secret to protect them from political and public pressure. Whatever the criteria are, they have shifted over time (on nudity, explicit sexual intercourse, and violence, for example). Furthermore, regardless of whether theaters enforce the proscription on admission of minors to R and PG-13 movies (which many don't), they are all accessible in homes on DVD including those films with the most severely restrictive rating of NC-17. Interestingly, the most scathing condemnation of the MPAA rating system was expressed in the independent documentary *This Film Is Not Yet Rated* (Lionsgate, 2006) by Kirby Dick, who, if anything, argued for less restrictiveness. The filmmaker denounced the system for being arbitrary, secretive, subject to major studio pressure, and for not meeting its own guidelines for selection of raters and their required training.

So, one might legitimately ask, "Are we better off with the current rating system?" The question is moot because unlike a VCR, life has no rewind button and there's no turning back. Still, my answer is "No." At least the Hays Code had a visible director and explicit criteria that had been publicly changed over time and would probably have been modified further to accommodate those worthy post-Code films that might have run afoul of it. Indeed, I was struck by an August 15, 1999, *New York Times* article titled "When the Spice of Choice Was Sin." While extolling pre-Code Hollywood movies, it cited a 1999 study by Thomas Doherty, which concluded that "the inconvenient truth is that Hollywood's most vivid and compelling motion pictures were produced under the most severe and narrow-minded censorship" (i.e., the Hays Code and the Legion of Decency). Not only were many of the most respected films in movie history made from the 1930s through the 1950s, an era universally called "The Golden Age of Film," but 1939 is often called "Hollywood's Golden Year" because it saw the release of so many excellent films, including *Gone with the Wind*; *The Wizard of Oz*; *Mr. Smith Goes to Washington*; *Stagecoach*; *Ninotchka*; *The Women*; *Goodbye, Mr. Chips*; *Gunga Din*; *Dark Victory*; *Young Mr. Lincoln*; and *Destry Rides Again* among others. Some argue that the great films made during the enforcement of the Code were made "in spite of the Code." If that were true, the period after the Code's demise would deserve to be called the Golden Age of Movies, and the output of great films would have increased, but it hasn't.

Another way of looking at that "in spite of" objection is to say that asking moviemakers to exercise judicious restraint was, on balance, beneficial to the creative process. Just as actors like Robin Williams are much more effective when kept under some control by experienced directors, so are movies with some controls over explicit sexuality, appalling violence, or the over-the-top trashing of ideas and institutions. An example of how the Motion Picture Production Code forced filmmakers to portray sexuality more subtly is the 1934 Frank Capra classic *It Happened One Night*, starring Claudette Colbert and Clark Gable. This is seen particularly in the famous hitchhiking sequence and the final scene when the blanket between their beds, dubbed the "Walls of Jericho," comes down to signal the consummation of their relationship, as opposed to today's predictable scenes of bed-rattling sexual acrobatics. In addition, few, if any, post-Code movies have ever scaled the romantic heights of Fred Astaire and Ginger Rogers dancing to the tunes of *Cheek to Cheek* or *Night and Day*.

Differing Treatment of Christian Groups

Fundamentalist Christians have the distinction of having been almost uniformly portrayed negatively as charlatan preachers, unenlightened dupes, and more recently as mean-spirited hypocrites. Their saving grace may only be that they have had relatively few films devoted to them—*Elmer Gantry* (1960), *Inherit the Wind* (1960), and *The Apostle* (1998) are the best known. Mainstream Protestant groups, which were once prominent in the background and occasionally in the foreground of many movies, have virtually disappeared from films, except for wedding ceremonies. Catholics turn out to be the most prevalent group dealt with in film, both in their predominantly favorable presentation in early films and their subtle and sometimes blatant disparagement in post-Code movies, beginning in the 1970s and escalating in the late 1980s. This may be because, since 1870, Roman Catholicism has been the largest Christian sect in America, and because of the Catholic Church's role in the National Legion of Decency and the strict enforcement of the Hays Code.

Still, anti-Catholicism is nothing new. As Penn State historian and former Catholic Philip Jenkins noted in his 2003 book, *The New Anti-Catholicism: The Last Acceptable Prejudice*, 50 years ago Harvard historian Arthur Schlesinger, Sr., called it "the deepest bias in the history of the American people." If you visit Old Town Philadelphia or Lower Manhattan, you can find churches where Catholics barricaded themselves from rampaging Nativist mobs in the late 1700s and early 1800s. The first Supreme Court Chief Justice, John Jay (1790–1795), erected a "No Popery" sign in front of his house on Guy Fawkes Day, November 5, the commemoration of the foiling of the Gunpowder Plot to blow up Parliament by a few dissident English Catholics in 1605. Opponents of immigrant Catholics flourished in the early and mid-1800s with the ascendancy of the Know-Nothing Party. Catholics remained the targets of the KKK and the Freemasons, who were well positioned to act against them politically and economically well into the 20th century.

In the 1930s, Catholics and other Christians began to join with Jews, blacks, and other groups subjected to blatant prejudice, to fight bigotry. When I was growing up in the 1940s, the National Council of Christians and Jews was a powerful force against anti-Semitism and racism as well as fostering tolerance toward Christians. Indeed, much of the Civil Rights legislation in the 1960s is owed to their efforts in support of black Protestant clergymen like Martin Luther King, Jr. The economic and social status of Catholics improved so much in the era beginning with World War II, that the decades from 1940 through 1960 are sometimes referred to as "the Catholic moment." Motion pictures played an important role in this rehabilitation of Catholicism in the public square and in the promotion of positive attitudes to invocations of God and Christianity.

The 1960 election of John F. Kennedy as the first Catholic president was thought to be the moment that anti-Catholicism would be buried. Indeed, as Colleen Carroll Campbell points out, it may have signaled the reverse, in that Kennedy was the first of many Catholic politicians to affirm that Catholic beliefs would not necessarily inform his policies. Realizing that his election hinged on distancing himself from his faith, in a speech before the Greater Houston Ministerial Association, he called the separation of church and state "absolute" and reversed his earlier stance in favor of state support for parochial schools. After Vatican II, as more Catholics entered the economic mainstream, they began to reject Catholic teaching, especially in the area of sexual ethics, and to espouse secular ideas. Many began by rejecting

Church teaching on birth control, premarital sex, and divorce. Some have moved on to rejecting its teaching on abortion, homosexuality, in vitro fertilization, embryonic stem-cell research, assisted suicide, and, in rare instances, even cloning.

In the meantime, mainstream Protestant denominations (e.g., Episcopalianism, Methodism, Presbyterianism) which were most responsible for founding many of the great American universities and philanthropic institutions, began to decline in membership and influence as they adapted to the prevailing secular beliefs. Their place in American Protestantism was taken by many large and small evangelical and fundamentalist denominations that stressed the importance of a literal interpretation of the Bible and religious beliefs. Interestingly, the once prevalent anti-Catholicism among fundamentalist Protestants has waned somewhat, as they began to find common ground with orthodox Catholics in opposing abortion and same-sex marriage, as well as uniting in the support of Israel. Instead, anti-Catholicism has taken on a new form. As Jenkins describes in *The New Anti-Catholicism*, the animus against the Catholic Church is now most evident in academic circles and among some of the media who notably seek out dissident Catholics whenever reporting on controversial moral issues.

Indeed, many of the contemporary films that ridicule Catholicism most severely have actually been made by "cradle Catholics" who (like me) attended Catholic schools. These directors have either abandoned their religion, becoming fallen-away Catholics (or, as some prefer to be called, "recovering Catholics") or "liberal" Catholics who profess still to be Catholics but simply choose to reject much Catholic dogma.

One prominent example is Robert Altman, the director of the influential 1970 film *M*A*S*H*, a very anti-institutional film that aimed some of its sharpest barbs at Christianity, especially in the famous "Last Supper" scene. Paul Giles in his 1991 essay, "The Cinema of Catholicism: John Ford and Robert Altman," gives an interesting insight into the motivations of the Jesuit-educated Altman. He quotes Altman saying, "Catholicism to me was school. It was restrictions; it was things you had to do. It was your parents. It was Mass on Sunday and fish on Friday. And then when I got out of that I got into the army. It was the same thing—you had to have a pass to get out." Giles concludes that in *M*A*S*H*, "Altman's compulsion is to lampoon religion as much as the U.S. Army." Giles contrasts this attitude with that of John Ford (p. 105), another great director who was raised a Catholic but was by no means a "Holy Joe." Yet he introduced little touches in his films that showed what religion meant to his often brawling, hard-drinking characters. New books contrast the messages and styles of early directors with a Catholic background such as Frank Capra, Leo McCarey, John Ford, and Alfred Hitchcock with more recent directors with Catholic roots like Altman, Martin Scorsese, Kevin Smith, John Waters, and others.

Ironically, such criticism of Catholicism, no matter how virulent, may still be seen as a positive insofar as attention is rarely paid to matters considered unimportant. In his 1987 book *Once a Catholic*, Peter Occhiogrosso summarizes interviews with prominent Catholics and ex-Catholics that illustrated the powerful influence the Church holds on them. Many ex-Catholics find themselves unable to escape their past allegiance to the Church, much as the protagonist in Francis Thompson's famous Victorian-era poem "The Hound of Heaven" cannot shake his implacable pursuer (see Backstory, p. 157). This may explain why they so often express their hostility in films and in public forums.

The Passion of the Christ as Rorschach Test

Nothing shows the hostility of media critics to Christianity better than the campaign against Mel Gibson's *The Passion of the Christ* (2004), which began almost a year before the film's release with the attempt to prevent its distribution. Many vitriolic articles accused the film of being anti-Semitic. Gibson countered that he drew his screenplay directly from the St. Matthew's Gospel account of the Crucifixion of Christ, depicting some Jews as culpable but making it clear the Romans were the most brutal and ultimately responsible for Christ's death. Adele Reinhartz, in her 2007 book *Jesus of Hollywood*, noted that the "betrayals, trials, condemnation and death of Jesus" have appeared in over a hundred films. Those faithful to the Gospels, especially to St. Matthew's Gospel, have pictured the responsibility of some Jewish leaders. D. W. Griffith deleted a number of scenes from the Judean Story segment of *Intolerance* replacing Jews with Romans at the Crucifixion after complaints from B'nai B'rith; Cecil B. DeMille made changes in his 1927 film *King of Kings* after concerns were expressed by Jewish groups. Gibson removed Matthew's reference to the Jews saying that Jesus's blood be upon them and upon their children whereas Pasolini's acclaimed *The Gospel According to St. Matthew* retained it, without outcry.

In contrast to most critics, many viewers, both believers and nonbelievers, reported being moved by "The Passion." Conversely, some believers were turned off by the relentless brutality. Others, like me, accepted it for what it was and remained unmoved. Many critics seemed both incredulous and almost threatened by its broad popularity. What was particularly striking was the fact that many of the same critics who expressed high dudgeon at the film's violence had heaped extensive praise on other very violent films like *Pulp Fiction* (1994), *The Matrix* (1999), and the two *Kill Bill* films (2003, 2004). The Academy of Arts and Sciences voted it only three minor Oscar nominations for cinematography, makeup, and music and it won none; one wonders how it would have fared with the Academy of the 1940s and 1950s. That the film went on to earn over $700 million did not escape Hollywood's notice as exemplified by recent films appealing to Christians, such as *The Nativity Story* (2006) and *Amazing Grace* (2007).

Why Should Christians Care About Their Portrayal in Film?

One might ask, "Why should Christians care about how film and the other media portray them?" The simple answer is that feature films remain, as they have been since their inception, powerful tools for framing public opinion. However, the best answer was given by a non-Christian, A. M. Rosenthal, the former executive editor of the *New York Times*. He waged a lonely campaign against media silence about the persecution and killing of Christians in many parts of the world. In a June 1997 *Times* Op-Ed piece ("Questions from West 47th Street"), Rosenthal reported being asked by an Orthodox Jew, "Why are you writing so much about Christians?" Before he could answer, the man added, "I know . . . it will be good for Jews, right?" Rosenthal replied that his main reason was the consistency with which the atrocities against Christians were taking place in Muslim-dominated countries in Africa, the Middle East, and Asia with so little outcry, but he also agreed that tolerating hostility toward one religion sooner or later fosters intolerance toward all.

Similarly, Orthodox Rabbi Daniel Lapin, in a 1999 article in *American Enterprise* magazine titled "Why Jews Should Pray for a Christian America," noted that the erosion of social institutions that Jews and other Americans depend upon for safety and tranquility is the result not of "too much Christianity," but rather the failures of secular liberalism. Indeed, many of us grew up in a country suffused with the Judeo-Christian heritage. At the Catholic institutions I attended we were reminded of the words of Pope Pius XI,

"Spiritually we are all Semites." We share with our brethren of other faiths a profound concern about the coarsening of the culture in which our grandchildren are being raised—one that, in the late Senator Daniel Moynihan's words, "has defined deviancy down."

Just in my lifetime, we have gone from questioning whether couples should kiss on the first date to whether they should have sex, and popular romantic ballads by Rodgers and Hart, Gershwin, Porter, Kern, and Berlin have been replaced by misogynistic and profane rap and hip-hop. Although Hollywood may have facilitated these changes, it didn't create them. To paraphrase Shakespeare in *Julius Caesar*, "The fault, Dear Brutus, lies not in our stars [or the movies they make] but in ourselves." The restoration of a better movie culture, like the return of civility and good manners in everyday life, is our responsibility both individually and collectively. If we want movies that are more reflective of our values, we can use the power of the purse and our voices to let Hollywood know that. As Father James Keller, founder of the Christopher movement pointed out, if one of us lights a candle, we can illuminate our space but if each of us does, we can illuminate the world.

My purpose in this book is not to argue for a return to yesteryear when films were often too saccharine in their approach to religion and Christianity. Indeed, I am not a big fan of many overtly religious films, believing that some of the best religious films are those where spirituality evolves in the characters as the story unfolds. Instead, my intent is to suggest that Christians, including Catholics, may not have been as good as they were depicted in their glorification days, but are certainly nothing like the hateful stereotypes in today's movies. In short, it's time to restore balance. Constant negativity is not only detrimental to institutions and professions but has a polarizing and corrosive effect on society as a whole.

PIETY AND PASSION: THE SILENT ERA

T he decades during which the motion picture industry developed, essentially 1890 to 1930, were full of turmoil around the world. The most consequential were the collapse of European empires, a devastating world war with more than 37.5 million casualties, the rise of Communism in Russia, and a large flow of immigrants, especially from southern Europe, to the United States. It was also a time of strong government activism in the United States beginning with the exuberant progressivism of Teddy Roosevelt, who became president after McKinley's assassination by an anarchist in 1901. These decades were a period of great social change with the passage of the first Pure Food and Drug Acts in 1906; the rise of unionism; and especially Constitutional amendments imposing a federal income tax (1913), the direct election of senators (1913), the prohibition of the manufacture, sale, and transportation of intoxicating beverages (1919), and granting women the right to vote (1920). The decades saw the development and proliferation of such amazing machines as the airplane, the automobile (especially Henry Ford's Model T that allowed a middle-class American to own a car), and a plethora of electrically-generated devices including lightbulbs and an array of household devices, such as vacuum cleaners, toasters, refrigerators, stoves, and dishwashers, as well as the phonograph, radio, and motion pictures.

The 1920s, dubbed "The Roaring Twenties" or the "Jazz Age," were marked not only by a sense of relief that we had fought "the war to end all wars," but by the excitement of a world that had changed completely in a mere two decades. Its flair was captured in such icons as the Art Deco Chrysler Building in New York City; the music of George Gershwin; the artistic flourishing known as the Harlem Renaissance; the writings of F. Scott Fitzgerald, Ernest Hemingway, and others who came to be known as the Lost Generation; and the popularity of such celebrities as Charles Lindbergh, Babe Ruth, and Jack Dempsey. An "anything goes" attitude prevailed as bootleggers and speakeasy patrons (especially "flappers") flouted Prohibition that, in turn, fostered the rise of gangsters. During the 1920s, the stock market climbed into the stratosphere and the good times seemed never-ending. But in October 1929 it all came crashing down.

As for moving pictures, building on work by the Lumiere brothers, Eadweard Muybridge, and others, William Kennedy Dickson at the Edison Laboratories in New Jersey developed a celluloid strip that allowed for projecting moving images. In 1893, Thomas Edison introduced the Kinetograph (a movie camera) and the Kinetoscope (an early film projector) at the Chicago World's Fair. Soon many short films were being shown in storefront "theaters" and as part of vaudeville acts or in tent shows, and it was evident that showing longer films to larger audiences could be a lucrative venture.

During the early years of film development, the "sound" associated with movies was music, often created on a piano, organ, or with small orchestra located in the theater itself. The notion that one could actually hear actors speak on film seemed impossible, and for most of this era, "silent" films seemed sufficient. The early movies reflected the societal shift from rural farms to industrial cities as they waxed nostalgic about the loss of the traditional values but also showed the excitement of the big cities. Most American films were made in a small studio in Astoria, Queens, just outside New York City. By the early 1920s, filmmakers needed more space to accommodate the new technology and more clement weather in which to film. A small suburb of Los Angeles called Hollywood ended up being a perfect place, and filmmakers moved there in droves. "Going Hollywood" soon became synonymous, not only with filmmaking, but with the glamorous, opulent, and risqué lifestyle that came to characterize the Roaring Twenties. Movie actors like Charlie Chaplin, Mary Pickford, Douglas Fairbanks, the Gish sisters, and Rudolph Valentino became international celebrities.

Christians in the Movies

In 1902, a 30-minute production called *The Life and Passion of Jesus Christ* was made in France by Pathé and was expanded to 45 minutes for wide release in 1905. Encouraged by its success, American filmmakers produced *From the Manger to the Cross* in 1912. Filmed on location, it was remarkably sophisticated given the newness of the industry. From the beginning, filmmakers recognized that the Bible was a rich source of dramatic material and used Biblical stories, most particularly the story of the life of Jesus Christ, for their more serious works.

By 1915, a quantum jump in the quality of film technique and storytelling had occurred. This was best exemplified by the work of the acknowledged master director of the silent era D. W. Griffith, who helped transform silent films from static tableaux to dramatic narratives in the controversial *Birth of a Nation* and the more intricate *Intolerance* that was acclaimed by critics but not by the public. Griffith paved the way for Cecil B. DeMille, the king of epic extravaganza. DeMille took many liberties with the biblical texts enabling him to blend content and entertainment. His progress as both storyteller and showman is illustrated in the 1923 version of *The Ten Commandments*, which is evenly split between a biblical spectacle and a theological tract set in modern-day San Francisco. In his 1927 *King of Kings*, he reserved his moral commentary to his introduction and concentrated on the biblical stories that he embellished. In so doing, he created a decidedly more entertaining spectacle that set the pattern for his later films, such as *The Sign of the Cross* (1932), *The Crusades* (1935), and the 1956 remake of *The Ten Commandments*. The treatment of Christianity in silent films is capped by Carl Theodor Dreyer's 1928 masterpiece *The Passion of Joan of Arc,* one of the greatest films of all time. The story of this much beloved saint would be filmed many times, but never better.

The Life and Passion of Jesus Christ (1905)

Originally made in 1902 by the French company Pathé, whose trademark rooster appears in every scene, this colorized expanded 1905 version is available on DVD. It consists of tableaux-like segments beginning with the Annunciation, as Mary puts down her jug of water to kneel before an angel to receive the news of the virgin birth. The film continues with the birth of Jesus, the star guiding the shepherds and the Three Kings, the Massacre of the Innocents, and the Flight into Egypt. In the segment of the Holy Family in Nazareth, Joseph is shown cutting down a tree and teaching Jesus carpentry. Highlighted during Jesus's public life are His Baptism, numerous miracles including the turning of water (which looks like milk) into wine, and His walking on or really coming up out of the water. The numerous events from His triumphant entry into Jerusalem to His crucifixion and death are also shown. The film concludes with His Resurrection and Ascension into heaven to join His Father and the Holy Spirit. Although the film is more of a historical curiosity, the various segments, identified by placards, may be useful as illustrations in educating children about the important elements of Christ's life.

From the Manger to the Cross (1912)

This 71-minute film is subtitled "A Review of the Saviour's Life According to the Gospel Narrative." It is divided into approximately nine segments consisting of a series of biblical passages followed by vignettes. They include: The Annunciation and the Infancy of Jesus; The Flight into Egypt; Christ's Youth; The Heralding of John the Baptist; The Beginning of the Miracles such as the driving out of the devils in the epileptic and the Marriage Feast of Cana; Christ's Ministry and teaching including Lazarus and the healing of the blind man; The Last Days of Christ's Life; The Last Supper, and His Crucifixion and Death. All these vignettes are faithful to the biblical verses that accompany them. At the end, the earth quakes and the rocks are rent and the film becomes colorized. The last caption is from John 3:16: "For God so loved the world that he gave his only begotten son that whosoever believeth in him shall not perish but have life everlasting."

Commentary

The film is available in video, having been preserved by Warner Bros. in 1994. It's quite an ambitious and successful film given the limited camera options and cast at director Sidney Olcott's disposal. He himself plays the blind man and screenwriter Gene Gauntier played Mary. One must look past the fake beards and some of the stilted language on title cards, such as

Figure 2.1. *From the Manger to the Cross*. Mary, Joseph, and the donkey rest during the flight into Egypt (filmed on location).

when Joseph hears that Mary is with child and the caption reads "Joseph, a just man, was minded to put her away privily." Its greatest asset is that the scenes were all filmed in Jerusalem, Bethlehem, and other authentic sites in Palestine. So when Jesus, Mary, and Joseph flee to Egypt, the viewer sees the real pyramids and the Sphinx. The extras (local shepherds, women carrying urns on their heads, and the fishermen recruited to be disciples) also lend an air of realism. So do the animals! I must admit that one of my favorite shots was of the very active donkey during the visits of the shepherds and the Three Wise Men. In summary, the film treats the story of Christ's life with reverence and biblical verisimilitude.

Intolerance (1916)

Director D. W. Griffith's stated purpose was to show "how hatred and intolerance have battled against love and charity." Four separate stories are repeatedly intercut with one another using as the connector a mother (Lillian Gish) rocking a cradle and a quote from Walt Whitman's "Leaves of Grass," "Out of the cradle, endlessly rocking. Uniter of here and hereafter."

The modern story, the most coherent and the only one that Griffith scripted, opens at the Jenkins Mill where contented workers support their families. However, the owner (Sam DeGrasse) is convinced by his socialite sister to fund a group of "do-gooders" labeled "The Vestal Virgins of Uplift" (The Uplifters) who campaign to raid the workers' parties filled with dancing and drinking of wine and beer. Hauled off to jail, the women later turn to prostitution and the men to bootlegging. They also take babies away from mothers they consider unfit only to have them die of negligent care. The accompanying subtitle says, "When women cease to attract men, they often turn to reform as a second choice."

Ultimately the Jenkins Foundation projects become so costly that the mill owner must cut the workers' pay by 10 percent, and the workers strike. The National Guard is called in and workers are shot, and the lives of two happy children are forever altered: Dear One (Mae Marsh), whose father is imprisoned, and the Boy (Robert Harron), whose father is killed. Meanwhile the Uplifters revel in their "success" as portrayed in the newspapers and celebrate with a posh party at the opulent Jenkins home.

The second or Judean story is the briefest and consists of three vignettes in, as Griffith describes, "Ancient Jerusalem the golden city whose people have given us many of our highest ideals and from the carpenter shop of

Nazareth, sent us the Man of Men, the greatest enemy of intolerance." Wine, said to be an important part of Jewish familial and community life, again sets off the do-gooders when Christ turns water into wine at the Marriage Feast at Cana. The Uplifters' counterparts are the Pharisees described as a "learned Jewish party, the name possibly brought into disrepute by hypocrites among them." The Pharisees turn their noses up at Christ and are shown thanking God for being better than the others. The other vignettes involve saving the woman from being stoned to death by asking the one who is without sin to throw the first stone. Last there is the crucifixion of an innocent man that resonates with the deaths of the innocents in the third vignette and the near-death of "the Boy" in the first.

The third story is set in 1672 and involves Catherine de Medici (Josephine Crowell) convincing her son King Charles IX (Frank Bennett) to exterminate the Huguenots in the Saint Bartholomew's Day Massacre. Griffith notes that the Queen Mother "covers her political intolerance of the Huguenots (described as "the Protestant party of the period") beneath the cloak of the great Catholic religion." In the process, two young lovers of different religions, who are about to be married, are killed.

The fourth story is the most spectacular, recreating Babylon of 539 BC as a peaceful place under King Nabonidus (Carl Stockdale), where the first code of Justice (the Code of Hammurabi) is in effect. After fending off Cyrus the Persian (George Siegmann), there is a seemingly endless party during which the King's son Belshezzar (Alfred Paget) is betrayed by the local priests who worship Bel rather than Ishtar and help Cyrus enter the gates to destroy Babylon. This contains the most entertaining and lively character in the almost three-and-a-half hour film, the tomboy-like Mountain Girl (Constance Talmadge) who loves Belshezzar from afar and tries to protect him until the end.

Commentary

D. W. Griffith was a man of paradox. On the one hand, he was considered to be the "father of film" by Lillian Gish and "the teacher of us all" by Charlie Chaplin. On the other, his wildly successful 1915 film *Birth of a Nation*, based on a popular play *The Clansman*, led to his being vilified as a racist for its sympathetic portrayal of the Ku Klux Klan and of blacks as villainous. Born on a Kentucky farm, he was the son of a Confederate colonel who was wounded during the Civil War and died when Griffith was 10. Largely self-schooled, he portrayed history through the eyes of an unreconstructed Confederate, although much of *Birth of a Nation* is antiwar. At a time of overt racism with separate facilities for blacks and whites, Jim Crow laws, and ubiquitous blackface stereotypes, it's interesting that the film produced the reaction it did. It probably marks the first realization of the power of a well-made and well-received film to affect cultural attitudes and views of history in an enduring way.

Upset by the attempts of the NAACP and other groups to ban and censor *Birth of a Nation* rather than let his views (and those of a number of others, it must be admitted) be heard, he concocted the idea for *Intolerance*. The techniques he used involved spectacle, close-ups, and intercutting four stories to depict the effects of schemes by those who considered themselves morally superior or used religious beliefs to wreak havoc on innocent citizens.

The modern story was said to be modeled on John D. Rockefeller Jr. who was aided by the National Guard in breaking a strike at his Colorado Fuel and Iron Company that led to the Ludlow massacre where 23 workers were killed. Griffith considered him a hypocrite for his callous disregard for the workers by poor pay and brutal strike-breaking, while supporting a foundation presumably to help the poor and society. The Judean segment has an interesting history. When B'nai B'rith was informed that Griffith was seeking stereotypic Jewish characters for the crucifixion scene, Joseph Brandeis and others threatened to lead boycotts if changes were not made. Already sensitive to criticism of his handling of blacks in *Birth of a Nation*, the director decided it would be best to burn all the relevant scenes (the reason this segment is so short) and cast Romans in the crucifixion scene. The Pharisees remain as the segment's hypocrites, but they are seen as garnering this reputation only because of a minority among them.

Similarly, although the third segment features Catholics killing the Huguenots in the Saint Bartholomew's Massacre, Griffith puts the blame on Catherine de Medici and her allies for inflaming the Catholics and calls the Catholic religion "great." In short, while Griffith was an equal opportunity basher of institutionalized religions and believers, he tried to mitigate his presentations so as not to alienate his audience completely. Nonetheless, the result is long, often confusing and, although lauded by cineastes, unsatisfying to them as well. Pauline Kael, the *New Yorker* critic, called *Intolerance* "perhaps the greatest movie ever made and the greatest folly in movie history." Even Griffith considered it his "great failure."

The Ten Commandments (1923)

The film, which is divided into the biblical and the modern eras, opens with Cecil B. DeMille's prologue in the form of a sermonette:

> Our modern world defined God as a "religious complex" and laughed at the Ten Commandments as OLD-FASHIONED. Then through the laughter came the shattering thunder of the World War and now a blood soaked and bitter world cries for a way out. There is but one way out. It existed before it was engraven upon Tablets of Stone. It will exist when stone has crumbled. The Ten Commandments are not rules to obey as a personal favor to God. They are the fundamental principles without which mankind cannot live together. They are not laws—they are the LAW.

Part 1: Exodus. As "Rameses the Magnificent"(Charles de Rochefort) passes, the Jewish slaves pulling the Sphinx are called "Jewish dogs" and are told by their Jewish overseer "Dathan the Discontented," "If a man clog the wheels of the Pharaoh, he shall be ground to dust." "Moses the Lawgiver" (Theodore Roberts) petitions Pharaoh to let his people go, and on being refused, God unleashes a plague on Egypt. Pharaoh remains resolute and God punishes him (through Moses) by killing the firstborn of every house in Egypt. The destroyer "passes over" the Jewish houses, marked by the blood of lambs on the lintels and two doorposts. Pharaoh finally relents, and the Jews flee. Pharaoh has a change of heart and sends his chariots to exterminate the Jews but God sends a Pillar of Fire to separate them and then empowers Moses to part the Red Sea, which engulfs the Egyptians once the Israelites are safely across.

Three months later they arrive at Mount Sinai and Moses leaves his brother Aaron in charge while he climbs the forbidding mountain and fasts 40 days and 40 nights. Then, the screen lights up as God writes each of the Ten Commandments. Meanwhile, the Israelites, who have lost faith in God and Moses, ask Aaron (James Neill) to help them build a golden calf to worship. A woman caresses the calf, and she and many of the Israelites engage in racy dancing and orgiastic behavior. God tells Moses, "Save my people," and he brings down the tablets which he hurls to the ground breaking them and destroying the calf. Then at God's command, he orders the wicked—numbering 3,000—to be slain.

Part 2: Modern Day. The scene shifts abruptly to a living room in 1920s San Francisco where an old woman (Edythe Chapman) is reading the Bible to her two grown sons. Dan McTavish (Rod La Rocque), a college student, laughs at her saying, "That's all bunk, Mother. The Ten Commandments were alright for a lot of dead people but that sort of stuff was buried with Queen Victoria." She chases him from the house. He stops at a diner where a homeless girl named Mary Leigh (Leatrice Joy) steals his sandwich. After chasing her down in the pouring rain, he takes her to his house where he apologizes to his mother "but not to God" in whom he doesn't believe. Mary proves to be Dan's soul mate saying, "Nobody believes in the Ten Commandments these days, Elinor Glyn's more interesting" (see Commentary). Dan tells his brother Johnny (Richard Dix) that he and Mary are getting married, and "We're going to break all of your Ten Commandments. Keep them and you'll end up what you are, a poor carpenter." His mother blames herself because she taught him to *fear* God rather than *love* Him.

Dan becomes a wealthy contractor who cuts corners by substituting jute he gets from Calcutta for cement. He cheats on his wife with an exotic named Sally Lung (Nita Naldi) who, unbeknownst to him, stowed away from the leper colony at Molokai on one of his ships from Calcutta. Proud that Dan is building a church, his mother goes to inspect it when it collapses because it stands on landfill. Distraught at her death and needing money, Dan goes to Sally who refuses to give back the jewels he gave her. He kills Sally but not before she tells him she is a leper and declares, "Danny Dear, I'll tell the Devil you won't be far behind." He returns to his office where he finds the picture of his mother that he had hidden in a closet, and the words "Thou Shalt Not Kill" flash from it. Dan dies trying to escape to Mexico. Mary, now a leper, is saved by Johnny who tells her, "Only One Man can save you—One you have forgotten." He then reads the biblical passage about Christ healing the leper who believed in him, and Mary is cured.

Commentary

The most perplexing thing about this movie is how disjointed it is. Tagging on a very long and moralistic modern-day parable to an otherwise well-done spectacle for the time is incomprehensible. The film was reissued in DVD along with the 1956 version and some excellent commentary. Comparing the film not just with the remake but with *King of Kings*, shows how much DeMille learned from making this film. The introduction and the heavy-handed moralizing in Part 2 make clear, however, that DeMille was a believer and a proselytizer, although later on that would be sublimated as he created the spectacles for which his name became eponymous. As noted in Lopate's *American Movie Critics*, even acclaimed playwright Robert E. Sherwood praised the picture saying "the day would come, I knew, when I should have to utter praise for a Cecil B. DeMille picture." Conversely, as the Keysers point out, John Steinbeck famously dismissed it with the epigram, "Saw the movie. Loved the book."

In a sense, the second half links the seminal history of Judaism with latter-day Christians, for whom the stories in Genesis and Exodus, as well as the Ten Commandments, are foundation stones. Of particular interest is Dan's sainted mother who blames herself for emphasizing the fear of God rather than love to steer Dan on the straight and narrow. She does this without referencing the New Testament where Christ says that the two greatest commandments are "To love God with thy whole heart, thy whole soul, and thy whole mind" and "To love thy neighbor as thyself." While these commands don't gainsay the importance of the Ten Commandments, they do embody the Christian message.

Mary's reference to Elinor Glyn being more au courant than the Ten Commandments is also interesting. Glyn was a well-educated woman from an "aristocratic" background who worked as a scriptwriter in silent films in the 1920s. Bored with her marriage, she began writing erotic fiction, the most "notorious" being her 1907 novel *Three Weeks* about a torrid affair between an older married Queen of the Balkans and an Englishman. Its denunciation from pulpits earned her permanent celebrity. She is best known for coining and ascribing the term "It" for the possession of an intangible quality of sexual attraction and energy to Clara Bow, who became forever known as the "It Girl." Popular references to Glyn include a line in a 1957 Broadway musical, *The Music Man* by Meredith Willson, as well as in the 1927 song "My Heart Stood Still" by Lorenz Hart, and the following doggerel inspired by *Three Weeks*: "Would you like to sin With Elinor Glyn on a tiger skin? Or would you prefer to err with her on some other fur?"

Ben-Hur: A Tale of the Christ (1925)

The introduction states, "Pagan Rome was at the zenith of her power . . . In Judea, the glory that was Israel's lay scattered in the dust." It's December 24 and thousands, including an ancient-appearing Joseph (Winter Hall) and a young beautiful Mary (Betty Bronson), are on the march to register for the census. The next scenes are of the birth of Christ followed by the visit of the Wise Men. The scene then shifts to Judah Ben-Hur (Ramon Novarro) at the Jerusalem Gate where he sees Messala (Francis X. Bushman) his old boyhood friend heading a Roman legion into Jerusalem. He invites Messala to visit the opulent Hur home where they grew up together. Judah expresses pleasure that the garrison will be led by "a Roman who understands my people." Messala responds, "Rome rules the people she has conquered. It is up to them to understand Rome . . . No offense, but you are a stiff-necked people . . . To be a Roman is to rule, to be a Jew is to crawl in the dirt."

Later, while the Roman troops are parading past the Hur house, a brick accidentally falls injuring the Roman governor, and Judah is convicted and sentenced to be a galley slave. On the brutal march, the slaves pass a carpenter's shop on the Nazareth road, and the outstretched hand of the unseen Christ answers Judah's plea for water. After three years on the galley where almost all die in a year, Judah tells the captain of the galley Quintus Arrius (Frank Currier) that revenge keeps him alive. The captain replies, "Spoken like a true Roman." Judah says, "I am a Jew." While other slaves are shackled during a pirate raid, Judah is not, which allows him to turn the tide of the battle and also to save the captain. Adopted as a son by Quintus, he becomes the foremost athlete in Rome.

He travels to Antioch where he meets Esther (May McAvoy), the daughter of his father's faithful servant Simonides (Nigel De Brulier), and pledges his troth. He then agrees to ride for a sheik in a chariot race when he hears that the principal opponent is Messala. Interestingly, Arabs and Jews are shown getting along well. The spectacular race and its preliminaries occupy 15 minutes of screen time. Messala, despite dirty tricks, is beaten. As Judah is being congratulated, Balthasar the Egyptian (Charles Belcher), one of the Three Wise Men, appears to announce that Christ is the Messiah that the Jews have been awaiting. Judah leaves to raise two legions, one consisting of Arabs, to fight alongside Jesus.

Then the focus shifts back to Christ where a woman is being stoned, and Christ stops them. The Last Supper, shown in early Technicolor, is followed by Christ's trial and the Way of the Cross. Meanwhile, Esther finds Judah's mother and sister Tirzah (Kathleen Key), whom Messala had imprisoned years before and who are now lepers. Over their objections, she takes them to see Christ. Meanwhile Judah brandishes his sword and says to Christ that he has two legions to rescue him. Christ (unseen) says, "My kingdom is not of this world. Put up thy sword for the Son of man is not come to destroy men's lives but to save them." Judah drops his sword, and Christ moves on whereupon Judah sees Christ cure his mother and sister. After the crucifixion, Tirzah says, "Our King is dead. He bade us hold our peace, forgive our enemies, love one another, and pray." Judah responds, "He is not dead. He will live forever in the hearts of men."

Commentary

Despite the subtitle, this film, based on a book by Lew Wallace, is only marginally about Christ and mostly about the relationship between Judah Ben-Hur, the Jewish hero, and Messala, his Roman ex-boyhood friend. Indeed, the presence of Christ at infrequent intervals seems superimposed. Even so, the film can be seen as a strong affirmation of the link between Judaism and Christianity with the fictional Ben-Hur providing a connector. Christ is the Jew whom the noble Judah is seeking, and he recognizes Jesus as the Messiah who will lead the Jewish people out of bondage. Believing it will be by conquering the Romans in battle, he raises troops for Christ's army only to find that Christ's kingdom is not of this world and that Jesus even allows himself to be crucified. At the end, seeing the wonders Jesus performs in curing his leprous mother and sister, Judah accepts Christ. In the 1959 remake (see chapter 5), the conversion is not so overt.

Not showing Christ's face harks back to Wallace's refusal to sell the rights of his enormously successful book for the stage until he was assured that Christ would not be impersonated by an actor but represented by a radiant beam of light. The stage play was such a success that an early crude and unauthorized short film using firemen from Coney Island in the chariot scene was produced in 1907. Wallace's heirs challenged it all the way to the Supreme Court and their copyright was upheld, forming the basis for copyright protection for transforming books to film.

Though overshadowed by the much-acclaimed 1959 remake, this film is very much worth seeing. It cost $4 million and despite its great success, which established the fledgling MGM studio, it took six years to make a profit. The sea battle, filmed in Italy, resulted in an accidental fire, and those people jumping ship are actually fleeing for their lives. The chariot race was filmed in Culver City, California, on a vacant area that is now Venice and La Cienaga Boulevard using 42 cameras and 3,000 extras including such luminaries as Douglas Fairbanks, Mary Pickford, Harold Lloyd, Lillian Gish, Clark Gable, and John Gilbert. In the old days, when they bragged about having a cast of thousands, they meant it, but then they only had to provide lunch, although that was not as easy as it sounds.

BACKSTORY

Lew Wallace: Author of *Ben-Hur*

Born in 1827, Wallace served as a first lieutenant during the Mexican War and was elected to the Indiana State Senate in 1856. With the outbreak of the Civil War, he was appointed a colonel and rose to major general in March 1862 after exemplary actions in the Battle of Fort Donelson under Ulysses S. Grant. In the Battle of Shiloh, a miscommunication between him and General Grant led to the late positioning of his troops and a high casualty rate. He was never able to regain his once lustrous military reputation, although he was later credited with delaying Confederate troops and preventing their capture of Washington. He also served on the commission for the trials involving the Lincoln assassination and the commander of the notorious Andersonville prison camp.

While governor of the New Mexico Territory, he published *Ben-Hur*. Historian Victor Davis Hanson suggests that the fictional Ben-Hur, who is unjustly punished for an accidental injury to the Governor of Judea and pays a heavy price, bears a striking resemblance to Wallace's travails. The relationship with Messala also seems analogous to his once warm relationship with Grant, who refused to exonerate him in his memoirs.

How the story became *A Tale of the Christ* is fascinating. In the preface to his book, *The First Christmas*, Wallace recounts an encounter with noted agnostic Colonel Robert Ingersoll who sought him out during a train trip to the Republican Convention in Indianapolis in 1876. Wallace asked him, "Is there a God?' Ingersoll answered, "I don't know, do you?" The same answer was repeated when Wallace asked about the existence of a Devil, Heaven, Hell, and a Hereafter. Ingersoll then argued for two hours against belief in God. Wallace admitted that, at the time, his attitude with respect to religion was "one of absolute indifference." He went on to say, "I was aroused for the first time in my life as to the importance of religion." He then went back to a story he was writing about the first Christmas and decided to continue it to the crucifixion and learn as much as he could about Christ. The first result was *Ben-Hur*. The second, in Wallace's words, was "a conviction amounting to absolute belief in God and the Divinity of Christ." In short, it took an all-out assault on the existence of God for him to become a believer and a formidable one at that.

The King of Kings (1927)

C. B. DeMille once again sets the scene in his prologue: "This is a story of Jesus of Nazareth. He Himself commanded that this message be carried to the uttermost parts of the earth. May this portrayal play a reverent part in the spirit of that great command!" The opening scene is in Technicolor and features a garishly dressed Mary Magdalene (Jacqueline Logan) described in the accompanying text as a "beautiful courtesan who laughed alike at God and man." She is reclining at a lavish banquet surrounded by admirers, scantily clad women, men carrying food, and assorted animals including leopards. She asks for her lover, Judas, and is told that he has become enthralled by Christ, who heals the blind. She says that she has blinded more men than Christ can heal. She then calls for her chariot complete with zebras and sets out to find Judas who is described as the "ambitious one who joined the disciples in the belief that Jesus would become the nation's king and reward him with honor and high office." The other disciples are introduced singly and then generally as "men who were to fight the good fight of faith through sacrifice and martyrdom."

Meanwhile, a beautiful little blind girl asks to be taken to Jesus (H. B. Warner), who is seen through her eyes as she is cured, beginning with a light surrounding His head and then His face. This is followed by a remarkable scene in which the haughty and defiant Magdalene is blinded by Christ who says, "Be Thou clean," and she is serially exorcised of each of the Seven Deadly Sins: Lust, Greed, Pride, Gluttony, Indolence, Envy, and Anger. As soon as this is done, she is conscious of being scantily clad and covers herself up and kisses the hem of his garment. There are many biblical citations followed by numerous scenes from Christ's public life, the path to Calvary, the Crucifixion, and the Resurrection. The many scenes include a marvelous depiction of a playful Christ repairing the broken leg of a child's doll with the children gathered around Him, the resurrection of Lazarus from the dead, and especially the scene where Christ dissuades the crowd from stoning a prostitute by writing their sins in the sand.

Other noteworthy scenes include Christ's telling Judas that his failure to cure a "lunatic" was due to his "unbelief" and when a Jew responds to those bribing the crowd to call for Christ's death rather than Barabbas, "You cannot bribe me a Jew to cry for the blood of an innocent brother." Again radiance is used to highlight Christ on the cross and the stone at the tomb when He rises from the dead. This scene is in color as is the very powerful scene of Thomas placing his hand in Christ's wounds. The film concludes with Christ saying, "Go therefore and teach you all nations and preach the gospel to every creature." He then leaves as a dazzling white blur ascends, and we see skyscrapers in the background as the words "Lo, I am with you always," appear on the screen.

Commentary

C. B. DeMille took the admonition to "Go teach ye all nations" seriously. As noted in the film's introduction, he hoped it would be seen as "reverent." On the first day of shooting in August 24, 1926, he invited members of the clergy to offer their blessings on the enterprise. He was joined by a Rabbi, a Mohammedan (as they were then called), as well as representatives of Catholicism, Buddhist, Episcopalianism, Baptists, the Salvation Army, Christian Science, Presbyterianism, and the Church of Christ in America. Father Daniel Lord, an advisor for the film, said daily Mass on the set before filming began.

The premiere was the first film shown at Grauman's Chinese Theater. After four months, it had become the longest running film on Broadway, leading DeMille to say in a promo, "Does New York like clean, wholesome, powerful pictures? The answer is *King of Kings*." Will Rogers said that "the only way to make a greater picture than *King of Kings* is to have a better subject and I doubt if there will ever be a better subject."

DeMille exercised considerable artistic license, especially at the beginning with the story of Mary Magdalene and Judas. Nonetheless, the focus on Mary Magdalene provided the opportunity for one of the most powerful movie scenes ever, involving the cleansing of her sins. DeMille also demonstrated great imagination in the use of the newly available Technicolor process in a scene when Matthew, not yet an apostle, comes to collect taxes. DeMille juxtaposes this with the challenge to Christ about what one owes Caesar. Christ asks Peter to cast for a fish and when Peter lifts it from the water, he finds a gleaming gold coin in its mouth. Christ then asks whose visage is on the coin and when told that it's Caesar's, he says, "Render to Caesar the things that are Caesar's and to God the things that are God's." In a playful addendum, DeMille has two Roman soldiers trying to catch more

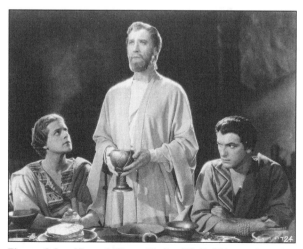

Figure 2.2. *King of Kings.* **Christ (H. B. Warner) at the Last Supper.**

fish, but to their dismay the fish have no more coins to yield. This scene and the ones with the blind girl and the healing of the doll convey Christ's humanity in ways that few other films about Jesus have been able to do.

The Passion of Joan of Arc (1928)

Made in France, the film focuses entirely on the trial of Joan of Arc using the actual court records as guides to the action and for the accompanying titles. It opens with a pair of hands turning the pages of an ancient book and then cuts to the entrance of the portly and self-satisfied judges into the courtroom. The prosecutor Bishop Pierre Cauchon (Eugene Sylvain) hovers over Joan (Renee Maria Falconetti) after her testimony that St. Michael the Archangel had appeared to her to tell her to lead the French to victory. Cauchon badgers her with rapid-fire questions: "Had he wings? A crown? Was he robed? Was he naked? How could you tell if it was a man or woman?" One judge objects that this is not a trial but a persecution and refuses to take part. And indeed it was, as Cauchon had made a deal with the English enemies to deliver Joan to them so that she could be destroyed.

Joan's request to be heard by the Pope is denied, and the Eucharist is withheld from her as part of unrelenting mental and physical torture. Threatened with being burned at the stake unless she signs a confession that she lied about the visions, she does so but almost immediately she recants. Knowing the fate that awaits her, she says, "My gentle Savior, I accept death with a good heart. Let me not suffer too long." A man in the supportive crowd shouts, "You have burned a saint." Although she was exonerated of her "crimes" 30 years later, what the bystander proclaimed in 1431 wasn't officially recognized by the Catholic Church until 1920.

Commentary

The brilliant director Carl Theodor Dreyer condensed the trial which lasted five months and consisted of 29 cross-examinations, as well as torture, into about 90 minutes of screen time. The film was believed lost when the original negative and other prints were burned in a fire and later after Dreyer's reconstruction met the same fate. In 1981, a complete print was found in a janitor's closet of an Oslo Norway mental institution. This print was beautifully restored and reissued on DVD in 1999 by the Criterion Collection. Two versions are provided: one in silence and the other with "Voices of

Light," a Latin oratorio composed by Richard Einhorn, consisting of the sounds of monks chanting. Inspired by the film, the new score marvelously enhances its extraordinary power.

Much of the film's success derives from Dreyer's insistence on making it as a silent film despite the advent of talkies. As Roger Ebert points out, Dreyer eschewed elaborate costumes and scenery so common to historical films. He opted instead for a stark angular set, a model of which is on display in Copenhagen's Film Museum. He juxtaposed unrelated images with close-ups of Joan and her interrogators, achieving a surrealistic effect that conveyed a sense of claustrophobia, discontinuity, and menace.

For his actors, he chose novices and unknowns. His greatest coup was to select as his Joan a comedienne who was appearing in a Parisian review while he was making preparations for the film. Falconetti, an accomplished stage actress who had never made a movie before, appeared for the screen test without makeup. Dreyer saw the naturalness he wanted and proceeded to cast other unknowns who also performed without makeup.

The film consists mainly of close-ups with Falconetti's face as the principal means of conveying the mood. As Todd Ollis recounts, Dreyer made her kneel on stones to achieve a painful expression. The filming took 18 months during which he had her endure take after take to get the expression or lack thereof he sought. The result of what can only be called merciless treatment was what Pauline Kael, the *New Yorker* critic, aptly called "the greatest performance ever captured on film." In my opinion, it's the closest we will ever get to seeing a soul on film. As a result of the experience, Falconetti would never make another picture, returning to comedic roles on the stage.

This picture provides a vivid example of the fallibility of what Catholic believers consider to be a divine institution entrusted to human hands through the abuse of power by corrupt clergymen cloaking themselves with the mantle of "The Church." By contrast, Falconetti conveys the inner turmoil of the devout saint as she pleads that she is "a good Christian" using myriad facial expressions and exquisite body language. Her humanity is evinced in her initial acquiescence to renounce her visions, whereas her sanctity is demonstrated in her recanting, knowing the fate that awaits her.

Saint Joan is the saint most frequently portrayed in film; at least four important films have been made of her life and a number of other films allude to her. Why the fascination with her? Was it simply that she was a strong woman who can be portrayed in a suit of armor or that the battle and death scenes make good theater? Maybe the best answer comes from Mark Twain, who labored for years on his *Personal Recollections of Joan of Arc*, which he considered to be his best work and the one that gave him the most pleasure. He called her "easily the most extraordinary person the human race has ever produced" and the embodiment of a selfless patriotism. That's pretty high praise from someone who was not a religious man and one who often took a jaundiced view of human nature.

Hallelujah! (1929)

This sentimental portrayal of Negro sharecroppers in the South during the Depression opens with the family, consisting of Mammy (Fanny Belle DeKnight), Pappy (Harry Gray), and six children, harvesting cotton and then eating dinner as their young son Spunk (Everett McGarrity) reads the Bible. Their dinner is interrupted by a couple named Adam and Eve who ask Pappy, a parson, to marry them. "It's about time," he says because they already have eleven children. During the post-wedding dance the eldest son Zeke (Daniel L. Haynes) makes a move on the adopted daughter Missy Rose (Victoria Spivey) who, although she loves him, pushes him away. Zeke says, "The Devil is in me tonight."

In a touching scene, Mammy rocks two of her sons to sleep and prays for a good price for their six months' worth of cotton when Zeke and Spunk sell it in town. Zeke gets a hundred dollars but is drawn by gamblers and a sexy honky-tonk dancer named Chick (Nina Mae McKinney) who first rejects him as a dirt poor farmhand but on learning about his money sets him up with a city slicker, Hotshot (William Fountaine). Accusing Hotshot of cheating him, Zeke pulls out his razor, and Hotshot pulls a gun. In the ensuing struggle, Spunk, who has been searching for Zeke, is shot. The repentant Zeke takes Spunk home to Mammy thinking she can save him, but he dies on the way. Pappy tells him that God forgives and will show him the light. On seeing it, Zeke is transformed into "Ezekiel the Prophet" and becomes an itinerant preacher. Arriving in his hometown on a train car labeled "Repent Ye Sinners," like Christ, he rides into town on a donkey. Chick ridicules him but finally gets religion and after being baptized, goes into a frenzy which excites Zeke who chases her to her tent, where he is prevented from ravishing her by Mammy.

That evening before the Jubilee, Zeke laments that "The Devil done take hold of me" and he pledges to marry Missy Rose to escape the devil. The obviously delighted Missy tells him, "You ain't never going to stop sinning; it's in your blood." That evening Hotshot tries to prevent Chick from attending the Revival, but she beats him with a poker saying, "That's what I'll do to anybody that stands in my Path to Glory." At the Jubilee, Zeke preaches while acting out a boxing match with the devil, fighting the gamblers, the backbiters, and the midnight ramblers. Just when the "Devil is down and out," Zeke sees Chick in ecstasy, and they run off together. He works in a sawmill, but Chick is bored and runs off with Hotshot in a horse and carriage. As Zeke chases them, they crash, and Chick is mortally injured. Zeke kills Hotshot and, after serving time on a chain gang, returns to the bosom of his family.

Commentary

The DVD of this film is introduced with the disclaimer that it is "a product of its time" and that it may reflect the prejudices that were commonplace in American society especially when it comes to the treatment of racial and ethnic minorities. The distributor, Warner Bros., while calling it wrong and not reflecting its views, rightly has not altered the content. The DVD contains an excellent commentary by noted African-American critic Donald Bogle, author of *Toms, Coons, Mulattoes, Mammies, and Bucks: An Interpretive History of Blacks in American Films*. He explains that director King Vidor put up his salary to make the film and that some African-Americans and liberal whites were offended by the scene of the late marriage and the move Zeke makes on Missy Rose as well as the violence when Zeke is cheated. Their concern was that, although comparably negative images existed of whites, they appeared in a wide range of films, whereas this was only one of two films with an all-black cast; the next, *Green Pastures*, wouldn't appear for seven years. W. E. B. DuBois objected to the fact that the film did not depict whites who were bearing down on the black community. Nonetheless, many blacks liked the film because it was very naturalistic, showing actual workplaces like the sawmill and the cotton fields almost in a documentary style, as well as the importance to blacks of family and religion. It also was a potent antidote (which director Vidor wanted) to what Bogle calls the "classic racist masterpiece *Birth of a Nation*." The film, shot mainly on location in and around Memphis, west Tennessee, and eastern Arkansas, captured actual local religious scenes. It could not be done in sound because of the primitive nature of the equipment in 1929, and the sound track was later dubbed.

The acting is remarkable, especially when one considers that none of the actors had much film experience. Nina Mae McKinney, who was only 16 when she was discovered by Vidor in New York, acts more naturally at times than her more experienced counterpart, the excellent Daniel L. Haynes. Harry Gray, who played the parson, was 82 when he was discovered working at the *Amsterdam News*, the New York City paper for blacks. The marvelous music ranges from spirituals to blues to jazz to tunes Irving Berlin wrote for the movie. Not only are Haynes, McKinney, and Spivey wonderful singers, but they are backed up by the Dixie Jubilee singers, a group from Fisk College that was dedicated to training black vocalists. From a Christian point of view, it captured a time when evangelists traveled the country preaching in makeshift tents. It also shows how religious ecstasy and charismatic preaching may sometimes cross the line to sexual predation, or as Zeke would say, those who genuinely may be trying to follow Christ are not immune from being tempted by the devil (even Christ was). Then again, Missy Rose may have it right when she tells Zeke, "You ain't never going to stop sinning; it's in your blood."

CHAPTER THREE
HE AIN'T HEAVY,
HE'S MY BROTHER: THE 1930s

Best remembered for the devastating world-wide depression, the 1930s were filled with other major events. These included the consolidation of power by the Nazis in Germany as Hitler ascended to the chancellorship in 1933; the fascist takeover in Italy by Benito Mussolini; the rise of nationalism and authoritarianism in Japan under Emperor Hirohito; and Stalin's purges of millions of his "enemies" including Trotsky. Japan waged war on China and retook Manchuria, while Spaniards fought a bloody and bitter Civil War viewed by many as a trial run for World War II in Europe involving backing by Germany and Italy on one side and Russia and a coalition of people from other countries including the United States on the other.

In the United States, extreme unemployment in the cities and abject poverty in both rural and urban areas led Franklin Roosevelt, who was elected president in 1932, to implement many New Deal programs using federal funds to ameliorate the lives of the poor. Although some initiatives like the Civilian Conservation Corps, the Works Progress Administration, and the Social Security Act were moderately effective, as Amity Shlaes documents in her landmark book *The Forgotten Man*, it took the outbreak of World War II in Europe and the rise in America's industrial growth aimed at sustaining the efforts of the Allies to lift the country out of the Depression.

Amid all the gloom, some bright spots emerged. Radio became ubiquitous and many classic radio programs helped unite rural and urban America. Sensing its great power, FDR began his "Fireside Chats," speaking directly to the people. Other noteworthy events included the building of the Empire State Building, Amelia Earhart's first successful solo flight across the Pacific, the exploits of Jesse Owens in the 1936 Berlin Olympics, the discovery of sulfa drugs, and an attempt at fostering optimism at the World's Fair in New York City in 1939–1940, when many nations came together to hail a brighter future. Unfortunately, that illusion was shattered by Hitler's invasion of Poland and the outbreak of World War II in 1939.

The Films of the Thirties

The 1930s was a transitional decade in film history as talkies supplanted silent movies, famously trumpeted with the advertisement for *Anna Christie*, "Garbo Speaks." The decade was also marked by other technical improvements such as the development of three-strip Technicolor, which beautifully reproduced colors, as well as better sound recording and cameras. Combined with the increased skill and sophistication of the actors, actresses, directors, and screenwriters under the studio system that required their appearance in two and usually many more films annually, the film industry experienced such a rapid maturation that 1939 is still considered Hollywood's Golden Year, because of the plethora of outstanding movies that were released.

If one dramatic theme predominated in the films of the 1930s, it was the fascination with gangsters, crime, and crime-solvers. In addition, up to 1934 some films featured healthy doses of sex and seduction, leading many to be concerned about film's profound cultural impact. In March 1930, responding to public concerns about film content, filmmakers established the Motion Picture Code of Conduct (or Hays Code), which regulated the depiction of scenes involving sex, violence, religion, and other sensitive subjects (see p. 5). Shortly thereafter, in 1933, clergy, predominantly Catholic, established the Legion of Decency (see p. 6), which rated films according to their moral acceptability for adults and children. The ability of both organizations to affect film content was enhanced by the Depression's economic downturn in studio profits that heightened the receptivity of filmmakers to public concerns about content. Gangster films were toned down into lighter fare like *The Thin Man* series featuring two perfectly matched stars playing off one another with sophisticated repartee and light comedy. Filmmakers buoyed the country's spirits with screwball comedies, such as *It Happened One Night*, *My Man Godfrey*, and *Bringing Up Baby*. Walt Disney's animation company came into its own, not only with fine cartoons (especially those featuring the Disney icon, Mickey Mouse) but feature-length animated tales, such as *Snow White and the Seven Dwarfs*. Films highlighting the dancing of Fred Astaire and Ginger Rogers and the singing of Nelson Eddy and Jeannette MacDonald were also immensely popular.

Christianity in Depression-Era Films

Although a few biblical epics were produced in the early 1930s, most notably *The Sign of the Cross* and *The Crusades*, these films were really a carryover from the silent era courtesy of the legendary Cecil B. DeMille; the genre would not flourish again until the 1950s. During the last half of the 1930s, sympathetic Catholic clergy began to make their appearance in the person of Spencer Tracy, Pat O'Brien, and Sir Cedric Hardwicke, who also played a kindly Episcopal Dean. For the most part, the films of the 1930s were stories of redemption. Christian influences were shown transforming a reckless, selfish playboy in *Magnificent Obsession* into a life-saving humanitarian; and helping wayward boys see that crime doesn't pay in *Angels with Dirty Faces* and *Boys Town* as well as a doctor reclaiming his shattered career by extraordinary service to others in *The Green Light*. In short, the 1930s began a three-decadelong positive attitude toward Christianity and Christian beliefs in film.

The Miracle Woman (1931)

A biblical quotation opens the film: "Beware of false prophets who come to you in sheep's clothing" (Matthew 7:15). The viewer is then drawn by the ringing of church bells into a typical small town Protestant church, where the choir is singing "Holy, Holy, Holy." The church is filled to hear the final sermon by an old minister whom the congregation's leaders have fired after 25 years of service. Instead of the minister, his devout and devoted daughter Florence Fallon (Barbara Stanwyck) ascends the pulpit and announces that her father died while dictating a sermon, just after saying, "You have chosen to hire a younger man." She then goes on to scold the deacon and his clique whom she accuses of crucifying her father just as Jesus was crucified. She says, "This is not a House of God. This is a meeting place of hypocrites. You don't pay your ministers what you pay your chauffeur." She decries the bootleggers who preach temperance and the "righteous" who cheat on their wives.

As the congregation flees, a traveling salesman who has seen Florence's potential as a charismatic speaker tells her that: "Religion is like anything else, great if you can sell it." Together they found the Temple of Happiness, and she becomes Sister Fallon. John Carson (David Manners), a blind ex-pilot and war hero, is about to jump out a window when he hears her speak on her radio station WGOD. He asks his landlady to take him to the revival meeting. The chorus sings "Over There" and Sister Fallon enters in a flowing white robe to the tune of "Onward Christian Soldiers." She then invites someone to come up and enter a cage with a lion ("The

Lion's Den"). The audience plant who usually performs the stunt is drunk and doesn't appear, and Carson goes up. She tells him that "You have shown faith and you shall see again."

Later, her manager scolds the various shills who feign being miraculously cured as the "crummiest crew of come-ons he's ever hired." He wants more "sincerity" from them. When Sister Fallon decides that she wants to work without them, he accuses her of "falling for her own ballyhoo." Naturally, she falls in love with Carson, and the manager, who covets her himself, threatens to expose her as a charlatan. She decides to confess to being a liar and a cheat and, as she does so, the tabernacle burns in a chaotic scene during which she is reunited with her lover. The film ends on a street in New York City with her working for the Salvation Army and receiving a telegram from Carson, who is in a hospital where he hopes to regain his sight so that they can marry.

Commentary

Filmmakers have not been kind to evangelicals and fundamentalists. Heavily influenced by Sinclair Lewis's 1927 novel, *Elmer Gantry*, and the writings of H. L. Mencken, many filmmakers have portrayed them as hypocrites and charlatans more intent on obtaining the audience's money and seducing them, both literally and figuratively, than saving their souls. This early Frank Capra film anticipates films like *Elmer Gantry* (see p. 150) where true believers get exploited by charlatans who fleece the masses hungry for that old-time religion. Capra uses an old-fashioned introductory crawl to state his purpose: "*The Miracle Woman* is offered as a rebuke to anyone who, under the cloak of religion, seeks to sell for gold, God's choicest gift of humanity, FAITH."

Still, Barbara Stanwyck's superb performance does manage to show a more human and sympathetic side in that she begins as a truly devout Christian anxious to carry on her father's mission by spreading the biblical message. However, she allows herself to be manipulated by a huckster and gets overtaken by the rich trappings and an entourage of sycophants. In conformity with the 1930s theme of redemption, she herself is saved by rescuing another lost soul and ends up living out her genuine beliefs not as an evangelistic grande dame but a humbler foot soldier in the Salvation Army.

The role is clearly based on Aimee Semple McPherson, a famous touring evangelist in the 1920s and 1930s. Born Aimee Kennedy she married Robert

Figure 3.1. *The Miracle Woman.* **Sister Florence (Barbara Stanwyck) assures the suicidal, blind war hero John Carson (David Manners) that he will see again.**

Semple, an Irish Pentecostal missionary in 1908 at the age of 17. In 1910, they went to China as missionaries where they both contracted malaria and Robert died. In 1913, she married Henry McPherson, an accountant, but left him in 1915 to become a full-time preacher, traveling the country in a 1912 Packard called "The Gospel Car." In 1925, she completed the building of the over 5000-seat Angelus Temple in Los Angeles.

She would appear onstage in a flowing white gown with flowers and preach the Four Square Gospel, which incorporated faith healing and speaking in tongues with calls to ecstasy. The first woman to give a sermon on radio, she also was the first to get an FCC license with the opening of Four Square Gospel's radio station KFSG. She also established lighthouses similar to the Salvation Army, which she called the Salvation Navy. After disappearing and staging a "kidnapping" in 1926 (presumably to cover up a tryst), she surfaced after 32 days. Although she continued her career until she died in 1944 of a barbiturate overdose deemed accidental, she never recaptured her initial fame.

The Sign of the Cross (1932)

It's AD 64 and a larger-than-life Nero (Charles Laughton) is "fiddling while Rome burns." When told of the destruction and loss of life, he says "Let us hope that most of the dead are Christians. We have hunted them like rats but they still multiply." The major plot, which anticipates such epics as *Quo Vadis* and *The Robe*, involves the pagan Marcus Superbus (Fredric March) as prefect of Rome rejecting the advances of Nero's wife Poppaea (Claudette Colbert) and, instead, falling for Mercia (Elissa Landi), a beautiful Christian who, despite her love for him, refuses to renounce Christ.

The film features an orgy with nude dancers and a lesbian seduction scene whose music is drowned out halfway through by the chanting of Christians imprisoned in the dungeon. Scenes of depravity in the Colosseum include bear-baiting, elephants stepping on the heads of Christians, crocodiles eating maidens, a gorilla seducing a young girl at the stake, and pygmies getting pitchforked by wild women. Christians recite the Lord's Prayer and the Beatitudes as they bravely enter a real "Lion's Den" to certain martyrdom. As Marcus and Mercia march into the arena arm-in-arm to their deaths, the image of a Cross lights the screen.

Commentary

This over-the-top Cecil B. DeMille extravaganza was one of the last films to flout the newly established Hays Code and is credited by some with playing a part in ending "pre-Code" Hollywood's "anything goes" portrayal of sex and religion in favor of the Code's more rigorous enforcement. DeMille resisted making the changes requested by the Hays office before distributing the film because they would detract from its box office appeal. He also believed that his bona fides as a committed Christian (see Backstory, p. 126) had been amply demonstrated in his previous very devotional film *King of Kings* (p. 27). Interestingly, the portrayal of Christians, as with many of DeMille's films, was indeed very sympathetic. Nonetheless, when the film was reissued in 1935, the contentious scenes were cut. Both versions are now available on DVD.

What probably offended many Catholics was that the title *Sign of the Cross*, which conjured up the blessings Catholics use devotionally as preludes to prayer, couldn't have been more misleading as to the content. Indeed, the film is best known among cineastes for Claudette Colbert's scene as Empress Poppaea, where she takes a bath in asses' milk. Parenthetically, the filmmakers used cow's milk that turned sour during the many days it took to film the scene, making it very unpleasant for Colbert. Indeed, what's most striking about the film, even more than the blatant sexuality, is the violence! The

Figure 3.2. *The Sign of the Cross.* **An elephant steps on a Christian in the colosseum.**

images of the animals having their way with the Christians are not pretty to watch. Still, film critic Pauline Kael probably characterized the film best with her comment: "DeMille's bang-them-on-the-head-with-wild-orgies-and imperiled-virginity style is at its ripest; the film is just about irresistible."

The Crusades (1935)

The Crusades begins in AD 1187 with the Saracens sweeping over the Holy Land and capturing Jerusalem. They are shown killing and enslaving Christians as well as pulling down the Cross with ropes and burning religious objects. Nuns say the Lord's Prayer while Saracens sell the golden-haired Christian princess as a slave with the statement "May Allah give you joy; of all the captives, this is the best." A hermit (C. Aubrey Smith) pledges to lead a Crusade to recapture Jerusalem and enlists Richard the Lionheart (Henry Wilcoxon) who professes "no love for monks and bald pates." He agrees to go if, by taking up the sword, he can renounce his pledge to marry Alice (Katherine DeMille), daughter of the king of France.

Cut to France where Berengaria (Loretta Young), the devout daughter of the king of Navarre, sees Richard and his men and shouts, "They're going to the Holy Land to free the tomb of Our Lord." Richard needs cattle and grain before embarking for the Holy Land, and Berengaria's father barters these in exchange for his daughter's hand. She is not thrilled, having discovered that Richard is not a saint but a womanizing, brawling boor. Richard sends his sword to represent him at the ceremony, so she says "I do" holding the sword which she kisses and flings away. He, in turn, disdainfully wraps her veil around his horse.

Berengaria and Alice share a cabin in the women's boat on the trip to Acre where the kings of France, England, Norway, Sicily, Hungary, and Germany meet with Saladin (Ian Keith) the Muslim leader at a great feast. Saladin tells them to "go in peace while you can, go and live, or stay and die." Richard answers, "From you Sultan of Islam, I accept only war." Meanwhile Richard starts to appreciate Berengaria who refuses to consummate the marriage, preferring to sleep with the sword in a bed whose four posts she names "Matthew, Mark, Luke, and John."

As they quarrel, Saladin attacks. Acre holds, and Saladin puts on Christian armor to go through the lines for reinforcements. Berengaria also suits up and is almost killed. Saladin scoops her up and nurses her back to health saying, "Allah has sent her to me. I will not let her die." Saladin proposes to her and after much more bloodshed, she acquiesces. Saladin agrees to release his captives if the Christians release the Islamic captives in Asia. He opens the gates to Jerusalem, the Crusaders enter singing "Alleluia, Alleluia," and the Cross goes back up on the Church of the Holy Sepulcher. Richard breaks his sword and says, "O God I was blind and now I see. Your cross has burned deep into my heart. Give her back to me. Have pity on a penitent fool." Finally, Saladin makes the ultimate sacrifice and releases Berengaria to Richard. The film ends with Berengaria making the Sign of the Cross and placing the broken sword on the altar as light plays on the cross and shield.

Commentary

This film, based on Harold Lamb's book *The Crusades: Iron Men and Saints*, was another Cecil B. DeMille extravaganza depicting the Third Crusade. In a typically overblown theatrical trailer, DeMille trumpets his message:

> Reissued as the eyes of the world focus on Palestine, Paramount re-presents Cecil B. DeMille's mighty production *The Crusades*, preserving for all the ages the Glory of Palestine's most spectacular struggle, the War of Faith. The glorious love story of the age of chivalry when faith in God carried the flower of knighthood on History's most Gallant Quest. Faith that gave strength to Christian women sold into the slave marts of the Saracens. Faith that sent Christian soldiers into battle against the mighty host of Islam.

It's so campy that even critics forgave its historical inaccuracies. As the critic for *Time* magazine said, "As a picture, it's historically worthless, didactically treacherous, artistically absurd. None of these defects impairs its entertainment value."

It is particularly interesting to compare the film with present-day views of the Crusades as evidenced by the decidedly not entertaining 2005 film *Kingdom of Heaven* (p. 321). Here the fictional hero is a nonbeliever who fights at the urging of his father, a Christian knight respected by the Muslims. The latter are portrayed as generally good in contrast to the bloodthirsty, evil, and hypocritical clergy and Christian Knight Templars. By contrast, *The Crusades*, at least at the outset, appears to be saying the reverse (Christians are good, Muslims are bad); however, as the film progresses, the luster fades from the Christian knights, although at the end Richard also gets the Thirties Redemption treatment. The Muslim leader Saladin is portrayed in a very favorable light, becoming decidedly heroic at the end, giving *The Crusades* a sense of balance that is missing from the newer film. In fact when DeMille asked permission of Egyptian strongman Gamel Abdel Nasser to film his remake of *The Ten Commandments* on location, Nasser replied, "Mr. DeMille, we grew up on your movie *The Crusades*. We saw how you treated our religion. You can do anything in this country."

The history of the Crusades and the struggles between Christianity and Islam are too complex to cover here, but the reader is referred to a number of contemporary works in the bibliography. Indeed, it might prove useful to explore the Crudades in a film series since very few today know its

Figure 3.3. *The Crusades.* **Berengaria (Loretta Young) holds a broken sword, Richard the Lion-hearted's "stand-in" at their wedding.**

real history. It should aim at examining the truth about the Crusades and placing them into the context of the spread of Islam over formerly Christian lands, their defeat by the Franks under Charles Martel in the battle of Tours in 732, and the defeat of two other invasions by the Ottoman Empire at the battle of Lepanto in 1571 and at the Gates of Vienna in 1683 as well as events in the 19th and 20th centuries in Tripoli and Armenia, as well as in many Islamic countries today.

Les Miserables (1935)

In this version of Victor Hugo's 1,400-page novel, Jean Valjean (Fredric March) is sentenced to 10 years in the galleys for stealing a loaf of bread to feed his starving family. On his release, Valjean, a bitter man, is taken in by kindly Bishop Bienvenu (Sir Cedric Hardwicke) who calls him his brother and serves him dinner on his best silver plate. When Valjean asks why he does not fear being murdered in his sleep, the bishop says he has faith in him. During the night, Valjean steals the silver and is brought back by the police. The bishop says that he gave it to him and that Valjean forgot to take the two other candlesticks. Sending Valjean on his way, he says, "Life is to give, not to take" and secures a promise that he will do likewise. Valjean stops by a wayside shrine and kisses the Blessed Virgin's foot to the strains of "Ave Maria."

Five years later, having resurrected an obsolete factory and a town, combined with paying fair wages and charitable giving, Valjean, now Monsieur Madeleine, is asked to be town mayor and magistrate. Here he crosses swords with Inspector Javert (Charles Laughton) who, with his quivering lower lip hiding his repressed emotions, implacably refuses to temper justice with mercy. Realizing that Madeleine is Valjean who is wanted for breaking parole, he begins a merciless chase. Valjean with his young ward Cosette (Marilyn Knowlden) are sheltered in a convent that Madeleine had supported. The film ends with Javert pursuing Valjean through the Paris sewers, a suicide, and the strains of "Ave Maria."

Commentary
The Christian theme is pervasive and except for a priest who is an agent of the state mouthing pious platitudes as the abused prisoners are paroled, the portraits are uniformly positive starting with the kindly bishop whose name is Bienvenu (or "welcome"). This extends to the nuns who gently minister

to Cosette's mother, Fantine (Florence Eldridge), and to the nuns who shelter Madeleine and Cosette. Rituals like Cosette's Confirmation, during which the children sing "O Salutaris Hostia" at Benediction, are handled reverently. Even more powerful is the portrayal of the lived Christian ethic of charity, social justice, the giving of oneself, forgiveness, and redemption. For the alternate view, I turn to *New Yorker* critic Pauline Kael. In her usual acerbic style, she commented that "after Valjean's spiritual rebirth, Fredric March acts impossibly virtuous . . . and Cedric Hardwicke is so saintly as the Bishop who gives Valjean the silver candlesticks that you wish Valjean had bopped him over the head with them." As they used to say in Brooklyn, "you pays your money and takes your cherce."

Magnificent Obsession (1935)

This "redemption" film is based on a 1929 novel by Lloyd C. Douglas, a former Lutheran (and later Congregational) minister (see Backstory, p. 46). It opens with Bobby Merrick (Robert Taylor), a rich playboy being saved from drowning with an "artificial respirator" after an accident while show-ing off his speedboat. At the same time a beloved older physician, Doctor Hudson, for whom the respirator had always been available on standby while he took an afternoon swim, dies from drowning. Like many early films, the introductory crawl states the theme to ensure that no one misses it: "To save him (Merrick), a man on whom thousands depend had to die."

The shiftless Merrick, missing his alcohol and life of partying, signs out of the hospital as soon as he is up on his feet. He gets drunk, smashes up his car, and seeks shelter in a nearby stonecutter's cottage surrounded by statues of angels and saints. The owner, Randolph (Ralph Morgan), tells him about Doctor Hudson, who had taught him how "to make contact with the source of infinite power." The secret is to help people by giving them money in absolute secrecy and, rather than being repaid, telling the recipient to do the same for others when they can afford to do so. He tells Merrick that Hudson had made several fortunes and given them all away.

The melodrama continues when, after his car is repaired, Merrick gives a lift to Hudson's widow (Irene Dunne), who is unaware of his connection with her husband's death. As she steps out of the car, she is blindsided both literally and figuratively by an oncoming car. The distraught Mer-rick quietly finances her visits to eye specialists from around the world, but without success. So, what does this medical school dropout do? He returns to school, becomes a world-famous doctor, and in a breathtakingly short period of time, wins a Nobel Prize. He seeks out Randolph to learn Mrs. Hudson's whereabouts. Randolph lauds Merrick for his good deeds in very explicitly Christian terms, saying, "Through one, all may be reached. Christ believed that he died for all humanity." Then he gives Merrick his last test, which is to save the now gravely ill Mrs. Hudson, and to restore her sight, which, of course, he does.

Commentary

The "magnificent obsession" refers not to a passionate love between the two main characters, but to Christ's admonition to help others secretly and without thought of recompense. This spirit underlies the actions of Doctor Hudson and all those he helped. It is this obsession that saves a wretch like Merrick and leads to a happy ending.

The film was remade in 1954, starring Jane Wyman and Rock Hudson in his breakthrough role. The story is basically the same except that, as

---

BACKSTORY

Lloyd C. Douglas: Minister Turned Best-Selling Author

Biblical subjects were among the most popular sources for early filmmakers, and it didn't take them long to figure out that other best-selling books would make great motion pictures, too. Perhaps the most famous example of a best-selling-novel-turned-movie is Margaret Mitchell's *Gone with the Wind* (1939), but it was, by no means, the first. In 1935, *Magnificent Obsession*, a story taken from a huge 1929 best-seller of the same name, was released to great acclaim.

The author of the book was a retired clergyman named Lloyd C. Douglas. The son of a Lutheran pastor, Douglas was born in Indiana in 1877, graduated from Wittenberg College (a Lutheran school) in Springfield, Ohio, in 1903, and spent the next three decades as a minister, first in the Lutheran Church and later in the Congregational Church and the United Church. *Magnificent Obsession* was his first novel, written when he was 50 years old, and was an immediate sensation. The "obsession" of the title was not, as is popularly believed, about sexual passion between a man and a woman, but about moral obsession and the love of God.

Indeed, all of Douglas's subsequent novels were concerned with morality and were distinctly religious. He went on to write eight more novels over the next twenty years, all of which enjoyed great success (*The Robe* sold over two million copies). Several were made into movies, including *The Green Light* (1937) and *The Robe* (1953), which starred a young Richard Burton. Unhappy with some of the adaptations, Douglas stipulated that his last novel, *The Big Fisherman*, not be dramatized in any other medium. Despite this, after his death, it was made into a forgettable movie by Frank Borzage, director of *The Green Light*, and starring Howard Keel.

Merrick helps Mrs. Hudson cope with her blindness, again without her knowing his connection with her husband's death, they fall in love. So, he completes medical school to become an expert eye surgeon to cure her. Also, the religious references are more subtle in the later film with Christ being alluded to rather than explicitly mentioned. Instead, when Randolph (Ralph Morgan) issues the same challenge to Merrick, he says that what he is asking Merrick to do is "dangerous stuff; the first man who used it died on the cross at thirty-three."

A Tale of Two Cities (1935)

London and Paris are the two cities in the title of this best movie version of Dickens's classic novel of the same name. Based on Carlyle's history of the French Revolution, the novel begins with one of the most famous opening lines in all of literature: "It was the best of times; it was the worst of times." The plot highlights injustice on both sides of the Revolution, beginning with the release of Dr. Manette (Henry Walthall), who had been unjustly imprisoned in solitary confinement for years by the king of France. Temporarily mad, he is brought over to England by Charles Darnay (Donald Woods) and reunited with his family. Charles falls in love with the doctor's daughter, Lucie (Elizabeth Allan), as does his good friend Sidney Carton (Ronald Colman), an alcoholic lawyer who defends the aristocrats who are being hunted down by the revolutionaries. Carton forswears his dissolute lifestyle and, like Darnay, seeks Lucie's hand, but when she marries Charles, the crestfallen Carton resumes his heavy drinking and sardonic attitude. He is persuaded by Lucie to accompany the family to midnight mass on Christmas Eve where he stands outside the church and hears the strains of "Hark the Herald Angels Sing." Later, the English version of "Adeste Fidelis," "O Come All Ye Faithful," echoes in the background as he talks about starting life anew.

The film is best known for the scenes involving Madame Defarge (Blanche Yurka), a revolutionary who furiously knits as she directs which aristocrat's head will next roll at the guillotine. Darnay heads her list because, although he is sympathetic to the Revolution, he is the nephew of the callous nobleman Marquis St. Evremonde (Basil Rathbone), whose carriage ran over and killed innocent peasants in front of the Defarge wine shop. Darnay is imprisoned and scheduled to ride the tumbrel for his rendezvous with the guillotine. Motivated by his love for Lucie, Carton, who is Darnay's look-alike, locates a nobler inner self and is smuggled into the Bastille where he drugs the reluctant Darnay and has him spirited out of jail. As Carton approaches the guillotine, he speaks the book's closing lines—words that kept Ronald Colman impersonators employed for years: "It's a far far better thing that I do than I have ever done; it's a far, far better rest that I go to than I have ever known."

Commentary

Although filled with action such as the storming of the Bastille, during which 17,000 extras were used, the film is at its core a moving story of love and friendship. Although the film is not an overtly Christian film, I have included it because of the indirect role Christianity plays in the redemption of the rejected suitor. The sardonic Carton seems to care for nothing or no one until he falls in love with the gentle Lucie. Rejected, he quickly returns to his dissolute lifestyle, only to be coaxed out of it by Lucie and the intervention of two very moving traditional Christmas carols.

When this film was released in 1935, movies with sound had been in existence for less than a decade. Filmmakers had long understood the ability of music to create mood and meaning, but in the silent era they were restricted to theater accompaniment on the "Mighty Wurlitzer" organs. With the arrival of sound, film scores by such prolific composers as Max Steiner began to be commissioned to match the action on the screen. The music in this film does more; it is an excellent illustration of the powerful ability of music not just to enhance the emotional content of a film but also to play the role of an offscreen character. In this case, the Christmas carols provide substitutes for Christian clergy or any other distinctly Christian character to aid Carton in his path to redemption. As an unseen "player," the carols project a Christian message more subtly and powerfully than an actor could.

Interestingly, although the words to "Hark the Herald Angels Sing" were written in 1739 by Charles Wesley whose brother, John, founded the Methodist Church, the tune in the film was composed by Felix Mendelssohn in 1840. Similarly, the English translation of "Adeste Fidelis" has been traced to Reverend Frederick Oakley in 1841, 50 years after the French Revolution and the historic moment depicted in the film. But, why quibble about 50 years? Let's just call it an effective bit of cinematic and artistic license. In a sense, Carton internalizes the message of the carols and lives it out when he decides to take Darnay's place in the Bastille and on the guillotine, in essence laying down his life, like Christ did for us. To be sure that the viewer does not miss the meaning, as he does so, we hear an unseen voice intone, "I am the Resurrection and the Life, sayeth the Lord."

The Green Pastures (1936)

The Hall Johnson Choir sings "Thank You Lord" as a bell rings in a wooden church and a young boy resists going to Sunday school. His grandfather asks, "Do you want to grow up to be a transgressor?" The boy joins the other children as they pass into a fantasy vision of heaven with a fish fry every day and men smoking "seegars." It begins with the creation story, after which Jehovah or "De Lawd" (Rex Ingram), unhappy with his handiwork, sends the flood, while saving only Noah, his family, and the animals. The film continues in a series of skits centered on Bible stories involving Abraham, Moses, and Joshua. Once again things go badly as Babylon is likened to "an all-night time in New Orleans with dancing girls." Finally, with Sodom and Gomorrah, De Lawd gives up on them, but the people are told that they "have a new Lawd now, a God of mercy. We fast a bit and gain mercy from suffering. Even God must suffer. They made him carry the cross up that high hill." The film ends with "Hallelujah! It's Jesus, God of Mercy, God of Love," and a smiling grandson.

Commentary

The first major feature film in the talkies era with an all-black cast was a milestone; yet, it would probably not be shown today because of its racial stereotyping. That's sad because it offers a more human and entertaining retelling of biblical stories than many of the more famous and sophisticated religious extravaganzas that came before and after it. The play by Marc Connelly, on which the film was based, was in turn based on a 1928 book by Roark Bradford, *Ol' Man Adam An' His Chillun*. Though banned in some states and cities, the play ran for five years in 39 states and won the 1930 Pulitzer Prize. The movie was also banned in some Southern cities as well as Finland, Australia, and Britain. Warner Bros. reissued it on DVD in 2006 with commentary by black filmmaker and actor LeVar Burton, along with Herb Boyd and Ed Guerrero, scholars of black cinema and culture, to put the film into perspective. The cast is excellent, and the Hall Johnson Choir's renditions of about 25 Negro spirituals like "Let My People Go" and "When the Saints Go Marching In" are alone worth the rental. More important, it

Figure 3.4. *Green Pastures.* **De Lawd (Rex Ingram) is surrounded by angels in heaven.**

is an enduring classic, which, while clearly a product of its time, transcends it by being a heartwarming validation of Christianity, rendered simply and without pretension.

San Francisco (1936)

One of the great disaster movies in movie history, *San Francisco* also features the good guy/bad guy buddy scenario that was so popular in films of the 1930s. Here, the two buddies are Father Tim Mullin (Spencer Tracy) and his boyhood friend, gambler, and saloon owner Blackie Norton (Clark Gable). Scripted by Anita Loos, it also stars Jeannette MacDonald as Mary, a budding opera singer, who falls for Blackie and agrees to sing and dance in his saloon, "The Paradise." Blackie tries to bed her, but she resists. Seeing that she isn't the ordinary chorus girl, he agrees to sleep in another room with the key on her side of the door. Later, he sends Mary to Father Mullin's parish, St. Anne's Mission, which he identifies as "a joint on Kearney Street," to sing in the choir, and a lovely job she does.

The film takes various twists and turns both in Mary's relationship with Blackie and in her career as a showgirl, an opera star, and then a showgirl again. In the process, she becomes the means by which Father Tim achieves his lifelong dream of redeeming his "good-hearted," albeit shady, friend Blackie. Just before the 1906 San Francisco earthquake, Mary enters a contest with a $10,000 prize that she hopes to win and give to Blackie, who is now down on his luck. She sings a rousing rendition of "San Francisco, Open Your Golden Gate" to a standing ovation. As she collects the prize, Blackie, not wanting charity, rushes the stage and angrily dumps the money out of a loving cup. Distraught, Mary starts to walk off stage just as the earthquake hits.

As he frantically searches for Mary in the fiery rubble, Blackie performs many good deeds saving people because he's really a softie at heart. He seeks out Father Tim who is tending the wounded at the mission, and they joins forces in the search for Mary. Just as they begin to despair, they hear her singing "Nearer my God to Thee" as she stands disheveled next to a woman mourning her dead child. Blackie, at Father Tim's suggestion, falls on his knees and gives thanks and all's well that ends well. Rather than end the film with destruction all around, the filmmakers panned the 1936 San Francisco skyline that showed the Golden Gate Bridge being built. Audiences stood up and cheered the rebirth of the city from its ruins.

Commentary

I've included this entertaining hunk of schmaltz in this book about Christianity in the movies because it marks the first appearance of the inimitable Spencer Tracy as the quintessential tough-yet-holy Irish priest, an image that he would come to personify and a few years later make famous in the classic film *Boys Town*. It also was the first in a string of priest-ne'er-do-well buddy films such as *Angels with Dirty Faces* starring the other ubiquitous actor/priest, Pat O'Brien.

Indeed, the Catholic Church was fortunate to have Tracy as its exemplar of the American priesthood because of his ability to portray gentleness as well as toughness; conveying the image of a priest as manly while still being a do-gooder. One of this film's best scenes is illustrative. Blackie and Father Tim are working out as sparring partners at the local gym. When Blackie gets Father Tim's Irish up, Tim flattens him with a haymaker. In his book *American Catholic*, Charles Morris notes that Joe Breen, an overseer for the Hays Code, suggested that they add this scene "to offset a later scene where Gable slugs Tracy. This way, the audience would know that Tracy was the better fighter, and the clergy would not be humiliated." This favorable image continued into the 1960s to be replaced later in the century by priests who were either sexual predators, physically abusive, uncharitable, effete, or

Figure 3.5. *San Francisco.* **Father Mullin (Spencer Tracy) kayos his friend Blackie Norton (Clark Gable) at the gym.**

saintly loners constantly challenging the hierarchy. From being portrayed as celibate despite their proclivities, they were later more likely to be pictured as having homosexual tendencies and regarding the vow of celibacy as an unreasonable constraint.

Lost Horizon (1937)

Directed by Frank Capra, and based on a popular 1933 novel by James Hilton, *Lost Horizon* tells the story of five survivors of an airplane crash in the Himalayas. They are taken to Shangri-La, an opulent Art-Deco lamasery founded by a Belgian priest, Father Perrault, in 1713, where people live in excellent health for hundreds of years and do not need doctors. The hero Robert Conway (Ronald Colman), a British diplomat, asks what religion they follow and is told: "Moderation: moderately obedient, moderately honest, moderately chaste, and moderately happy." Conway asks, "What about law and order?" The response is "We have no crime here. What makes a criminal is lack. There can be no vice where there is sufficiency." Finally, Conway asks, "What about women?" The reply is "No one would take another man's woman. A little courtesy all around smoothes out every problem." How civilized!

Conway is brought to see the High Lama who is none other than the 250-year-old Father Perrault (Sam Jaffe), who tells Conway that the crash and their rescue were planned and that he was awaiting his arrival. Given the Lama's wizened appearance, Conway has arrived none too soon. As with many late-1930s films, *Lost Horizon* has overtones of the impending war in Europe, such as when the High Lama notes that "Europe is rushing headlong into destruction because of greed and lust for power, but brotherly love will spread when the strong have devoured each other and the Christian ethic will be fulfilled and the meek will inherit the earth." Conway is urged to stay by the lovely Sondra (Jane Wyatt), with whom he has fallen in love, but he acquiesces to his brother's plea to return to England where he is looked upon as a teller of tall tales. Conway comes to his senses and struggles back across the massive snows to Shangri-La and Sondra.

Commentary

Lost Horizon is suffused with Christian philosophy about brotherly love blended with the Tibetan ethic of tranquility and moderation. Shangri-La is patterned after Shambhala, a mystical city in the Tibetan Buddhist tradition isolated from the turmoil of the world where people could live in peace, harmony, and relative prosperity. Indeed, such a place was something greatly to be wished for after a devastating World War and the dawn of another. The film reminds us that the entertainment community's love affair with Tibet and Buddhism did not begin with the Beatles or Richard Gere, nor did the attempt to develop a syncretism, that is, a combining of different beliefs and practices as between Eastern and Western religions, begin with Thomas Merton. For example, Swami Vivekananda, whose hostel I stayed in during my three months in Calcutta while taking care of cholera patients in 1963, attempted to bridge Eastern and Western religions. He introduced Hinduism and especially the Vedanta philosophy as well as yoga to America in 1893 at the World's Parliament of Religions in connection with the Chicago World's Fair. As the French say, "plus ca change; plus ca meme chose" or the more things change, the more they remain the same.

Angels with Dirty Faces (1938)

The film begins in Hell's Kitchen, a tough New York neighborhood where two kids commit a robbery. "Rocky" Sullivan (Frankie Burke) gets caught, refuses to "rat" on his friend, and is sent to reform school where he gets an education in crime and grows up to be a hardened criminal (James Cagney), in and out of jail for robbery and gambling. The other, Jerry Connolly (William Tracy), is a faster runner and gets away. He later becomes Father Jerry (Pat O'Brien), a priest devoted to keeping the rough neighborhood of Dead End Kids, led by Bim (Leo Gorcey), on the straight and narrow.

Years later, Rocky appears at Father Jerry's church where the priest is leading the boys' choir in Latin hymns. Sullivan pledges to develop a recreation center for these "angels with dirty faces," but instead shows them how to steal. He tells them: "Always remember, don't be a sucker." He becomes their hero and they, his acolytes. He always greets them with the questions, "Whadda ya hear? Whadda ya say?" a line that was copied by film lovers. He tells them to aim big and never bother anyone in their own neighborhood. Father Jerry confronts Rocky saying, "What good is it to teach that honesty is the best policy when they see that dishonesty is the best policy?" He asks his friend not to give them money and not to encourage them to admire him. When the smug Sullivan leaves his office, Father Jerry says, "There but for the grace of God go I," something many Christians were encouraged to articulate when inclined to be too judgmental.

A subplot involves Humphrey Bogart as a sleazy lawyer, Jim Frazier, who refuses to give Rocky the hundred thousand he stashed with him before going to prison. Realizing that Frazier and his partner are out to kill him, Rocky kills them first. Rocky who, until now, has been protected by the police, is arrested, convicted, and sentenced to the electric chair. As Rocky is about to "walk the last mile," Father Jerry appears. Rocky, in best Cagneyesque fashion, tells him, "None of that incense and holy water stuff." Instead, Father Jerry asks Rocky "to scream for mercy and to go to the chair yellow" in order to let his hero-worshipping kids down and possibly ensure their salvation.

After initially refusing, Rocky appears to comply, and the next day's headlines read "Rocky Dies Yellow" and "Killer, Coward at the End." The camera then pans on the Dead End Kids who read it and weep. Bim says, "You were dere, Fodder. You saw everything." Father Jerry tells them, "It's true boys, every word of it." He then adds, "Let's say a prayer for a boy who couldn't run as fast as I could."

Commentary

This is another priest/ne'er-do-well film that's schmaltzy, moralistic, somewhat melodramatic, and very entertaining with Cagney reeling off one-liners at a rapid pace. Because of concern about the glorification of gangsters, the film was banned in China, Denmark, Finland, Poland, and parts of Canada and Switzerland. Even so, it earned Academy Award nominations for Cagney (who lost to Spencer Tracy in *Boys Town*), director Michael Curtiz, and screenwriter Rowland Brown for best writing, original story.

For his role, Cagney drew on his boyhood growing up in New York's Hell's Kitchen. As for the famous tagline, he credited a drug-addicted pimp who used to stand on the corner, hitching up his trousers and twitching his neck while repeating "Whadda ya hear? Whadda ya say?" This film was the first appearance of Pat O'Brien as a tough Irish priest, a role he later played in *The Fighting 69th* and *Fighting Father Dunne*. Two scenes in this film are of particular note. In one, angered by the boys' dirty play in a church basketball game, Father Jerry decides to stop refereeing and to get in the game. He starts throwing a few elbows and punches; the boys get the message to play by the rules. In another, he tracks the kids to a local pool hall and urges them to leave. When they rebuff him, a wise guy asks him, "Can't ya get them to go to heaven with ya?" and Father Jerry decks him.

Despite the hard-hitting persona, these pictures also portrayed O'Brien as a concerned clergyman, always looking out for men or boys under his charge, as well as the society at large. For example, although conflicted, Father Jerry leads a public campaign against his friend Rocky and his corrupt associates to clean up the town. As with Spencer Tracy

Figure 3.6. *Angels with Dirty Faces.* **Father Jerry (Pat O'Brien, right) asks his boyhood friend Rocky Sullivan (James Cagney) to die in the electric chair like a coward.**

(who, coincidentally, was a boyhood friend of O'Brien's), this tough but compassionate film image not only benefited Catholic priests but probably increased priestly vocations.

Boys Town (1938)

The film opens with the customary 1930s on-screen prologue: "This is the story of Father Flanagan and the city for boys that he built in Nebraska. There is such a place as Boys Town. There is such a man as Father Flanagan. This picture is dedicated to him and his splendid work for homeless abandoned boys, regardless of race, creed or color." Father Flanagan (Spencer Tracy) is visiting a man he knew as a youth, now on death row. The man asks him how much time he has, and Flanagan answers that "eternity begins in 45 minutes." The man tells his story about being a starving kid at 12 years old, stealing and being sent to a state reformatory where he learned to be a criminal. He needed a friend, he says, and is sorry for his mistakes.

Three years before, Father Flanagan had set up a refuge for homeless men. The doomed man's story makes him realize that perhaps saving wayward and homeless boys would be more beneficial, and his bishop reluctantly agrees. Flanagan sweet talks a furniture store owner, Mr. Morris (Henry Hull), out of money and supplies, saying, "Before you go to sleep you'll feel a lot better about yourself." Finally, he rents a house, but he and the boys spend their first Christmas eating cornmeal mush and singing "Silent Night" in a dispirited way until Morris arrives with a turkey, as well as presents for everyone, and the mood turns from downcast and rebellious to "Jingle-Bells" happy.

Flanagan then drives Morris out of Omaha to see a property for sale on which he envisions building a town with no wall or fence for 500 boys of all faiths. It will operate on the honor system, governed by an elected mayor, and everyone will be expected to work on the farm. He enlists the help of a skeptical newspaper editor, and the town takes shape. Flanagan is called to federal prison to take in a convict's kid brother, a tough guy named Whitey Marsh (Mickey Rooney). "What am I going to do at a broken-down nursing home like Boys Town?" Whitey asks. Flanagan pulls him up by the collar, knocks him down, and takes him to Boys Town. Predictably Whitey gets into a series of scrapes with the law, but everything is cleared up and Whitey is made Boys Town's mayor. The movie ends with Father Flanagan's signature line, "There's no such thing as a bad boy."

Commentary

Spencer Tracy won his second consecutive Oscar as Best Actor (his first was as Manuel in *Captains Courageous*) and donated it to Boys Town; afterward, he received a replica that mistakenly read "Best Actor Dick Tracy." The film also won Oscars for best writing, original story (Eleanore Griffin and Dore Schary), and garnered three more nominations, including one for best picture. Not only did the film demonstrate that an audience for such feel-good overtly Christian films existed, but that they could also be honored by the Academy of Motion Pictures Arts and Sciences, a far cry from today.

Ironically right after the release of *Boys Town*, donations dropped because everything seemed to be hunky-dory. So, in 1941 MGM made a sequel, *Men of Boys Town*, again starring Spencer Tracy and Mickey Rooney, now the charismatic mayor of Boys Town and Father Flanagan's right-hand man in keeping the boys under control. In this film Lee J. Cobb plays Dave Morris, who risks his health to help Flanagan with the mountain of debt incurred by building more residential units to meet the tremendous demand to replace reform schools. The movie suffers from being too long and filled with silliness, corn, and fake bonhomie, but perhaps the actors were content to play the roles for what they considered to be a good cause.

Nonetheless, on the strength of these movies, Boys (now Girls and Boys) Town became one of the best supported charities in America. Indeed, when my parents and I drove West so that I could interview for a

Figure 3.7. *Boys Town*. Father Flanagan (fourth from left) joins Mickey Rooney, Bishop James Ryan, Louis B Mayer, and Spencer Tracy at MGM Studios.

BACKSTORY

Are All Catholic Priests Irish?

Watching films made from the 1930s to the 1960s that portrayed Catholics, you would think that all priests were Irish. These include Spencer Tracy as Father Tim Mullin in *San Francisco*, as Father Flanagan in *Boys Town* and its sequel, as well as Father Doonan in *The Devil at 4 O'Clock*; Pat O'Brien as Father Connolly in *Angels with Dirty Faces*; Father Duffy in *The Fighting 69th* and as *Fighting Father Dunne*; Bing Crosby as Father Charles Francis Patrick O'Malley, Barry Fitzgerald as Father Fitzgibbon, and Frank McHugh as Father Timothy O'Dowd in *Going My Way*; Alan Hale as "Big Mike" in *God Is My Co-Pilot*; Preston Foster as Father Donnelly in *Guadalcanal Diary*; Karl Malden as the labor priest Father Barry in *On the Waterfront*; Don Murray as Father Clark in *Hoodlum Priest*; Dan Frazer as Father Murphy in *Lilies of the Field*; Tom Tryon as Stephen Fermoyle in *The Cardinal*; and Cecil Kellaway as Monsignor Ryan in *Guess Who's Coming to Dinner?* Okay, Gregory Peck played a Scottish priest in *The Keys of the Kingdom*, but even he gets half-credit because he was of Irish descent.

The reasons for the preponderance of Irish priests reflect both the makeup of the clergy and hierarchy of the American Catholic Church at the time, as well as the fact that many prominent actors as well as directors like Leo McCarey and John Ford were of Irish extraction and were products of Catholic schools. The Hollywood moguls, although primarily Jewish, also respected their Catholic audience for both personal and business reasons. In his excellent book *American Catholic*, Charles Morris quotes Louis B. Mayer's daughter as saying that her father "loved the Catholics" and "may have considered converting." He "kept a priest at his bedside during a long illness, was great friends with Cardinal Spellman (of New York) and displayed the Cardinal's portrait in his library." Morris also points out that both the wives of Harry Cohn, the tyrannical founder of Columbia Pictures, were Catholic and "his children were raised in the Church." In addition, the most prominent administrators of the Hays Code and the National Legion of Decency, both of which had a great impact on a film's box office, were Irish Catholics: Joe Breen and Martin Quigley respectively. Morris quotes Douglas Fairbanks, Jr., who was active in Hollywood at the time, as remembering "that the Irish Catholic audience was considered very important, and it never hurt to have the parish priest touting a movie like *Going My Way*."

Another major reason for the prevalence of Irish priests was the encouragement given by Irish immigrant parents to their sons to enter the priesthood as well as government, social services like policemen and firemen, the law, and the stage. They had the advantage of speaking English and overcame overt discrimination, such as signs saying "Irish need not apply" to ascend in the ranks of various professions including the priesthood. As a consequence of their preponderance, a number of real-life Irish priests had eminently filmable autobiographies as noted above.

By contrast, immigrant Italians, most of whom had been peasants in southern Italy and had been wary of the government and the Italian clergy, which were controlled by Northern Italians, did not gravitate toward education or these professions. Unable to speak English, they were often pictured negatively in 1930s films as wine-drinking and knife-wielding (e.g., in *Mary Stevens, M.D.*, and *Society Doctor*). As with the society at large, which had hierarchical gradations from WASPS (White Anglo-Saxon Protestants) at the top to blacks at the bottom, a similar hierarchical caste system was evident in the American Catholic Church. This hierarchy consisted of the Irish and a few Germans at the top and the Poles, Italians, Lithuanians, French-Canadians, and blacks lower down a scale that sadly, too often, manifested itself as overt discrimination in churches, schools, and seminaries.

medical internship in 1960, we stopped at Boys Town. I still have the little statue with a boy carrying his brother over his shoulders. The inscription taken from one of Whitey Marsh's lines in the original movie reads "He ain't heavy, he's my brother."

Short Subjects

The Bitter Tea of General Yen (1933)

In this exotic Frank Capra film, Megan Davis (Barbara Stanwyck), from "the finest Puritan family in New England," travels to war-torn Shanghai to marry her childhood sweetheart Bob Strife (Gavin Gordon), a missionary who delays the wedding to rescue Chinese orphans from the burning of Chapei. Separated from him in the chaos, Megan is rescued by a ruthless but cultured Chinese warlord General Yen (Nils Asther), who falls hard for her and risks control of his province to win her affection. The film is included because of the frequent references to the clash of cultures between the well-meaning Protestant missionaries and the "500 million people" they are trying not just to convert but to Westernize. Even the good-hearted Strife doesn't understand Chinese. An Episcopal bishop likens his 50 years there to "persistent ants trying to move a great mountain." He recalls a lesson he learned just the month before. Discussing the crucifixion with a band of Mongolian tribesmen, he misinterpreted their rapt attention as having captured their hearts. He pauses and then adds, "The next caravan of merchants that crossed the Gobi desert was captured by them and crucified. That's China!" Selected to open the Radio City Music Hall, it was a box office failure, probably because its portrayal of an interracial romance was ahead of its time. Despite the caricatures, this strange, absorbing and well-acted film is worth seeing.

Manhattan Melodrama (1934)

Manhattan Melodrama has the distinction of having drawn John Dillinger out of hiding to Chicago's Biograph Theater where FBI agents, having been tipped, gunned him down as he left the theater. It opens with a little-known disaster (which was actually greater than the Titanic), the sinking of the excursion boat General Slocum in New York's East River in 1904, killing over one thousand German and Irish immigrants, mostly women and children. A priest, Father Joe (Leo Carrillo), saves two boyhood friends and then disappears from the film. The two orphans take different paths. One becomes

Blackie the gangster (Clark Gable); the other, Jim Wade, a conflicted district attorney (William Powell), whose prosecution lands Blackie in the electric chair. Complicating matters, the two men are in love with same girl (Myrna Loy). Wade tries to save Blackie from the chair, but he will have none of it, knowing it would ruin his friend's career. He marches to his fate with his head high and a smile on his face. This "gangster with a heart of gold" theme will turn up again in the 1938 film *Angels with Dirty Faces* with a priest in place of the district attorney.

The Garden of Allah (1936)

The film opens with Domini (Marlene Dietrich) returning to the Convent school of Ste. Cecile, the only place she was truly happy. She had forgone marriage to care for her ailing father, now dead. The Mother Superior sends her to the desert "to find happiness in its solitude." On the way, she meets Boris (Charles Boyer), a dour Trappist monk, the only one who knows the secret of their liqueur. He has broken his vows by leaving the monastery and professes "no use for the Church," throwing away his crucifix. They stop to get their fortunes read by a sand diviner (John Carradine) who tells Boris that "A man who fears to acknowledge his God is unwise to set foot in the desert, the Garden of Allah." To Domini, he says that she will find the happiness she seeks but then blanches at what will happen later, and Domini refuses to hear it. Domini and Boris are married by a priest against Boris's better judgment. Their bliss is ended when his secret is revealed, and the unhappy pair profess to meet in heaven as she drops him off back at the monastery. This film is mainly a vehicle to show Dietrich in beautiful flowing clothes, marvelous desert scenery, and luxurious full silver service desert banquets. Pauline Kael called it "heavenly romantic kitsch" and "just about perfection of its insanely goopy type."

Green Light (1937)

The film is based on a book of the same name by the former Lutheran minister Lloyd C. Douglas, whose Christian-themed novels were adapted into a number of films (see Backstory, p. 46). The protagonist is Doctor Paige (Errol Flynn), who is falsely accused of the incompetence of his mentor, Doctor Endicott (Henry O'Neill), that resulted in the death of Mrs. Dexter (played with the utmost serenity by Spring Byington). Adhering to the Hippocratic admonition to respect one's teachers, Paige refuses to blame Endicott and is cashiered by the hospital director. He then enters into a dialogue with the Episcopal Dean Harcourt (Sir Cedric Hardwicke) whose sermons Mrs. Dexter had credited for her willingness to accept whatever outcome might befall her. Paige questions how Harcourt's concept of eternal life squares with life's unfairness and admits to having no "religion," which his dictionary defines "as an opiate used by people with hurt sensibilities to dull them into drowsiness." Harcourt says that, on the contrary, Paige has a "fine religion characterized by loyalty, devotion, and honor." He praises Paige for having won a moral victory over his mentor.

Harcourt tells Paige that he has been stopped by a "red light," but that if he perseveres, he will get the "green light" and see the meaning of his life. Harcourt explains that he found his own faith after being ravaged by polio. As a result, he put away despair, recovered, and found "something to live for." Paige adds, "and something to die for." This he finds when he volunteers to be infected by a tick, the principal vector of Rocky Mountain Spotted Fever, in order to develop an antiserum. After teetering on the brink of death, Paige receives the "green light" and recovers, having submerged himself in the service of others. He also gets a bonus, the hand of Dexter's daughter (Anita Louise) who had blamed him for her mother's death. Though not yet on DVD, the film is shown on the Turner Classic Movies Channel. It is particularly noteworthy for the excellent sermons given by Dean Harcourt and how he commands the pulpit. It also continues the theme of redemption which permeated so many of the films of the 1930s.

"THERE ARE NO ATHEISTS
IN FOXHOLES": THE 1940s

T he first half of the 1940s was dominated by World War II, while the second was noteworthy for the postwar recovery in Europe and Asia, as well as marked growth in the economic fortunes of most Americans. In the late 1930s and early 1940s, America's entry in the war was opposed by many conservative isolationists like Joseph P. Kennedy, Charles Lindbergh, and a number of Senate Republicans. President Franklin Roosevelt managed to secure passage of the Lend Lease Act which helped support Britain's war with Germany, but it was not until the bombing of Pearl Harbor on December 7, 1941, that America declared war on the Axis powers of Germany, Italy, and Japan. The deployment of troops and the rapid wartime industrialization led to women, symbolized by Rosie the Riveter, entering the workforce in droves, as well as the development of women's armed service corps. Blacks, who were originally only able to serve in the Merchant Marines and in noncombat roles, were finally, like Japanese-Americans, allowed into combat where they served with distinction, as documented in Capra's *The Negro Soldier* (1944). On the home front, rationing of food, gasoline, and luxury items like nylon (which was needed for parachutes) was accepted as the price for victory. Radio continued to be the major means of unifying Americans and maintaining a common language and culture.

In Europe, Britain's withstanding the Nazi Blitz, the defeat of General Rommel at El Alamein, D-Day, the subsequent march by Patton's army to Berlin, and the defeat of the Germans by the Russians at Stalingrad were among the most important events leading to the end of the war in the European theater (V-E Day). In the Pacific theater, the American victory at Midway and the ability to secure an air base in Iwo Jima put America in position to defeat the Japanese who vowed to defend the homeland until the last man. President Harry Truman's decision to use the atom bomb on Hiroshima and Nagasaki led to a rapid unconditional surrender on V-J Day.

As the war ended, the evils of the Holocaust were made painfully visible with the liberation of the Nazi concentration camps and highlighted in the Nuremberg trials of the Nazi leaders. Other notable postwar events were the founding of the United Nations in 1945, Churchill's 1946 "Iron

Curtain" speech that officially signaled the start of the Cold War, Truman's institution in 1947 of the Marshall Plan to help Western European recovery and his articulation of the Truman Doctrine that same year, warning the Soviets not to advance into Greece and Turkey, and the establishment of the state of Israel.

As for the achievements of the decade, the principal one involved the availability of penicillin, which led to a marked reduction in mortality in wounded soldiers and later, along with other antibiotics, in deaths from pneumonia, tuberculosis, and other infections. The most notable societal event in the United States was the return of the GIs who reclaimed their jobs from women, enrolled in large numbers in college as a result of the GI Bill of Rights, and helped initiate a "Baby Boom" whose effects were felt in the 1960s and will be economically profound in the millennium. The computer ENIAC, weighing 30 tons and reaching two stories high, debuted in 1945, and television, which had been showcased at the 1939 World's Fair, became available in 1947.

Films of the Forties

The films of the early 1940s strove to bolster public morale in the face of war. Most notable were Noel Coward's and David Lean's Academy Award–winning *In Which We Serve* (1942), Frank Capra's documentary series *Why We Fight* (1942), and Laurence Olivier's *Henry V* (1944). Other popular patriotic films of the era included *Yankee Doodle Dandy* (1942), *Watch on the Rhine* (1943), and *Mrs. Miniver* (1942), which ends with the British survivors singing "Onward Christian Soldiers" in a bomb-ravaged church. Despite the preoccupation with war, the art of film was maturing, as evidenced by all-time classics like Orson Welles's *Citizen Kane* (1941), David Lean's *Brief Encounter* (1945), and Carol Reed's *The Third Man* (1949). There were also a plethora of films featuring strong women (and strong actresses) such as *Now Voyager* (1942) starring Bette Davis, *Double Indemnity* (1944) starring Barbara Stanwyck, and *Mildred Pierce* (1945) starring Joan Crawford.

In the immediate postwar years, the tone of films turned darker. No longer needing to bolster morale on the home front, filmmakers could deal with the consequences of the war. The 1946 Academy Award–winning *The Best Years of Our Lives*, which chronicled the difficult reentry of returning servicemen, is illustrative. The late 1940s saw the emergence of the so-called film noir genre epitomized by *The Killers* (1946), *Kiss of Death* (1947), and *The Naked City* (1948), all of which dealt with the seamier side of life.

Christian Attitudes in Forties Films

Throughout the 1940s, Hollywood films continued to reflect positive attitudes toward Christianity (particularly Catholicism and the Catholic clergy) in such films as *The Song of Bernadette* (1943), *The Keys of the Kingdom* (1944), *Going My Way* (1944), and *The Bells of St. Mary's* (1945), all of which were Academy Award nominees or winners. However, nowhere was the concept of faith better seen than in the war films of the first half of this decade, most of which were made while American soldiers were fighting and dying in Europe and in the Pacific. It's estimated that approximately 418,500 Americans died in combat during World War II. Not surprisingly, a large number of 1940s war films pictured chaplains, as in *The Fighting 69th* (1940) and *Guadalcanal Diary* (1943), playing important roles in keeping up morale and ministering to the wounded and the dying. This contrasts with today's war films, even those set in World War II, such as *Saving Private Ryan* (1998) and *Flags of Our Fathers* (2007), where the chaplains are hardly seen and the calls are universally for medics, not clergymen.

Journalist Ernie Pyle, who was killed in World War II while covering the Battle of Okinawa, is frequently credited with originating the saying, "There are no atheists in foxholes." The phrase made it into the screenplay of the World War II movie *Wake Island* (1942) and was widely published in *Reader's Digest* and other publications during and after the war. The implication, of course, is that when faced with imminent death, we all believe in God. While this notion is not universal, as witnessed by a statue honoring atheist soldiers in Alabama, war does bring out reflections on mortality and questions concerning why a benevolent God would permit such carnage.

Andrew Carroll, author of *Grace Under Fire: Letters of Faith in Times of War*, says that the "comfort and strength" brought by faith "does not explain why so many soldiers go to extraordinary and potentially fatal lengths to worship a higher power" such as exposing themselves to enemy fire during battlefield religious services. He cites "sacrificial concern" for their brothers-in-arms and for those on the home front as well as a deep reservoir of faith as the impetus. Sergeant York, who did not want to serve in World War I because war was killing and against the Bible, said he performed the extraordinary actions in which he killed 28 Germans who were manning the deadly machine gun nests because he was saving many more lives.

Christian-themed films of the late 1940s were also weighted to the darker side, although they usually ended on an upbeat note. A good example is *It's a Wonderful Life* (1946), voted "Number 1" among American Film Institute's "100 Most Inspiring Films of All Time." A perennial favorite today, it had only a modest box-office success, probably because audiences weren't ready for a despairing, self-pitying, and suicidal Jimmy Stewart. Nonetheless, the postwar films included inspirational films like *Miracle on 34th Street* (1947) and *Come to the Stable* (1949), as well as one of the best movies about Christianity, the 1947 French film *Monsieur Vincent*. So, although the pall of war hung over the decade, in the end, hope sprang eternal.

The Fighting 69th (1940)

Dedicated to "Father Francis Duffy, a beloved chaplain and great humanitarian," this film chronicles the activities of "The Fighting 69th," a New York infantry regiment in France during World War I. Given its nickname during the Civil War by Robert E. Lee in recognition of its dogged battle tactics, it was part of the Rainbow Division so-called because every state of the Union was represented. It opens at Camp Mills, New York, in 1917, where the division is training. A fight erupts to the strains of "Garry Owen" and "Dixie," symbolizing the lingering resentments from the Civil War. The regimental commander, Wild Bill Donovan (George Brent), pleads for comity and introduces Father Duffy (Pat O'Brien) to bless the troops.

Jerry Plunkett (James Cagney), a troublemaker, complains: "You can't get away from these Dominus Vobiscums." After offering prayers, Duffy announces that he will be holding midnight mass and confessions in the afternoon. "I'm a Methodist," says Plunkett. "What about non-Catholics?" Duffy replies that Mike Murphy (Sammy Cohen), who changed his name from Misha Moskowitz to join this all Irish regiment, would build the pulpit, adding that "If people knew how well faiths get along here, it would upset some pious souls." Plunkett says, "I came over here to fight not to pray. I don't go in for the 'Holy Joe' stuff. I'm not here to convert." "I'm not asking you to convert," Duffy responds, "just to come back to your religion." Later to the strains of "Silent Night" and "Adeste Fidelis," Plunkett goes into the church, and Duffy is reminded of the Good Shepherd who is concerned with the sheep that went astray.

The scene moves to France where at the height of battle during the Argonne offensive, Plunkett starts firing too early and then runs, trapping his fellow soldiers and causing many deaths. Father Duffy crawls to the front to give Last Rites to the dying men and calms everyone during the bombardment by reciting the Lord's Prayer. After the battle, Duffy arranges buses for the Jewish boys to reach the Rabbi for services. Donovan wants to court-martial Plunkett and have him shot but relents when Duffy argues that "the 69th makes men out of cowards." He reaches out to Plunkett who redeems himself by leading the charge to save his comrades and dies bravely after asking Father Duffy for the Last Rites. The picture ends with the Fighting 69th marching down Fifth Avenue with the Washington Square arch in the background. The final shot bears the statement: "Monsignor Duffy 1871–1932 served in four wars" as well as his prayer asking that "America's lost generation (who) loved life, O Lord . . . but accepted painful wounds and death that an ideal might live" not be forgotten.

Commentary

Although the character of Plunkett is fictional, Father Duffy was real, a much-decorated chaplain. So was Wild Bill Donovan, who was awarded the Congressional Medal of Honor for bravery and later ran unsuccessfully as a Republican for governor of New York in 1932. He was commissioned by President Franklin Delano Roosevelt to start the Office of Strategic Services (OSS), the precursor of the CIA. The film is remarkable on several levels. First, it was released in 1940, before the United States entered World War

Figure 4.1. *The Fighting 69th*. Father Duffy (Pat O'Brien) blesses the troops before battle.

BACKSTORY

Father Duffy: The Prototypic Wartime Chaplain

Father Francis Duffy (1871–1932) was born in Canada, educated in the United States, and ordained in the Archdiocese of New York in 1896. A well-known and popular teacher at St. Joseph's seminary and editor of the *New York Review* (a progressive Catholic theological publication), Duffy became regimental chaplain to the famed "Fighting 69th" New York National Guard Regiment. His service in France during World War I is celebrated in *The Fighting 69th* (p. 66). Duffy could be seen on the front lines and in the trenches, recovering the wounded, comforting the dying, and performing other military duties far beyond the role of a conventional military chaplain. The regiment's commander, "Wild Bill" Donovan, credited Duffy's so-called ministry of presence as being pivotal to the unit's morale. Duffy was later awarded the Distinguished Service Cross and the Distinguished Service Medal, the Conspicuous Service Cross (New York State), the Legion d'Honneur (France), and the Croix de Guerre for his service. After the war, Duffy went on to serve as a pastor of Holy Cross Church, a few blocks from Times Square, ministering to Broadway players. Duffy Square, a portion of Times Square, is named for him and features a monument of the popular priest in military dress standing in front of a Celtic Cross.

II. Although talk of war was in the air, at this point, the United States was leaning toward isolationism. Still, in a sense, the film makes strong statements about patriotism and such Christian virtues as courage, forgiveness, and redemption, as well as Father Duffy's wish for all major faiths to live harmoniously and the need to respect and to provide for different faith choices.

Another real personage was poet Joyce Kilmer, best known for his poem "Trees," which was hugely popular with the public but not among critics. The film shows him reciting "Go to Sleep, Farewell" and other poems. Raised as Anglicans, he and his wife, also a poet, converted to Catholicism in 1913 after the death of their daughter. A graduate of Rutgers and Columbia, he enlisted shortly after America entered the War in 1917. He repeatedly refused a commission, saying he would rather be a sergeant in the 69th than an officer in any other regiment. He was killed by a sniper bullet on July 30, 1918, at age 32 while leading a scouting party to ascertain a German machine gun position. He is memorialized at a rest stop on the New Jersey Turnpike as well as at his nearby birthplace in New Brunswick.

Knute Rockne, All-American (1940)

Knute Rockne (Pat O'Brien), a Norwegian immigrant, works in the post office for six years in order to save up to go to Notre Dame, where he is said to be "born to be a great scientist." Working with Father Callahan (Donald

Crisp) on research to manufacture synthetic rubber, he graduates magna cum laude, teaches chemistry, and coaches football. Deciding to abandon science to coach full-time, he apologizes to Father Callahan who tells him, "Anyone who follows the truth in his heart never makes a mistake . . . You're helping mankind and anyone who helps mankind, helps God."

Rockne sees George Gipp (Ronald Reagan) kick a football the length of the field and recruits him for the team. Named All-American and just hitting his peak, Gipp develops a fever and a strep throat and dies (not uncommon in the days before antibiotics). After receiving the Last Rites, Gipp utters the famous lines that Rockne uses during halftime when his team is getting dominated by Army: "I'm going to tell you something I've kept to myself for years. None of you ever knew George Gipp. He was long before your time, but you all know what a tradition he is at Notre Dame. And the last thing he said to me, Rock, he said, 'some time when the team is up against it, and the breaks are beating the boys, tell them to go out there with all they got and win just one for the Gipper. I don't know where I'll be then, Rock,' he said, 'but I'll know about it, and I'll be happy.'" Of course, they won.

Commentary

The film is included for a variety of reasons. First, it is inspirational and moving, especially with the tremendous outpouring of affection for Rockne after he dies in a plane crash on his way to do a favor for a friend. The movie ends with a funeral mass in a packed church, with beautiful singing and a sermon in which Father Callahan eulogizes Rockne, a lifelong Protestant who contributed so much to the Catholic school of which he was such an integral part. The film is well acted and is noteworthy for giving Ronald Reagan the nickname of "The Gipper" that forever stuck. Finally, the film includes a brief but important scene that represents how immigrant families (including mine) felt after coming to America, which has resonance today. It involves Rockne's father Lars (John Qualen), a Norwegian immigrant carriage maker who won second prize in the Chicago World's Fair and decided to stay in America. Early in the movie, when the family says grace in Norwegian, Lars says, "Don't talk Norwegian, talk American. We're Americans now."

One Foot in Heaven (1941)

A Canadian medical student, William Spence (Fredric March), attends a Methodist revival and gets the call. His well-to-do fiancée Hope Morris

(Martha Scott) prefers that he had joined the Episcopalians but accompanies him to an ugly Iowa parsonage where he tells her, "Don't wear nice clothes. We're not their betters; we're their servants." The congregants tell him there's not enough sin in his sermons. They next move to Fort Dodge, Kansas, where they are poorer than ever. The minister invokes the Methodist discipline: "No hoarding money, no debts, no movies, dancing, gambling, or divorce." Their son complains about playing "Questions and Answers" every Sunday and is told that "The Discipline says 'No levity on the Sabbath.'" When told that his son attended the movies, Spence joins him to see William S. Hart in "The Silent Man" to prove that movies are evil but finds it morally uplifting. He tells the congregation "he who speaks to only one generation is dead. He who listens to only one generation is deader."

After serving as a wartime chaplain, he is sent to a dilapidated Denver parsonage where a rich church member berates him for talking to her black handyman when she was away from home, thus putting them on the same level. He refuses to apologize, and she becomes a Baptist. Another major donor withholds money when Spence disbands the choir, which can't sing and just wants to be seen, in favor of a youth group. Caught spreading slander about the minister's son, the donor and his wife wind up paying for a new church, parsonage, and recreation center. The rich woman also returns and pays for a carillon. Just then, Spence is asked to go to a church in trouble in Iowa. His wife (a true saint) says, "Whither thou goest, I will go." Before they leave, he plays "The Church is One Foundation" on the carillon, and everyone sings and marches to the new church.

Commentary

Based on Hartzell Spence's biography of his father, the film, which is not available on DVD or VHS, but is shown on Turner Classic Movies, is noteworthy for the sympathetic portrayal of a selfless and poorly paid minister and the difficult life of his family. Hartzell who, as founding editor of the Army weekly *Yank* during World War II, made the "Pinup" famous, chose a different path. After the war, he became a gentleman farmer at Gaston Hall, a 30-room, 700-acre estate in Virginia, with his wife and two children, whose experiences he chronicled in *Happily Ever After*. The most intriguing aspect of the film is the portrayal of the inhabitants of rural America as less than wholesome. Most of the churchgoers are hypocrites, or as Spence puts it when he refuses to go abroad as a missionary, "the real heathens are in the church." Finally, it seems strange that this unprepossessing film was nominated for an Oscar for Best Picture of 1941. True, that was when the number of nominees was ten rather than five but much better films like *The Lady Eve* and *Meet John Doe* were not nominated. My guess is that the scene where the Methodist minister approves going to the movies was what swayed the voters.

The Devil and Daniel Webster (1941)

Based on a short story by Stephen Vincent Benet, this variation of the Faustian bargain is about the battle between the Devil aka Scratch (Walter Huston) and Senator Daniel Webster (Edward Arnold) for the soul of a down-on-his-luck New Hampshire farmer, Jabez Stone (James Craig), living in Cross Corners, New Hampshire. Webster is quoted at the beginning saying: "I'd fight 10,000 devils for one New Hampshire man." Stone is 27, married, childless, and about to lose his farm to loan sharks. Deciding not to go with his Bible-reading wife Mary (Anne Shirley) and mother (Jane Darwell) to church, he is approached by Scratch who proffers a contract for his soul. When Jabez expresses concern, Scratch says, "A soul is nothing. Can you see it, smell it, touch it? No, this soul (pointing to another he just claimed), and your soul are nothing against seven years of good luck. You'll have good money and all that money can buy."

Jabez signs the contract and becomes the richest farmer in the state. He gambles, builds a mansion, and lives there with the lovely maiden Belle (Simone Simon) whom Scratch sends to steal his heart and with whom he has a bratty son named Daniel (Lindy Wade) after Webster. Meanwhile, Jabez's wife lives in the old house and prays that the evil spirit be removed from her husband. As the day of reckoning approaches, Jabez becomes more afraid, and Daniel Webster agrees to defend him. Eager for Webster's soul, Scratch agrees to let Jabez have his day in court and handpicks the judge and jury from the "quick and the dead," a collection of knaves, villains, and thieves, including Benedict Arnold. Webster must convince them that a man's soul belongs to him, to his community, and to his maker. The rest of the picture is excellent, especially the last scene with Scratch sitting on a fence and eating a peach pie and looking for another victim before pointing at the viewer. When first released, the film ended with a quote from Benet: "The Devil was never seen again in New Hampshire, but I'm not talking about Massachusetts or Vermont."

Commentary

Among the film's many excellent features is Bernard Hermann's Oscar-winning score, which incorporates "Springfield Mountain" music, violin solos of "Pop Goes the Weasel," and other rustic American tunes. Walter Huston is magnificent and was nominated for an Academy Award, but he and Orson Welles (*Citizen Kane*) lost to Gary Cooper (*Sergeant York*). The film was released as "All That Money Can Buy," reputedly because films with "devil" in the title were not well received in the South. It was not a box office success and was later rereleased under the new title and with the ending about Vermont and Massachusetts dropped. Butchered for airing on television, the film has been reissued on a DVD that includes a reading of Benet's story by Alec Baldwin.

I have included the film because of its discussion of the existence of a soul and to whom it belongs. At one point, Jabez is reassured by another Faustian bargainer that he shouldn't be "worried about losing something that isn't there." Interestingly, Scratch's targets are men who don't seem to put as high a premium on the existence of a soul. Maybe it's because they are more literal-minded and don't go to church as often as women. They also may be more susceptible to the sins of greed and lust that Scratch is eager to satisfy.

The courtroom scene is marvelous, as Webster and Scratch debate to win the hearts and minds of the scoundrels who constitute judge and jury. For example, when Webster challenges the contract on the basis that the devil is a foreigner and that an American cannot be forced into the service of a foreign prince, Scratch claims American citizenship asking "who has a better right?" After all he was there "when the first wrong was done to the first Indian" and "when the first slaver put out for the Congo." Another great scene involves Daniel Webster giving the bratty son an American history lesson.

Sergeant York (1941)

As the film opens, Preacher Rosier Pile (Walter Brennan) leads his congregation in the hymn "When the Roll is Called up Yonder" in a church in the Valley of the Three Forks in the Woods in the Cumberland Mountains of Tennessee. Meanwhile Alvin York and his hell-raising friends ride around the church, and York shoots his initials into a tree with perfect precision. Pile suspends the service, saying the "Devil be a knocking at the door of worship." York's mother (Margaret Wycherly) allows how it was mighty good shooting for a man in his liquor but asks the preacher to talk to Alvin about religion. York and his friends go to a bar that straddles the border between "wet" Kentucky and "dry" Tennessee, where liquor can be bought on one side and drunk on the other. They start a fight, and when it's over Alvin's younger brother George (Dickie Moore) tells him that their Ma wants him to come home.

York takes a fancy to Gracie Williams (Joan Leslie) and decides to raise money to buy some "bottom land" where the soil is richer so he can ask her to marry him. He gives a down payment and works like a dog to pay the rest by the due date. Falling short, he asks for a four-day extension until the Turkey Shoot. The owner and he shake on it, but when he wins and has enough to pay it off, he learns that the land has been sold to his rival for Gracie's hand. He gets drunk and sets off in a terrible storm to kill the farmer but is knocked off his horse as lightning strikes his gun. Chastened, he enters the church and joins the congregation in singing "Give Me That Old-Time Religion." He asks pardon of the two who had wronged him and starts teaching Sunday school.

When World War I breaks out, he applies for conscientious objector status because "war is killing" but is refused three times. Pile counsels him to serve and though clearly the best shot in the unit, he still has reservations. The commanding officer gives him leave to read American history and the Bible. After much soul-searching, he decides to "render to Caesar the things that are Caesar's" and in the Argonne-Meuse offensive on October 8, 1918, armed with only two weapons, he manages to silence 25 machine gun nests while killing 28 Germans and capturing 132. He is given the Croix de Guerre by Marshal Foch, the Distinguished Service Cross, and the Congressional Medal of Honor by General Pershing. Feted in a ticker tape parade up Broadway and offered a quarter of a million dollars in endorsements and screen and stage roles, he refuses to trade on his exploits. He returns home where he finds that the state has built a home on the bottom land he wanted. The last line is "God works in mysterious ways."

Commentary

The film received 11 Oscar nominations but only two awards: Gary Cooper as Best Actor and William Holmes for Film Editing. The score by Max Steiner blends in a number of hymns and patriotic anthems. Jesse Lasky, the producer, traveled to Tennessee to convince York to permit the movie to be made. York's major concerns were that his wife be portrayed by someone who didn't drink, smoke, or swear. Joan Leslie was the perfect choice because she was Gracie's age (16) at the time portrayed in the movie and had been voted Hollywood's Girl Next Door because of her naiveté and innocence. York asked that Cooper play him and that his exploits not be portrayed in the film, but he later relented. On his deathbed York asked his son if God would forgive him for killing the Germans. He gave much of the moneys he received from his fame to a Bible school he founded.

When the movie was released in September 1941, much of America was isolationist and Senator Nye held hearings before the Commerce oversight committee accusing Jesse Lasky, a practicing Jew and fervent anti-Nazi, of trying to get America into the war. Before the second set of hearings, Pearl Harbor had made any reservations about entry into the war, moot. York became a believer in the importance of the film and agreed to a publicity tour for which he was savaged and accused of being a traitor. The false notes in the film include the dramatic portrayal of his conversion as being similar to Saint Paul's "road to Damascus." Actually, Gracie, his mother, and the pastor were responsible for his conversion, and it took a while for him to accept religion. In addition, Tennessee gave them land but not a house, and York had to pay the mortgage. On the DVD film historian Jeanine Basinger points out how in addition to "Ma, Sis, and the girl back home," the idea of fighting for a home of one's own resonated with the soldiers of World War II and that the last scene was a particular favorite of veterans.

Figure 4.2. *Sergeant York.* **Sergeant York (Gary Cooper) reads the Bible as he wrestles with his conscience over the commandment "Thou Shall Not Kill."**

The Song of Bernadette (1943)

This story of Bernadette Soubirous, to whom the Virgin Mary appeared in Lourdes in 1858, is captured in the prologue: "For those who believe in God, no explanation is necessary. For those who do not, no explanation is possible." Bernadette (Jennifer Jones), an asthmatic, lives in a cold, dingy former jail cell with her father (Roman Bohnen) an unemployed miller, her mother (Anne Revere) who was a laundress, and her two sisters. When the girls go to get wood for the fireplace, Bernadette sees the Blessed Virgin (Linda Darnell, uncredited) who asks her to come daily for 15 days but warns, "I cannot promise to make you happy in this world, only the next."

The imperial prosecutor, Vital Dutour (Vincent Price), considers Bernadette to be a religious fanatic and a menace to civilization and jails her. Bernadette stops eating, and Dutour is forced to let her go, after large crowds are attracted to the village. The Virgin instructs Bernadette to tell the Dean of the local Church (Charles Bickford) to build a church at the site, but he chases her away. At the next visit, the Virgin tells Bernadette to dig and drink of the resulting spring, but when no water appears, she is led off in disgrace. Later, a spring appears and miraculous cures begin to occur. The local doctor Dozous (Lee J. Cobb) admits that certifying the miracles is very difficult because he is not used to believing in things he can't see. The Dean, now a believer, responds, "Unlike a doctor, a religious must believe a great many things he cannot see."

After another apparition, Bernadette tells the Dean that the Virgin says, "I am the Immaculate Conception," a dogma that had been long debated, though she had never heard of it, nor does she know what it means. The Dean is astonished, and a church commission is convened to determine whether she's mad, a fraud, or "the rarest of the rare." When she is vindicated, the Dean, who had warned her that she was playing with celestial fire, tells her that she must enter the convent rather than marry her friend Antoine. Her mistress of postulants is her old teacher Sister Vauzous (Dame Gladys Cooper), a cruel nun who believes that "Only in suffering can we hope to gain the Kingdom of God." She harasses Bernadette, telling her that she has tortured herself and never been favored by a vision, so how could Bernadette, who has never suffered, see the Virgin? Bernadette then uncovers her leg revealing a painful tuberculous tumor of the bone, which she has borne without complaint. The nun confesses to being consumed with hate and envy and dedicates herself to helping this chosen soul. As

Bernadette is dying, the Bishop tries to get her to say that she was lying, but she refuses. After despairing that she will ever see the Virgin again, she raises herself in bed and says, "I love you, Holy Mary Mother of God" and falls back, dying peacefully.

Commentary

This beautiful and touching film was adapted from a best-selling book of the same name by Franz Werfel, a Jew, born in the Austro-Hungarian empire, who was best known as a playwright and for his novel *The Forty Days of Musa Dagh* about the Armenian genocide in Turkey. He warned of similar events under the Nazis whom he criticized in a number of plays. When Germany annexed Austria in 1938, Werfel fled to Paris, but he and his wife, Gustav Mahler's widow, had to flee again in 1940. Unable to escape into Portugal, they sought refuge in Lourdes where nuns and families offered shelter as the Gestapo searched for him. He promised to write a story about Lourdes and Bernadette if he survived, and did so in 1941. The novel was a best-seller, and the film was a box office smash and was nominated for 12 Oscars, including Best Picture, and won four: Best Actress (Jones); Best Musical Scoring (Alfred Newman); Best Cinematography (Arthur C. Miller); and Best Art Direction (James Basevi, William Darling, and Thomas Little). However, it confounded critics like Bosley Crowther of the *New York Times* who called it "tedious" and filled with "dialectic discourse that will clutter and fatigue the average mind." Conversely, as noted in Lopate's *American Movie Critics*, famed critic James Agee who said he went to see the film "gritting my teeth against my advance loathing" for what he suspected would be "pseudo-religious," admitted that he "was unexpectedly and greatly moved by a great many things."

At two-and-a-half hours long, the film certainly requires that viewers be ready to sit quietly and let the story and the music draw them in. It's worth seeing for Jennifer Jones's performance alone; she portrays Bernadette with radiance, honesty, and simplicity. Indeed, the film should not be written off as pious hagiography, but one that should provoke thought and serious discussion of such difficult questions as: Why did the Virgin Mary choose Bernadette, a simple, unschooled peasant as an instrument for one of the most enduring miracles and as a messenger of important dogma that she could not comprehend? Why did God let this innocent suffer so much? What does the response of the nun, the Bishop, and, initially, the Dean say

Figure 4.3. *The Song of Bernadette*. **The Blessed Virgin Mary appears to Bernadette (Jennifer Jones) at Lourdes.**

about the openness to God's workings by the clergy when politics, appearances, and the legal system intrude? Why did the atheist imperial prosecutor, like atheists of today, feel so threatened by this simple girl that he had to suppress her message?

The Fighting Sullivans (1944)

This true story of the five Sullivan brothers from Waterloo, Iowa, who went down with the same ship during World War II is a paean to faith, family, and country. The paterfamilias (Thomas Mitchell) is a railroad signal man who never misses a day of work. The children are brawlers, but they all rally around one another. After Pearl Harbor, the brothers petition the U.S. Navy to be assigned to the same ship. Al, the only married brother, is conflicted but opts to enlist as well. The father mortgages the house to pay the bills. The mother, Alleta (Selena Royle), hangs a service flag in the window with five stars indicating that five family members are in the Armed Services; initially blue, they will soon turn to gold indicating that they all are dead. The brothers' ship, *The Juneau,* leaves New Caledonia on November 8, 1942, to take supplies and reinforcements to marines on Guadalcanal. A naval and air battle ensues, and the ship is torpedoed. The scene when the family learns that all five have perished is heartwrenching.

The last scene shows the mother, accompanied by the father and sister who has joined the Waves, christening a new battleship, The USS *Sullivans* (now a permanent museum in Buffalo, New York). She says, "May God bless and protect this ship. Our boys are afloat again," and the five brothers in their navy uniforms are shown rising from the sea to heaven. Since then, no brothers have been allowed to serve together on the same ship.

Commentary

Nominated for an Academy Award for screenwriting, the film is available on DVD, which includes the brothers singing "When Irish Eyes Are Smiling" and an interview with the last survivor of *The Juneau*. Although the DVD says that the Sullivans inspired Steven Spielberg to make *Saving Private Ryan*, that film is based on the story of the Niland brothers of Tonawanda, New York, two of whom died on D-Day, another who survived in a Japanese POW camp, and a fourth who was searched for in northern France and brought home after his two brothers had died.

The DVD does flesh out the fate of *The Juneau*, which had survived a first torpedo and sought refuge in a cove. The next day, it was struck again and sank within minutes. Anyone who was below deck died instantly. The approximately 110 survivors, many badly wounded, thought their sister ships would recover them. Instead, they hightailed it out of what was called "torpedo alley." A plane flew overhead the next day but failed to pick up the men, who remained on the rafts for seven days until help arrived; only ten were left alive by then. George, the oldest brother, was one of those who jumped off the raft "to take a bath" and was eaten by sharks.

The *Fighting Sullivans* captures a simpler and more innocent time in America. It pictures what were ordinary events then, like using a string attached to a doorknob to remove a loose tooth and the father having the children smoke a cigar when he catches them smoking, to discourage the habit. It also shows the innocence of courtship when Al falls in love with Katherine Mary (Anne Baxter) and, after they marry, their difficulty in paying for medical care. When she becomes pregnant, they send the doctor $5 a week until the baby comes, and they buy a layette on layaway. When the baby arrives, Al has a tougher time than his wife with the delivery.

It also depicts a time when the Catholic Church was in ascendance in America, providing an enduring record of the Irish-American Catholic culture of the 1920s through the 1940s. The centrality of their Catholic faith is shown in the opening scenes of the five being baptized in turn and later in a First Communion service, as well as when they go to church to light candles and pray after enlisting. In this way, it shows the ties between faith and a willingness to risk one's life for a cause and one's country. Finally, it's a story about a family that gave so much for our freedom without asking for recompense. Rejecting bitterness, they were willing, as painful as it was, to tour the country to support the war effort. How many of us would have done that?

The Keys of the Kingdom (1944)

Monsignor Sleeth (Sir Cedric Hardwicke) is sent to evaluate Father Francis Chisholm (Gregory Peck) an elderly former missionary who has raised concern among his parishioners in Tweedside, Scotland, by statements such as "All atheists are not godless men. I met one who I hope is now in heaven" and "A good Christian is a good man but I found that the Confucians had a better sense of humor." To a wealthy parishioner, he says, "Eat less; the gates of heaven are narrow." Ready to prepare a negative report, the Monsignor reads Chisholm's journal and learns that he was a child of a Catholic father and a Protestant mother who told him, "You and your father are Catholics, son. Some people fear and hate Catholics." One rainy night, a gang yells "there goes that dirty papist" and beats his father; when his mother goes to help him cross a bridge, they are both swept away. Satisfying his aunt's desire, he enters the seminary where he challenges the declaration that Catholicism is the one, true religion, asking, "Did God set such an exclusive value on creed or on an accident of birth?" His kindly mentor, Hamish MacNabb (Edmund Gwenn), teaches him patience by showing him how to fish and later suggests he be reassigned as a missionary to China.

Two "Rice Christians" who promise him crowds if paid in money and rice, meet him and take him to a burned out mission. He drives them away and unsuccessfully tries to set up a mission, until his boyhood friend Willie Tulloch (Thomas Mitchell), an atheist doctor, sends him medical books and equipment. With the help of a young Chinese Christian Joseph (Benson Fong), Chisholm sets up a dispensary and lances the badly infected arm of the local mandarin's son. The grateful mandarin says, "If I as a mandarin accept Christian belief so should my people." Chisholm responds that there is "no difference between buying a man's soul and taking it for services rendered." Still, the mandarin donates a hilltop for a new mission, and there is a touching dedicatory scene with Chisholm holding a beautiful little girl and saying the Magnificat.

He is joined by three nuns including a descendant of Austrian royalty, Sister Maria Veronica (Rosa Stradner), who calls Chisholm a "peasant priest" and admits that she has difficulty accepting that these "lowliest of God's subjects are my equal before God." Nonetheless, the mission thrives because of her efficiency. Tulloch, who calls himself "The Devil's Number One Boy," also comes to help. The missionaries are caught in the middle of a civil war, and the doctor is shot. Before dying, he tells Chisholm, "I still can't believe in God. Are you mad with me? Are you disappointed that I can't let you save me?" When Chisholm demurs, the doctor says, "I've never loved you as much as I do now, because you haven't tried to bully me into heaven."

Years later, Chisholm welcomes two Methodist missioners (James Gleason and Anne Revere), reflecting that it must confuse the Chinese with different Christian sects saying, "come over here, this is the true sect." His ambitious friend Father Angus Mealy (Vincent Price) visits and deplores how little Chisholm has accomplished ministering to the poor Chinese rather than the wealthy, adding to Chisholm's sense of failure. His reassignment to Scotland provokes a moving good-bye from Joseph and his flock, as well as the nun who had come to respect him. Sleeth changes his mind about his report, saying, "I came here thinking you were nobody and after reading your journal, I come away feeling it's an honor to have known you."

Commentary

Based on a popular novel by physician A. J. Cronin, this long, slow-moving but earnest film is distinguished by its cast, especially Gregory Peck who won one of the film's four Academy Award nominations. Cronin, a Scot, also had a Catholic father and a Protestant mother. Alienated from the Church in early adulthood, he returned to Catholicism after a long convalescence from a duodenal ulcer when he began writing novels starting with *Hatter's Castle* in 1931. His family background undoubtedly affected his desire that faiths work together and that emphasis be placed not solely on accidents of birth or espoused beliefs but good works. The film's dialogue, especially regarding the atheist doctor, also reflected the views of the screenwriter Joseph Mankiewicz. As his son says in the DVD commentary, Mankiewicz was at "the height of his atheist period" and had said that Sinclair Lewis and he would be having more fun "down there shooting craps" than the believers in heaven. His son said that the character who most represented his father's beliefs was the doctor who signs his name "M.D., heathen." Ironically, Mankiewicz was married to Rosa Stradner, the

Figure 4.4. *The Keys of the Kingdom*. **Father Chisholm (Gregory Peck) arrives in China to find that his mission church has been destroyed.**

acclaimed Austrian actress who played the Mother Superior and who, as a devout Catholic, had their sons baptized.

Mankiewicz, who is best known for writing and directing *All About Eve*, was called an "idea writer" rather than an "action writer," and this film presents many ideas to ponder. The messages about searching for goodness in everyone regardless of their religion or other different characteristics, and the importance of kindness, humility, and charity as central to the Christian ethos are timeless and make this film well worth watching. It also takes dead aim at those in the clergy who use their position, not in service of the poor and needy, but for their own comfort by catering to the wealthy and powerful. The film's title comes from Christ's charge to Peter, "And I will give thee the Keys to the Kingdom." It suggests that those priests like Chisholm, MacNabb, and even Sleeth, who, through their humility, genuine care for others, and openness to the truth, "get it" and thus are true successors of Saint Peter as possessors of the keys to the kingdom of heaven.

Going My Way (1944)

A banker threatens elderly pastor Father Fitzgibbon (Barry Fitzgerald) with foreclosure of St. Dominic's Church. To the rescue comes his new "assistant" Father Charles Francis Patrick O'Malley (Bing Crosby) who, with his St. Louis Browns jacket, golf clubs, tennis racket, and fishing pole, is clearly an unorthodox priest. O'Malley develops a choir out of a bunch of young toughs with the help of Tony (Stanley Clements) who tells him, "I'm on the hook for you, Fodder, that you won't try to get them to be holy Joes. If you do, we'll drop you like a hot potater."

While praying, Fitzgibbon hears them singing "Three Blind Mice" and resolves to ask the Bishop to remove O'Malley, only to learn that O'Malley is his unstated replacement. So, he puts off dinner and "runs away from home" in the pouring rain. At midnight, McCarthy the policeman (Tom Dillon) brings a reluctant Fitzgibbon to the rectory provoking a delightful exchange between the two. The crestfallen Fitzgibbon is helped out of his wet clothes and sent upstairs for a bath, after which he polishes off a hearty dinner. In a touching scene centering on their mothers, he and O'Malley sample some Irish whiskey hidden in Fitzgibbon's bookcase "behind *The Life of General Grant*" in a music box which plays "Toora Loora Loora."

Later, O'Malley drops by the Metropolitan Opera to see his old flame, opera star Jenny Linden (Risë Stevens). As she prepares for the next scene, she asks why he stopped writing while she was on tour in Europe and South America. He says, "You must not have gotten my last letter." When she enters the room and sees that he is a priest, she says, "Father Chuck, it's going to take a while to get used to that." Stevens sings "La Habanera" in her signature role as Carmen and later "Ave Maria."

A far-fetched subplot involving a romance between an 18-year-old runaway (Jean Heather) and the banker's son (James Brown) serves to explain the title. As the two lovers discuss their big decision to marry, O'Malley tells them, "I had quite a decision to make whether to write the nation's songs or go my way." Asked if he has any regrets, he replies, "No. I get great happiness out of helping people realize that religion doesn't have to be like this (he plays low chords), taking all the fun out of everything. It can be bright (he plays brilliant higher chords), and bring you closer to happiness." Then he plays and sings "Going My Way." The rest of the film involves getting money for St. Dominic's by selling O'Malley's new song "Swinging on a Star," and an ending that will bring tears to the eyes of even the most hard-boiled.

Commentary

This good-natured, heartwarming film won seven Oscars including Best Picture, Best Actor (Bing Crosby), Best Supporting Actor (Barry Fitzgerald), and Best Director (Leo McCarey). Jean Renoir, the great French director and son of the famous artist, called McCarey "one of the few directors in Hollywood who understands human beings." What he turned out is an

Figure 4.5. *Going My Way.* After sharing some Irish whiskey, Father O'Malley (Bing Crosby) sings Father Fitzgibbon's (Barry Fitzgerald) favorite song "Toora Loora Loora."

unabashed encomium to traditional Catholicism and the Irish. It is doubtful that it could be made today, let alone garner any Oscar nominations. The film also features the excellent singing of Risë Stevens and the Robert Mitchell Boys Choir.

Like Spencer Tracy, Pat O'Brien, and Gregory Peck had done before him, Crosby imbued the priest with his distinctive persona. Though unorthodox, O'Malley uses humor and a genuine humility to win the hearts of those around him. The pairing with Barry Fitzgerald was a stroke of genius, providing the opportunity for much comedy as well as pathos. Add to that the disclosure of his preseminary relationship with an opera singer (Risë Stevens at that), which bolsters the scene where he tells of having to make a difficult choice. It's no wonder that Pope Pius XII granted Crosby a personal audience and credited his portrayal with being one of the greatest stimuli to priestly vocations.

The Bells of St. Mary's (1945)

Father O'Malley (Bing Crosby) moves to St. Mary's, where the housekeeper tells him that the previous pastor was taken away to a rest home in a wheelchair, mumbling to himself because the Sisters wanted their way in everything. While meeting Sister Benedict (Ingrid Bergman) and a dozen nuns, he's upstaged by a cat who cavorts in his straw hat on a mantle behind him. Sister Benedict hopes their neighbor Mr. Bogardus (Henry Travers), chairman of the City Council, will give them the building next door because they don't have a playground. Instead, wanting to buy the school, he threatens, as chairman of the City Council, to condemn the property if they refuse.

Sister Benedict shows her prowess by hitting a softball and also teaches a bullied boy (Dickie Tyler) how to box using Gene Tunney's handbook. After he wins their next encounter, she tells O'Malley, "We try our best to raise masculine men with our limited knowledge of the outside world." A charming scene involves the first graders putting on a Christmas play with one shepherd using a golf club for a staff. Conversely, a weak subplot involves Patsy (Joan Carroll), a runaway over whom the priest and nun clash about how to help her succeed. Her essay assignment about the five senses leads O'Malley to play the Oscar-nominated song "Aren't You Glad You're You." Upset with her mother, Patsy fails her test on purpose so she can stay and become a nun. Sister Benedict says, "You don't become a nun to run away from life. It's not because you lost something; it's because you found something." She tells Patsy that she has a lot of living to do, going to dances, her first love, before she can decide.

In the end, Bogardus has a change of heart and turns the new factory into a school, leading to a stirring rendition of "The Bells of Saint Mary's." Then, Sister Benedict is diagnosed with tuberculosis. The doctor tells Father O'Malley not to tell her (which is bad medicine), making her believe that O'Malley wants her sent away. Sister Benedict prays: "Dear Lord, remove all bitterness from my heart. Help me see your will" and she cries. As she leaves, O'Malley calls her back and tells her the truth. She is thrilled and promises to be back soon. He tells her, "If you're in trouble, just dial O for O'Malley."

Commentary

Leo McCarey wrote this story as a tribute to his aunt, Sister Mary Benedict, who helped build the Immaculate Heart Convent in Hollywood and who died in a typhoid epidemic. It was written before *Going My Way* and was intended to precede it. Fortunately, that didn't happen, because although it received eight Academy Award nominations, winning one Oscar for Best Sound recording, it's really a lightweight film, though entertaining because of the stars. The Christmas pageant scene is responsible for the film being shown frequently at Christmas.

Figure 4.6. *The Bells of St. Mary's.* **Sister Benedict (Ingrid Bergman) gives boxing lessons to a boy who has been bullied.**

Homages to the film have been made in such disparate films as *It's a Wonderful Life* (the title is on a theater marquee) (p. 89), *The Godfather* (p. 199) (Michael Corleone and Kay are watching this movie when the Don is shot), and particularly in *The Magdalene Sisters* where the sadistic nun cries while watching the final scene, hypocritically identifying with the sweet image of Sister Benedict (see p. 305). Indeed, this film cemented the image of the kindly nun for many and probably helped in the surge in vocations that occurred over the next decade. It also affected Ingrid Bergman who was typed with a nun persona in the public's mind. Later, *Joan of Arc* (p. 97) added to her aura of sanctity, so that in 1949 when she left her husband and ran off with Roberto Rossellini, who directed her in *Stromboli*, the public was shocked and outraged, and her stock plummeted. She was relegated to making films only in Europe until returning to Hollywood for the 1956 film *Anastasia* for which she won an Oscar.

God Is My Co-Pilot (1945)

Based on a book by Robert Lee Scott, Jr., the film traces the development of a boy who rejects the notion of a black farmworker that he needs "someone else up there" to fly. While serving in the Air Force transporting oil over the Himalayas ("The Hump") to the Flying Tigers headquarters in Kunming,

China, Scott (Dennis Morgan) meets "Big Mike" (Alan Hale) a missionary priest who is bringing "some supplies for my people,—the Chinese not the Irish," he laughs. Scott tells him, "You sound like a soldier not a missionary," and Big Mike responds, "There's not too much difference, only different weapons. We both fight the forces of evil."

American Claire Chennault (Raymond Massey), the commander of the Flying Tigers, refuses to let Scott fly the operations protecting the "Burma Road." Scott goes to see Big Mike who tells him he'll need faith in God to persevere. Later, having contracted malaria and being grounded, he is disconsolate and hears "Believe, believe in me. I'm the strength you seek" and has a revelation. He says, "Not knowing where to turn, I prayed. I never believed in miracles. If it's your will, let me go with them." Chennault gives him his plane. Big Mike says, "More things have been wrought by prayer than this world dreams of," words that are repeated as the pilots fly toward their target in Japan.

Commentary

I have included this film because of its title and because in contrast to today's films that play down religion, this features an Irish priest and discussions about God, both of which were seen as assets in films of the 1940s. Actually, the only reference to God in Scott's book is when he recalls having five rivet heads removed from his back and the Cantonese surgical assistant, trying to distract him from the pain, commented on how he was all alone in the plane: flying, navigating, dropping bombs, firing machine guns, changing fuel tanks, and talking on the radio. Before Scott could respond, the surgeon said, "No, son—you're not up there alone—not with all the things you've come through. You have the greatest co-pilot in the world, even if there is just room for one in that fighter ship—no, you're not alone." Scott then added, "When this war is over we will be closer to God than at any time in the past. I believe this because I have seen instances of real faith on several fronts in this war." In short, contrary to the film's plot, there was no Irish priest influencing Scott, who grew up a Southern Baptist.

Black Narcissus (1946)

This British film is about the Anglican Order of the Servants of Mary of Calcutta, asked to establish a school and a hospital in what was the House of Women, a palace where the general Toda Rai (Esmond Knight) kept his concubines. A dirty old woman caretaker, who yearns for the good old days, lives there alone among a series of erotic pictures. Set in the mountains above Darjeeling at an altitude of 8,000 feet, it's a forbidding place where a Holy man sits day in and day out while the wind whistles steadily. An order of Brothers on a similar mission only lasted five months. The local English agent Mr. Dean (David Farrar) tells the directress Sister Clodagh (Deborah Kerr), "I give you until the rains break."

When the general's son Dilip Rai (Sabu) falls ill, the drums beat all night. If they stop, he's dead and presumably so are the nuns. The old general is pleased at the boy's recovery, and he pays people (whom he calls "children") to go to the school and hospital (echoes of *The Keys of the Kingdom*). He warns the nun that if someone dies, the people will blame them. Sure enough, Sister Honey (Jenny Laird), the sweetest of the five nuns, gives a baby some castor oil, and she dies. The drums start beating, testing everybody's sanity. Sister Philippa (Flora Robson) is already crazy. Sister Ruth (Kathleen Byron), who is not renewing her annual vows, applies lipstick, dresses up, and goes to seduce Dean. He rebuffs her and she goes off the deep end, literally and figuratively. Trying to kill Sister Clodagh—her seeming rival for Dean's affections—she missteps and falls to her death.

Sister Clodagh, a cool and rather haughty superior, is momentarily taken aback but then recovers. She reveals to Dean, who also fascinates her despite his drunken bouts, that before she became a nun, "I wanted to marry. I had shown I loved him. I had to get away first. That's why I entered the order." She adds, "God works in strange ways. The first time I came here was the first time I thought of him." He tells her, "You must all get away before something happens," and they do. The title comes from a distracting subplot in which Dilip, after his recovery, uses the strong scent of the black narcissus to seduce a sexy, nubile Kanchi played to the hilt by Jean Simmons.

Commentary

Given the murkiness and weirdness of this melodramatic story, as well as the almost stylized stringing together of the scenes as if they were portraits, viewers may, like me, wonder what the film's "classic" and "four star" status is all about. Based on a novel by Rumer Godden (see *In This House of Brede* p. 211), it is a favorite of cineastes because of who made it and how it was made. The film's directors, producers, and screenwriters were the duo of Michael Powell and Emeric Pressburger, who were responsible for the highly acclaimed British films *Stairway to Heaven*, *The Red Shoes*, and *Tales of Hoffman*. More important were the cinematography and the art direction/ set design for which Jack Cardiff and Alfred Junge respectively won well-deserved Oscars. Considering that the film was entirely made in Britain's Pinewood studios, it was a tour de force. In a DVD extra, director Martin Scorsese discusses how the film's color washed over him and was a major influence on his work.

As Sister Clodagh explains, not all nuns are alike. This group can reconsider their commitment year by year. In addition, she tells about giving up her virginity for someone she thought was in love with her. Film critic Leonard Maltin noted that this scene was originally censored from American prints, probably to appease those who wanted nuns to be seen as "pure" their whole lives rather than having ever engaged in sexual activity. All in all, this film paints an unflattering picture of nuns as repressed, neurotic at best, and psychotic at worst. This will be a recurring theme as the decades pass, first in foreign films and later in American films after the demise of the Hays Code. In short, the film is tailor-made for those who appreciate the technical aspects of film and armchair psychoanalysts who love to discuss films filled with eroticism, repression, madness, and, mysterious settings. For everyone else, it may disappoint.

Figure 4.7. *Black Narcissus*. Sister Clodagh (Deborah Kerr) does needlework to relieve the stress of directing a remote nunnery in the Himalayas.

It's a Wonderful Life (1946)

The film opens in heaven with Angel Second Class Clarence Oddbody (Henry Travers) being told by his superior the story of the life of George Bailey (Jimmy Stewart), a despairing resident of Bedford Falls, who is standing on a bridge about to commit suicide. The scene shifts to George's childhood where he saves his younger brother after he falls through the ice and, in doing so, loses hearing in one ear. He is next seen as an errand boy for a distraught pharmacist (H. B. Warner) who has just received news that his son has died in World War I and absentmindedly mixes poison in a prescription. When George refuses to deliver the prescription, the pharmacist boxes his ears before learning how George has saved him.

After his father dies, George runs his family's Savings and Loan while putting his younger brother through college. He awaits his brother's return so he can take a vacation and see the world, only to find that his brother is going to work for his father-in-law and can't take over the business. The day George marries his childhood sweetheart Mary (Donna Reed), there's a run on the banks, and he uses the $2,000 he was going to spend on their honeymoon and future home to tide over the Savings and Loan depositors. Finally, when things are going well, his absent-minded Uncle Billy (Thomas Mitchell) misplaces $8,000, which is discovered and withheld by their competitor, a mean-spirited bank owner named Potter (Lionel Barrymore). The bank auditor discovers the discrepancy, and George is threatened with jail. George becomes nasty and offensive to family and friends and decides to commit suicide.

Clarence, needing to perform a good deed in order to earn his wings, jumps in the water, and George dives off the bridge to save him. As they dry off in the bridgemaster's office, George tells Clarence that he wishes he never was born. Clarence arranges for his wish to come true, and George suddenly has his hearing back and a new set of dry clothes. Clarence then proceeds to show George how bereft the lives of so many would have been if he had not been there for them. In short, his has been truly a wonderful life. George then pleads to heaven to be restored to his previous life and is reunited with friends and family in a poignant ending at his house around the Christmas tree on Christmas Eve. As he stands with his daughter in his arms, a bell rings and she says, "Look, Daddy, teacher says, every time a bell rings, an angel gets his wings." George agrees and winks, saying, as he looks up to heaven, "Attaboy, Clarence."

Commentary

Although this film was nominated for five academy awards (Best Picture, Actor, Director, Film Editing, and Cinematography), it won none and was a box office failure, losing over $500,000 and sank into oblivion, much to the dismay of Stewart and Capra who thought it was their best

---

BACKSTORY

Frank Capra and His Secular Saints

Director Frank Capra directed 43 films, three of which made the American Film Institute's top 50 all-time best films and four were named to the top 100 most inspiring films. Called the most American of directors, Capra was born in Sicily and came to Los Angeles at age six in what he described as 23 days without a bath or change of clothing, including "thirteen days of stench and misery in steerage and two more days of panic and pandemonium at Ellis Island." After serving in World War I, he graduated from the California Institute of Technology. Unable to get a job as a chemical engineer, he worked as a comedy writer for Hal Roach's "Our Gang" and Mack Sennett comedies.

After directing Barbara Stanwyck in *The Miracle Woman* (p. 137) and *The Bitter Tea of General Yen* (p. 159), he had his big breakthrough in 1934 with Claudette Colbert and Clark Gable in *It Happened One Night* for which he won his first Oscar for Best Director. He said that his resolution to make films illustrating faith in the common man and the philosophy of love thy neighbor was instilled in him after recovering from a serious illness in 1935. While secular, his films expounded Christian values as well as a syncretic melding of Christianity with the tenets of Tibetan/Buddhist beliefs (see *Lost Horizon*, p. 152). The string of classics involving secular saints included, most notably, *Mr. Deeds Goes to Town* (1936), for which he also won an Oscar as Best Director. It stars Gary Cooper as a poet of greeting cards and a tuba player who inherits $20 million and gives it away to needy farmers. This was followed by another Oscar as Best Director for *You Can't Take It With You* (1938); a nomination as Best Director for *Mr. Smith Goes to Washington* (1939) starring Jimmy Stewart as an idealist senator trying to help young people and fight corruption; and *Meet John Doe* (1941) starring Gary Cooper as a homeless man who, thrust into the spotlight by an unscrupulous newspaperwoman and her publisher, advocates continuing the Christmas spirit year-round by "tearing down the fences of hate and prejudice that separate neighbors."

During World War II, Capra took three years off from directing feature films to serve in the armed forces, heading a unit that made the acclaimed seven-part documentary series called *Why We Fight*, as well as *The Negro Soldier*, a landmark for its time. He returned to Hollywood in 1944 to make another classic film, *Arsenic and Old Lace*, starring Cary Grant. In 1947, he was again nominated as Best Director for *It's A Wonderful Life* (p. 89) in which the suicidal George Bailey (Jimmy Stewart) finds that "no man is a failure who has friends." The film, which would later be regarded as his masterpiece, was a box office disappointment. Along with many of his other films, it was denigrated as "Capracorn" by some film critics. Capra stopped making films in 1961 but did produce such noteworthy documentaries as the Bell Laboratory Science films. His stock rose after *It's Wonderful Life* (see p. 89) came off copyright, and it began to be shown on television. For the last two decades of his life, he toured the country, receiving the acclaim that he had been denied earlier, and he was able to say that his had truly been a wonderful life.

film. Decades later, it was saved by a clerical error or possibly Clarence's intervention. In 1978, the inadvertent failure to renew the copyright thrust the film into the public domain, and it became available for viewing on television without any fee. Through repeated airings, it found a wider and wider audience and became a Christmas perennial and the most celebrated of Frank Capra's films. Voted #1 in the American Film Institute's 2006 list of top 100 most inspiring films, it's near the top of almost everyone's "Best Film of All Time" list, including the Vatican's. The only downside to the copyright loss was that users could cut the film and more importantly produce a colorized version that Stewart appealed unsuccessfully to Congress to have recalled from circulation.

Bailey does not profess any religion and seems to be a prime example of Capra's secular saints (see Backstory, p. 90). So, why include the film? During his directorial years, Capra had drifted away from the Catholicism of his youth, only to return to it with fervor during the last half of his life. Nonetheless, his early Christian upbringing strongly influenced his moviemaking. This film is no exception in that it is a profoundly Christian film, albeit with only a few Christian overtones. The most overt Christian elements are briefly at the beginning with the angels in heaven, then when George falls on his knees and tells God that he's not a praying man but if He's up there, he asks to live again, and finally at the end when family and friends gather around the Christmas tree to sing the hymn "Hark the Herald Angels Sing." It's an excellent example of how symbols and overt religiosity are unnecessary when the story and its realization on film provide such a resounding affirmation of the Christian ethic, particularly the notion of self-abnegation, a fancy way of saying doing good for others even at the expense of oneself.

The Bishop's Wife (1947)

A nativity scene in a downtown department store window combined with the sound of a choir singing "Hark the Herald Angels Sing" sets the scene and gives this film a warm glow. Even the acerbic Professor Wutheridge (Monty Woolley), who professes no religion, buys a tree, albeit a scrawny one, to remember the Christmases of his youth. To raise money for a new cathedral, the Anglican Bishop Henry Brougham (David Niven) meets with the wealthy Mrs. Hamilton (Gladys Cooper), who will only donate if the church is built to her design in her husband's honor. Afterwards Henry tells his wife Julia (Loretta Young) that he "had the most un-Christian feeling of hitting her over the head." She asks, "Henry, what's happening to you? What's happening to us?" Promising to spend the day with her, he instead meets with financiers to get the necessary $4 million, and then moans, "God, can't you help me?"

Dudley (Cary Grant), a guardian angel who had previously been shown leading a blind man across the street and saving a runaway baby carriage, appears and tells him, "I'm an angel helping people who deserve to be helped." To the Bishop's disbelief, Dudley responds, "But you're a Bishop. You, of all people, can trust the word of an angel. You'll have to take me on faith" and disappears. Later Henry visits Mrs. Hamilton and caves in to her demands but is stuck to the chair when he wants to leave. Meanwhile Dudley takes Julia out to lunch as the Bishop had promised to do, after which they take a taxi and he saves the taxi driver Sylvester (James Gleason) from a crash. To celebrate, they stop off at a skating rink for one of the best scenes in the movie with Julia, Dudley, and Sylvester doing some fancy skating. Sylvester refuses a fare, saying, "My pockets are bulging with coins of self-satisfaction because you and the little lady have restored my faith in human nature."

Dudley decides to be bolder with Henry saying, "Sometimes angels must rush in where fools fear to tread." He tells him, "You are sacrificing your principles for the cathedral. These are lean years. There are so many needy." The Bishop thinks Dudley is trying to steal his wife and challenges him to a fight. Dudley leaves but returns later to dismiss the parish secretary, Matilda (Elsa Lanchester), who has been kept working on Christmas Eve, and writes the Bishop's sermon. He confronts Mrs. Hamilton, who is acting out of guilt because her husband was not her true love. After their meeting, she tells Henry "that meeting Dudley has been the greatest spiritual exercise of my life. I've changed my mind about the cathedral. I will give money to poor, needy and homeless and you will direct the money. Dudley is no mortal man. He's an angel." Dudley would like to stay, but he must return to heaven. He tells them, "When I'm gone you will have no memory of an angel being here. Nor will anyone else." On learning of Dudley's departure, the professor who has overcome his writer's block and returned to the church says, "I should have known. Only an angel would have set me to work. There are few people who know how to make a heaven on earth." Asked if he is expecting any mail from Dudley, he replies, "No, but if I do get some, you can be sure the stamp will be worth something."

Commentary

The film did not do well early in its run. Market research showed that people were avoiding it because they thought it would be too pious or serious. So, the advertising in magazines and newspapers was given more pizzazz by featuring Cary Grant and Loretta Young with the headline "Cary and the Bishop's wife." Indeed, the best scenes are those involving the twosome, especially when they go skating. The film, which is pure hokum, won an Oscar for Best Sound and received four other Oscar nominations for Best Picture, Director, Music, and Film Editing. My wife loved it, and given its standing as a Christmas perennial, so do a multitude of others. The marvelous cast is reason enough to see this film and the Bishop's (or should I say, Dudley's) sermon about how materialism has overwhelmed the spirit of Christmas is one of the best Christian affirmations in film:

> Tonight I want to tell you the story of an empty stocking. Once upon a midnight clear, there was a child's cry. A blazing star hung over a stable and wise men came with birthday gifts. We haven't forgotten that night down through the centuries. We celebrate it with stars on Christmas trees, with the sound of bells, and with gifts. But especially with gifts. You give me a book. I give you a tie. Aunt Martha has always wanted an orange squeezer. And Uncle Henry could do with a new pipe. Oh, we forget nobody. And our stockings are stuffed. All that is, except one; we

Figure 4.8. *The Bishop's Wife.* **The Bishop (David Niven) is not pleased with Dudley (Cary Grant), an angel sent after he asks God to help him build a church.**

have forgotten to hang up the stocking for the child born in a manger. It's His birthday we're celebrating. Don't let us ever forget that. Let us ask ourselves what He would wish for most, and then let each put in his share: loving-kindness, warm hearts, and a stretched-out hand of tolerance. All the shining gifts make peace on earth. (Screenwriter: Leonardo Bercovici and Robert E. Sherwood)

Now that's a sermon worth hearing every Christmas!

The Fugitive (1947)

This John Ford film is based on the Graham Greene novel, *The Power and the Glory* (originally titled *The Labyrinthine Way*, a reference to Francis Thompson's poem "The Hound of Heaven," p. 157). It chronicles the flight of the last priest in Mexico, where the Catholic Church was being suppressed in the 1930s and priests were being executed. A fugitive priest (Henry Fonda) returns to his village and meets Maria Dolores (Dolores Del Rio), who tells him that her baby and many others have not been baptized. He rings the bell and holds a mass baptism to the strains of "Agua Bendita" or Blessed (Holy) Water.

The scene shifts to the military headquarters where a lieutenant (Pedro Armendáriz) is shown a picture of the fugitive priest. The lieutenant lays out his plan to shoot a hostage if the priest doesn't reveal himself. He starts with the priest's old village where they are having a fiesta (the only bright spot in the movie). Coincidentally, the lieutenant happens to be the father of Maria's baby. The priest volunteers to be a hostage, but the mayor is chosen instead. The priest escapes to a neighboring country where he tells a doctor that he had no stomach for being a martyr and let others die for him. Yet, he is lured back by a brigand (J. Carrol Naish) to administer Last Rites to a gringo (Ward Bond) who saved him. The fugitive priest is arrested, tried, and found guilty. Despite having given up safety twice to administer Last Rites to those in need, the priest calls himself a coward. He says that he was always too small for the priesthood but gains courage as he faces death. As the sound of his firing squad dies down, and the military declare that they have finally gotten the last priest, there's a knock on the door of a pious group of peasants in hiding. The man says, "I'm the new priest, Father Serra."

Commentary

The only saving graces of this languorous film are the exquisite black and white cinematography and the frequent appearance of the luminously beautiful Dolores Del Rio, who mercifully does not emulate Fonda's acting, which alternates from agonized anxiety to zombie-like. That the lieutenant was the father of Maria's baby seemed contrived. In fact, in the book the child is the priest's illegitimate daughter. This was probably changed to comply with the Hays Code, and if so, it's too bad, because it would have made a more interesting story and the character of the priest more human and less insufferable. Still, the movie has strong moments, especially when the priest risks his own safety to perform his duties and the ending when, just as it looks like the forces of evil have won, the Church sprouts a new shoot.

Monsieur Vincent (1947)

The most intriguing aspect of this movie is that in almost two hours, the film barely scratches the surface of the extraordinary life and times of St. Vincent de Paul (Pierre Fresnay), which could have filled three films. Still, what was left in was quite enough. It covers the period beginning when Vincent at age 41 leaves a comfortable sinecure in Paris as confessor to a countess (Lise Delamare) and tutor for her children to take over a rural church that has been abandoned for 17 years and now serves as a chicken coop. After a long walk from the bus stop, he must run the gauntlet of stone-throwing villagers who are afraid that any new visitor will bring the plague. He compounds their enmity when he breaks into a home the town had boarded up three days before, fearing its inhabitants had the plague. He removes a woman who had died of another ailment, gives her a decent burial, and after feeding her starving daughter insists that she be cared for not by a rich person but by one who is just getting by. When a mother with five children of her own steps forward, the townspeople are shamed and, slowly but surely, he wins over the rich and poor as he starts a soup kitchen.

The countess entices him back to Paris with promises of money and the help of other prominent women to expand his mission. He gives away all his possessions, and these women become the Ladies of Charity who provide additional funds. They are, however, honest enough to admit that they are temperamentally ill-suited to care for the poor. So, with the help of Louise de Marillac (Yvonne Gaudeau), he recruits hard-working young women from the so-called lower classes into the Daughters of Charity, a community without walls that serves in hospitals, orphanages, and soup kitchens.

The ending is especially poignant when he chooses to speak to a new Daughter of Charity recruit rather than a papal envoy just before he dies. He tells her that:

> You'll find that charity is a heavy burden, heavier than a bowl of soup or a loaf of bread, but keep your guilelessness and your smile. The poor are your masters, terribly sensitive and exacting, as you will see. The dirtier and uglier they are, the more vulgar and unjust, the more love you must show them. It is only because of your love, your love alone that the poor will forgive you for the bread you give them. (Screenwriters: Jean Bernard-Luc and Jean Anouilh)

Commentary

This remarkable film easily makes my top 10 list of films about Christianity. You know it's something special when even film critic Pauline Kael praises it. The film was released in a new DVD in French with English and Spanish subtitles in 2008. Directed by Maurice Cloche, this film is the product of the confluence of three major talents. Jean Anouilh, the playwright, co-wrote the screenplay with Jean Bernard-Luc. The photographer was Claude Renoir, the grandson of the famed Impressionist painter and nephew of the renowned Jean Renoir with whom he worked on many great French films. Most importantly, Pierre Fresnay, who starred in another classic, Renoir's *La Grande Illusion*, plays Saint Vincent de Paul in a down-to-earth believable manner, combining earnestness and good humor. There's no self-conscious suffering, histrionics, or long speeches—just an obsessive and charismatic desire to help the poor, the sick, the aged, and the orphans.

As noted, much of St. Vincent de Paul's life is left out. Not shown is his youth in poverty and his studies for the priesthood, after which he was captured by Turkish pirates and sold into slavery for two years to an apostate priest who converted to Islam and taught him the art of medicine. Later he would reconvert his master to Christianity. He returned to Avignon and then Rome where he became a papal envoy to Henry IV and later alms distributor for Margaret of Valois, Queen of France. He became a confidant of Cardinals Mazarin and Richelieu who appointed him Chaplain General of the Fleet and Grand Almoner of the galleys where, appalled by the treatment of the galley slaves, he is shown spelling one of them and arguing for more

Figure 4.9. *Monsieur Vincent.* **Vincent De Paul (Pierre Fresnay) washes the clothes of the sick.**

humane treatment. These powerful connections proved useful in getting money and land to help the poor by building hospitals and asylums.

My only quibble is the treatment of Louise de Marillac, who is shown in the film recoiling from the poor like the rich benefactresses (the Ladies of Charity). Actually her story is also remarkable in that she wanted to become a nun but was advised to marry. She did so and was happily married for 12 years until her husband died. She chose not to remarry but took care of her son and devoted herself to Christian service. Described as "self-effacing, un-flappable, and gracious," she was a natural to head the Daughters of Charity. De Paul told her that her "convent will be the house of the sick, your cell a rented room, your chapel the parish church, your cloister the city streets or hospital wards." She took the first four recruits into her home for training and though never intending to found an order of nuns, it expanded into the Sisters of Charity with 40 convents in 25 years. She was canonized a saint of the Roman Catholic Church in 1934 and later was declared patroness of social workers by Pope John XXIII.

Joan of Arc (1948)

It's 1920, and the Church of Rome makes reparations for the burial of Joan as a heretic 500 years before and declares her a saint. The scene shifts to Joan's birthplace Domremy, France, in 1412 when the English, who had ruled much of France, claim the right of succession to the French throne. The semi-literate Joan (Ingrid Bergman) is very religious and hears voices from God telling her to lead an army against the English and restore the Dauphin to the throne, fulfilling a prophecy that a Maid of Lorraine would save France.

She asks to be allowed to go to Orleans to see the Dauphin. Examined by an archbishop and a priest for three weeks, she is declared not to be a sorcerer and is sent to Orleans. The court tries to trick her by presenting her to a false Dauphin while the real one (José Ferrer) hides in the crowd. She picks him out and tells him: "What you need is faith in God, then you will have faith in yourself." She heads the army, winning the soldiers' respect despite telling them that she will tolerate no gambling, swearing, or camp followers, and that they must go to confession. She says, "It's not enough that God must be on our side, we must be on His. Our strength is in our faith. We can win only if we become God's army." In battle, the wounded Joan rallies the retreating French and snatches victory from defeat. Surveying the battlefield, Joan weeps at the carnage.

The spineless Dauphin is crowned at the cathedral in Rheims amid much pageantry and then makes a deal with the enemy not to pursue his advantage. Joan's voices desert her, and she goes it alone leading the army, knowing that she will be taken prisoner and will die in one year. She is captured at Campeigne by the Duke of Burgundy. The archbishop of Rheims tells Burgundy that if he were a true Christian, he would give her up for nothing. He responds that she is a sorceress and that her death is a political and military necessity. She undergoes a five-month trial mainly by French bishops in league with the English and the Burgundians who can be counted on to declare her a heretic. She is guarded by men in an English cell and not allowed to enter a church or receive communion until she forswears the voices in public. Under duress, she does so and is condemned to prison, but recants saying: "The Voices said I did a wicked thing in denying them, but they have forgiven me. To live without faith is worse than death. Send me back to God from whence I came." A cross is given to her by a soldier and after affirming that she is "a good Christian," she is burned at the stake. "Jesus" is her last word and rays appear in the heavens as the film ends.

Commentary

Based on Maxwell Anderson's play *Joan of Lorraine,* this straightforward and reverent retelling of the story of Joan of Arc is the most complete film

Figure 4.10. *Joan of Arc.* **Joan (Ingrid Bergman) leads the French soldiers against the English.**

treatment of Joan's story. It is light-years better than 1999's *The Messenger* (see p. 294) but much less powerful than the 1928 film *The Passion of Joan of Arc* (see p. 30). Made watchable by the performance of Ingrid Bergman, it's hard to believe that the film was originally released at 145 minutes. The film won Oscars for cinematography and costume design. Both Bergman and José Ferrer in his film debut received Oscar nominations. My favorite line is spoken by Isabelle d'Arc (Selena Royle), Joan's mother: "A mother raises her children and thinks she knows them, but she doesn't know them at all." Then again, how many mothers raise saints!

Come to the Stable (1949)

Sister Margaret (Loretta Young) and Sister Scholastica (Celeste Holm), two nuns of the French order of the Holy Endeavor come to a Connecticut crossroads with signs saying Jordan, Bethlehem, Nazareth, and Galilee. Arriving in Bethlehem, they see a nativity scene and hear two angels singing "Adeste Fidelis." It turns out to be two children singing outside the studio of an absent-minded painter of religious art, Miss Potts (Elsa Lanchester). The nuns reveal that during the war, they worked in a children's hospital and had 100 critical cases that couldn't be moved. They made a promise to St. Jude, the patron of the impossible, that if the hospital was spared during an Allied bombing, they would go to America and build a hospital. Seeing a reproduction of her painting "Come to the Stable" with a hill that seemed perfect for the hospital, they came. They bury a St. Jude's medal on the hill and borrow a jeep from the neighbor, Bob Mason (Hugh Marlowe), a music composer. They visit the local bishop (Basil Ruysdael) to tell him that they only have two needs: land and money. He gives them $50 and comments when they leave: "Simple blind faith of such sisters." His secretary, a monsignor (Regis Toomey) adds: "disturbing," but the bishop corrects him: "No, sublime."

Mason tells them the hill is owned by Luigi Rossi, who can be found by asking any policeman in New York. Sister Margaret (Loretta Young) drives down Fifth Avenue and parks in front of St. Patrick's Cathedral. As a policeman writes them a ticket, they get directions to Luigi Rossi's business, a front for a bookmaking establishment. Lo and behold, Corporal Luigi Rossi, Jr., died near Rouen close by where their hospital was located. Rossi Sr. (Thomas Gomez) tells them, "Put a stained glass window with Luigi Rossi, Jr., on it and the land is yours." He gives them the deed to the land and receives a medal of St. Jude to protect him.

The nuns say the rosary while driving the jeep very fast. A tire blows out, and while fixing it, they see a witch hazel bottling plant for sale and take out a $50 option on the building for three months. They need $30,000 and start trying to raise money with bake sales. Sister Scholastica, a French tennis champ before entering the order, wins $500 playing in full habit. Mason fights the hospital but capitulates after realizing that his new neighbors helped end his songwriter's block. His new song (played by Dooley Wilson of *Casablanca* fame) was based on a Gregorian chant and plainsong sung by the nuns. The film ends in the new chapel with the stained glass window reading "In Memoriam Luigi Rossi, Jr." with all the principals in attendance.

Commentary

If one is looking for a single film to show how times have changed, look no farther than this illustration of a time when filmmakers didn't shrink from making wholesome films. It received seven Academy Award nominations and is highly recommended for family viewing. Loretta Young and Celeste Holm are marvelous as two enterprising nuns who manage to merge sanctity and savvy. So is Elsa Lanchester as the somewhat dotty artist. All three received Oscar nominations.

The film is loosely based on the founding of the Abbey of Regina Laudis in Bethlehem, Connecticut, in 1947 by Mother Benedict Duss. Born in Pittsburgh in 1910, her maternal grandparents were part of an experimental

Christian commune and her maternal grandmother was a spiritualist. Her parents, who had met at a Baptist college, split up when she was three and her French-American mother, a Catholic convert, took her and her younger brother to France. Vera (Mother Benedict's given name at birth) was baptized at five and attended convent schools. When she was 17, her mother refused her request to become a nun, and she graduated from the Sorbonne as a doctor in 1936. Entering a Benedictine abbey in Jouarre, France, in 1938, she ran their infirmary and during World War II took care of the townspeople who lost their doctor. She had to be especially careful because the Gestapo had been tipped off about an American nun in the abbey.

She had no intention of returning to America until August 27, 1944, when the Americans liberated the town. Climbing to the abbey tower, despite being ill with hepatitis, she was moved by the sight of the White Star on the vehicles and the American flag. She asked another nun to take a rose to one of the soldiers with a message that it was sent by an American nun, and was told that he "burst into tears." Thus began her effort to thank the liberators whom she later learned were headed by General Patton, whose granddaughter entered the convent at Regina Laudis years later.

Given permission by her order to proceed, she was taken in by artist Lauren Hall, who lived in Bethlehem and saw the hill where she did bury a St. Benedict medal. She overcame the objections of Bishop O'Brien of Hartford who saw no need for an order of French nuns. Although the abbey is run according to the Rule of Saint Benedict, Mother Benedict felt strongly that the nuns should develop as persons and not renounce their past. One nun is a lawyer and a former Connecticut state representative, another is a social worker, and others include an artist, a doctor of animal science with a Ph.D. from Yale, and a chemist. Their most famous member is Mother Dolores the prioress, formerly Dolores Hart, who starred in films like *King Creole* opposite Elvis, *Where the Boys Are,* and *Francis of Assisi* (see p. 158). All are allowed to keep up with their professions; for example, Mother Dolores is the only nun who is a voting member of the Academy of Motion Picture Arts and Sciences (see Backstory, p. 160). At the same time, Mother Benedict believed in their wearing the habit all the time as a way of "giving evidence to the fact that a vocation is not a forty hour week." As she said, "It isn't that it makes you act in a holier or phonier way." Instead, it "signs, seals, and encloses you— a constant reminder that you are witnessing to something else."

The impetus for the movie came from Clare Boothe Luce, journalist and author of *The Women*. Married to Henry Luce, publisher of *Time* magazine

Figure 4.11. *Come to the Stable.* **French nuns, Sister Scholastica (Celeste Holm) and Sister Margaret (Loretta Young), discuss their plans to build a hospital in the United States.**

and a Catholic convert, she had completed two terms as a Congresswoman from Connecticut, when she began visiting the Abbey in 1948. Luce thought a film would be helpful given the nuns' debt, and Mother Benedict was sent a script and a contract that Bishop O'Brien forbade her to sign. They were not compensated until years later when Twentieth Century Fox asked Luce to offer them $30,000. Mother Benedict, who didn't see the film until 1950, said that much of it was fiction including the introduction of the gangsters.

Short Subjects

Brother Orchid (1940)

Little Johnny Sarto (Edward G. Robinson) decides to quit the rackets to fulfill his lifelong dream of acquiring "class." After five years of being cheated by the so-called high-class people, he returns to find that his second-in-command Jack Buck (Humphrey Bogart) has taken over the business. Buck tries to kill Sarto who, badly wounded, finds help at the Monastery of the Little Brothers of the Flowers, whose motto is "Be poor of purse, pure of heart, kind in word and deed, and beautify the lives of men with flowers." Healed, he spends an awkward but happy six months with the brothers before leaving, when his girlfriend Flo Addams (Ann Sothern), thinking he's dead, agrees to marry Clarence Fletcher (Ralph Bellamy), a rich cowboy from Montana.

After handing Buck and his gang over to the police and giving his blessing to the wedding, Sarto returns to the monastery saying, "I thought class came in dough, nice clothes, and society. I was wrong. I sure traveled a long way to find one thing" and pointing to the brothers assembled at table, "This! This is the real class." Pure corn, the film has a good message and a number of light-hearted scenes provided by Robinson, Sothern, Bellamy, and Allen Jenkins as Willie the Knife, a good-hearted mug who spouts malapropisms.

Joan of Paris (1942)

Paul Lavalier (Paul Henreid), a French Resistance leader piloting planes for the RAF, and his four buddies are shot down over occupied France. They escape to Paris where they are hidden by Father Antoine (Thomas Mitchell) and a waitress Joan (Michèle Morgan), who is devoted to Joan of Arc. Paul is finally caught by a persistent Nazi agent and his slimy Gestapo supervisor Herr Funk (Laird Cregar) but is released to lead the Germans to the remaining four pilots. They meet in the church where one who had been wounded (Alan Ladd) dies after Father Antoine reads the 23rd Psalm (The Lord is My Shepherd) and blesses him. Father Antoine leads the four to a secret passage to the Paris sewer. Joan, realizing Lavalier's identity and his importance to the cause of freedom, delays the Nazis, sacrificing her life, thereby allowing them to escape. Just before she is taken to be shot, Father Antoine comforts her with the Litany of Mary, Our Queen. The film ends in Latin spoken by the priest.

This is a great example of a B film that one watches for pure entertainment and escape. It was clearly meant to be a morale booster in the early days of World War II. There's even a rendition of La Marseillaise by middle schoolers who shout down a Vichy sympathizer (shades of *Casablanca*). As in *Casablanca*, the heroic Freedom Fighter is played by Paul Henreid. The good priest and the devotion of the heroine to Saint Joan give a Christian overtone to the film, as does their willingness to risk their lives in a noble cause.

Guadalcanal Diary (1943)

Based on a book by war correspondent Richard Tregaskis about the Guadalcanal campaign, a turning point in the war with Japan, the film is filled with stock characters like Brooklyn Dodger fan Taxi Potts (William Bendix), a tough marine sergeant (Lloyd Nolan), a boyish recruit (Richard Jaeckel), and an Irish priest, Father Donnelly (Preston Foster), who is told not to go ashore with the first wave. "Why not?" he asks, "That's when I'll be needed most." After Donnelly says the Last Rites over a soldier, he says, "I'm no hero. I'm just a guy. I came out here because nobody else would." The film is briefly mentioned here because the priest is a central character. Strong, caring, and manly, he selflessly puts himself at risk to minister to the souls of his comrades. In this respect, he's like Father Logan (James Bell), who provides the mechanism for telling the story in *Dead Reckoning* (1947). In that film, he is known as the "Jumping Padre" for being the first to parachute out of a plane with his men.

Miracle on 34th Street (1947)

This film is filled with wonderful scenes, including the opening when Kris Kringle (Edmund Gwenn), a Santa look-alike who says he really is Santa, informs the person decorating a store window that the reindeer are mixed up. The plot involves Macy's events organizer Doris Walker (Maureen O'Hara), a divorcée, who shields her daughter Susan (Natalie Wood) from believing in Santa Claus and fairy tales because Doris's Prince Charming turned out not to be too charming. Her new suitor, next-door neighbor lawyer Fred Gailey (John Payne), tells her that "Faith is believing in something when common sense tells you not to."

Filmed on location during Christmas 1946, *Miracle on 34th Street* was chosen "Number 9" on the American Film Institute's List of Most Inspiring Films in 2006. The acting is excellent, especially by Edmund Gwenn, who deservedly won an Academy Award for Best Supporting Actor. Also awarded Oscars were George Seaton (Screenplay) and Valentine Davies (Original Story) who fought Darryl Zanuck, who was against making what he considered a corny film and was surprised when it ran over six months in theaters. What is striking, however, is that this whimsical Christmas staple never mentions Christ, nor shows a nativity scene, nor enters a church. Furthermore, one gets no notion that Santa is a saint; the religious significance has been leached out of him just as when "holy day" became "holiday." It also criticizes the commercialism of Christmas while at the same time being one long promo for Macy's and the Macy's Thanksgiving Day Parade, during which Santa makes his annual entrance into New York City.

3 Godfathers (1948)

This sentimental movie has been called a Christmas western and the most underappreciated John Ford film. I saw it in the theater when I was 11 and

---

BACKSTORY

John Ford: A Directorial Paradox

When Orson Welles, whose *Citizen Kane* is considered by many to be the best film of all time, was asked to name the three best movie directors, he replied, "John Ford, John Ford, and John Ford." In *Directed by John Ford*, a masterful documentary tribute to Ford first produced in 1971 and updated in 2006, director Peter Bogdanovich interviewed Welles, Walter Hill, Martin Scorsese, Steven Spielberg, and Clint Eastwood. All acknowledged the debt they owed to Ford. Hill was especially incisive, calling Ford a "Catholic poet." He went on to say that "what set him apart was his sense of spirituality, his sense that death is not the end." Bogdanovich illustrates this with scenes from such films as *Young Mr. Lincoln* (1939), where Lincoln (Henry Fonda) talks to Ann Rutledge at her grave and in *She Wore a Yellow Ribbon* (1949) in which the Colonel (John Wayne) visits his wife's gravesite to share the news of his retirement from the Army. *How Green Was My Valley* (1944) begins with grace before meals and ends during the funeral of the paterfamilias, whose wife says, "He came to me just now and spoke to me of the glory to be seen."

Paradoxically, Ford, whose pictures are suffused with the importance of family, had a disordered one. He was profane, had affairs, drank heavily, and was far from a model Catholic; yet his films respectfully portrayed Catholics, their rituals, and imagery. Although his films radiated warmth, he was often very cold and off-putting. It sort of reminds me of my response to the film *Amadeus* in which Mozart's behavior is portrayed as incongruous with the excellence and otherworldliness of his work. To the extent that the portrayal was true (and many dispute it), I say, "So what! Just enjoy the works and leave him to God's mercy where his oeuvre should speak for him." The same holds for Ford. Indeed, nothing says it better than the line in Ford's classic *The Man Who Shot Liberty Valance* (1962). Senator Ransom Stoddard (Jimmy Stewart), whose career was built on his being the hero who shot the evil Valance, admits to reporters that it wasn't him but his friend Tom Doniphon (John Wayne), who wouldn't take the credit. When he expresses dismay that the reporters won't print the truth, one replies, "This is the West. When the legend becomes the fact, print the legend."

---

liked it, but for adults, it requires a major suspension of disbelief. Three cattle rustlers, Robert Marmaduke Hightower (John Wayne), Pedro "Pete" Roca Fuerte (Pedro Armendáriz), and William Kearney "The Abilene Kid" (Harry Carey, Jr.) rob a bank in Welcome, Arizona, and are pursued across the desert by sheriff Perley "Buck" Sweet (Ward Bond) and his posse. They come across a pregnant woman (Mildred Natwick) in an abandoned prairie schooner. She has a boy, asks the threesome to be the baby's godfathers, names the child Robert William Pedro Hightower, and then dies. The men dig a grave for her, and the Abilene Kid sings the hymn "Let Us Gather at the River" and puts up a cross. The film becomes an allegory of the Three Wise Men as they use a Bible to follow a star to a nearby town, which just happens to be called New Jerusalem. They say their prayers ("Our Father" and "Now I Lay Me Down to Sleep"). The Abilene Kid says, "God Bless Mom, Papa and sister" before dying of a wound. Pedro breaks his legs and says, "Tomorrow is Feliz Navidad" and realizing he is slowing down Hightower and the baby, he stays behind to die. Hightower reaches New Jerusalem and brings the baby into a bar where the sheriff and others are playing chess while a pianist plays "Silent Night." He is given a light sentence because of the extenuating circumstances and vows to come back to see his godson when he is released.

The Miracle of the Bells (1948)

Despite a screenplay by respected writers Ben Hecht and Quentin Reynolds, this is just a low-budget Republic Studio production about an actress, Olga Treskonva (Alida Valli), who dies after playing Joan of Arc in her first film. When the film's producer Marcus Harris (Lee J. Cobb) refuses to release it, her publicist Bill Dunnigan (Fred MacMurray) returns her body to her Pennsylvania coal town and pays for all the town's church bells to ring. This causes the Blessed Virgin's statue in a poor Polish church to move to face Olga's casket. Although the priest, Father Paul (Frank Sinatra), says it's due to the structural effects of the unusually large crowd, Dunnigan calls it a miracle and attracts nationwide publicity. Harris relents, releasing the film, and Olga becomes the star she always wanted to be. After seeing this film, James Agee, noted author and film critic, declared himself "a founding father of the Society for Prevention of Cruelty to God." The best scenes involve Lee J. Cobb and a flashback to a Christmas Eve the publicist and Olga spent in a Chinese restaurant and its starry aftermath. It's also noteworthy for Ol' Blue Eyes in a priestly role, but he is no match for Crosby.

CHAPTER FIVE
THE AGE OF THE EPIC: THE 1950s

It has long been fashionable to label those, like myself, who came of age during the 1950s as the "Silent Generation." We may have been silent about accomplishments during the decade, unlike the hype promulgated by the 1960s generation, but I can attest that the 1950s was actually a period of enormous growth and considerable social progress. For example, the groundwork for the Civil Rights Movement was laid in the 1950s with the landmark Supreme Court decision *Brown v. Board of Education of Topeka* in 1954, which outlawed the concept of "separate but equal." The law was tested in 1957 when Governor Orval Faubus of Arkansas refused entry to nine black students at a Little Rock High School. President Eisenhower federalized the Arkansas National Guard and sent in the 101st Airborne Division to escort the children safely into school, an action memorialized in a famous Norman Rockwell *Saturday Evening Post* cover. In addition, President Eisenhower got the Congress to pass the 1957 Civil Rights Act that affirmed the voting rights for blacks by eliminating discriminatory voting requirements and established a Civil Rights division in the Justice Department. Racial and ethnic barriers to immigration established in the 1920s were removed by Congress, and discrimination against Catholics and Jews in Ivy League and other "elite" universities and medical schools were laid bare and reversed. These revolutionary events occurred relatively peacefully amid social stability.

During the 1950s, the crime rate fell to an all-time low, as did unemployment. Higher wages allowed Americans to become better educated and increased homeownership. Other dramatic events on the home front included the introduction in 1955 of the Salk polio vaccine, followed within a few months by the Sabin oral vaccine, which removed the specter of a disease that struck fear in parents. Other medical breakthroughs included the discovery of ACTH and related hormones, as well as organ transplantation and cardiopulmonary resuscitation. Combined with the further development of antibiotics and the provision of medical care benefits, they allowed average life expectancy to climb to age 70. In addition, the discovery of oral contraceptives and their wide availability were to have profound effects a decade later.

The automobile became the primary means of transportation, as Eisenhower championed the building of an interstate highway system. Jet plane travel premiered domestically in 1958 and also began to supplant luxury liners as modes of foreign travel. The notion of the nuclear family became fully entrenched in the 1950s, probably because for the first time in history, the nation's growing affluence permitted the majority of women (most notably working-class women) to stay home to raise children. This ideal was reinforced by popular television sitcoms, such as *Father Knows Best, The Adventures of Ozzie and Harriet,* and *I Love Lucy,* while the quintessential 1950s businessman was defined by Sloan Wilson in his novel *The Man in the Gray Flannel Suit.* Men not only wore suits and ties to work and church but even to baseball games. Women traded the big-shouldered suits of the 1940s for the stylish fashions of Dior and Givenchy, as exemplified by Audrey Hepburn in *Roman Holiday* and *Sabrina.* On the other hand, teenagers began to reject their parents' music by Nat King Cole, Dinah Shore, and Perry Como for rock and roll featuring Bill Haley and the Comets, Elvis Presley, Buddy Holly, etc. That simmering spirit of rebellion that would burst forth in the mid-1960s was captured in such films as *The Wild One* (1953), *Blackboard Jungle* (1955), and *Rebel Without a Cause* (1955).

While it's easy to ridicule the "duck and cover" school exercises and the bomb shelters people built in the event of a nuclear attack, it's important to remember the vast cloud of fear created by the threat of nuclear attack by the Russians, especially after they launched Sputnik, the first space satellite, in 1957. This fear was compounded by the Korean War that began as a United Nations "police action" after Communist-dominated North Korea invaded South Korea with the help of Communist China. Although a truce was declared in 1953, its effects linger to this day.

Hollywood in the Fifties

The biggest problem for Hollywood was the rapidity with which television sets became a fixture in every home. Concerned that fans would stay home and watch TV rather than spend money at the movies, filmmakers developed new technologies, most notably Cinerama and CinemaScope, a dramatic wide-screen format developed by 20th Century Fox. The use of 3-D glasses was another attempt to lure audiences, but it didn't catch on. As it turned out, television ended up being a fertile training ground for many film actors and writers as Hollywood studios wound up producing many television programs. Another form of competition was the influx of foreign films by directors such as Ingmar Bergman, Roberto Rossellini, and Federico Fellini. Their gritty and neorealistic themes, as well as increased sensuality, had a great impact on American filmmakers such as Elia Kazan and Otto Preminger, moving the focus away from big and glossy films to smaller, hard-edged, more personal stories. All these factors increased the pressure for the abolition of the Motion Picture Code.

Finally, the "studio system," best exemplified by the megastars and top-notch filmmakers assembled by MGM, began to disintegrate. Actors, writers, and producers started making films independent of the studios or on a limited contractual basis. Additionally, the last of the studio-owned theaters disappeared, severely cutting into studio revenue. Despite these problems, a number of great movies were made during this decade, including *All about Eve, Sunset Boulevard, High Noon, Stalag 17, The Bridge on the River Kwai,* and *Some Like It Hot.*

Christians in the Movies: The Golden Age

In the mid-1950s, a poll quoted 49 percent of Americans as saying they had attended a church or synagogue in the previous week, and in 1952, 75 percent said religion was "very important" in their lives. As Charles Morris points out in *American Catholic*, steadily growing affluence had a particularly strong effect on many formerly working-class Catholics (Irish, Italian, Polish, German, French Canadian, etc.), Their population doubled from 20 million in 1940 to 40 million in 1956, and the urban centers where they were concentrated boomed economically. Morris quotes Protestant historian Martin Marty as saying in 1959, "Catholicism controls the urban centers with few exceptions outside the South and America is a nation of urban dominance." The innocence and earnestness of the 1950s as I knew it growing up in New York City was best captured in Paddy Chayefsky's academy award winning 1955 film *Marty*.

Not surprisingly, Catholicism was the dominant religion portrayed in movies, music, and even television. From 1952 to 1957, Bishop Fulton Sheen hosted a prime-time show called *Life Is Worth Living*. As Reeves documents in "America's Bishop," Sheen, given a seemingly impossible time slot (opposite comedian Milton Berle, known as "Uncle Miltie" and "Mister Television"), attracted 30 million viewers, many of whom were non-Catholic. Berle became a good friend of Sheen's, whom he called "Uncle Fultie." When Sheen received an Emmy Award in 1952, he thanked his "four writers Matthew, Mark, Luke, and John." Messages of hope were also promulgated by Protestant denominations, most notably by Norman Vincent Peale in his best-seller *The Power of Positive Thinking* and Billy Graham who was in the forefront of a growing Evangelical Christian movement.

During the 1950s, Hollywood produced a series of top-flight religious-themed films. A number were epic blockbusters, such as *Quo Vadis, Ben-Hur, The Robe, Spartacus,* and *The Ten Commandments.* Others with religious overtones were *On the Waterfront; Friendly Persuasion; Heaven Knows, Mr. Allison;* and *The Nun's Story.* The production of memorable films about Christianity continued into the 1960s such that the period from the 1940s through the mid-1960s might be considered "The Golden Age of Christianity in the Movies."

Stars in My Crown (1950)

As the camera pans over a Protestant chapel in Wellsburg, the narrator, John Kenyon (Marshall Thompson), begins his reminiscences about Parson Josiah Gray (Joel McCrea) who took him in as a young boy (Dean Stockwell) after his parents died. When Gray, a Civil War veteran-turned-preacher, arrived in town, the first thing he did was walk into the saloon and say, "I'm your new parson and I aim to give my first sermon right here and now." He and his wife Harriet (Ellen Drew) ran a boarding house, and he won people over, much as Abraham Lincoln did, by telling stories. He led services in barns until the townspeople built a church. The title comes from the parson's favorite hymn with which he began every service.

The major plot line involves a kindly black farmer, "Uncle Famous" Prill (Juano Hernandez), who teaches everyone how to fish. He refuses an offer by a white churchgoer, Lon Backett (Ed Begley), who wants to buy him out to extend his profitable mine. After harassment doesn't work, Backett and his friends burn Famous's place to the ground. Jed Isbell (Alan Hale), a farmer and his five sons, who don't go to church, help rebuild it. "You're a real Christian, Sir," says Famous. The Parson also stands up to the Ku Klux Klan Night Riders (all members of the Church) who terrorize Famous. In a climactic scene, the Parson reads from what he says is Famous's will that he intends to give the property to the town when he dies, thus shaming the Klanners. Picking up the blank piece of paper, the boy says, "No will here." The Parson replies, "Yes it is, it's the will of God."

The subplot involves the conflict between the Parson and the scientifically trained Dr. Harris, Jr., (James Mitchell), who takes over the practice of his father (Lewis Stone). Arriving to minister to the Widow Smith, and finding her dying, Harris Jr. tells the Parson that he should have been called earlier and disparages the effectiveness of prayer. The Parson replies that "If the Lord wants someone bad enough, it's not for me to stand in his way." When a typhoid fever epidemic breaks out, the doctor works tirelessly to help the victims and wins over the town and the schoolmarm (Amanda Blake). However, it is the Parson who discovers the epidemic's cause, which is a well at the school, and thereby ends the outbreak. This raises his esteem in the doctor's eyes and at the end, the church is full, including the Isbells and the young doctor.

Commentary

This is one of the films with which people should be more familiar and one of the reasons I am writing this book. This unapologetic bit of nostalgia, in which the young boy recalls his Granny telling him that she saw George Washington and a drummer boy at Bull Run, was directed by Parisian-born Jacques Tourneur. Tourneur liked the story so much, he agreed to work for scale. Best known as the director of the horror film *Cat People,* he is just getting his due because of praise by Martin Scorsese. The outstanding cast is headed by one of the most underappreciated actors, Joel McCrea, who was called Mr. Nice Guy by all who worked with him.

The take-home messages are clear. First, the churchgoers are not necessarily Christian, and nonchurchgoers may be better Christians. This is a

Figure 5.1. *Stars in My Crown.* **Parson Gray (Joel McCrea) prays at the bedside of a dying woman while a young doctor (James Mitchell) takes her pulse.**

theme that recurs in many films, notably *The Keys of the Kingdom* (p. 79). The second message relates to the supposed conflict between science and religion. Interestingly, the vehemence is all on the side of the doctor, who is not content to exercise his skills but must disparage belief in an invisible presence. In the end, this difference is also reconciled.

The film harks back to an era that some say never was. As the boy says, "We are promised a city of gold in the hereafter. Now I know we had a city of gold in the city of my youth." That the Parson can overcome evil and reconcile enemies with his stories and his own moral presence may seem simplistic. However, it is a trait much to be desired. That's why Atticus Finch in *To Kill a Mockingbird* and George Bailey in *It's a Wonderful Life* (p. 89) resonate with moviegoers. So, ignore the cynics and sit back and enjoy this fine family film.

Quo Vadis (1951)

The tribune Marcus Vinicius (Robert Taylor), returning in triumph to Rome, is welcomed by Nero (Peter Ustinov), who has murdered his wife and uncle and married a "harlot," Poppea (Patricia Laffan). Nero's advisor Petronius (Leo Genn), Vinicius's uncle, has adopted Lygia (Deborah Kerr), a Christian, as his daughter. Vinicius asks Nero to award him Lygia as his prize and takes her from Petronius to the House of Women, whose mistress is a closet Christian. She helps Lygia escape to her Christian friends. There she is guarded by Ursus (Buddy Baer), a giant who thinks it's a sin to kill. Vinicius seeks her in the catacombs where he listens to the preaching of Peter and Paul but cannot accept Christ's teachings,

Back at the palace, Nero, vowing to build the new city of Neropolis, orders Rome burned and then asks for his robe of grief and his lyre. Poppea, who has been rebuffed by Vinicius, suggests Nero blame the Christians. Petronius says doing so will assure their immortality, but Nero responds that when he's through, no one will know they ever existed. As the Christians are herded together to be fed to the lions, Peter and his young companion flee Rome. A sign appears from heaven, and Peter says, "Christ Jesus you are here. Quo vadis Domine? (Whither goest thou Lord?)" Christ tells him that if Peter deserts His people, he will have to return to be crucified once more. Peter returns and is imprisoned. Vinicius, who has joined Lygia in prison, asks Peter to marry them before he is taken to Vatican Hill to be crucified.

Peter says, "To die as Our Lord died is more than I deserve," so he is crucified upside down.

The Christians sing as they are led into the arena, and Nero wonders
why they are not afraid. On being told that they believe that death is a tran-
sition to a better life, he says that "it's monstrous for them to die smiling."
Lygia is tied to a stake and a bull is let out with only Ursus to protect her. I
will stop the story here. Suffice it to say that many events take place before
the film ends with the words, "I am the Way the Truth and the Life."

Commentary

Based on the book by Polish Nobel Prize winner Henryk Sienkiewicz, the
film, whose title comes from John's Gospel, is very sympathetic to Christ and
Christianity. This grand spectacle was filmed in a four-block square replica
of ancient Rome constructed at Cinecitta Studios. The film featured 30,000
extras, including Elizabeth Taylor who was a big star at the time, and Sophia
Loren. Although almost three hours long, it maintains interest due to the
acting and the musical scoring by Miklós Rózsa. *Quo Vadis* boasts outstanding performances by Peter Ustinov and Leo Genn, who were among the
film's eight Oscar nominees. None won. There are many marvelous scenes
between Nero, who is besotted with himself, and Petronius, whose dialogue

Figure 5.2. *Quo Vadis.* **The triumphant Tribune Marcus
Vinicius (Robert Taylor) is given a Christian, Lygia (Deborah Kerr), as his prize, but she wants no part of him.**

is brimming with irony as when Nero tells Petronius, "It's lonely being the Emperor. It's lonely being a genius." Then turning to the crowds, he says, "You were right, Petronius; how they love me." Nero's calling for the vial to hold his tears, on learning of Petronius's suicide, is precious. Both Ustinov and Genn had remarkable screen careers, but Genn's other career was even more noteworthy. A lieutenant colonel in the British army during World War II, he was awarded the Croix de Guerre. After the war, he was one of the prosecuting officers at the war crimes trial at Bergen-Belsen, the concentration camp where Anne Frank, among many others, was imprisoned and died of illness and starvation.

The Robe (1953)

The film begins in the 18th year of the reign of Tiberius. The narrator intones that there are more slaves in Rome than citizens and that its soldiers are the scum of the empire and its officers are no better as evidenced by Marcellus the Tribune (Richard Burton). A drunkard, gambler, and womanizer, he is sent with his slave Demetrius (Victor Mature) to Jerusalem. The film covers the events from their arrival on Palm Sunday to the crucifixion which Marcellus oversees. Marcellus wins the Robe in a game of dice and winds up with blood on his hands. Just then, Jesus says, "Father, forgive them, for they know not what they do." Demetrius, who has been won over by Christ, tells Marcellus, "You crucified Him" and escapes with the Robe.

Marcellus writhes in pain and believes that he is mad and cursed by the Robe, which he vows to find and destroy. Returning to Rome, he helps Caligula (Jay Robinson) to capture Demetrius and the Robe which appears to be an ordinary garment. Caligula asks, "Is it really bewitched?" Demetrius says, "It changed my life and soon it will change the world." Demetrius and the Robe are rescued and taken to Galilee. The subplot involves Marcellus falling in love with Diana (Jean Simmons), a Christian, who convinces him to convert. Declared an enemy of Rome, Marcellus is tried and sentenced to death. Diana denounces Caligula and asks to join Marcellus as he goes into the Kingdom. The film ends with "Alleluia" as they march to their death.

Commentary

Based on Lloyd C. Douglas's book of the same name, *The Robe* was the first film released in CinemaScope, a large curved screen which was Hollywood's

Figure 5.3. *The Robe.* **The Centurion Marcellus (Richard Burton), who won the Robe, cowers as his slave Demetrius (Victor Mature) berates him for crucifying Christ.**

answer to television. Though not nearly as good as *Quo Vadis*, it was very popular and was nominated for five Academy Awards, including Best Picture and Best Actor (Burton) and won for Art Direction/Set Design, and Costume Design. It has a marvelous score by Alfred Newman. The film has become an Easter staple. The conversions of Marcellus and Demetrius are well handled, and though the tribune and the Christian marry, they are not as fortunate as the couple in *Quo Vadis*.

The Silver Chalice (1954)

This CinemaScope bomb, based on a novel by Thomas Costain, should have killed the religious epic genre but didn't, although through no fault of the director Victor Saville, who never directed again. Basil (Paul Newman), a silversmith, is brought to Jerusalem out of bondage by Saint Luke (Alexander Scourby) to the home of Joseph of Arimathea (Walter Hampden). The silversmith is commissioned to build an ornate silver cup holder for the Holy Grail, the cup that Christ used at the Last Supper. Basil is in love with a slave, Helena (Natalie Wood), who escapes with his help and reappears years later as a heavily made up courtesan (Virginia Mayo). Meanwhile, Joseph's radiant granddaughter Deborra (Pier Angeli) becomes a devout Christian against her father's wishes and also falls for Basil, who she thinks loves her, while he's romancing Helena. Still, Basil agrees to marry Deborra because she needs a husband to inherit Joseph's riches that she intends to use for Christian evangelization. However, Basil refuses to consummate the marriage. Also, in the mix is Helena's protector, Simon Magus (Jack Palance), who vows to do miracles that will equal and even surpass Christ. He is recruited by a militant Jewish sect to help them draw the Jews who have embraced Christianity to return to their Jewish roots and, he hopes, later to him.

Everything comes to a head in Nero's Rome with the de rigueur epic Roman feast featuring terrible dancing and a menu consisting of roast peacock, wild boar, oysters, plover's eggs, fried aged grasshoppers, ortolans, and hummingbird tongues. Basil succeeds in capturing the likenesses of the apostles for the chalice but is unable to sculpt Christ until Christ appears to him, and he falls to his knees and becomes a believer. The cup is stolen by Simon's friends, and he organizes one last stunt where he will fly from a high tower. Simon plunges to his death, and Helena pays the price for Simon's failure to please the crowd. Basil and Deborra consummate their marriage, and Saint Peter (Lorne Greene) blesses them as they return from Rome to Antioch.

Commentary

As Bernstein notes in Paul Newman's obituary, this debut film is best known for Newman's taking out an advertisement in a Hollywood paper in 1966 when it was to be shown on television calling it "The worst motion picture filmed in the fifties." Apologizing for his performance, he asked that people refrain from watching it. Of course, viewership went sky-high. Newman was right about his performance, which resembles a marble statue of Adonis. With his blue eyes and handsome face and figure, he seemed to have been urged to just stand there regardless of whatever the scene called for. Virginia Mayo also seems to have been told to just stand there, look beautiful, and forget the acting, which was never her forte anyway.

The sets are just about the worst cinematic reproductions of Rome, Jerusalem, and Antioch. The futuristic domes, artificial-looking walls, and eerily immaculate streets and rooftops are totally distracting, but the story line is so slight and convoluted that this may be a blessing. An over-the-top performance by Jack Palance is the only thing that adds life to the movie. Based on a character in the Acts of the Apostles, he actually supplies insights into the early Christian church. Simon allowed himself to be baptized when he saw the miracles that Peter wrought and then asked him to sell him the power to perform miracles but was rebuked by Peter. The sin of simony (buying indulgences or ecclesiastic preferment) was named after him. He then became an early Gnostic and rival of Peter. The film's other interesting features involve the issue of women not inheriting the family's wealth and the inclusion of the Holy Grail as well as of Luke and Joseph of Arimathea, disciples who are not usually seen in such epics.

On the Waterfront (1954)

Terry Malloy (Marlon Brando) is a punch-drunk fighter who "coulda been a contender" if he hadn't thrown a fight on the advice of his mob-connected brother Charlie the Gent (Rod Steiger). An errand boy for Johnny Friendly (Lee J. Cobb), the corrupt longshoremen union boss, Terry unwittingly sets up a friend, Joey Doyle, who has agreed to talk to the Crime Commission investigating union corruption on the docks. After Joey is pushed from a roof to his death, Terry tells Charlie that he thought they were just "going to lean on him" so that he would "dummy up."

Father Barry (Karl Malden), an activist waterfront priest, holds a meeting in the church basement, against the advice of his fellow priest who warns Barry that he shouldn't get involved and not to blame him if the Church authorities send him to "Abyssinia." When Barry tries to get the longshoremen to fight back and take control of the union, he is told that "on the docks we're 'D and D' (deaf and dumb)." Barry challenges Terry to tell what he knows and is laughed off. Terry does the same to Joey's sister Edie (Eva Marie Saint), whom he escorts to safety when Johnny Friendly's goons go after the attendees. Edie is an idealist who has been sent to a convent school by her father to get her out of the neighborhood. She tells him "shouldn't everyone care about everybody." Terry calls her a "fruitcake," saying that his philosophy of life is "Do it to him before he does it to you."

A feisty dockworker, Kayo Dugan, agrees to talk if Father Barry promises to "go all the way" if he gets killed. When Dugan is killed in an "accident," Barry gives an impassioned speech in the hold of the ship, saying that "Christ stands with you in the shapeup." He compares Doyle and Dugan's deaths to the crucifixion of Christ and those who keep silent to those who threw rocks at Him. Terry is subpoenaed to testify and goes to see Barry who tells him to listen to his conscience and to tell Edie of his role in Joey's death. As he does so, foghorns drown out some key words of contrition, and she runs away. In turmoil, Terry meets with Charlie who tries to dissuade him from testifying. He pulls a gun on Terry but then he relents knowing that he will be killed for not silencing his brother and gives the gun to Terry.

After Charlie is killed and left hanging from a longshoreman's hook, Barry convinces Terry that rather than kill Johnny Friendly, he can hurt him more by testifying. Terry decides to do so and, after getting beaten to a pulp by Friendly and his goons, manages to lead the longshoremen in defiance.

Commentary

This screen classic garnered 12 Academy Award nominations and won eight Oscars including for Picture, Actor (Brando), Supporting Actress (Saint), Director, Writing, Art and Set Design, Cinematography, and Film Editing. Other nominees were Leonard Bernstein for his musical score and the three supporting actors (Steiger, Malden, and Cobb) who split the vote, enabling Edmond O'Brien to win for *The Barefoot Contessa*. Originally, director Elia Kazan planned to make a film about the longshoremen in Red Hook in Brooklyn with Arthur Miller. However, Kazan and Miller had a falling out when Kazan agreed to testify about Communist infiltration in Hollywood before The House Un-American Activities Committee. Kazan then collaborated with Budd Schulberg who had also testified before the committee. Schulberg had been working on a screenplay drawn from exposés about corruption on the New York/New Jersey docks that appeared in a series of 24 articles in the *New York Sun* by Malcolm Johnson in 1948. What resulted was a perfect storm of excellence in screenplay, acting, and direction.

One poster used to promote the film contained the subtitle "The Redemption of Terry Malloy." Although Kazan said that the film is not about his self-vindication for risking opprobrium by testifying, one cannot help but feel it is. This is especially so when one considers that Arthur Miller took the opposite tack in his play *A View from the Bridge*, in which someone turning in a relative who broke the law leads to tragedy rather than a more upbeat ending as in *On the Waterfront*.

The film's authenticity and mood were heightened by filming on the docks of Hoboken in cold weather with real longshoremen as extras. Father Barry, one of the strongest, most sympathetic priests in movie history, is based on a real-life priest, Father John Corridan. A tall, chain-smoking Jesuit, he ran a labor school with Father Phil Carey who was allied with an activist Association of Catholic Trade Unionists. The organization was committed to improving the plight of workers in accord with the principles set forth in two Papal encyclicals: Pope Leo XIII's highly influential encyclical Rerum Novarum in 1891 on the condition of the worker and the reciprocal duties

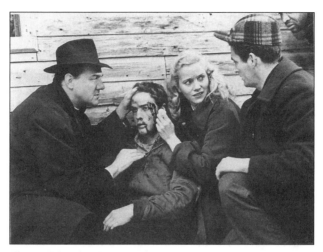

Figure 5.4. *On the Waterfront.* **Father Barry (Karl Malden) and Edie Doyle (Eva Marie Saint) comfort Terry Malloy (Marlon Brando) after he is savagely beaten by mobsters.**

of capital and labor as well as Pope Pius XI's encyclical Quadrigesimo Anno issued 40 years later in 1931 in the midst of the Depression on reconstructing the social order. The association's other aims were fighting corruption and Communist infiltration in the unions. An economist, Corridan documented the cost of the union corruption and management shakedowns.

Corridan served as an advisor on the film, and screenwriter Schulberg cited him as a major influence in his life. The sermon in the film when K.O. is killed was taken directly from Corridan's speech to the Jersey City longshoremen. The film shows Barry's words having an impact on Malloy. While Malloy's character is fictional, Corridan's words did encourage one longshoreman, Joe Dwyer, a World War II veteran, to cooperate with an investigation which helped turn around a longshoreman's local on New York City's West Side.

A Man Called Peter (1955)

The "Peter" in this film is Peter Marshall (Richard Todd), a Presbyterian minister who was born in Scotland and rose from poverty to be chaplain of the United States Senate. Based on the book of the same name by his widow Catherine Marshall, it is billed as "The story of a man who had a close relationship with God." Losing his father at age four and constantly berated by his stepfather, Peter tries, at age 14, to stow away in a canvas bag on a ship but is caught. He then gets a job and goes to night school. At age 24, he decides to become a minister and arrives penniless in America, where he works on roads and digs ditches in New Jersey while attending Columbia Theological seminary for four years.

After graduation, he goes to a big parish in Atlanta, then a small parish in Covington, Georgia, then to Atlanta again. While there he courts an Agnes Scott College student named Catherine Wood (Jean Peters) with such comments as "I wonder what's in that fine mind of yours" and "One thing I've learned about Southern girls is the cake is almost finer than the icing." While flattering her, he is also self-deprecating, calling himself "a stupid lump" and saying that "God just spun me around and said, 'Peter, you idiot, this is my greatest plan for you.'" And that "God plants his own tree in the human heart." They marry in 1936, and the next year he becomes pastor of the New York Avenue Presbyterian Church in Washington, D.C. His wife's illness brings a crisis of faith, but he surrenders himself to God and she recovers. Ten years later, he is asked to be the United States Senate chaplain. He is so effective that he makes the cover of *Newsweek* in connection with an article on the religious revival in D.C. In 1949, he has a heart attack but insists on opening the new Senate session because he is worried about a time when we "will believe that this nation is no longer founded under God." After being introduced by Senators Wiley and Prescott, he offers a prayer and then dies suddenly of a heart attack at 47.

Commentary

This somewhat overlong but earnest film, which received an Academy Award for Cinematography, is very complimentary to the ministry and Christians generally. While Christians will find it uplifting, today's audiences would probably regard it as "hokey," because of the interpolated reflections at critical moments, such as when he is caught as a stowaway and he says, "When God slams a door in your face, he guides you to the door which he wants you to enter." After completing night school, he is, in his words "saved from the abyss" after hearing voices which he believes convey God's plan: "He wants me to be a minister. He's sending me to America." He had to wait, in his words, for "word from the chief, which took a long time."

Richard Todd, a fellow Scot, who had parachuted into France on D-Day to capture a crucial bridge, studied Marshall's sermons, which had been re-

Figure 5.5. *A Man Called Peter.* **A Man Called Peter opens at the Roxy theater in New York City.**

corded on the Caedmon label. Todd beautifully captures Marshall's eloquence in the portions of many sermons that are heard throughout the film. As a minister in Washington, D.C., Marshall's Sunday services were attended by senators and Dwight Eisenhower; hundreds had to be turned away. There's no question that Marshall could give powerful sermons on the spur of the moment, which made him the ideal Senate chaplain, a post he held on two occasions. His greatest assets were his humility and sense of humor as illustrated by his telling his wife one evening when they sat down to dinner: "Catherine, I'm afraid you'll have to ask the blessing. The Lord knows I'm not grateful for the turkey hash and I can't fool Him." Most impressive, however, is his envisioning 60 years ago that many in our nation would no longer believe that America was founded under God.

The Prisoner (1955)

The Cardinal (Alec Guinness) of an unnamed Eastern European country is saying mass in a crowded cathedral, assisted by many priests and altar boys with all the pomp and ceremonies of the 1950s Latin Rite. He receives a note reading, "The police are here to arrest you." After mass, he blesses the crowd and on reaching the police, he is accused of treason against the state. He reassures his assistant that any confession he is said to have made will be a lie or a moment of weakness. At the police station, he is told that in the pulpit he is a danger to the state. The interrogator (Jack Hawkins), who fought alongside him against the Nazis, tells his assistant, "Bring me the completed confession." To the Cardinal, he says, "You wouldn't want to sign it right away and save us trouble?" The Cardinal replies, "I'd like to read it first."

They put a spotlight in his cell that can't be dimmed. He is not allowed to doze or talk to anyone but the interrogator and the jailer. "Psychology, they call it," says the interrogator who adds, "I wish that physical exhaustion wasn't so important in the beginning. It's your mind that we want." After months of captivity, the public is restless wondering why there has been no trial. The interrogator says, "We are up against a good man. He must show us where his weakness lies so that we can destroy him." They make noise outside his cell, and he is not fed for three days. The Cardinal does multiplication tables and tries to make a clock when they refuse to give him a watch. The interrogator threatens to kill his comatose mother if he refuses to sign. The Cardinal replies that he does not love his mother. Under a "sedative," he says that his mother was a whore and that he became a priest "to justify myself to myself not to God." The interrogator says, "Tell the whole world as you told me that your whole life is a fake." He confesses to everything. At the trial, they use false evidence and tapes to convict him. They commute his sentence, however, because dead he would be a martyr, but alive, he can't hurt the government. The Cardinal tells the guard on his release, "Try not to judge the priesthood by the priests." As he walks out of prison through a crowd of onlookers, his words are repeated, "Any confession I will have been said to have made will be a lie or the result of human weakness."

Commentary

Directed by Peter Glenville, the director of *Becket*, this intense film does not identify the locale, which is further obscured by the all-British cast. However, the film seems loosely based on the ordeal of Hungarian prelate Josef Cardinal Mindszenty and is noteworthy for the excellent acting by Alec Guinness and Jack Hawkins. Mindszenty's story had been the subject of a more factual anti-Soviet 1950 film, *Guilty of Treason*, starring Charles Bickford and Bonita Granville. *The Prisoner* portrays the Cardinal in a much more unfavorable light; for example, the lines about his mother are complete fiction. Actually, Mindszenty loved his mother, and his first book written when he was 24 was entitled *Motherhood*.

Mindszenty's real story, which spanned the time from the Austro-Hungarian empire to the Cold War, would make a fascinating movie even without cinematic embellishments. He was born Josef Pehm in 1892 in the Austro-Hungarian empire town of Csehimindszent and was ordained a priest in 1915. In 1941, he changed his name to reflect his town and joined the Resistance against the Arrow Cross party of Hungarian Nazi collaborators, fighting the Nazis and working to prevent the deportation of Jews. Made a Bishop in 1944, he was imprisoned and tortured by the Gestapo. After the war, he was released and continued to oppose the government, now a puppet of the Soviet Union. When religious orders were banned in 1948, he was declared an enemy of the state. He was imprisoned for treason and conspiracy after celebrating Mass on St. Stephen's Day, December 26, 1948. He did send a note to his mother saying that any confession he made would be false and coerced. He was given scopolamine ("truth serum") and confessed to crimes against the state and was tried and given life imprisonment. His story was broadcast worldwide, and he made the cover of *Time* on February 14, 1949. A "Yellow Book" detailing his confessions was made public by the Communists.

During the October 1956 Hungarian uprising, Mindszenty was released from jail and hailed as a hero. He made a radio broadcast supporting the revolution but counseled against revenge. After the Russians entered Hungary with their tanks a week later, he sought refuge in the American embassy where he remained for 15 years. He was allowed to leave the country in 1971 after a deal between the puppet Hungarian government and the United States and the Vatican. He died in 1975.

The Ten Commandments (1956)

In his prologue to this quintessential Hollywood epic, Cecil B. DeMille notes that "Thirty years of Moses's life is not in the Bible, from his discovery in the bulrushes to when he discovered he was Hebrew and killed the Egyptian." DeMille directed his screenwriter to fill in the gap using extensive research, especially through the works of the historians Philo and Josephus. DeMille calls the film "The Birth of Freedom," which asks the question, "Are men to be subject to a dictator or are they to be free?" His aim, he says, is not to create a story but to be seen as worthy to tell it.

When the Pharaoh declares that every firstborn Hebrew must die, Moses's mother hides him, and he is discovered by Pharaoh's daughter who sees him as gift in memory of her dead husband. She orders her attendant Memnet (Judith Anderson) to hide the Hebrew shawl used to wrap Moses and raises him as her son. The grown Moses (Charlton Heston) is considered a Prince of Egypt by the new Pharaoh Sethi (Sir Cedric Hardwicke). Moses is a rival to Sethi's son Rameses (Yul Brynner) as both Pharaoh's successor and the suitor for Nefretiri (Anne Baxter) who is promised as the next queen and who loves Moses. Many scenes depict the savage treatment of the Hebrew slaves as they struggle to build Pharaoh's monuments and cities. Where Rameses failed, Moses succeeds in building the city honoring Pharaoh because he has more sympathy for the slaves and feeds them. Just as he is poised to be named Pharaoh, Moses discovers his identity as a Jew and kills the evil Egyptian overlord Baka (Vincent Price). Nathan, the traitorous Jew (Edward G. Robinson), learns that Moses is a Jew and informs Pharaoh's son who denounces Moses as a traitor. Despite his many acts of loyalty, Moses is sent into the desert to die. Stopping at the Well of Midian, he protects the daughters of Jethro, the Sheik of Midian, from the Malachites. After one of the usual epic dancing scenes, Moses is rewarded with the hand of Sephora (Yvonne De Carlo) and becomes a shepherd. As he learns about his true heritage, he resists the idea that he is the one to lead the chosen people out of bondage, until God appears to him on Sinai in the form of a bush that burns without being consumed.

The rest of the film follows where DeMille's earlier version began with Moses importuning Rameses to let his people go, followed by the unleashing of the plagues, the killing of the firstborn Egyptians, the pillar of fire, and the marvelous reenactment of the Red Sea parting and its return to swamp the Egyptians. It shows Moses going up into the mountain for 40 days and 40 nights during which the Israelites worship a golden calf and engage in blasphemous and licentious behavior. The scene where the Ten Commandments are written by the finger of God is particularly striking. Moses throws down the tablets on the Golden Calf and destroys the sinners. After the Israelites wander in the wilderness for 40 years, Moses is shown the promised land but is not allowed to cross the Jordan River. Joshua (John Derek), Aaron (John Carradine), Sephora, and his son leave, and Moses disappears.

Commentary

Not satisfied with his 1923 silent version of the Ten Commandments, DeMille very much wanted to remake it and do it on location. He met with Egyptian strongman Gamel Abdel Nasser and the leader of the Egyptian army and began explaining his reasons. Nasser stopped him and said, "Mr. DeMille, we grew up on your movie *The Crusades*. We saw how you treated our religion. You can do anything in this country." He then put the Egyptian army at DeMille's disposal for four months of training and filming in such scenes as the march to the Red Sea.

The film was a monumental undertaking, especially for someone aged 75. As DeMille's brother once said, "The trouble with Cecil is that he bites off more than he can chew—and then chews it." A perfectionist even in the smallest details, the director suffered a heart attack during filming, while climbing to the top of a 103-foot ladder. He barely was able to get down from his perch before collapsing in a chair. He stayed in bed for three days, much of it in intense prayer, and then defied his doctors by going back to work and living for almost three more years. The film's many established stars included Edward G. Robinson, who credited DeMille with "restoring my self-respect" and resurrecting his career after he had been blacklisted, unjustly in DeMille's opinion. The stars' salaries plus the 20,000 extras, the 15,000 animals and the complicated filming logistics in the United States and abroad raised the film's cost to $13.5 million. Criticized by the studio heads for running over budget, he asked if they wanted him to stop and release the film as "The Five Commandments." The film ultimately brought in $80 million. DeMille donated his share of the profits to a fund for religious, charitable, and educational purposes.

Figure 5.6. *The Ten Commandments.* **Moses (Charlton Heston) parts The Red Sea.**

BACKSTORY

Cecil B. DeMille: The King of Religious Epics

Cecil B. DeMille is the most famous director of biblical epics in the history of the movies. Beginning in 1914 when he was 33, DeMille directed scores of films on an array of subjects, especially comedies, and helped establish the narrative form of storytelling in silent films as opposed to episodic tableaux. He first achieved monumental success with *The Ten Commandments* (1923) and *King of Kings* (1927). Over the next 30-plus years, he directed dozens of films but continued to find his lasting successes with films with Biblical themes, including *The Sign of the Cross* (1932), *The Crusades* (1935), *Samson and Delilah* (1949), and his last film, the spectacular remake of *The Ten Commandments* (1956).

Born in 1881, Cecil B. DeMille was the son of Henry Churchill DeMille, an Episcopal lay minister and playwright, and Matilda Samuel DeMille, a native of England and a schoolteacher. DeMille, who grew up in Pompton, New Jersey, and kept a home throughout his life in nearby Wayne, New Jersey, attended Pennsylvania Military College in Chester, Pennsylvania. He had a younger sister, Agnes, who died in childhood and an older brother William, who remained a close business and professional advisor throughout his life. William's daughter, also named Agnes, became a famous dancer and choreographer, best known for creating the dance sequences in the Broadway musical, *Oklahoma!* in 1943.

A larger-than-life showman, he was also one of the first directors to achieve celebrity in his own right with his trademark image featuring a bald head, a riding crop, boots, and a megaphone. He hosted the popular *Lux Radio Theatre* but quit when he refused to join the union. He frequently introduced his movies with reverent religious messages or, in the case of the 1944 film *The Story of Dr. Wassell*, with a patriotic message. The film starred Gary Cooper as a doctor who refused to evacuate the Philippines, when it was overrun by the Japanese to care for wounded soldiers. DeMille recounts how, once he heard the story, he called FDR to say it was a picture he had to make. He was also famous for having a great eye for acting talent, winning the support and affection of many well-known actors, as well as those of lesser stature. He was immortalized in Billy Wilder's 1950 classic, *Sunset Boulevard*, when Gloria Swanson, playing an actress living in the past, proclaims: "All right, Mr. DeMille, I'm ready for my close-up." And he appeared on cue. His film, *The Greatest Show on Earth* (1952), starring Charlton Heston and Betty Hutton, with a memorable role by Jimmy Stewart, won an Oscar for Best Picture and a nomination for DeMille as Best Director. However, his biblical epics are his enduring legacy. DeMille died of a heart attack in January 1959.

The connection of this film with Christian believers is not as explicit as DeMille's previous version in which the second half ties it into the New Testament. However, DeMille's belief about the importance of the Ten Commandments as the foundation for the New Testament and on which the freedom of all people rests, is underlined at the end when Moses says, "Woe unto thee O Israel. You have sinned a great sin in the eyes of God. You are not worthy to receive the Ten Commandments." They reply, "We are free." Moses responds, "There is no freedom without the law." In short, they may no longer be the slaves of Pharaoh but without the Law, they remain slaves to sin.

Heaven Knows, Mr. Allison (1957)

Set in 1944, the film opens with Allison, a marine corporal (Robert Mitchum) floating on a raft in the Pacific. He comes upon an island village where a nun, Sister Angela (Deborah Kerr), is sweeping the steps of a church, wearing a spotless white habit. When told there are no "Japs," he collapses. After waking and learning that she is the lone survivor of her mission, he catches a fish and says to the nun, "It's a cinch you would like fish, your religion and all. Those who need to eat fish on Friday, we call them mackerel snappers." He tells her that he was illegitimate and grew up in an orphanage on Allison Street and that he joined the marine corps, which he likens to the Church, and they compare notes of her overseer of novices and his drill instructor. Asked if he believes in God, Allison replies, "Sure, Ma'am, anyone with any sense believes in God."

The Japanese bomb and then invade the island, and Allison and Sister Angela retreat to a cave. He asks her what would happen if a nun changes her mind. She tells him that vows are not taken lightly but that the Holy Father can make a "rare" exception if the reason is serious. When told that she was completing her fifth year after her novitiate when she must take final vows, he asks her not to take final vows, saying, "I want to take care of you not just here but the rest of our lives. Is there a chance?" She tells him that she has already given her heart to Christ and shows him her ring, which he compares to an engagement ring.

He apologizes for the proposal with feigned marine bravado. He gets sloshed from sake left behind by the Japanese and then bemoans the fact that if she wants to be a nun, she should be old and ugly. She runs off in the rain, gets fever and chills, and he cares for her during three days of delirium. She wakes up and says that she was running from the truth. She prays that God will receive him into his holy presence. The Japanese return, and the Americans arrive. Allison is wounded but dismantles the Japanese guns before they can be used, and the Marines take over.

Commentary

Directed by John Huston, who also cowrote the Oscar-nominated screenplay, the film is a real tour de force for Mitchum and Kerr, who are the only credited cast members. The movie never leaves the island, yet Huston and his two superb actors never allow it to seem claustrophobic or the viewer to lose interest as their evolving and deepening relationship is chronicled. In

Figure 5.7. *Heaven Knows, Mr. Allison.* **After he is shipwrecked on a deserted island in World War II, a Marine (Robert Mitchum) falls in love with Sister Angela (Deborah Kerr).**

Charles Shaw's novel, on which it is based, the two fall in love. The plot was changed ostensibly to meet the Hays Code, but in a way, it provides the story more richness and the actors more range as they clearly do fall in love but then must deal with the consequences. Huston thought the film was one of his best and most underappreciated films, while Mitchum reportedly said that it was his favorite film. The treatment of Catholicism is very favorable. The dialogue, as can be seen from the above sample, is very true to the time period, both for the nun and the marine. In the end, it respects the characters and their struggles to stay true to their respective belief systems and their principles.

The Seventh Seal (1957)

The film opens with a quotation from chapter 8 of the Book of Revelations: "And when the lamb opened the Seventh Seal, there was silence in heaven about the space of half an hour and the seven angels which had the seven trumpets prepared themselves to sound." A knight, Antonius Block (Max Von Sydow), and his squire return from 10 years in the Crusades only to find Sweden in the midst of the Black Plague. Block kneels to pray and then encounters Death (Bengt Ekerot) with whom he plays a game of chess to spare his life. They come across Jof (Nils Poppe), a poor naïf, with his wife Mia (Bibi Andersson) and their child. Where the knight and his squire (Jons Bjornstrand) see sickness, devastation, and immorality all around, this Joseph, Mary, and Jesus trio are happy and see only visions of beauty.

Thinking the plague is a punishment from God, some people wander the land scourging one another and flagellating themselves doing the dance of Death. Scenes of people with purifying censors and others carrying a cross are interposed with the carefree play of the family. The Knight goes to confession in front of a tortured Christ, unaware that it's Death behind the screen. He wants knowledge from God, but God is silent. Not realizing it's his adversary, he reveals the chess gambit he is going to use against Death.

The squire tells him that "Our crusade was so stupid that only an idealist could have thought of it." The world seems entirely populated with thieves, hypocrites, and sadists, including the religious (maybe especially the religious since the one who recruited Block to go on the Crusade is now an atheist who steals from plague victims and ravishes young girls). A cruel priest burns a woman in oil for having carnal knowledge of the devil and for being the cause of the plague. A child is burned as a witch after a monk breaks her hands.

Block realizes he is losing the game so he overturns the chessboard which allows the holy family to escape Death's clutches. When Block finally arrives at his castle, he finds his wife who tells him that hidden in his eyes is the boy who went away so many years ago. She asks, "Are you sorry you went?" He says, "No, but I'm tired." His wife continues to read from Revelations as a storm rages outside. As Death enters the room to claim the Knight, the storm abates and the holy family is saved, ending the film on a happy note.

Commentary

This is one of the most powerful and haunting religious allegories in cinematic history. I saw it when it first came out, and it provided many hours of discussion about its meaning for many who saw it. It remained one of my favorite films. My wife, a devout, thoughtful, and cheerful woman, hated it. On reviewing it 50 years later, I can see why. It's almost unrelentingly grim, and one must be in a certain philosophical mindset to stay with it. It's definitely not entertaining but rather a film that is more renowned for its indelible images than as a story. It begs for postfilm discussion.

Swedish director Ingmar Bergman (1918–2007) was a certifiable genius, whose creativity was bought at a steep price. Married five times, divorced four times, with many mistresses and at least nine children, he was

129

Figure 5.8. *The Seventh Seal.* **Block (Max von Sydow) returns from the Crusades after ten years to a plague-ridden Sweden and plays chess with Death (Bengt Ekerot) to save his life.**

hospitalized for a nervous breakdown and lived for some time in exile. Yet, some of his 62 films were among the greatest films ever made In Bergman's 2007 obituary, Rothestein quoted director Woody Allen as calling him "probably the greatest film artist, all things considered, since the invention of the motion picture camera." Many of his films, especially during the first half of his career, involved struggles with an absent God and reflections about death. Given this, it isn't surprising to learn that he was the son of a very strict Lutheran minister who used to cane his children and banish them to a dark closet for such infractions as wetting the bed. He described his mother, whom he adored, as alternating between being very warm and very cold and rejecting. When his father was made chaplain to the king of Sweden, Bergman attended many services and while the sermons bored him, he soaked up the scripture and was fascinated by the religious imagery all around him. He recounted that he lost his faith at age eight and shortly after he traded his toy soldiers for a magic lantern that projected images of puppets in stories he created. Sent to Germany for a summer when he was 16, he became fascinated by Hitler and movies; the former fascination disappeared after a few years, but the latter was lifelong.

In this film, the clergy are uniformly un-Christian and the Crusades are deemed to be worthless. The Knight seeks God and only finds Death who resembles the Devil. The squire, on the other hand, chooses the presumed better part, living in the moment and romping in the hay with any woman he can find. Yet in the end, the Jesus, Mary, and Joseph figures survive the dark night of the plague, and the storm gives way to a radiant dawn. There is no question that Bergman had a profound effect on American moviemaking and when his *Virgin Spring*, a story of rape, won the 1960 Oscar for the Best Foreign Film, the contrast with American films constrained by the Hays Code couldn't have been more striking. As Bergman told a *Playboy* interviewer in 1964, "the manifestation of sex is very important, and particularly to me, for above all, I don't want to make merely intellectual films. I want audiences to feel, to sense my films. This to me is more important than their understanding them." He succeeded on both scores.

The Inn of the Sixth Happiness (1958)

An English domestic, Gladys Aylward (Ingrid Bergman), believes that we are all responsible for one another and that God wants her to go to China. In 1930, after being rejected by the China Inland Society because of her inadequate education and lack of knowledge of Chinese, she manages to get an invitation as an assistant to a 73-year-old missionary, Jeannie Lawson (Athene Seyler). Lacking any savings, she cannot go by ship, so she leaves London with two pounds nine pence, a passport, a Bible, and travel tickets. Beginning her trek on the Trans-Siberian railway, she reaches Vladivostok, but because Russia and China were skirmishing at their border, she sails to Japan and on to Tientsin, China. From there she goes by train, bus, and mule train to the inland city of Yangchen in Shansi province, south of Beijing, where she joins Lawson.

The two missionaries set up an inn for travelers in this overnight stop for mule caravans that carry coal, raw cotton, pots, and iron goods on six-week and three-month journeys. The inn's title is supposedly based on the Chinese wish for five happinesses: wealth, longevity, good health, virtue, and a peaceful death in old age. Each person must decide what the sixth happiness is. Gladys gets people to stop at her hotel by kidnapping the lead mules, so that the other mules and their riders follow. Gladys advertises that the hotel has no bugs and no flies; the drivers sleep 50 at a time together, fully-clothed. Realizing that the Chinese love stories, she tells Jesus and biblical stories during the meals and is accused of trying to save souls of people who don't want to be saved. Eventually, however, the mule drivers begin coming voluntarily because of the stories.

Gladys witnesses many horrors, including a beheading, babies left in ditches to die, and the poor preying on one another. After Lawson dies from a fall, Gladys carries on with the help of Chinese cook Yang (Peter Chong). She convinces the local mandarin (Robert Donat), a Chinese public official, to stop the practice of binding a woman's feet. The Chinese Army Colonel, Lin Nan (Curt Jurgens), a Eurasian, tells her, "Don't you know you are beautiful?" She responds, "Once in her life a woman should have that said to her. Thank you for being the one who said it to me." The colonel falls in love with her, and she with him. The Japanese bomb the city, so they must retreat to the mountains. The mandarin converts to Christianity in tribute to her and, although she and the colonel find one another, they are separated again. She risks her life to save 100 children from the Japanese by leading them over steep mountain passes to reach the Yellow River and safety.

Commentary

The film's screenplay was adapted from *The Small Woman*, a book by Anthony Burgess about Aylward's life. Because the film is set in China, some objected that the principal actors are Caucasian, and Aylward "was deeply embarrassed" by the movie because it was so full of historical inaccuracies. As noted by Samuel Wellman in his "Heroes of History" website, the greatest liberty Hollywood took was the bogus infatuation with the Chinese Colonel Lin Nan, even changing him into a Eurasian. Aylward was said to be horrified that the movie portrayed her in "love scenes." The name of the inn was also changed from "The Inn of the Eight Happinesses." The film is also somewhat confusing because the historical events involving clashes between the Japanese and the Russians and between the Chinese and the Japanese are unfamiliar to most viewers and are not explained until the epilogue.

Still, it is very complimentary to Christians by depicting a selfless Protestant missionary whose given Chinese name was "One who loves people" or "Virtuous One." The theme is set early with the hymn "Onward Christian Soldiers." Aylward was raised an Anglican and was not particularly religious but got the call to be a missionary at a revival meeting. Ironically, after being rejected for not knowing Chinese, she became fluent in the language and in 1935 became a Chinese citizen. She was very successful as an inspector assuring compliance with the law forbidding foot binding at a time when native Chinese inspectors were often assaulted. After the war, she was barred by the Communists from returning to China and settled in Taiwan where she died.

Despite Bergman's radiant portrayal, the last third of the film drags. However, it ends rousingly as she leads the children marching into town singing "This Old Man," an old nursery rhyme that became a popular ditty in England. Mitch Miller made it into a popular music hit in America as "The Children's Marching Song." In reality, after Aylward successfully brought the children over the mountain, she collapsed from typhus, malnutrition, and exhaustion. One final note: this was the great actor Robert Donat's final film before he died of longstanding asthma. His last movie line was "We shall not see one another again, I think."

The Nun's Story (1959)

The film opens in 1930 with Jesus's spoken exhortation "He that shall lose his life for me, shall find it. If thou wouldst be perfect, go sell what you have and give to the poor and Come Follow me." The young Gabrielle (Audrey Hepburn) prepares to leave for the convent by removing an engagement ring from her finger. She goes downstairs where her father (Dean Jagger), a doctor, tells her, "I can see you poor; I can see you chaste, but I can't see you, a strong-willed girl, answering to those bells." She is to be a postulant for six months and a novice for one year. The door is locked behind postulants signaling their withdrawal from the world. They are given a set of rules: They can't speak to one another because of the rule of interior and exterior silence from after chapel in the evening to after morning chapel. They must not talk loudly, saunter, or hurry and must walk close to the walls. They cannot retain keepsakes of their past life, which they must forget. As the Prioress says, "It's a life against nature, meant for us to come into communion with Our Lord Jesus Christ." The novices don't leave the motherhouse, and the year is designed to remove faults and destroy passion, pride, and self-will. They must proclaim their faults each week before the sisters. They must kiss the feet of the nuns in the refectory. Gabrielle's best friend decides it's not for her and leaves.

The film shows the Procession of the Brides of Christ and the cutting of the hair, a sign of mortification. Gabrielle takes the name Luke, in honor of the patron saint of her father's profession. She excels at tropical medicine but is denied her wish to go to the Belgian Congo by a mean-spirited Mother Superior and instead becomes a psychiatric nurse for which she is ill-suited. Trying to help a devious and homicidal patient (Colleen Dewhurst), she is almost killed. Finally, Gabrielle is sent to a hospital in the Congo as a nurse and technician. Because Jesus supposedly had a beard, the priests must wear beards in the Congo. No beards; no converts. Doctor Fortunati (Peter Finch) is considered by the staff to be a genius and a devil. He asks Sister Luke whether she ever went fishing and when she can't answer, he says, "It's impossible to talk to someone who is not allowed to remember." She works so hard that she succumbs to tuberculosis, which she diagnoses herself, and recuperates in a monastery. She leaves the Congo but can't regain her inner silence. When the Nazis invade Holland, Gabrielle is working in a hospital near the Belgium-Holland border. After her father is killed by the Germans, she decides to leave the convent to join the Underground.

Commentary

Based on a best-selling novel by Kathryn Hulme, this film shows the underside of convents, with the postulants having to examine their consciences twice a day and to maintain both exterior and interior silence. Sister Luke wants to tell at least one person of her accomplishments but is told that to do so would diminish her sacrifice of humility. As Donald Spoto notes in his 2006 *Enchantment*, an excellent biography of Hepburn, the humiliations, suppression of personality, putting aside normal feelings, and ignoring one's past were thought to be "guaranteed paths to holiness in some religious orders of monks and nuns." He adds: "To good effect, almost every community later abandoned these practices, under encouragement from the Vatican itself. *The Nun's Story* and Audrey's recognizably human Sister Luke offered neither a gratuitous endorsement nor a smug disapproval of this rarefied life of long ago." The film does show the sharp contrast between the rule-obsessed motherhouse convent nuns and the missionary nuns who had to live day-to-day among the people as they performed a valuable service.

As for Sister Luke's departure from the convent, Hepburn made changes in the script to mirror the book and real life so that it represented neither a failure nor a rejection of God. Indeed, the real Sister Luke never lost her Catholic faith saying, "Christ will not abandon me if I go out. I have given too many cups of water in His name and He knows I would go on doing it whether working for Him as a nun or a war nurse." Even so, as Spoto recounts in his book, almost every film reviewer "discussed the wonderful Hepburn film about a nun who failed in her vocation." It is true, as my wife commented, that there was "No good-bye, God Bless you, thank you for all you have done" from the Prioress. However, this was not so in real life, because the Prioress recognized that the death of Sister Luke's father and the need to care for the soldiers were sufficient reasons to leave.

The real Sister Luke was Marie Louise Habets, known as Sister Marie Xaverine, a Belgian nun in the community of the Sisters of Charity of Jesus and Mary from 1927 to 1944. Lou, as she was called, met Kathryn (Kate) Hulme while they worked in a former Nazi camp that held 20,000 displaced persons. After six years, they came to America where Kate resumed work as a writer and Lou as a nurse. Spoto said they were both on a spiritual journey which culminated in Kate's conversion to Catholicism and Lou's suggesting her own story as a basis for a book. After publication in 1956, it sold over three million copies in the United States and many millions more abroad.

Audrey Hepburn became very close to Lou and Kate during the making of the movie and remained so all their lives. In one letter to them she wrote, "Delving into the heart and mind of Sister Luke, I have also had to dig deep down in myself. Thereby having done a bit of ploughing of the soul—so to speak—the seeds of all I have experienced have fallen on neatly prepared ground, and I hope will result in harvesting a better Audrey." She called the experience "transformational" and her son recalled after her death that of all her films, she "was proudest of *The Nun's Story*."

Figure 5.9. *The Nun's Story.* **Sister Luke (Audrey Hepburn) and a friend are punished by the Mother Superior for an infraction of the rules.**

Ben-Hur (1959)

This remake of the 1920s epic tells essentially the same story as its predecessor (p. 24), beginning with the birth of Jesus and ending with Christ's crucifixion. The initial encounter between Messala (Stephen Boyd) and Judah Ben-Hur (Charlton Heston) is more cordial, with Judah inviting Messala to dinner with his mother Miriam (Martha Scott) and sister Tirzah (Cathy O'Donnell). They relive their boyhood, challenging one another by hurling the javelin at a target and drinking as comrades. Things start to turn sour when Messala asks for advice as he takes over the Roman garrison in Jerusalem, and Judah replies, "Withdraw your legions and give us our freedom." Messala responds that he is there on the emperor's orders and that the "Emperor is God, the only God on earth." When he adds, "You're either for me or against me," Judah tells him that he is against him.

When a tile falls from Judah's home, injuring the governor, Judah is blamed and sent back to Rome in a slave galley. On the way, the slaves enter Nazareth where Judah falls and says, "God help me." He sees Christ's face and is given water. The scenes on the galley profit from color and sound and are much more effective than the original. The filming of the sea battle is much more controlled than in the earlier film through the use of a man-made lake, not subject to the vagaries of the ocean. The interaction with the Consul Quintus Arrius (Jack Hawkins), whom Judah saves, is much stronger than in the original, and the panoply on their triumphant entry in Rome, more spectacular. The Consul adopts Ben-Hur who becomes a Roman patrician.

Anxious to find his mother and sister, he returns to Jerusalem and finds Esther (Haya Harareet) and her father Simonides (Sam Jaffe), who have kept his house and his treasure safe. Esther tells him that his mother and sister, who are now lepers, are dead, as they instructed her to do. He blames Messala and promises to exact revenge. Esther loves Judah but is saddened by how consumed he is with hate. Judah gets his chance through the assistance of Ilderin (Hugh Griffith), an Arab sheik who provides a chariot to race Messala, the odds-on favorite. Messala employs sharp rotating blades on his wheels to wreck his competitors' chariots. As one after another is eliminated, the two battle it out and Messala's chariot is destroyed. Messala is then brought under the stands where he tells Judah, before dying, that his mother and sister are lepers.

The rest of the picture involves scenes from the Sermon on the Mount and Judah's refusal to hear Christ (Claude Heater, uncredited). Esther takes

Miriam and Tizrah to see Christ while He is on the Road to Calvary. Judah recognizes Christ as the one who gave him water in Nazareth, and he returns the favor as Jesus falls. There is darkness at noon—thunder, lightning, and rain during which Miriam and Tirzah are cured of leprosy. Afterwards, Judah tells Esther that when he heard Christ say, "'Father, forgive them for they know not what they do,' I felt His voice take the sword from my hand." The film ends with "Alleluia."

Commentary

The film won 11 Academy awards, the most ever until the record was tied in 1997 by *Titanic* and in 2003 by *The Lord of the Rings: The Return of the King*. Best seen on the big screen, it starts with an overture and runs 212 minutes with an intermission. The marvelous score by Miklós Rózsa is one of the film's greatest assets. Paul Newman, who had been terrible in *The Silver Chalice* (p. 115), turned down the role of Judah saying, "Never again will I act in a movie in a cocktail dress. I don't have the legs for it." Director William Wyler, who had worked as an assistant director on the original film, won his third Oscar. He kept the tradition of not showing Christ's face and reportedly told his granddaughter that "It took a Jew to make a great picture about Christ." The picture was meant to have wide appeal, so one can read the enigmatic ending as Judah eschewing violence

Figure 5.10. *Ben-Hur.* **Judah Ben-Hur (Charlton Heston) recognizes Jesus as the one who gave him water while a galley slave in Nazareth.**

while either remaining a faithful Jew or accepting Christ. One interesting touch was the Arab sheik giving Judah the Star of David to wear in the race saying, "The Star of David will shine out for your people and my people together and blind the eyes of Rome."

The high point of the movie is the famous chariot race. Clearly, this scene benefits from the improved technology, the staging by the premier stunt man in Hollywood, Yakima Canutt, and the direction of Andrew Martin. There's a particularly harrowing scene in which Canutt's son Joe, acting as Heston's double, is actually thrown from the chariot but scrambles back. Finally, in neither film is it clear how Miriam and Tirzah contract leprosy while in solitary confinement together, since prolonged close interaction with lepers is necessary to become infected.

Short Subjects

The Flowers of Saint Francis (1950)

Made in commemoration of the 1950 Holy Year by Roberto Rossellini, who had just gone through a turbulent public affair with Ingrid Bergman, this film was named by the Vatican in 1995 as one of the 45 greatest films ever made. In collaboration with his protégé, Federico Fellini, Rossellini used actual Franciscan friars in nine episodes inspired by the "Fioretti," 14th-century legends about Saint Francis in the early days of the Franciscan order. The first shows their return from Rome, where Francis has gotten permission to start the order, in which they debate the concept of "joy" as they trudge blissfully through the pouring rain. In that respect, the Italian title, Francis, God's Jester, is somewhat more apt, except the real jesters are two of Francis's followers, Brother Sempliciotto ("Simple"), who echoes everything Francis says, and Brother Ginepro, who keeps giving away his tunic to the poor and returning home naked, even after being admonished not to do so. Although most critics said the friars seem like a group of naïve simpletons, Rosselini wasn't making fun of them but instead extolling their innocence as "Fools for Christ," if you will.

Diary of a Country Priest (1950)

Based on a novel by Georges Bernanos, the film uses diary entries to tell the story of a dour, self-absorbed priest (Claude Laydu) who is named pastor of a rural church. Because of stomach trouble, he deliberately removes vegetables and meat from his diet and eats only old bread dipped in wine with sugar.

His health is so bad that he can't go uphill on his bicycle without feeling faint. He is challenged for charging for funerals as exploiting the poor. The veteran pastor in a nearby village criticizes him, saying, "You dream of being loved. No true priest is ever loved" (not true in my experience).

My take on this film, which some consider to be a classic, is distinctly heretical. In my opinion, the priest is a rather pathetic advertisement for priests, who may, even more than the rest of us, need a sense of humor to survive. However, he is just the right priestly portrait to be drawn by a French intellectual. He spends too much time recording what he admits are insignificant secrets of a life lacking in mystery, and not enough connecting with the folks. In short, he is like the weak-minded priest in the 2000 film *Chocolat* (p. 302), except the latter has the saving grace of singing and being happy whereas this priest is a picture of despair. Despite his many failures, he does succeed in bringing a God-hating countess, who shuts herself off from the world after her son's death, into the state of grace before dying. The film is a favorite of cineastes for its acting and cinematography as well as of some devout Catholics as the portrait of a frail, unappreciated priest struggling against losing his faith during his "dark night of the soul." Others, like me, may feel that they are dying with the priest from stomach cancer.

The Miracle of Our Lady of Fatima (1952)

The film opens in 1910 with the forced abdication of the king of Portugal and the establishment of a Socialist police state that the film proclaims unleashed "a savage persecution of all religious orders." After seven years, rural churches are allowed to reopen but only under strict government supervision. The scene shifts to Fatima on May 13, 1917, where three shepherd children (Lucia, Jacinta, and Francisco) are saying the Rosary. The Virgin appears to the two girls and tells them to come for six months on the 13th day at the same hour. The Bishop, aligned with the authorities, presses Lucia to confess that she lied about seeing the Virgin, but she refuses. The children are imprisoned but escape and are told by the Virgin that in October she will give them a sign that will make the people believe. On the appointed day, October 13, 1917, the Virgin appears. Even hardened cynics believe as a crippled boy walks, the blind see, the sun plummets toward the earth, and three secrets are imparted to Lucia. The film ends with 1 million people in Fatima's square on October 13, 1951. As the Virgin predicted, Jacinta and Francisco died of influenza within a few years of the apparitions. Lucia became a nun and died in 2005.

BACKSTORY

The Fatima Story

The story of the Blessed Virgin appearing to three children in Fatima, Portugal, in 1917 and revealing three secrets was very popular in the 1950s. The specific mention in the Fatima revelations of the need to pray for Russia made it especially meaningful. At the time, Soviet Russia had expanded through Communist control of Eastern Europe, and the threat of a nuclear attack was on everyone's mind. The Catholic Church was particularly concerned because of religious suppression in formerly Catholic Eastern European countries.

The first two secrets dealt with a vision of hell and predicting the end of the ongoing world war and the beginning of World War II. The third secret was to be revealed by the Pope in 1960 and presumably was related to consecrating Russia to Mary. If it wasn't revealed, it said that Communism would spread—killing millions, the Church's influence would diminish with the ascendance of materialism, and a Pope would be in danger. Pope John Paul II's three predecessors chose not to reveal it. Communism did spread, killing millions, and the Catholic Church's influence in Europe and the United States did diminish with the rise of materialism and secularism.

As for the third part of the prophecy, on May 13, 1981, in St. Peter's Square, Pope John Paul II bent down to greet a little girl wearing a picture of the Virgin at Fatima which had caught his eye. As he did, two bullets passed where his head had just been. Although the would-be assassin later shot him twice, the Pope survived. Seeing this as further fulfillment of the Virgin's prophecy, he developed a special homage to the Virgin of Fatima. The Pope dedicated his papacy to the liberation of Eastern Europe, the conversion of Russia, and halting the spread of materialism. Many credit him with playing a large role in the fall of the Iron Curtain. In an emotional visit to a Roman prison, he forgave his assassin, a Bulgarian, who was later found to have been in the employ of the Soviets.

This pious retelling of the appearance of the Blessed Virgin at Fatima is disappointing because it fails to illuminate the import of this extraordinary event, little understood by many Catholics, let alone others (see the above Backstory and Bottum's article about "What Happened at Fatima"). Second, it marginalizes a potentially rich subject in the overthrow of the Portuguese government by a socialist, anticlerical group, just as *The Fugitive* (p. 94) failed to confront similar events in Mexico. The only one who gives any life to the film is Gilbert Roland who plays the children's uncle, a lovable rascal who, when asked if he believes in God, says, "Let's just say God doesn't believe in me."

High Noon (1952)

This classic western is about a marshal (Gary Cooper) who could leave town with his Quaker bride (Grace Kelly) but decides to stay and face three murderers who are arriving by train at high noon to kill him. It opens with the townspeople gathered in a Protestant church. As the marshal enters, the minister says, "You don't come to church often and you didn't come here to get married." The marshal replies, "because my wife is a Quaker." He tells the congregation that he needs special deputies and to get the children out of town. The congregation argues as to whether to help him. Almost everyone sits in church while the marshal faces the killers with little help. Unhappy that her husband will be involved in a shootout, his wife leaves town but has a crisis of conscience. She must decide whether to return and use a gun against her Quaker principles to protect him from being killed. Few of the devout churchgoers come off very well in this film.

When in Rome (1952)

This innocent and hokey film provides an interesting historical record of mid-20th Century Catholicism and of the 1950 Holy Year when the dogma of the Assumption of the Blessed Virgin Mary was promulgated. Holy Years were first proclaimed by Pope Boniface VII in 1300, a time of wars and plagues. Called every 25 to 50 years since, pilgrims would trek by foot to the tombs of Saints Peter and Paul seeking forgiveness for their sins and reconciliation with God and man. In her book *Rome and a Villa,* Eleanor Clark quotes a Vatican official as labeling 1950 as the last Holy Year of the Catholic Counter-Reformation, because the next one in 1975 occurred after the Vatican II Council and at a time when making the trek to Rome was no longer so arduous.

Among the three million pilgrims is Father John X. Halligan (Van Johnson), sent off at the film's outset by his Coaltown, Pennsylvania, parishioners whom he tells not to forget to go to Holy Communion. His shipmate is an escaped convict and ex–altar boy, Joe Brewster (Paul Douglas), whom Father John helps escape by exchanging clothes before debarking. Father John brings Brewster to a Roman monastery that he compares to a prison. Deciding not to turn him in, he and Brewster set out for the requisite 1950s movie tour of Rome (à la *Three Coins in the Fountain* and *Rome Adventure*), beginning with a procession of priests as far as the eye can see and the choir of St. Peter's singing "Panis Angelicus." At the Colosseum, Brewster, who is impressed by the depth of faith of the martyrs who died there, makes his first confession in 20 years. At St. John Lateran, he receives communion. After that, they visit St. Mary Major, St. Paul's Outside the Walls, and finally St. Peter's, where they go out the Holy Door, which is only open during a

Holy Year. Still chased by the police, Brewster agrees to retire to a lifetime "in solitary" in the monastery to the strains of "O Sanctissima" and speaks the film's best line: "I've been in places where it's all past and no future. I want to be in a place where there is all future and no past. There is a feeling of love not hate in this place." Father John promises to visit him during the next Holy Year in 25 years.

Angels in the Outfield (1952)

This harmless, lightweight fantasy is about a foul-mouthed Pittsburgh Pirates manager (Paul Douglas) with no interpersonal skills who makes a bargain with an angel to clean up his act if his hapless team gets divine help to win the pennant. It turns out that Bridget, a nine-year-old orphan at St. Gabriel's Home for Orphan Girls, has prayed daily to St. Gabriel for the Pirates. He answers her prayers by sending his assistants who appear in the outfield to help, although Bridget is the only one who sees them.

Her story is reported by the food editor of the local paper (Janet Leigh). There is a twist on the predictable ending in that the Pirates win the last game without angelic assistance, on the strength of the arm of a presumably washed-up Jewish pitcher who has less than a year to live. The reporter and the manager get together to adopt the girl. The nuns are portrayed as kind even though they find Bridget's vision hard to believe. The film has a nice ecumenical scene where a rabbi, a minister, and a priest testify before the baseball commissioner that they believe in the existence of angels and that the story is believable. An added feature is the appearance of Ty Cobb, Joe Dimaggio, and Bing Crosby, who was part owner of the Pirates.

I Confess (1953)

Alfred Hitchcock, seen in the opening scene, directed this absorbing movie starring Montgomery Clift as Father Michael William Logan, a priest who hears a murderer's confession. Falsely accused of the murder and of having an affair with a woman (Anne Baxter), he is brought to trial after refusing to break the seal of confession. Karl Malden and Brian Aherne round out the cast. Hitchcock's decision to film it in black and white in old Quebec gives it a somber, noirish effect. After seeing the film, you might compare it with later films that deal with breaking the seal of the confessional and truth-telling by priests on the witness stand (e.g., M*A*S*H, Sleepers, and Priest).

Demetrius and the Gladiators (1954)

Drawn from characters in Lloyd C. Douglas's novel *The Robe*, this sequel follows Demetrius (Victor Mature), who gives the Robe to Peter (Michael Rennie) to hide with Christian friends. Captured and made to become a gladiator, Demetrius says that it is against his religion to kill and purposely loses. Messalina (Susan Hayward), Claudius's wife, convinces the emperor Caligula (Jay Robinson) to spare Demetrius rather than kill him, the fate of losers. She repeatedly tries to seduce Demetrius, and he finally gives in and gives up God. Peter goes to the palace to see Demetrius, who mocks Jesus and sends Peter packing. Glycon (William Marshall), Demetrius's black gladiator friend, who is also a Christian, chastises him. Messalina tells Caligula to send Demetrius to retrieve the Robe, which is said to hold the secret to eternal life. Demetrius goes to the house and demands the Robe. Peter says if he wants the Robe, he should pray for it. Demetrius has a flashback to when he was at the foot of the cross and heard, "Father, forgive them for they know not what they do." Demetrius gets the Robe, falls on it and says "Father, forgive me." His ex-girlfriend Lucia, who had been in a coma clutching the Robe, wakes up and says she saw Jesus.

There are lots of other twists and turns as Caligula is killed, Claudius ascends to the throne, and Messalina decides to act the part of Caesar's wife and dumps Demetrius. Claudius and she vow to leave the Christians alone if they are not disloyal to the state. The film ends with Demetrius and Glycon doing an about-face and joining Peter to march down the palace steps with the Robe to a chorus of "Gloria in Excelsis Deo." Though the movies drawn from his books made him wealthy, Douglas (see Backstory, p. 46) was not happy with them, and he was right. Despite some nice touches, such as an excellent musical score by Franz Waxman and a bravura performance by Jay Robinson reprising his role as Caligula from *The Robe*, this picture is a dud. Mature was more convincing as a supporting actor than he is as the lead, playing Demetrius with the woodenness that typified most of his pictures. Indeed, as noted by Donnelly, he was very honest about his acting ability. When he retired he said, "I'm no actor and I have 64 pictures to prove it."

There's No Business like Show Business (1954)

This CinemaScope extravaganza consists of a lot of uneven Irving Berlin musical numbers starring Ethel Merman, Dan Dailey, Mitzi Gaynor, and Donald O'Connor. Along with Johnnie Ray, they comprise a vaudeville act called the Five Donahues until Ray decides he is going to be a priest. He tells his parents, "Consider it just a change of booking. You've got to admit the Church has had a long run." Ray sings a pretty terrible song called "If You Believe, You'll Get To Heaven" at his going-away party. During the film, he is ordained, officiates at his sister's wedding and his niece's christening, and becomes an Army chaplain. It's hard to say which is worse: his singing or his acting. The film also features Marilyn Monroe at what some consider her sexiest, but, to me, she seemed to be simply a parody of herself.

Father Brown (aka The Detective) (1954)

This literate piece of whimsy is based on the sleuth popularized by the prolific Catholic writer G. K. Chesterton. It stars Alec Guinness, who converted to Catholicism two years later, as Father Ignatius Brown, whose philosophy is "We are not born good and bad people, only people. There but for the grace of God go I, a man once said on observing a man going to his execution." The story focuses on Gustave Flambeau (Peter Finch), a connoisseur and thief of fine things, who is trying to steal a Cross that once belonged to Saint Augustine. Father Brown goes to France for the Holy Year with many priests, and he sees a priest order a ham sandwich on Friday and surmises that it is Flambeau. He follows Flambeau to the catacombs where they quote the Bible to one another. Returning to London, he finds the Cross missing, believing that Saint Augustine would have agreed with him that rather than turning him in, his dialogue with Flambeau was worth the gamble for his soul. The Archbishop gives him two weeks to find Flambeau, which Brown likens to "looking for a black cat in a coal bin during a solar eclipse."

In the course of the film, he preaches many sermons with numerous biblical references and other wise sayings like "The secret of the confessional is that the more you learn about other people, the more you learn about yourself. The more you learn about yourself, the more you understand other people." He and Flambeau confront one another at the end. See this film not just to learn the end but for the sheer delight of watching two superb actors act out a script that's worthy of them. Suffice it to say, I'll take this literate priest with a sense of humor any day of the week over the dreary French Country Priest.

The Left Hand of God (1955)

This film is based on a novel by William Barrett, author of *Lilies of the Field*. It opens with Humphrey Bogart in a priest's cassock riding on a donkey in "a remote province in China" during a raging rainstorm when, while crossing a bridge, they fall into the swirling water. Barely surviving, he manages to walk a great distance to a local mission, where he presents himself as the new priest Father O'Shea. He's actually Jim Carmody, a downed pilot who was rescued by a warlord, General Yang (Lee J. Cobb), and forced to act as his right-hand man for three years until he escapes in the habit of the priest killed by one of Yang's renegades. At the mission he meets Doctor David Sigman (E. G. Marshall), who, like many movie doctors, is an atheist (see *Keys of the Kingdom*). He doesn't "believe in an immortal soul." Also staffing the mission is the doctor's wife Beryl (Agnes Moorehead) and a nurse, Anne Scott (Gene Tierney).

Later admitting he hasn't been in a church since being an altar boy, he must immediately give Last Rites and has a backlog of 42 marriages, 36 baptisms, and countless confessions. He begs off saying mass (although he does preach) because he presumably lost his chalice and vestments in the stream. How he manages to convince them that he is the replacement priest strains credulity, and the temptation to gong the film at this point is almost overwhelming, but then something extraordinary happens. Jim Carmody becomes a priest through small and ultimately grand gestures. As he later explains it, "There may be a little bit of a priest in every man." Of course, he and Scott fall in love, but she is mortified at falling for a priest and nothing transpires between them (this is the 1950s after all). There are some marvelous scenes between Bogart and Cobb upon which rests the film's resolution that, while as implausible as the rest of the film, is quite satisfactory. It even induced a tear in the eyes of this viewer when Carmody says good-bye to the children whom he has taught, in the best "Bing Crosby as priest" fashion, to sing "My Old Kentucky Home." My advice is to suspend disbelief and simply enjoy the film.

The Night of the Hunter (1955)

The screenplay for this critical and cult favorite was written by noted author and critic James Agee, based on a Davis Grubb novel; although Robert Mitchum said that it was completely rewritten by director Charles Laughton. It begins with scriptural passages read by Lillian Gish. "Reverend" Harry Powell (Robert Mitchum) plays a psychopathic killer who communes with the Lord and has the words LOVE and HATE tattooed on the knuckles of his two hands. A car thief, he is arrested while in a burlesque house where he grabs his knife as he watches the woman gyrate. His cellmate Ben Harper (Peter Graves) is a murderer who stole $10,000 and is to be executed. Powell tries unsuccessfully to get Harper to tell him where the money is hidden. Upon his release, certain that the man's wife and two children know where it is, Powell goes to their town. He wins over the town gossips and the widow Willa Harper (Shelley Winters) with his pious talk and his demonstration of his two hands wrestling with one another such that LOVE defeats HATE.

The children know where the money is but have been sworn to secrecy. The son John (Billy Chapin) immediately senses Powell's evil and that he is not a preacher. Powell murders the widow and pursues John and his sister downriver. They are saved by a good Christian lady, Rachel (Lillian Gish), who shoots Powell. The film was a box office and initial critical failure, and Laughton never directed again. However, many critics, including Roger Ebert, have called it one of the greatest films ever made. This judgment is based partially on the many ways it pays homage to German and American filmmakers such as the use of Lillian Gish in a way that recalls her role in D. W. Griffith's *Intolerance* (see p. 19). More important, to my mind, is its staying power with the viewer. I agree with film critic Pauline Kael who called it "one of the most frightening movies ever made (and truly frightening movies become classics of a kind)." She went on to describe Powell as a "murderous sex-obsessed, hymn-singing, soul-saver with hypnotic powers." So, while not disputing that it is a great movie, I am not a fan of movies filled with menace, especially those where innocent children are preyed upon. There are enough scary things in the real world without seeking out frightening and potentially nightmare-inducing fare. Still, there's no question that the film has influenced many directors and screenwriters who have populated a number of films at the end of the millennium with murderous, terrifying Bible-spouters.

Friendly Persuasion (1956)

Set in 1862 in southern Indiana, this film classic tells the story of a proper Quaker minister, Eliza Birdwell (Dorothy McGuire), her fun-loving Quaker husband Jess (Gary Cooper), and their three children. There are many lighthearted scenes as Jess pushes his wife's limits by racing his Methodist friend Sam Jordan (Robert Middleton) on the way to Sunday meeting, his buying an organ (music is frowned on at Quaker meetings), the resolution of a quarrel with his wife, and his convincing Eliza to let the children go to the county fair, which is filled with such evils as dancing and gambling. Other marvelous scenes involve the widow Hudspeth (Marjorie Main) and her three marriageable and desperately isolated daughters, as well as the antics of Samantha, Eliza's pet goose, who opens and closes the picture and is at constant war with the youngest, Little Jess (Richard Eyer). The tone turns serious two-thirds of the way into the film when Confederate soldiers arrive and the family's pacifist beliefs are tested. Eliza stays true to her beliefs while her son Josh (Anthony Perkins) takes up arms but is reluctant to kill the enemy. The film garnered six Oscar nominations including one for Best Picture, Best Supporting Actor (Perkins), and for the theme song "Friendly Persuasion (Thee I Love)," which underscores a romantic subplot and became a popular hit.

THE TIMES, THEY ARE A'CHANGIN': THE 1960s

T he 1960s, often referred to as "The Era of Sex, Drugs, and Rock and Roll," is considered a watershed period in American society, and it was; however, actually, the first half of the decade was more a continuation of the 1950s. The major societal changes commonly associated with "the sixties" occurred between 1964 (or the assassination of John F. Kennedy in November 1963) and 1975, as postwar baby boomers came of age with their rallying cry, "Don't trust anyone over thirty." The political and social changes were numerous and shattering. They centered on the intensification of the anti–Vietnam War movement with its protest marches, draft evasions, and attacks on military facilities by antiwar protestors (some of whom were clergy). The decade also brought the Civil Rights Movement to a boiling point, manifested by urban riots and ultimately the assassination of the Reverend Martin Luther King, Jr., in April 1968. Within two months, Senator Robert Kennedy was also assassinated.

Socially, change was also quick and deep. Birth control pills became available in the early 1960s and were widely disseminated, even to students in small religious colleges, making sex outside of marriage seem less consequential. The rise of the Feminist Movement and the challenge to laws banning abortion led to the Supreme Court decision *Roe v. Wade* in 1973, which made abortion legal and easy to obtain. Drugs of every persuasion— marijuana, psychedelics, heroin—were readily available and casually used. The Free Speech Movement emanating from Berkeley made the public use of profanity in speech and writing more accepted.

Hollywood in the Sixties

While all these events were occurring in the world at large, major changes were also taking place in Hollywood, notably the dissolution of the Hays Code in 1967 and its replacement with a less stringent rating system. Simultaneously, the Catholic Church, which had exerted a strong influence on film content since the early 1930s, began undergoing major changes after the Vatican II Council. As Kenneth C. Jones documents in his book

Index of Leading Catholic Indicators: The Church since Vatican II, from 1965 to 2002, the number of those studying for the priesthood fell from 49,000 to 4,700, and the number of nuns, who had been the backbone of Catholic schools and hospitals, fell from 180,000 to 75,000, with an average age of 68. During the same period, half of the Catholic high schools closed, and enrollment in parochial schools dropped by half as well. Paradoxically, the number of Americans identifying themselves as Catholic increased, although attendance at Sunday Mass dropped threefold and the number of Catholic marriages decreased by a third. Not coincidentally, the Legion of Decency ceased to exist in 1965 and was replaced by a less-intrusive advisory film rating system that many Catholics chose to ignore.

The impact of this political, social, and religious turmoil did not take effect in Hollywood until the last third of the 1960s. The period from 1960 to 1964 saw the release of films which were a continuation of a 1950s sensibility: *The Apartment, Elmer Gantry, Inherit the Wind, Judgment at Nuremberg, The Hustler, West Side Story, To Kill a Mockingbird, Lawrence of Arabia, The Man Who Shot Liberty Valance, The Great Escape, My Fair Lady, Sound of Music, Mary Poppins*, and *Becket*. Indeed, Mark Harris, in his book *Pictures at a Revolution* (2008), designates the year 1967 as the birth of the new Hollywood, especially with the release of *The Graduate* and *Bonnie and Clyde*. These were followed by *Easy Rider, In Cold Blood, 2001: A Space Odyssey*, Sam Peckinpah's *The Wild Bunch*, and finally in 1969 by *Midnight Cowboy*, the first (and only) X-rated film to win an Academy Award.

Christianity in Sixties Films

Up to 1968, some of the most outstanding and reverent religious films ever made were released, including *Lilies of the Field, Becket, The Gospel According to Saint Matthew, The Greatest Story Ever Told*, and *A Man for All Seasons*. Nevertheless, a fitting marker for the transitions that occurred during this decade is the 1969 film *Change of Habit*, in which three nun/nurses doff their habits and wear mufti, while caring for the poor in a ghetto clinic. One, played by Mary Tyler Moore, falls in love with the doctor, portrayed by none other than Elvis Presley in his last film. Only in Hollywood!

Elmer Gantry (1960)

Adapting the 1927 Sinclair Lewis novel, the screenwriter changed the main character from a drunken disgraced minister to a drunken lecherous salesman

(Burt Lancaster). He hooks up with the evangelical Sister Sharon Falconer (Jean Simmons), probably modeled, as was *The Miracle Woman*, on Aimee Semple McPherson. Sister Sharon is skeptical of Gantry's religious commitment at first but then, captivated by his oratorical skills and raw sexuality, falls in love with him. Together they barnstorm the country with evangelical tent meetings and become rich and famous. She gets to build her temple off the money gained from those so-called ignorant folks that H. L. Mencken called "booboosie." Gantry's true character is unmasked with the appearance of the sultry Lulu Bains (Shirley Jones), a minister's daughter whom Gantry had deserted after "deflowering" her, and who subsequently was condemned to a life of prostitution. Gantry admits his past and vows to change his ways, asking Sister Sharon to marry him and settle down. She refuses to give up her missionary life and suffers a tragic fate as a fire destroys her temple.

Commentary

The film is a lot less vitriolic than the book, in which Gantry becomes a Baptist and then a Methodist minister who specializes in womanizing, alcohol consumption, and hypocrisy. Although the movie ends with the burning of the temple and Gantry having a life-changing epiphany, the Gantry of the book only feigns a conversion. He continues as an itinerant evangelist and then becomes a "respectable" married Methodist minister while keeping up his proclivities for women and alcohol and managing to evade all attempts to bring him down as a fraud. Sinclair Lewis, himself an alcoholic, researched this book through his friendship with William Stidger, a Methodist Episcopal pastor in Kansas City, Missouri, and Reverend L. M. Birkhead, a Unitarian and agnostic. Lewis dedicated the book to H. L. Mencken, which may be why the screenwriter changed Gantry's sidekick, an atheist seminary dropout in the book, to a Mencken-like journalist. Lewis may have also modeled Gantry on popular evangelist Billy Sunday, who called Lewis "Satan's cohort."

Burt Lancaster plays Gantry with a gusto that bursts off the screen and won a well-deserved Best Actor Academy Award. Shirley Jones, who was not director Richard Brooks's choice but Lancaster's, received little directorial guidance but won an Academy Award for Best Supporting Actress. She did a very good job but nonetheless may also have benefited from a Hollywood tradition of awarding Oscars to actresses with sweet, innocent personas who play against type as prostitutes. The film lost out for Best Picture, Music, and Screenplay.

Like *Inherit the Wind, Elmer Gantry* portrays Fundamentalists as believers who shout "Amen" and follow the Bible with literal-minded slavishness. As a result, they come across as unthinking dupes who fall prey to snake oil salesmen and hypocrites whose designs lie not in heaven but firmly on earth. Not until Robert Duvall's 1996 film *The Apostle* (p. 277) was this stereotype of Fundamentalist preachers and believers challenged by a more nuanced and sympathetic portrayal.

Inherit the Wind (1960)

Filmed in black and white, this adaptation of the 1955 Broadway play by Jerome Lawrence and Robert Edwin Lee is based on the Scopes or "Monkey" trial in 1925 in Dayton, Tennessee. Scopes was accused of teaching Charles Darwin's theory of evolution in a public high school science class, contrary to a recently passed Tennessee law forbidding the teaching of anything but creationism as professed in the Bible. The play and film are almost entirely fiction, with very little of the actual trial records used. (See Backstory, p. 154).

The film opens ominously as four men, one later identified as a fire-and-brimstone pastor, Reverend Brown (Claude Akins), march from the courthouse in Hillsboro to the high school, with Leslie Uggams singing "Give Me That Old-Time Religion" in the background. They arrest Bertram Cates (Dick York), modeled after Scopes, for teaching that man evolved from a protozoan. Enter E. K. Hornbeck (Gene Kelly), a fast-talking *Baltimore Herald* reporter meant to represent H. L. Mencken, who covered the trial. Declaring that his motto is "the duty of a newspaper is to comfort the afflicted and afflict the comfortable," he says that his paper will provide a lawyer and hires Henry Drummond (Spencer Tracy) representing Clarence Darrow. Three-time presidential candidate Matthew Brady (Fredric March), representing William Jennings Bryan, presumably agrees to be the prosecutor and is welcomed to town by a massive parade to the strains of "The Battle Hymn of the Republic" and "Give Me That Old-Time Religion."

A fictional subplot involves Rachel (Donna Anderson), Reverend Brown's daughter and Cates's fiancée, who refuses to condemn Cates. Rachel is damned to hell by the Reverend at an outdoor rally where he gives a sermon filled with hate, followed by Cates being hanged in an effigy. Conflicted between her loyalty to her father and love for Cates, Rachel is called to the stand. She breaks down as she tells of how her father damned

Cates to hell, as well as a 13-year-old boy, who later drowned after looking at protozoa in a microscope. Drummond succeeds in getting Brady to take the stand and makes a fool of him as he shreds the prosecutor's belief in the literal nature of the Genesis story. The film's highlight occurs when Brady says that God created the world in "six twenty-four hour days beginning on the 23rd of October in the year 4004 BC at—uh 9 AM." Drummond asks if that's Eastern Standard Time, and the courtroom bursts into laughter. After Cates is convicted and fined the minimum $100, Brady screams for a higher penalty and turns into a blithering idiot, as he tries to read a defense of his beliefs and collapses in apoplexy. Later, Drummond praises his old adversary and condemns the cynical Hornbeck who is delighted by Brady's death. As he packs to leave town, Drummond weighs the Bible and Darwin's *Origin of the Species* in each hand and places the latter on top of the former and carries them out together under his arm. Did that action signify compatibility of the two, albeit with primacy for Darwin's Theory?

Commentary

For much of the following commentary and the accompanying backstory, I am indebted to Edward Larson's excellent book *Summer for the Gods*.

Neither the film nor the play resembles the actual Scopes trial (see Backstory, p. 154). Like *The Crucible*, Arthur Miller's fictional description of the Salem Witch trials, the play and film owe more to the imagination of the playwrights and screenwriters who took broad liberties with history as they took aim at the so-called witch hunts conducted by Senator Joseph McCarthy and the House Un-American Activities Committee. The film's title comes from the Book of Proverbs: "He that troubleth his own house shall inherit the wind" and reflects the author's concern with the blacklisting of actors and writers. *New York Times* trial correspondent Joseph Wood Krutch, an avowed supporter of evolution, was very much bothered by the fact that "Most people who have any notions about the trial get them from the play, *Inherit the Wind*, or the movie." He said the townspeople behaved well and that far from being sinister, the atmosphere was like a circus. It was "a strange witch hunt," he went on to say, "where the defense instigated the trial" and one in which "the accused won a scholarship to graduate school and the only victim was the chief witness for the defense, poor old Bryan."

As the *New Yorker* drama critic said about the play, which ran for three years on Broadway, "History has not been increased but fatally diminished."

BACKSTORY

The Real Scopes Trial vs. *Inherit the Wind*

As documented by historian Edward Larson in his 1997 Pulitzer Prize winning book *Summer for the Gods*, contrary to what is depicted in *Inherit the Wind*, the Scopes trial was instigated by the American Civil Liberties Union (ACLU). Founded in 1920 by liberal, educated New Yorkers, the organization was concerned mainly about academic freedom and the policy consequences of majority rule. Its first annual report declared, "The chief activity necessary is publicity in one form or another for ours is a work of propaganda—getting facts across from our point of view." By 1925, when the Tennessee law banning the teaching of evolution in schools was signed, the ACLU had yet to win a court case. It immediately issued a press release, printed in the May 4 Chattanooga Times, stating: "We are looking for a Tennessee teacher who is willing to accept our services in testing this law in courts."

The civic leaders of Dayton, Tennessee, saw this as a way for them to get on the map. Two brothers, Herbert E. and Sue Hicks, agreed to prosecute the case if a local teacher could be found who said he taught evolution. Scopes, who taught physics and math and also coached football, had occasionally substituted for the biology teacher. A shy, earnest man with horn-rimmed glasses, he was summoned to a drugstore meeting and agreed to be the defendant, with the ACLU paying the costs.

Clarence Darrow, who considered Christianity to be "a slave religion that encouraged acquiescence in injustice, a willingness to make do with the mediocre, and complacency in the face of the intolerable" volunteered to handle the defense. William Jennings Bryan was a natural choice to assist the prosecutors. Although he had led the fight against evolution, Bryan was opposed only to its being taught as "true." Not mentioned was his concern that Darwin's theory of "survival of the fittest" was being used to justify eugenics and sterilization of "defectives," as in a Virginia statute authorizing the sterilization of the "feeble-minded," whose constitutionality was upheld by the Supreme Court in 1927. To Bryan's credit, when it became clear that Scopes would be found guilty, he asked for the lowest penalty of $100 that he offered to pay (in contrast to the movie where he goes ballistic and asks for a larger fine).

Rather than argue the case on constitutional grounds and have Scopes admit to having broken the law, Darrow wanted to try Bryan and the Fundamentalists' belief in creationism vs. reason and science. He succeeded in getting Bryan to take the stand to stage the attack on the broader issue. While not part of the trial itself in that the jury was dismissed for that day, his tactic had the hoped-for effect, which was trumpeted by the press (including Mencken), which favored his position. Also, rather than facing a hostile crowd, the town of Dayton, unlike much of the South which was Baptist and Fundamentalist, was mostly Methodist leading Mencken to joke that "A Methodist down here belongs to the extreme wing of liberals."

One comes away from the film with the idea that the trial was not about the freedom to teach the competing theories, but that Darwin's theory is the correct one and that Fundamental Christians and their beliefs in a creator whether literally (in the case of creationism) or by some divine intervention (intelligent design) were discredited once and for all. One would hardly know that many intelligent and reputable scientists, who are also committed Christians, believe in the existence of a creator. They also believe in intraspecies evolution but not in randomness of creation or evolutionary interspecies jumping the so-called missing link, which despite many false reports has never been demonstrated. Ironically, the ACLU led the support for the successful banning of teaching creationism and intelligent design in Dover, Pennsylvania, public schools in 2006, contrary to their founding concern about academic freedom.

The critic for *Time* said, "The script wildly characterizes the Fundamentalists as vicious and narrow-minded and just as wildly and unjustly idealizes their opponents." The same is true for the film as Pauline Kael, film critic for the *New Yorker,* wrote that Bryan, who never said the foolish words attributed to him, was portrayed as an "embarrassingly hollow imitation of a Bible-thumping fundamentalist" and that "the movie presents the fundamentalists as foolish bigots." By contrast, Kael noted that Darrow is portrayed in a "wise, humane, meant-to-be irresistible manner." One shouldn't be surprised that Scopes had no fiancée or that the sinister and demonic pastor was entirely made up, and that Scopes was not hanged in effigy.

Despite the negative reviews, even by critics sympathetic to Darwin's theory, the play and the film are widely used in high school courses and drama programs. One can legitimately ask "Why?" First it's a tribute to the playwrights and the filmmakers who caught the spirit of an age concerned with government intrusion in the arts and effectively used a courtroom setting, a surefire crowd pleaser, as in *12 Angry Men*. Second, they also were blessed with exceptional actors in Darrow's role, Paul Muni on stage and Spencer Tracy (who garnered a Best Actor nomination) in the movie, who gained the audience's sympathy against less charismatic actors Ed Begley and Fredric March, who got the disproportionately laughable lines. Thirdly, it won the support of the academy of historians, which was more sympathetic to the overarching thesis and less concerned with the play's accuracy and thus recommended it for incorporation in high school curricula. Finally, it shows the power of film especially in an age when history has been poorly taught. Think director Oliver Stone!

Viridiana (1961)

The "Hallelujah Chorus" opens this story of a dedicated novice, Viridiana (Silvia Pinal), who is on the verge of taking her final vows. Against Viridiana's will, the Mother Superior orders her to visit her uncle Don Jaime (Fernando Rey), who had paid her dowry for entry into the convent, as well as her expenses, but had never visited her. Viridiana unpacks her coarse linen nightgown, crucifix, and crown of thorns, prays, and then sleeps on the floor. Meanwhile her uncle wears his dead wife's wedding shoes and her girdle at night. He tells Viridiana that she looks just like her aunt, who died on their wedding night. He asks her to marry him, but she is repelled and prepares to leave. Don Jaime prevails on her to stay one more night and to wear his wife's wedding dress and veil, and she reluctantly agrees. The uncle's devoted servant Ramona (Margarita Lozano) puts some pills in Viridiana's tea that makes her pass out. Jaime then carries her to the bed, kisses her, and although he stops there, the next morning he tells her that they had sex. Seeing her angry reaction, he tells her the truth, but she still leaves. Then he gets a brilliant idea to leave the estate to her and his bastard son Don Jorge (Francisco Rabal) before committing suicide. The Spanish police (Guardia Civil) catch her before her return to the convent to tell of her uncle's death.

Viridiana decides to forego her vows and stays to do good works. She scours the highways and byways for the beggars, the lame, and the blind, and sets them up in the estate's outbuildings. Meanwhile, Jorge comes with his girlfriend and begins to get the place in order. He is appalled by Viridiana's piety but falls for her, and his girlfriend, bored to tears, leaves. Meanwhile, Ramona falls for Jorge and takes the girlfriend's place in his bed. At first, the homeless seem to fulfill Viridiana's belief that they can be saved by charity and kindness. They do the chores and placate their benefactress by stopping at noon for the Angelus (a devotion practiced in response to church bells at 6 AM, noon, and 6 PM, that was most vividly portrayed in Jean-Francois Millet's painting of a farm couple stopping in the field for prayer). However, when Jorge and Viridiana leave to settle the estate, the workers break into the main house and have a banquet with copious food and wine, using the best china. After posing for a Last Supper picture, which one of the women pretends to take by lifting up her skirt to show her mons veneris, they start fighting and carousing and destroy most of the china. When Viridiana and Jorge return early, two men subdue Viridiana, and one of them begins to rape her after chaining Don Jorge to a dresser. Jorge convinces the other, a retarded man, to hit the first man in the head and kill him. Viridiana is rescued before she loses her virginity. After reflecting on the events, Viridiana goes to Jorge's room where he is listening to rock music with Ramona. She turns to go but is convinced to stay and play cards as an allusion to their future ménage a trois.

Commentary

Not surprisingly, the Vatican condemned this strange film about the perversion of a nun, especially because of its Last Supper scene. When director Luis Buñuel (see Backstory, p. 157) was challenged by the actress Silvia Pinal about the final scene where Viridiana throws herself at Don Jorge, the director

BACKSTORY

Luis Buñuel: Lifelong Vendetta for a Catholic Education

Luis Buñuel (1900–1983), the film's director, grew up in Calanda in the Spanish province of Aragon and was taught by the Jesuits in a strict curriculum he described as "unchanged since the 18th Century." After moving to the University of Madrid, he met Salvador Dali and turned to filmmaking as his career. As noted in the Criterion DVD's extra commentary, Buñuel later said that "religious education and surrealism marked me for life." Uninterested in making commercial movies, he made films that consisted of harsh attacks on the Catholic Church, the bourgeoisie, and fascism. He collaborated with Dali to make his first film *Un Chien Andalou* (1929), which opens with a scene of an eyeball being sliced and later shows a man dragging two grand pianos with rotting donkeys, two priests (one is Dali), and the Ten Commandments tablets. The film set the pattern of the reaction he was to receive from critics and intellectuals as it left people asking what the film was all about, while also declaring it to be great. After his second film, *L'Age d'Or* (1930), based on the "Marquis de Sade 120 days of Sodomy" in which Jesus appears to be one of the participants, attendees rioted and tore up the movie theater.

In 1959, Buñuel made *Nazarin,* a film about a clueless priest who is forever being robbed or giving away money while he cadges food and offerings. All his attempts to help people backfire. His 1961 film *Viridiana* depicted the perversion of a devout nun and in *Simon of the Desert (*1965), a saint, after being tempted by the devil in the form of a girl, rejects asceticism for life in a jazz club. The anti-Catholicism in the latter films pales in comparison to *The Milky Way (1970)*, his savage parody of the pilgrimage to Santiago de Compostela and deconstruction of the history and dogma of the Catholic Church. He is best known for his more popular art house films *Belle de Jour* (1967), *The Discreet Charm of the Bourgeosie* (1974), and his last film *That Obscure Object of Desire* (1977). Buñuel was, like Robert Altman and Martin Scorsese, haunted by his Catholic education. While his targets were legitimate inadequacies and imperfections in a Church made up of people, imperfect as we all are, he couldn't let it go and escape thinking about it. In this way, he resembles the person (presumably the author) portrayed in Francis Thompson's "The Hound of Heaven," reproduced below in part.

The Hound of Heaven

I fled Him, down the nights and down the days;
I fled Him, down the arches of the years;
I fled Him, down the labyrinthine ways
Of my own mind; and in the mist of tears
I hid from Him, and under running laughter.
Up vistaed hopes I sped;
And shot, precipitated,
Adown Titanic glooms of chasmèd fears,
From those strong Feet that followed, followed after.
But with unhurrying chase,
And unperturbèd pace,
Deliberate speed, majestic instancy,
They beat—and a voice beat
More instant than the Feet—
"All things betray thee, who betrayest Me."

Buñuel reportedly told Pinal, "Look, she has been useless all her life at the convent, with the homeless, now she's going to have children and work the land and be of some use." Pinal then did as she was directed.

The extraordinary verisimilitude in mannerisms, speech, and interactions was achieved by Buñuel's recruiting the homeless and the retarded man off the streets. Acclaimed for its sacrilegious nature, the film was made in Franco's Spain and somehow got by his censors. Its best assets are its beautiful Spanish language and Fernando Rey, who later starred in *The French Connection*. However, there is no question that the film had profound effects on American directors. The use of ridicule in portraying what had previously been off-limits like the Last Supper was later mimicked by Robert Altman and Mel Brooks. In the same vein, Buñuel joined Fellini in portraying Catholic clergy in less than the felicitous ways that had characterized American films. Finally, the inability of censorship laws to prevent his and other sexually explicit or anticlerical critically acclaimed foreign films from being shown in art houses hastened the demise of the Motion Picture Production Code.

Francis of Assisi (1961)

Based on the novel *The Joyful Beggar* by Louis De Wohl, the film recounts the life of Saint Francis (Bradford Dillman), around whom many legends have arisen. A pleasure-loving rake, he decides to go off to war, much to the satisfaction of his rich merchant father, who is certain that his son will attain the rank of nobleman. After some initial success, Francis hears a voice calling him to turn back and he will be told what to do. His father and the townspeople are mortified by his apparent cowardice and aimlessness. His friend Paolo (Stuart Whitman), a knight whom he had admired, turns against him and vies with Francis for the love of a noblewoman, Clare (Dolores Hart), a seeming dramatic contrivance. Still, the basics of the story are there as he wears coarse clothes and gives everything he has to the poor. While praying in the ruined Chapel of San Damiano, he is told to rebuild the church. Taking the command literally, he begs to obtain stones not only for that church but two others as well.

His work begins to attract followers, ranging from a wealthy merchant and the local canon, to farmers and shoemakers. He goes to Rome to petition Pope Innocent III (Finlay Currie) to establish an order dedicated to living Christ's admonition of "Leave all and follow Me" but is turned away by Cardinal Hugolino (Cecil Kellaway). Recalled by the Pope, who recognizes him from a dream he had of a monk lifting up a falling basilica, he is told, "Your order will be an example to all of us."

As his followers go off two by two to various countries, the number increases to two thousand, and his original idea that they should not acquire property becomes impractical. There appears a schism whereby his disciple Brother Elias (Russell Napier) begins to rewrite the rules so that they are less ascetic and self-denying. Francis relinquishes control, and thinking that he is a failure, goes off to a cave where he prays and composes such spiritual classics as the "Canticle of the Sun." Before he dies, he receives the Stigmata, the first with the possible exception of St. Paul to be so linked to Christ's sufferings. Cardinal Hugolino, who had helped the order change but remained its protector, now Pope Gregory IX, declared Francis a saint within two years of his death at 45.

Commentary

Watching this film 45 years after it was made, I was struck by how it signaled the end of an era both for Hollywood and society. It could hardly be imagined that a major studio would now make a lavish and reverent production of the life of a Catholic saint, beautifully photographed on location in Cinema-Scope. The DVD even has a newsreel clip in which George Christopher, the mayor of San Francisco, holds a ceremony for the movie's premiere, saying that the film will profoundly move the city's citizens. Though the film has the advantage of an excellent director, Michael Curtiz (*Casablanca*), and cast,

Figure 6.1. *Francis of Assisi.* **Dolores Hart, who played Clare in Francis of Assisi, later became a nun.**

BACKSTORY

Dolores Hart: From Actress to Prioress

The only child of a Catholic father, an actor, and a Protestant mother who married at age 17 and 16, respectively, and later divorced, she lived in Chicago with her grandparents. Sent to a Catholic school for convenience and safety reasons, she asked to be baptized at age 10. Her grandfather was a projectionist, and she spent many days in the soundproof booth watching films and alerting him to change reels. When her mother remarried, Dolores returned to Hollywood at age 11 and played Saint Joan in the high school play. She earned a scholarship in drama at Marymount College where she was called out of charm class one day for a screen test to appear opposite Elvis Presley in his first film, *Loving You.* Later, in *King Creole,* she gave Elvis his first movie kiss. Asked about it years later by Barbara Cloud, she said, "I think the limit for a screen kiss back then was something like 15 seconds. That one has lasted 40 years."

While playing on Broadway in *The Pleasure of His Company* in 1959, for which she received a Tony nomination, she confessed to being weary and was persuaded to visit the Abbey of Regina Laudis (see *Come to the Stable,* p. 99), and kept returning. She asked the abbess Mother Benedict if she had a vocation and was told to "go back and do your movie thing." She starred in *Where the Boys Are* followed by *Francis of Assisi* during which she met Pope John XXIII. Introduced as the actress who played St. Clare, he said, "No you *are* Clara." Thinking he had misunderstood, she corrected him saying she was an actress and the Pope repeated the statement, which she said, rang in her ears. In 1962, after playing a stewardess in *Come Fly with Me,* she broke off an engagement to a wealthy Los Angeles businessman, gave up her film career, and joined the Benedictine order of Regina Laudis in Bethlehem, Connecticut. Her ex-fiancé never married and visits her every Christmas and Easter. As she told Barbara Middleton, "every love doesn't have to wind up at the altar."

She is currently the Abbey's Prioress and remains active in drama, having established a theater at the Abbey with the help of Patricia Neal, and remains the only nun who is a voting member of the Motion Picture Academy of Arts and Sciences. Her interviews have been occasioned by the release of a CD, "Women in Chant," her visit to Congress and Hollywood in 2006 to publicize the painful rare disease idiopathic peripheral neuropathy (which followed a double root canal in 1999) and Elvis anniversaries. Of Elvis, she told Nicole D'Andrea that he was "like a beacon in the dark" for many people and that his impact "allowed him to be something of a Christ presence for better or for worse. I think that is going to be the basis of salvation for him."

it is slow-moving at times. Yet, its focus on the most ecumenically popular of Catholic saints means that it will still appeal to the devout, those who are going through a reevaluation of their lives, and those who simply want to gather the family for an old-fashioned uplifting movie.

There are marvelous scenes showing Francis reciting his famous prayer on Palm Sunday and blessing the animals. He is shown living his motto Pax et Bonum (peace and good works) as he tends to a leper and when he receives the Pope's approval to visit a sultan in Syria in an unsuccessful attempt to gain peace as well as access for Christians to Jerusalem. Probably the most powerful and poignant scene involves the reception of Clare into the monastic life, as her hair is cut and she joins the Benedictine nuns, in what will later be called the Poor Clares, that mirror Francis's rules and vision. This is an example where life imitated art because two years later actress Dolores Hart, who played Clare, entered a convent.

El Cid (1961)

Set in 1080 in a Spain described as "a war torn, unhappy land, half Christian, half Moor," this three-hour spectacular tells the story of the legendary Rodrigo of Vivar (Charlton Heston) known as El Cid (1040–1099). The country had been left fragmented by the death of the Christian King Ferdinand I with the various provinces divided among his three sons and two daughters, leading to sibling warfare. The film depicts cities in flames and a priest lamenting the burning of the Cross and praying for someone to lead them against the Moors. Rodrigo appears and captures two Moorish emirs. He refuses to have them killed, however, and wins their undying loyalty when he releases them on the condition that they pledge not to take arms against the Christians. One says, "In my country, we have a name for a warrior who has the vision to be just and the courage to be merciful, 'El Cid' (The Lord)." He is correspondingly honored by the Spanish Christians as "El Campeador" (The Champion). The rest of the film is part love story and part action film, blending fact and fiction and ending with the legendary account of how El Cid turned back the African invaders with the help of his Moorish comrades, reuniting Spain for three hundred years.

Commentary

This slow-moving spectacle, filled with pomp, pageantry, and battle scenes, was meant to be seen on the big screen. The opening sequence has an eerie resonance to today as the North African Moorish leader Ben Yussuf (Herbert Lom) urges his Spanish Moorish brethren to turn away from their great achievements in medicine, philosophy, and the arts to become killers. He says that:

> The prophet has commanded us to rule the world. Where in all of Spain is the rule of Allah? When they speak of you, they speak of poets. Where are

your warriors? You call yourselves sons of the Prophet! You have become women. Burn your books. Make warriors of your poets. Let your doctors invent new poisons for our arrows. Let your scientists invent new war machines. Then kill! Burn! Encourage the infidels to kill each other. Then when they are weak, I will sweep up from Africa and then the empire of the one God, the true God Allah, will spread across Spain, then across Europe, and the whole world. (Screenwriters: Fredric M. Frank, Philip Yordan, and Ben Barzman)

In contrast to Ben Yussuf, the film favorably portrays other practitioners of Islam who stand with El Cid and fight for Spain, which characterized the true brotherhood between Christians and Muslims that flourished there for centuries. It also has numerous positive scenes of Christians as when the nuns provide a sanctuary in their abbey for Jimena (Sophia Loren), El Cid's wife, and their children, as well as when El Cid gives water to a leper to drink from his pouch. Unfortunately, much of this is buried under a strange love story and many long, noisy battles. In short, the movie suffers from its stars. In those days, getting the biggest box office stars was considered essential. This is a case where the real identities of Charlton Heston and Sophia Loren and their star power obscure their characters. Although Heston is okay, he has played too many of these roles (Ben-Hur, Moses, Michaelangelo, etc.) to be submerged into El Cid. And Sophia Loren is, dare I say, terrible in this movie. Now, as for *Yesterday, Today, and Tomorrow* and *Gold of Naples,* that's different!

Barabbas (1962)

Based on a novel by Nobel Prize winner Pär Lagerkvist, this film imagines what happened after Barabbas (Anthony Quinn) was pardoned by Pontius Pilate instead of Christ. Returning to his old haunt upon release, Barabbas stumbles by Christ, who appears in a radiant glow. His friends at the bordello are ready to party, but his girlfriend Rachel (Silvana Mangano) rejects him because while he was in jail, she became a follower of Jesus. The film's premise is that Barabbas is tortured by why he, a murderer, was spared and Jesus, a just man, was killed. Still, he continues to struggle against believing in Christ even as he watches Rachel being stoned to death for proselytizing.

Caught after returning to a life of robbery and murder, he cannot be executed because he had been spared death. Sent to the sulfur mines of Sicily, where he amazingly survives 20 years, he winds up being chained to a devout Christian, Sahak (Vittorio Gassman). Revolted on first learning it's Barabbas, Sahak realizes Barabbas is the only one he knows who saw Christ, and he tries to convince Barabbas to affirm God. Sent as slaves to Rome to be gladiators, they encounter the mean Torvald (Jack Palance), the Emperor's favorite. Sahak is sentenced to death for being a Christian and when the guards purposely miss him with their lances, Torvald steps forward and kills him. Barabbas kills Torvald in the arena and is freed by Nero. Finally accepting Christianity, Barabbas is crucified for presumably burning Rome. His last words are: "I give myself up to your keeping. It is Barabbas."

Commentary

One of the lesser-known Roman epics, the film benefits from its novelistic roots and an intelligent screenplay by Christopher Fry that challenge the viewer to contemplate why the good must die while evildoers are allowed to go free. Was there a purpose to the wretch's life? The film is certainly reverential to Christianity with convincing witness to Christ given by the superb Italian actors Mangano and Gassman, as well as the American actor and Academy Award winner Ernest Borgnine, whose character helps convert Barabbas. Indeed, a few reviewers panned it for its religiosity.

The film more than earns its sobriquet as a "sword and sandal epic" with its gladiator scenes that outdo those even in the 2000 film *Gladiator*. This is best shown in the scenes of the schooling of neophyte gladiators, the menacing presence of Jack Palance, and the well-orchestrated final competition between Torvald and Barabbas. Also noteworthy is how director Richard Fleischer took advantage of an actual solar eclipse on location in Nice to film the crucifixion scene when there was "darkness at noon."

Lilies of the Field (1963)

Homer Smith (Sidney Poitier), an itinerant black veteran and handyman on his way to California, stops for water for his car's radiator in a remote part of Arizona at a mission run by nuns who escaped from East Germany. He reluctantly agrees to work to get money for gas to move on but continues to get delayed by the tough Mother Superior Mother Maria (Lilia Skala), who keeps giving him more work and no money. Finally, she tells him that God sent him to build their chapel. At first, he refuses, but then remembering his desire to be an architect like the one who designed the Golden Gate Bridge, he decides to take it on. Insisting on doing it alone, he spurns the help of the local Mexican-Americans but then gives in, and it becomes a community affair.

There are many lighthearted scenes as when Smith stares at his solitary egg that he scoops up in one bite and says, "That's a Catholic breakfast, ain't it!" In another, he pits his knowledge of the Bible from his Baptist upbringing against Mother Maria's, and in yet another he teaches the nuns English with a humorous twist. The most poignant involves the singing of the movie's theme "Amen" at the end as Homer departs.

Commentary

James Poe's screenplay for this uplifting classic was taken from a novel by Manhattan College graduate William Barrett who also wrote *The Left Hand of God*, which was made into a film in 1955 (p. 144). As recounted in Jeffrey Marlett's excellent contribution to *Catholics in the Movies*, Barrett based the story on a group of German nuns who had fled Nazi Germany in the 1930s and established a Benedictine convent near his Colorado home. The title derives from Christ's counsel about not being anxious about worldly things: "Consider the lilies of the field, how they grow, they neither toil nor spin, yet I tell you, even Solomon in all his glory was not arrayed like one of these" (Matthew 6:27–28). The film was voted 46th on the American Film Institute's top 100 inspirational films in 2006. Nominated for five Oscars, it is best known for Sidney Poitier's performance that earned him the first Oscar for Best Actor awarded to a black.

Still, the film almost didn't get made. Some studios considered the screenplay as "soft" consisting of nuns, a black handyman, faith, and redemption while lacking sex, violence, and white stars. Harry Belafonte had turned down the role, but as Poitier recounts in his autobiography, he liked the quiet plea for tolerance, understanding, and interracial friendship, and jumped at the chance to play Smith. United Artists gave director Ralph Nelson a budget of only $240,000 even though Poitier's usual salary alone at the time was half that. Nelson convinced Poitier to take $50,000 and a percentage of the profits. He also put his house up as collateral and hired Skala, a former Viennese stage actress before the Nazi takeover who was working at a factory, and four other professionals to work at the union scale of $350 a week. Cutting corners, Nelson filmed the movie in two weeks. Most critics praised the film, although, as Vickie McClare Darson notes, the *Newsweek* critic complained that "the screen overflows with enough brotherhood, piety, and honest labor to make even the kindliest spectator retch." Released at the peak of the Civil Rights Movement, Poitier's soft sell was seen by some black critics as a "sell-out."

Clearly, the filmmakers were very sympathetic to the religious elements. Smith reserves the reverent placement of the Cross on the chapel, the final step in its building, to himself. Mother Maria, whose toughness was responsible for them escaping and making the trek of almost 3,000 miles from Communist East Germany, finally shows a softer side. She is surrounded by other nuns who are rather simple, sweet, naïve, and committed to their vocation. The film does show a darker side as well. Father Murphy (Dan Frazer), the circuit-riding Irish priest who says Mass on Sunday off the back of his van, is said to be a drinker, one of the reasons Juan (Stanley Adams), the Mexican-American owner of the local diner, gives for not attending Mass. Murphy tells Homer that he is disillusioned by the priestly life and advises him not to get involved in building the chapel. When Homer stays and the work is completed, Murphy's faith is renewed as he says the first Mass in the new chapel. Even Juan pitches in to build the chapel saying, "To me, it's insurance. To me, life is here on earth. I cannot see further, so I cannot believe further. But if they are right about the hereafter, I have paid my insurance."

Figure 6.2. In *Lilies of the Field*, Baptist Homer Smith (Sidney Poitier) teaches English to a group of East German nuns whose superior ropes him into building a chapel.

The Cardinal (1963)

As Stephen Fermoyle (Tom Tryon) awaits elevation to Cardinal, his mind flashes back to his ordination and his assignment to a Boston parish, headed by Monsignor "Dollar Bill Monaghan" (Cecil Kellaway) in the 1920s, when his sister, Mona (Carol Lynley), is accused of "going out with a dirty rag-picking Jew." She professes her wish to marry Benny Rampell (John Saxon) but is told that their difference in faith is insurmountable and that only Catholics can get to heaven. She correctly responds that "the Church teaches that anyone can go to heaven if he acts according to God's will."

Considered by his future in-laws to be destined for hell, Benny refuses to become a Catholic or to raise their children Catholic. After their civil wedding, Fermoyle tells Mona there's no living in mortal sin, and she must give Benny up. He gives her three rosaries as her penance. Mona runs away from home, saying, "I'm through with your pious mealy-mouthed religion. I'm through with your God." Mona becomes a prostitute, and Fermoyle is asked to pay for her abortion in Albany. Told that a fetal craniotomy (crushing the child's head) must be done to save Mona, he refuses to give permission and leads Mona in the act of contrition and blesses her as she dies. Again Fermoyle must have been studying theology in Hollywood, not Rome.

He is reassigned to a rural parish with Father Halley (Burgess Meredith), an incompetent pastor but a first-rate individual, who suffers from multiple sclerosis. Halley tells him that his major character trait is overweening pride, which seemingly destines him for the highest ranks in the Church hierarchy. Fermoyle works with the Mafia to pay for Halley's medical expenses. Later, he becomes secretary to the Cardinal of Boston and accompanies him to Rome where Pope Pius XII appoints him to the Secretariat of State office. Fermoyle refuses saying he must leave the priesthood, for which his parents destined him from birth. He says despairingly, "I had to deny myself the softness of a woman. The time came when my being a priest meant my sister had to die. I couldn't do what layman could do, pretend I never heard of the law." He starts teaching in Vienna where he meets Annemarie (Romy Schneider), whom he dumps, in a completely phony and tedious scene in the Vatican.

Back at the Vatican, a black priest, Father Gillis (Ossie Davis), pastor of St. Jude's (patron of the impossible) in Lamar, Georgia, comes to complain that the superintendent of the only Catholic school refuses to accept blacks and the local bishop won't intervene. His church has been burned to the ground by the KKK. An anti-American Cardinal rebukes him saying, "It's hardly a tribute to your discretion to use methods that are inflammatory." Fermoyle accompanies Gillis to Georgia and is met with racial epithets. He and Gillis are beaten by a KKK member who is convicted of disorderly conduct.

Fermoyle is made a Bishop and is sent to Austria where the Cardinal is shown welcoming Hitler saying "the Bishops extend best wishes and blessings for the Nazis' efforts for the underprivileged. We expect faithful Catholics to vote 'Yes' in the plebiscite." When Hitler repudiates all his promises by dissolving Catholic schools and taking Church property, the Austrian Cardinal is humiliated. It's Alleluia vs. Seig heil. All of this and more passes through Fermoyle's mind. It may not have been a wonderful life, but it certainly was a full one.

Commentary

Based on a popular novel by Henry Morton Robinson, the film lasts over three hours, with a screenplay that begged to be edited with pruning shears. It received six Oscar nominations including Best Supporting Actor (John Huston) and Best Director (Otto Preminger). In my opinion, this is a thinly veiled anti-Catholic film. Why would anyone think that Otto Preminger, whose *The Moon Is Blue* was condemned by the Catholic Church in 1953, would make a film even moderately favorable to the Church? Yet, there is Preminger, in the coming attractions, meeting with the Bishop of Bridgeport and visiting various holy sites in Boston, the Vatican, and Vienna in a promotional campaign to gain "Catholic cred" so that a potentially large audience would not be alienated (actually, its condemnation helped inflate box office receipts). It would have been better if the Bishop had watched the film and helped Preminger with Catholic theology.

The movie contains a laundry list of complaints about Catholicism (some quite legitimate), with only the Crusades and the Spanish Inquisition left out. First, there's the focus on anti-Semitism which was beginning to be confronted. *Abie's Irish Rose*, the popular musical about a Jewish man who marries an Irish girl over the objections of both families, ran from 1922–1927 on Broadway. Then there is the argument that only Catholics can be saved, because "it is the one true Church." Fortunately, the priest's sister was paying attention in catechism class because he wasn't. Most important is the abortion issue and the need to obey the law spouted by a priest who seems not to remember that Catholic teaching permits sacrificing the child to save the life of the mother.

Next, there's Fermoyle's work with the Mafia to get cash for Father Halley. Even the Mafiosi are puzzled since they have never had a priest working with them before (this will be rectified in later films). There's also the celibacy theme with his confessing to having become a priest to satisfy his parents, and his little dalliance in Austria. Finally, there's the racism in the Church theme. This is quite legitimate historically, but at the time the film was made, Catholics, laity and clergy alike, had been marching for civil rights for years. Finally, there's the Church's relationship with Hitler.

If Preminger had decided to pursue only one or two of these admittedly contentious and important issues, the film would have benefited. For example, in the initial discussion between Fermoyle and his future brother-in-law, there is a good back and forth exchange about squaring Adam and Eve with Darwin, and whose side God was on during World War I, when both sides claimed him. However, after that, Preminger made Fermoyle seem like Woody Allen's *Zelig*, who pops up everywhere that history is being made. In so doing, he treats the issues in a simplistic fashion, like a hit-and-run driver, determined to get all of them in, while sacrificing complexity, nuance, and context. Nonetheless, segments of the film may be useful to discuss these issues. I did learn from the film about the American Cardinals being shut out of papal elections (the sea crossing could not be made in the allotted

Figure 6.3. *The Cardinal.* **Father Fermoyle (Tom Tryon) confronts a picket line of Catholics supporting segregation.**

time before the Cardinals were sequestered after a Pope's death) and of the disdain for Americans by the mainly Italian Curia.

Becket (1964)

Based on Jean Anouilh's play *Becket*, the film explores the relationship between Henry II of England (1133–1189) and Thomas Becket (1118–1170), ending with Becket's murder in Canterbury Cathedral. It opens with black-robed monks marching out of the cathedral, followed by King Henry II (Peter O'Toole), who takes off his crown and robe in front of the tomb of Thomas Becket (Richard Burton) and asks: "Well, Thomas, are you satisfied?" He kneels and is scourged by Saxons.

The film then flashes back, and shows the two men in their days of drinking and wenching together. Early in the film, Henry asks Becket: "Who rules the kingdom, the clergy or me?" He then makes Becket the Lord Chancellor of England with the idea that Becket will aid him in keeping the clergy in check. Meanwhile, Becket ruminates, "Where honor should be, in me there is a void. While I wear the seal, I am servant to my King. What if one day I should meet my honor face to face?"

King Henry, fearing that the power of the bishops is rising, declares Becket primate of England, Archbishop of Canterbury, a role he is to hold simultaneously with that of chancellor. After his consecration, Becket gives the seal of chancellor back saying, "The honor of God is greater than the King's," and he begins giving away the gold plate and church treasure to the poor. Realizing that he made a mistake elevating Becket so high, the king suggests that Becket embezzled funds while chancellor. The sheriff of London summons Becket to a court of law, but he escapes across the Channel under the protection of King Louis of France and the Pope, who refuses to relieve Becket of his archbishopric. He spends the next six years living a monastic life at the Abbey of Saint Martin.

Finally, Becket decides to return to England and confront the king. Despite an attempted reconciliation, played out in a great scene on a gray wintry beach in Britain, the two are now mortal enemies. Becket returns to Canterbury, and the king, in the presence of several ambitious noblemen, asks: "Will no one rid me of this meddlesome priest? Are all around cowards like myself?" Four knights take him at his word and ride directly to Canterbury. Becket knows that they are coming but makes no attempt to flee and is murdered on the altar on December 29, 1170.

The film ends with a return to the first scene, with Henry kneeling at Becket's crypt. After the flogging, Henry says, "Thank you, Saxon pigs. There is nothing so certain to win them over than the King humbling himself under the lash . . . Thomas Becket is a martyr and will henceforth be prayed to as a saint." Indeed, a number of miracles occurred shortly after Becket's death at the site of his tomb, and he was declared a saint in 1172, a mere two years after his murder. The shrine at Canterbury became a favorite pilgrimage site, made famous by Chaucer's *Canterbury Tales*.

Commentary

Becket, both the play and the film, is a wonderful story, especially because it shows that saints need not have been saintly all their lives. Immensely popular when it first came out, a restored print of the film was reissued in 2007 for reshowing in select theaters. The complex story is dramatic; the dialogue, rich; the acting, excellent; and the on-location cinematography, beautiful. It garnered 12 Oscar nominations, losing out in the major categories to *My Fair Lady*, and won only for Best Adapted Screenplay.

It's important to note that Anouilh admitted to taking dramatic license with the historical facts that were carried through by the screenwriter. Consequently, the movie operates on the premise that Becket was a Saxon (that is, a peasant) rather than the son of a Norman merchant, who was educated in London and at the University of Paris. As Thomas Craughwell points out in his book *Saints Behaving Badly*, Becket's first job was as a clerk for a London banker where he started "overdressing, took up falconry, and ran with a boisterous, frivolous, and fashionable young crowd." At 26, he became a clerk to Theobald, the Archbishop of Canterbury, who was so impressed with Becket's diplomatic skills that he made him an archdeacon, one step below a priest. Like many other archdeacons, who were supposed to be chaste and not bear arms, Becket remained very worldly—hunting, gambling, and given to ostentatious displays. At age 37, Becket was made Chancellor of England by Henry II, then 22, and began to live even more lavishly.

At Theobald's death, as shown in the movie, Henry made Becket Archbishop of Canterbury the day after being ordained a priest. Henry reasoned that he would gain control over the Catholic Church, which gave allegiance to the Pope and which operated its own legal system for clerical miscreants who were treated much more leniently than ordinary Englishmen in secular

Figure 6.4. *Becket.* **Becket (Richard Burton) defies his old friend Henry II (Peter O'Toole) who wants control over the Catholic Church in England.**

courts. At the feast celebrating his elevation, however, Becket signaled the beginning of a change when the jesters asked him to bestow his usual reward on them. As Craughwell notes, Becket was reported to have said, "I am not the man I was when I was Chancellor. Church funds are for the Church and the poor. I have nothing to give you."

From that point, the film follows the historical record fairly faithfully in that Becket refused to compromise with Henry knowing that his aim was to take control of the Church. In this respect, the story anticipates the story of Sir Thomas More about 350 years later (see *A Man for All Seasons*, p. 179). Interestingly, according to Craughwell, three years after Henry VIII became head of the Church of England, he had Becket's Canterbury shrine stripped of its treasure and the saint's tomb opened and his bones destroyed.

The Gospel According to Saint Matthew (1964)

As the film opens, the camera moves from a placid, pregnant Mary to a disillusioned and disconsolate Joseph who runs away at the sight of his future bride with child. Then an angel appears and tells him the circumstances of the forthcoming birth of Jesus. The film consists of a series of tableaux of key moments in the life of Christ from Bethlehem through the flight into Egypt to the slaughter of the innocents (with the Negro spiritual "Sometimes I Feel like a Motherless Child" playing in the background), to His ministry, and ultimately His death on the cross.

Commentary

Roger Ebert, in *The Great Movies II* in which he listed his second hundred great movies, tells the following story: Pasolini was in Assisi "in 1962 to attend a seminar at a Franciscan monastery. Although it was well known that he was an atheist, a Marxist, and a homosexual, he had accepted the invitation after Pope John XXIII called for a new dialogue with non-Catholic artists." He found a copy of the Gospels in his hotel room and read them straight through, and a film was born. Consequently, the film is dedicated to: "The beloved, happy, familiar memory of Pope John XXIII."

Filmed in black-and-white in the barren birthplace of my maternal grandparents, Basilicata and the Province of Matera in Italy, it features local peasants in all the roles except for the young man who plays Christ. The film begins slowly with long close-ups, no dialogue, and lots of traveling to and fro, but the pace picks up a third of the way through the film, and by the end there is much exposition by Christ. The dialogue is faithful to Matthew's Gospel, although the portrayal of Christ tends more toward his being a revolutionary or a union organizer than a God of mercy. The austere surroundings, the plain rough-hewn actors, and the director's neorealist technique give a sense of authenticity and gravitas to the production.

The handling of the Passion is much more subdued certainly than Mel Gibson's *The Passion of the Christ* (2004), which was filmed in the same location. There is none of the scourging, and Christ falls only once rather than the traditional three times while carrying the Cross; the rest of the time he walks behind Simon who helps Him with the cross. A thief is pictured being nailed to a cross, but there is only one shot of Christ getting a nail driven into His hand followed by a brief scream by Mary. The film was much acclaimed by the critics as a very sensitive and faithful rendition of the life of Christ, made all the more surprising given director Pasolini's atheism. What is particularly interesting is that Pasolini uses Matthew's record of the role of the Jews in Christ's trial and sentencing as well as the Jewish crowd saying, "His blood be upon us and on our children," whereas Mel Gibson removed that line from the subtitles (but not the Aramaic dialogue) before releasing his version. Yet, there were no accusations of anti-Semitism leveled against Pasolini as there were against Gibson for his faithfulness to Matthew's gospel. To quote Cicero, "O tempora! O mores!"

The Greatest Story Ever Told (1965)

The film begins with the words "In the Beginning was the Word and the Word was with God," and the Sistine Chapel ceiling is shown depicting the Creation. This is followed by scenes of the Birth of Christ and the Magi bearing gold for the sovereignty of God, incense for the worship of God, and myrrh for preservation of life everlasting. When Herod declares that every child under age two in Bethlehem must die, there is weeping for the slaughter of the innocents like Rachel weeping for her children as proclaimed in Jeremiah.

Some high points are scenes depicting John the Baptist (Charlton Heston) prophesying, the Devil (Donald Pleasance) tempting Christ, the Beatitudes, and Peter's designation by Christ as the rock on which to build His Church. Other scenes involve Christ curing the blind man (Ed Wynn), the recitation of the Lord's Prayer, and the raising of Lazarus from the dead before an awed crowd with the "Hallelujah Chorus" in the background. Judas (David McCallum) is shown worrying about the cost of the perfumed oil used to bathe Christ's feet, which could be used to sell and give to the poor, with Jesus responding, "The poor you will always have with you." There are very powerful scenes of the cleansing of the temple and of a conflicted Judas bargaining to hand over Jesus with the high priests reassuring him that "We will do everything to see that no harm comes to Him."

The most powerful part of the movie shows how the disciples, though well-meaning, are flawed: Judas the betrayer; Peter the denier; and Peter, James, and John who cannot stay awake in the Garden showing that "The spirit is willing but the flesh is weak." The Way of the Cross is very movingly filmed, with little dialogue. It shows Veronica wiping the face of Jesus and Simon of Cyrene (Sidney Poitier) helping carry the cross. Christ's death is intercut with Judas committing suicide. Then clouds burst, and there is thunder and lightning. "Truly this man was the son of God" says a Centurion (John Wayne) standing on a hill. After Jesus rises from the dead, He tells the disciples, "Go now and teach all nations. Make it your first care to love one another and to find the Kingdom of God. Don't fret about tomorrow for today's troubles are enough. I am with you forever even unto the end of the world." The film ends with Christ's Ascension into heaven.

Commentary

Based on the Bible and Fulton Oursler's book of the same name, this film story of Jesus was written, produced, and directed by one of Hollywood's

Figure 6.5. *The Greatest Story Ever Told.*
Max von Sydow as Christ wearing a
Crown of Thorns.

greatest directors, George Stevens. As Stevens's son recalled in an interview on the DVD, his father "wanted to tell Jesus's story by removing the Jews as 'Christ-killers.'" Stevens had worked as a photographer with the Army in World War II and had filmed the liberation of Dachau and had seen the extreme consequences of anti-Semitism. The movie's star-studded cast was Hollywood's attempt to pull out all the stops to compete with television. Unfortunately, the film was a decade out of sync. On the flight to New York for the opening, the flight attendant gave Stevens a copy of *Time* magazine, whose cover asked the question "Is God Dead?"

Critics panned the film because of the many cameo appearances by established stars; John Wayne as the centurion at the foot of the cross was especially ridiculed, although it didn't bother me. The film was originally 260 minutes before being shortened to 195 minutes and finally to 141 minutes. Although long and slow-moving, the story is very reverential and biblically accurate, and the film picks up considerably halfway through with a very moving portrayal of Christ on the Way of the Cross. From there on, it's hard to take one's eyes off it. Max von Sydow is superb as Christ. The film certainly can be used in segments for teaching and classroom discussion.

The Sound of Music (1965)

This film adaptation of Rodgers and Hammerstein's Tony-winning Broadway musical is based on the story of the singing von Trapp family. When it begins, Maria (Julie Andrews) is a carefree, exuberant postulant training to be a nun in an Austrian convent. The Mother Superior (Peggy Wood) realizes that the young woman is not cut out for the life of a cloistered nun, which is well captured in the lyrics of the nuns' song, which asks the question "How do you solve a problem like Maria?" Counseling her to go back out into the world, the Abbess secures her a job as the governess for the seven children of a widower, Captain von Trapp (Christopher Plummer). Though a loving father, his strict discipline takes much of the fun out of their childhood. Maria helps them recapture it especially in such musical numbers as "My Favorite Things," "Do-Re-Mi," and the title song marvelously filmed on a beautiful hilltop in Salzburg.

Maria finds herself falling in love with the Captain, who seems set to marry a rich and beautiful baroness (Eleanor Parker), and so she returns to the abbey in a state of confusion. The Mother Superior wisely encourages her to return to the children, and soon it becomes clear to all, including the Baroness, that the Captain loves Maria as she does him. She says good-bye to the nuns, and the couple is married in the cathedral and go off on a blissful honeymoon during which time Hitler annexes Austria. On their return home, the captain is billeted to take over a ship. A fierce anti-Nazi, he agrees to a "farewell concert" for the family in Salzburg, but they escape and hide in the Abbey where they are protected by the nuns. Discovered as they rush to their car, the von Trapps are chased by the Nazis who are delayed enough for them to escape to Switzerland because a nun sabotages the Nazi's car by putting sugar in the gas tank.

Commentary

Maria von Trapp was quoted as saying about the movie, "It's a nice story, but it's not my story." Many elements were fictionalized including the personalities of Maria and the Captain and especially the how, when, and where of their escape whose true story is told in the extra materials in the 40th anniversary DVD. It's a good example of that great line from *The Man Who Shot Liberty Valance*, "When the legend becomes fact, print the legend." Indeed, *The Sound of Music* received 10 Oscar nominations and won 5, including Best Picture and remains one of the most popular movies of all time (ranking 40th in the American Film Institute's 100 Greatest Films 2007 poll). Its earnings adjusted for inflation place it third on the list of all-time top-grossing movies.

Until *The Passion of the Christ*, it was probably the best example of a disconnect between the critics and the public. As Wilk notes in "Making the Sound of Music," *New York Herald Tribune* film critic Judith Crist warned diabetics to stay away from the movie for fear of overdosing on

Figure 6.6. *The Sound of Music.* **The Mother Superior (Peggy Wood) tells postulant Maria (Julie Andrews) that she is not cut out to be a nun.**

sugar. The *New Yorker* critic Pauline Kael wrote an extraordinary self-revealing critique: "Whom can this operetta offend? Only those of us who, despite the fact that we may respond, loathe being manipulated in this way and are aware of how cheap and ready-made are the responses we are made to feel. We may become even more aware of the way we have been turned into emotional and aesthetic imbeciles when we hear ourselves humming the sickly goody-goody songs." Wow!

Although not essentially a religious movie, it is included because of the sympathetic treatment of the Catholic nuns who are portrayed in a manner that mirrors my experience during eight years of schooling by nuns from three different orders. The Mother Superior knows from the beginning that Maria doesn't have the temperament to be a cloistered nun and that her loving, effervescent nature is perfectly suited to the role of governess (and eventually mother) to a passel of children. Later in the movie, the nuns play a pivotal role, helping the von Trapps escape the Nazis who are after them by showing great bravery and some humor. They even lie to the Nazis to save the family.

The Sandpiper (1965)

Laura Reynolds (Elizabeth Taylor), a member of the artist colony on Big Sur, homeschools her 12-year-old son Danny (Morgan Mason). The boy gets into trouble for shooting a deer because his mother says that man is the only animal who kills other animals for fun, and he wants to see why. He also has released the neighbor's horses and put his hands on a girl's thigh uninvited. Danny is a wunderkind who recites the prologue from Chaucer's *Canterbury Tales* in olde English. The Judge (Torin Thatcher) gives them a choice of sending Danny to reform school or Saint Simeon's Episcopal School where he is a board member. Headmaster Dr. Edward Hewitt (Richard Burton), dressed in a black cassock (the only time he wears religious garb until the end), meets with Reynolds. A professed naturalist, she believes that man is doomed by his myths and that there will be no peace on earth until people shed their religious beliefs. He counters by saying that the school is perfect for Danny because when he inevitably rebels, it will be against their beliefs—not hers.

At the suggestion of his clueless wife Claire (Eva Marie Saint), Hewitt visits Reynolds in a breathtakingly appointed house overlooking the Pacific "to get to know her" and starts visiting regularly. On one occasion Reynolds's current lover Cos Erickson (Charles Bronson) is sculpting the semi-nude Laura. Cos calls him Reverend, whereupon Hewitt corrects him saying that "Reverend" is an adjective, not a title: "Call me doctor or mister." Cos scoffs at the Virgin birth and says, "No well-educated priest or minister could believe the greater part of Christian dogma in this day and age."

Hewitt offers Reynolds a commission to design the stained glass windows for the school's new church. Being an atheist, she refuses to glorify a creed she doesn't believe in. He tells her, "It's not at all rare to find religious vision more perfectly apprehended by non-believers than by the saint. Saints tend to be myopic, whereas atheists are almost always innocent." She capitulates, but in her initial sketches, man is left out because man lacks innocence. She rails against the male establishment's enormous conspiracy against women since "Adam stool-pigeoned on Eve." She decries how women are unfulfilled, and how men like doctors and presidents "make women feel worthless." She tears up her designs and tells him that he shouldn't spend money on a church with so many needy.

He lusts for her and, saying he has lost all sense of sin, lies to his wife about going to San Francisco. Instead, he and Laura spend an idyllic weekend picnicking on the beach and going to a Club Nepenthe ("oblivion") where young people drink, do drugs, dance, and presumably find peace and wisdom. Later he persuades the school board that instead of building a new church, they should use the money to educate gifted underprivileged children rather than continue to foster racial and class ideas that are inconsistent with Christian dogma. His affair is exposed by a jealous married board member, Hendricks (Robert Webber), who once had Laura as his mistress. Confessing to his wife, Hewitt says he is no longer a man of religion. He expresses regrets at his sinking into corruption with fundraising, sloganeering, and becoming a businessman by altering grades to keep children in school for a hefty contribution. She reminds him how when they started 20 years before, "We were God's sweet fools" dedicated to ministering to the poor, living in perfect trust in the footsteps of Francis of Assisi in a "ministry of love."

From the pulpit, he announces his resignation as headmaster in a service in which the boys' choir opens with "Ye Watchers and Ye Holy Ones" and closes with "There's a Wideness in God's Mercy." He praises the freedom and rebellion and other things he has learned "from a generation younger than my own," also mentioning "Nepenthe," which this time he defines as peace not oblivion. He says good-bye to his wife, who needs time to think, and Reynolds, who loves him as he does her, and drives down the coast.

Commentary

There is no film that better illustrates how authority figures in the religious and educational establishments ceded the intellectual and moral high ground to the rebellious youth of the 1960s, described by Harvard Law School's Archibald Cox as "the best informed, the most intelligent, and the most idealistic this country has ever known" (see Charles Sykes's book, *A Nation of Victims*). In this film, a married Episcopal minister and director of a prestigious boys' prep school who falls in love with an artist, a Beatnik, and professed atheist finds innocence and wisdom (not to mention, lust). The film's opening credits are its high point, as the cinematographer surveys the beautiful and rugged coastline of California's Big Sur while the Academy Award–winning song "The Shadow of Your Smile" plays in the background.

It's interesting to note that in contrast to today when mainly evangelicals and devout believers homeschool their children, it's the freeloving freethinkers who do it in this film. In addition, the 1930s convention of a judge sending a wayward boy to a religious school is still in evidence. However, this is not *Boys Town*. This is an affluent school meant to show the hypocrisy of those who profess to be religious. This is illustrated by the minister's greater concern with money and golfing at Pebble Beach, as well as the Episcopal school board's makeup of immoral and hard-edged men. The latter contrasts with the "innocence" of Reynolds and her drug-taking fellow artists, although to my eye it looks more like hedonism. When the film was shot, Burton and Taylor had finally married after the torrid affair that began on the set of *Cleopatra*. Perhaps that is why some lines caused titters in the audience, especially "I want you, Laura" and "I never knew what love was before."

A Man for All Seasons (1966)

Based on the play by Robert Bolt, this is the story of the martyrdom of Sir Thomas More (1478–1535). The crux of the story involves Henry VIII (1491–1547), played by Robert Shaw, appointing his good friend Thomas More (Paul Scofield) as Lord Chancellor to replace Cardinal Wolsey (Orson Welles) in 1529. The latter had been unsuccessful in obtaining Pope Clement VII's approval of an annulment of Henry's marriage to Catherine of Aragon, the daughter of the king of Spain and his brother's widow, whom he had married after obtaining a papal dispensation in 1502. All their male progeny had died at birth, and Henry took a fancy to Anne Boleyn, one of Catherine's ladies-in-waiting, who might bear him a son. More objects and refuses to sign a letter petitioning the Pope to grant the annulment.

Henry, with the help of the compliant Archbishop Cranmer (Cyril Luckham), severs the Church of England from Rome and declares himself its head. More, a devout Catholic, resigns as chancellor without publicly stating his position. He hopes by moving away from the court and keeping silent, he can live in peace with his family. Thomas Cromwell (Leo McKern), the king's new chancellor, urges Henry to force More to agree that Henry is head of both the Church and the State or to admit that he had spoken against the king. More continues to refuse and is falsely betrayed by an ambitious young man, Richard Rich (John Hurt), whose request for a place at court More had refused. More once again refuses to take the oath of allegiance to the king as head of the Church and is imprisoned in the Tower of London for high treason. After forgiving his executioners, he says that "I die his majesty's good servant, but God's first" and is beheaded. His head was placed on public display for one month at the Traitor's Gate on the Thames.

Commentary

A Man for all Seasons is a timeless classic that can be viewed on many levels. It is above all a film about a man who puts principle, in this case his allegiance as a Catholic to the Pope, above worldly possessions, his family, and life itself. On another level, it is the story of the clash between Church and State, which led to the Reformation in England and later to the persecution of Catholics during the Counter-Reformation. Ironically, More had helped Henry in his writing of "Defense of the Seven Sacraments," which argued against Protestantism and for which Pope Leo X awarded Henry the title of "Defender of the Faith" in 1521.

Robert Bolt, an agnostic who can hardly be called a hagiographer, adapted his play for the screen, using More's own words as much as possible. The following dialogue epitomizes the literate Oscar-winning screenplay and captures the essence of the dispute between More and the king. More asks, "Why does your Grace need my poor support?" Henry answers, "Because you're honest . . . and what is more to the purpose, you're *known* to be honest. There are those like Norfolk who follow me because I wear the crown; and those like Master Cromwell who follow me because they are jackals with sharp teeth and I'm their tiger; there's a mass that follows me because it follows anything that moves. And then there's you."

What is especially good is that the actors avoid over-the-top performances that such spectacles and speeches often bring out in performers. The film also won Oscars for Best Picture, Best Actor (Paul Scofield), Best Color Cinematography, Best Costume Design, and Best Director (Fred Zinneman), who also directed *High Noon* and *From Here to Eternity*.

This film was very well received by the public and the critics, although a few historians have denounced More for having persecuted Lutherans, especially the followers of William Tyndall, whose Bible translation was the precursor of the King James Bible. In particular, Richard Marius, a radical historian at Harvard and author of a revisionist biography of More (I recommend Peter Ackroyd's biography), wrote an essay in which he decried the favorable representation of More as a "Catholic Abraham Lincoln." He said that the real More "shrieked for the blood of Protestants and gloated when they burned." There is a wealth of contrary evidence bearing on More's character, but Marius cites none of it. His essay concludes by saying that "most of us would have done what all More's family did—take the oath that he refused." That's hardly an objective statement. He also accused those who bought the story as being "gullible, unable to bear ambiguity, incapable of thought, self-righteous and transfixed by appearances." I leave it to the reader to decide. In essence you either believe him or More's contemporary, Erasmus, who said his "heart was whiter than snow" and called him "a genius such as England never had before or ever will have" as well as countless

Figure 6.7. *A Man for all Seasons*. Thomas More (Paul Scofield) refuses the request of Henry VIII (Robert Shaw) to support the annulment of his marriage.

others commentators, such as Samuel Johnson who said of him, "he was the person of the greatest virtue these islands (Britain) ever produced" (see Hubbard). More's *Utopia* and other writings established him as one of the world's greatest humanists. More was canonized by the Catholic Church in 1935 along with John Fisher, the only Bishop during the English Reformation to refuse to take the Oath. More was even added to the Anglican calendar of Saints in 1980.

The Shoes of the Fisherman (1968)

Taken from Morris L. West's book of the same name, the story builds to the election of a Pope who was a prisoner behind the Iron Curtain. It opens in Siberia where Kiril Lakota (Anthony Quinn), a Metropolitan (an Eastern Rite Bishop) made a cardinal in secret by the now dead Pope, had spent 20 years as a political prisoner. He is taken to see the Russian premier Kamenev (Laurence Olivier), who tells him that the Chinese are threatening the Soviet Union with atomic war. Concerned about the future of the world, Kamenev is releasing him to go to Rome for the conclave, but he is to keep silent about his treatment in the Soviet Union.

The scene shifts to Rome affording great shots of the Colosseum and Saint Peter's Square where George Faber (David Janssen), an earnest network reporter, though much more restrained than today's crop, has been sent to televise live. Faber reveals many arcane things that follow the death of the Pope, such as the sealing of the Pope's apartment, the defacing of the former Pope's ring, the breaking of the papal seals, the various caskets, the nine days of masses and absolutions, and the Pope's lying in state. Faber comments that:

> when a president dies in office, his replacement is sworn in within hours. When a king dies, they say "The King is dead, Long Live the King." When a Pope dies, time is suspended. Atomic war may be on the horizon but in the Vatican, the only question is "Who will stand in the shoes of the fisherman?" and "Who will deliver Christ's message to a troubled world?" The cardinals are sealed in from the world, and two ballots are cast daily. If no Cardinal receives enough votes, they are burned with wet straw to produce black smoke. If successful, ballots are burned dry to produce white smoke. (Screenwriters: James Kennaway and John Patrick)

With great pomp, the Cardinals march into the consistory. The interplay of the Cardinals is interesting as they weigh personal and political considerations in the voting. Meanwhile large crowds wait in St. Peter's Square because, as Faber notes, the Pope speaks for Catholics who comprise one-fourth of the world. Finally, there are joyous tidings. "We have a Pope, Pope Cyril." Then he adds with apprehension, "They have elected a Russian. He is the first non-Italian Pope since Adrian VI 400 years ago." Half a million people crowd into St. Peter's Square for the ceremony, which Faber says "will be antique and obsolete to many; but to others, it will appear as a sign of continuity." The Pope gets a triple tiara crowning and makes brief remarks.

Noting that he had 11 brothers and sisters and that they lived in two rooms, the Pope pledges the wealth of the Church to help the poor. The Pope dresses in a black cassock and leaves the Vatican to get out to meet the people. He sings a Hebrew hymn over a dying Jewish patient and leads prayers, and then covers the man's eyes. He quotes Sholem Aleichem, "The dying is easy. It is the living that defeats." Determined to be a broker of peace, the Pope, dressed in civilian clothes, meets privately with Soviet and Chinese leaders (presumably what that sly Kamenev had hoped for), and the film moves slowly to its improbable conclusion.

Commentary

Like *The Cardinal*, this film is a relic of a time when pictures were overblown with overtures and intermissions. Still it is better than *The Cardinal*, although that's not saying much. The story is far-fetched, but it has an excellent cast going for it. Particularly good are Leo McKern (Cardinal Leone), Vittorio De Sica (Cardinal Rinaldi), and John Gielgud as the former Pope. Another plus is the narration by Janssen, who played "The Fugitive" on television. Since few knew the workings of the Vatican, the highlight of the film is his clear explanation of the selection process.

There are many subplots, the most important being the appointment by the Pope of a maverick priest, Father David Telemond (Oskar Werner), as his secretary even though the Pope admits that in their discussions, he finds little of the Christian faith as he knows it and that Telemond's ideas are full of errors and omissions. Telemond is thought to represent Jesuit philosopher Pierre Teilhard de Chardin, whose book *The Phenomenon of Man* was very influential in Catholic intellectual circles in the 1950s and 1960s and had a major effect on the deliberations of Vatican II. As informative as the film is, it suffers from a dour atmosphere mirroring the Siberian opening and the specter of atomic war. For example, the Pope is told, "You are in this chair until the day you die. The longer you live, the lonelier you will become. You are condemned to a solitary pilgrimage from the day of your election until the day of your death." That's about as cheerful as this film gets.

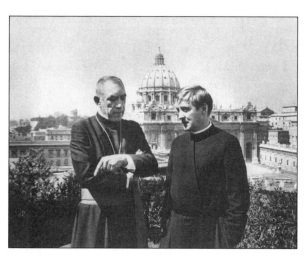

Figure 6.8. *The Shoes of a Fisherman.* **Pope Cyril (Anthony Quinn) talks with his maverick secretary Father Telemond (Oskar Werner) with St. Peter's in the background.**

Change of Habit (1969)

The film's opening credits show Sister Michelle (Mary Tyler Moore) and two other nuns deciding to leave the convent and donning civilian clothes to work in a free clinic in an impoverished neighborhood. Their reasoning for doing so was consistent with the feminist doctrine at the time, namely, "We've got to escape the old order, got to be accepted as women first, then as nuns." Having received permission from their Mother Superior Mother Joseph (Leora Dana), the credits show them buying new clothes, getting hairdos, wearing makeup, and getting outfitted before they venture out of the convent. However, they have been in the convent so long that they are clueless, and a policeman has to help them cross the street.

The film is filled with 1960s costumes, activism, and sing-alongs led by Doctor John Carpenter (Elvis Presley), who directs the ghetto clinic where they work. He is unaware that his new nurse is a nun, and of course they both fall in love. When he gets serious, she bolts for the convent along with the black nun Sister Irene Hawkins (Barbara McNair) who, as her name Irene connotes, finds peace there. Meanwhile Sister Barbara Bennett (Jane Elliott) leaves the order to become a community activist. Carpenter visits Sister Michelle to try to get her to leave the order. Sister Irene, recognizing that she is conflicted, recommends that they go to the neighborhood church in full habits for Sunday Mass. There they find Carpenter singing "Let Us Pray Together" in Las Vegas style with backup singers while Mass is going on—in seeming disconnect. Everybody's rocking to the new liturgy, except two old women who never liked the nuns. One says, "Give me the old ways when you could go to Mass and never think of a blessed thing." Meanwhile, Sister Michelle is alternately thinking of Doctor Carpenter, the crucifix, and the Blessed Virgin. The picture ends with the viewer wondering, "Will she or won't she?"

Commentary

Seeing this film is like opening a 1960s time capsule as it provides a convenient demarcation in Hollywood's treatment of the clergy and the liturgy. The title signals the change in nuns from somewhat distant figures in iconic habits to being indistinguishable from social workers. In this case, there is an added twist as they are also nurses who were simultaneously doffing nurse's uniforms and caps that designated the programs from which they graduated. In both cases, the use of ordinary work clothes may have had the liberating effect in that nurses and nuns no longer had to wear starched caps, wimples, or more confining and less comfortable garb. However, it came at the price of a loss of signs that often were both attractants to the nursing profession or vocation as nuns, and marks of distinction. One need only recall films where the cornettes (headwear) of the Daughters of Charity, who were both nuns and nurses, were visible in crowd scenes or films like *Vigil in the Night* where the nurse's distinctive uniform was an inducement to explore the profession. One nun put it well: "The habit makes us available, readily visible to ourselves and others in the choice we have made and are making each day. It's also a source of encouragement and strength to us . . . reminding us of the meaning of our life and our commitment to one another and to God."

The profound drop in the number of nuns beginning in the 1960s is noted in this chapter's introduction. Not only did women have more employment opportunities outside of secretarial or teaching positions, but there seemed no point in entering a convent when you looked the same and could do the same work as a social worker or a regular teacher without vows of poverty, chastity, and obedience. Indeed, many public school systems actively sought ex-nuns while others found jobs as nurses. In her excellent book *The Habit: A History of the Clothing of Catholic Nuns*, Elizabeth Kuhns chronicles the evolution of the habit and its falling out of favor associated with the decline in vocations. She also documents today's reversal of the sharp decline in vocations, especially in orders that have reinstated the distinctive habits and the discipline that had often been jettisoned with it.

Figure 6.9. *Change of Habit.* **Elvis Presley plays a doctor who falls in love with a nurse (Mary Tyler Moore) who turns out to be a nun sans habit.**

Short Subjects

The Devil's Eye (1960)

Like *Smiles of a Summer Night*, this film illustrates director Ingmar Bergman's lighter side while still grappling with moral issues. Based on an Irish proverb, "A woman's chastity is a sty in the devil's eye," it opens with a narrator bringing us to hell where the Devil (Stig Järrel) is holding a hand mirror and complaining of a sore eye. The source of his discomfort is a 20-year-old Swedish girl, Britt-Marie (Bibi Andersson), who is intelligent, lovely as a rose, about to be married, and still a virgin. The Devil worries that heaven will exult, that her friends may follow her lead, and that more happy and monogamous marriages will follow. After consulting with his advisors, he calls in Don Juan (Jarl Kulle), who has been tormented daily for 300 years by women coming to his bedroom and always being interrupted at the point of conquest. The Devil proposes that he be sent back to earth to seduce Britt-Marie before her wedding with the promise of getting 300 years off his sentence if he succeeds.

Along with Pablo his retainer (Sture Lagerwall), Don Juan crawls out of a well and is met by the girl's father, a hopelessly naïve vicar (Nils Poppe), who can't understand why his wife rejects him. The vicar invites Don Juan and Pablo to his home. The film unfolds in three acts whose events lead the Devil to conclude: "The heavenly powers have tricked us. Our evil has been worsted by their joy, their calculated goodness. I am weary and fed up. I think I'll retire. Heaven will have to manage without hell. That will teach Him up there a lesson. My profession irritates me. I'm getting old." Then he gets some news that brings a smile to his face, and his eye clears up. The narrator intones the moral, "A tiny victory in hell is often more fateful than a great success in heaven."

King of Kings (1961)

Director Nicholas Ray's talky remake of the silent classic tries to tell the whole story of Christ from birth to His Resurrection while giving a tutorial about the politics of Judea and Rome from 63 BC on. It also adds long subplots involving Barabbas (Harry Guardino), Judas (Rip Torn), and John the Baptist (Robert Ryan). The latter story gives the opportunity for a sultry dance by Salome (Brigid Bazlen) that many consider the high point of the film. The various scenes are held together by Orson Welles's narration. The musical score by Miklós Rózsa remains a favorite of classical music aficionados. Ray, who was an early devotee of Frank Lloyd Wright, creates a rather cold atmospheric setting with minimalist modernistic architecture and splashy color. One is not drawn into the film and thus, except for occasional set pieces, the totality is long, artificial, soporific, and inferior to the earlier silent version.

Nonetheless, there are some who consider Jeffrey Hunter, who plays Christ, with his piercing blue eyes to be the most handsome and compassionate Jesus on film. The critic Leonard Maltin called this life of Christ "intelligently told and beautifully filmed, full of deeply moving moments such as the Sermon on the Mount and Christ's healing of the lame." He concluded that it was "Not without flaws, but worthwhile; grandly filmed in widescreen." Most critics were less kind and were turned off by Hunter's appearance which, even though he was 33 at the time, his youthful appearance earned the film the nickname, "I was a Teenage Jesus," a play on the title of a cult film, *I was a Teenage Werewolf.*

The Hoodlum Priest (1961)

Father Clark (Don Murray), a teacher at a St. Louis Jesuit high school, spends more time helping his "parishioners" (burlesque dancers and hoodlums) than with his students. Questioned by his superiors, he says, "There are 3 million in college; 4 million in the armed forces, and 5 million in jails. Two-thirds of released inmates have no place to go, no jobs, and go back to prison." With $40,000 from a Jewish friend, Louis Rosen (Larry Gates), whose real name was Morris Shenker, he established a nonsectarian house, named after Dismas the Good Thief who was hanged with Christ. Its stated mission was that "friendless, homeless, powerless men could have lodging, food, clothes, and a helping hand until they got a job." Calling capital punishment "legalized murder," he fights for a convicted death row inmate (Keir Dullea) who was falsely accused of a crime and then foolishly pulled a robbery with a gun and killed somebody. Intertwined is the boy's far from believable love affair with a rich girl (Cindi Wood). The film portrays a gruesome picture of capital punishment and all ex-cons as good boys. In that their efforts spawned many similar houses across the United States, Clark's and Shenker's stories deserved better than this "Boys Town Revisited."

The Devil at 4 O'Clock (1961)

This film about a disillusioned priest and three convicts who are redeemed by their selflessness is so bad you can't take your eyes off it. Father Doonan

(Spencer Tracy) has labored for decades in a French-speaking leper colony near Tahiti. His replacement, Father Perreau (Kerwin Matthews), arrives with three convicts: Charlie (Bernie Hamilton), Marcel (Gregoire Aslan), and Harry (Frank Sinatra). When Harry points out that the priest drinks cognac and buys sex magazines, Doonan replies, "Whom did you expect to meet here, a Saint Damien?" referring to Damien the leper priest of Molokai. Of his buddy, the cynical good-hearted Doctor Wexler (Martin Brandt), Doonan says, "Scratch a doctor and you find an atheist" (shades of *The Keys of the Kingdom*, p. 79). Wexler says, "religion is for busybodies," but admits his admiration for Doonan with whom he once spent half the night "arguing the important questions: God, life, science."

The island's volcano acts up, and Harry, previously a paratrooper in Korea, helps lead the children to the mainland. Charlie is severely injured saving a child. He asks Doonan, "Don't you ever give up?" The reply is "Sure we do. Priests fail. I stopped speaking to God a long time ago, but you, Marcel, and Harry gave it back to me." Charlie says that he didn't buy religion. Doonan says, "A lot of people don't buy it. It's never too late to change. Another thief (Dismas) once died on the cross next to Christ. He didn't chicken out. He just got smart at the last moment and stole heaven." He then says a prayer over the dying Charlie and an act of contrition. The volcano erupts, and the remaining principals are killed, while the children and Father Perreau escape to safety.

Satan Never Sleeps (1962)

Noted director Leo McCarey tried unsuccessfully to recapture the magic of *Going My Way* in this, his last film, set in Southeast China in 1947 when the Red Army closed all the Christian missions. William Holden is terribly miscast as Father O'Banion, who saves a young woman, Siu Lan (France Nguyen). By Chinese tradition she now belongs to him, so she constantly follows him mooning and trying to get him to renounce his vows. Clifton Webb plays his crotchety superior Father Bovard, who is prevented from leaving China by his former altar boy, Ho San (Weaver Lee), now a ruthless Communist colonel. After raping Siu Lan and ransacking the church, Ho San stands by while his devout parents are shot as they try to restore the crucifix to its place on the altar. The priests refuse to sign a confession that they misled the people and are tortured. Ho San reconverts and tries to save Siu Lan, their baby, and the priests. It's too bad the film is so lame because the issue of religious repression in China under the Communists is as relevant today as it was four decades ago.

The Agony and the Ecstasy (1965)

Based on Irving Stone's popular novel of the same name, this overlong and talky film begins with a short but good documentary-like history lesson about Michelangelo from his birth in Caprese to his stays in Florence and Rome. In one particularly good scene Michelangelo (Charlton Heston) explains to Bramante, the architect of St. Peter's Basilica, how God set Moses in the marble for him, the artist, to let loose. Pope Julius II (Rex Harrison) commissions Michelangelo to paint the Sistine Chapel, named for his uncle Pope Sixtus. Then Julius is off to war, saying, "I will remain at war until I recover the Papal States for the Church. I will use art as I do the sword for the glory of the Church." He is shown armed for battle leading his army, but the film does not give much background on this battle for Bologna in Romagna.

About the Pope, Michelangelo says, "He gives me work. I give him monuments. Both our ambitions are satisfied." Much of the film is devoted to their bickering about the plan for the ceiling and how long it is taking. The Pope asks, "When will this be finished?" Michelangelo answers, "When I'm finished!" The love-hate relationship is illustrated when the Pope makes comments like "I planned a ceiling and he planned a miracle" and then sending in Cardinals critical of naked bodies to evaluate the ceiling. When he does, Michelangelo asks, "Why do you bring fools in to judge my work?" At the end, the Pope says: "What you have painted there is not a portrait of God but a proof of faith. You are an artist. I am merely a Pope." Alleluia resounds as the camera pans the magnificent ceiling. The greatest asset of the movie is the cinematography.

The Singing Nun (1966)

This saccharine and pretty much unwatchable film purports to tell the story of a Belgian nun, Sister Luc-Gabrielle. Promoted as Soeur Sourire (Sister Smile) by Phillips records, she recorded "Dominique," a French song about Saint Dominic's love for God and his fight against the Albigensian heresy. The song, which became a worldwide sensation in 1963, is the best part of the film, which squanders the talents of Debbie Reynolds (called Sister Ann), Ricardo Montalban as a priest, and Greer Garson and Agnes Moorehead as nuns. Sister Ann rides around Ghent on a scooter and dedicates her life to helping troubled children. Her singing voice is discovered, and she makes a hit record and appears on *The Ed Sullivan Show* (true). Fame brings conflict with her vocation and rekindles a romance with a young man (Chad Everett) whom she knew before entering the convent (not true). She remains faithful to her vocation and leaves to be a missionary in Africa (not true). This is a case where the real story, some of which was unfolding as the film was being made, is much more interesting—in a sad way—than the movie version. Sister Luc had a female partner and left the convent to live with her in 1965, and the record label dropped her. She left the Church and after financial reverses, she and her partner committed suicide in 1985.

The Trouble with Angels (1966)

Based on a novel of the same name, this film is a juvenile pastiche of hoary clichés about a Catholic girls' boarding school, which the rebellious Mary (Hayley Mills) declares to be "positively medieval; all that's missing is the dragon." She gives the Mother Superior (Rosalind Russell) a "Heil Hitler" salute behind her back and says, "The only thing different between this place and a girls' reformatory is the tuition and that we were enrolled, not committed." She and her friend Rachel (June Harding) smoke in the bathroom setting off the fire alarm, break into the off-limits cloister, put bubble bath in the sugar bowls, and iron a girl's hair, all of which endears her to Mother Superior who says that "Mary has a will of iron. She will bend but not break, yield but not capitulate."

A teacher of manners and charm played by stripper Gypsy Rose Lee is brought in to teach the girls how to walk and dance. Although the nuns seem dotty and simple-minded, they are good-hearted; for instance, Sister Ursula hid 34 Jewish children in the cellar of a convent. When she was found out, "she was imprisoned and submitted to many indignities." Another nun tells Mary that she wants to go to a leper colony. At the Christmas pageant for elderly women, Mary watches as Mother Superior rocks an old woman in her arms and tells her to be happy. When a much-loved nun's heart gives out, the very reverential handling of the religious observance and the wake also shows Mother Superior's softer side. On graduation day, the girls are all dressed up in gowns with bouquets. Mother Superior reads the names of the girls who have decided to enter the convent, which includes Mary. Rachel calls Mary a traitor and says she was brainwashed. Mary says that she didn't yield, but chose. They hug, and Rachel says, "You'll make some crazy nun." The picture did well enough to spawn a lame 1968 sequel, *Where Angels Go, Trouble Follows* starring Rosalind Russell and Stella Stevens. Even more anachronistic, given the tenor of the times, it did not find an audience.

Guess Who's Coming to Dinner (1967)

This film is about a supremely overqualified black doctor, John Prentice (Sidney Poitier), unaccountably wanting to marry Joey (Katharine Houghton), the young ditzy daughter of a white San Francisco newspaper editor named Matt Drayton (Spencer Tracy). Drayton wants nothing of it and tries to dig up reasons to block the marriage. Though non-Catholic, Drayton's best friend and golfing partner is Monsignor Ryan (Cecil Kellaway), who adds comedy to the movie as he gently tweaks his liberal friend about practicing what he preaches. Ryan also adds lightness to the movie as he joins Drayton's wife Christina (Katharine Hepburn) and Prentice's mother (Beah Richards), who try to persuade Drayton and Prentice's father (Roy E. Glenn, Sr.) to recognize the couple's love and to sanction the marriage. The Monsignor represents the last entirely sympathetic and unalloyed paean to Irish priests by Hollywood.

BACKSTORY

Capturing Atmosphere and Conveying Seriousness in Black-and-White

Just as Theodor Carl Dreyer eschewed the use of sound after the silent era in filming his masterpiece *The Passion of Joan of Arc*, many directors chose to film certain movies in black-and-white (even long after excellent color processes had been perfected) to convey a feel and, in some cases, a seriousness of purpose. The most obvious examples are the "film noir" movies of the 1940s and such classics as *Casablanca*, *The Third Man*, and *Citizen Kane*. It's hard to imagine that Woody Allen's *Manhattan* or *To Kill a Mockingbird* would have been so evocative in color, and the same can be said for many of the films included in this book, such as *It's a Wonderful Life*, *Lilies of the Field*, *On the Waterfront*, *The Seventh Seal*, *Inherit the Wind*, and *Viridiana*, as well as *Schindler's List*, where Spielberg uses a dash of "blood red" to great effect in a few brief scenes.

The most flagrant example of the invidious effect of color in selected cases is *It's a Wonderful Life*, which came off patent and into the public domain in the 1970s. Not only was it crudely cut for television, but a colorized version was made. Jimmy Stewart, who played the common man in *Mr. Smith Goes to Washington*, felt so strongly about the liberty taken in transforming the film that he testified before Congress to have the colorized version withdrawn. Unfortunately, this is one case where "Mr. Smith" did not prevail.

CHAPTER SEVEN
THE FLOWER CHILDREN'S HOUR: THE 1970s

Like the 1960s, sociologically the 1970s don't conform to a neat bracketing of the years 1970 to 1979. Whereas the first part of the sixties had been a continuation of the fifties, the first part of the seventies was a continuation of the turbulent sixties. Those in power were considered to be the enemy. "Do your own thing" and "Don't trust anyone over thirty" were the rallying cries. The younger generation, the post–World War II "Baby Boomers," many of whom had known nothing but peace and prosperity and now were subject to the draft, were consumed with opposition to the Vietnam War. The mantra "Hell No, We Won't Go" was chanted in angry demonstrations against President Lyndon Johnson and then President Richard Nixon. The peaceable demonstrations of the Civil Rights Movement of the mid-1950s through the mid-1960s were replaced by riots, angry confrontations, and occupations of academic and other institutions.

President Nixon was driven from office in 1974 for trying to cover up the break-in at the Democratic Party office at the Watergate. His pardon by President Gerald Ford as a gesture of national healing turned out to be very unpopular. The rest of the decade featured the sad aftermath of the United States withdrawal from Vietnam with the massacre of millions by the Pol Pot regime in the Cambodian killing fields, as well as the boat people trying to escape the savage recriminations of the Communists in South Vietnam. The presidency of Jimmy Carter, who succeeded Ford, ended on a down note with the failed mission to rescue American hostages, a gasoline shortage, stagflation, and what Carter described as a national "malaise."

Labeled the "Me" decade by journalist Tom Wolfe in *New York* Magazine in 1976, this period in American history has become strongly identified with attitudes of self-absorption and self-fulfillment. Concern for individual autonomy trumped concern for community. After the ending of the unpopular Vietnam War, the "Boomers," having partaken of the pleasures of "sex, drugs, and rock-and-roll," began establishing careers and starting families, some with "open marriages" as captured in the 1969 film *Bob & Carol &*

Ted & Alice. This narcissistic decade is often characterized and lampooned by the clothing styles of the time, including polyester, leisure suits, platform shoes, hot pants, bell-bottom trousers (for both men and women), and other garish—and self-conscious—fashions that were satirized in John Waters's film *Polyester* and rendered iconic by John Travolta in *Saturday Night Fever.*

The 1970s was also the decade in which the United States Supreme Court, in the famous 1973 *Roe v Wade* decision, made abortion a constitutional right and therefore legal under federal law, overturning state laws. At the time, even liberals, like Harvard professor Alan Dershowitz, a supporter of legalized abortion, found the decision's constitutional rationale (based, in large part, on the right to privacy) flawed. To this day, *Roe v. Wade* remains in effect, and the war between those in favor of legalized abortion, called "pro-choice," and their pro-life opponents continues to be played out in various media, including film.

In the 1970s, post-Vatican II Catholicism underwent a sea change, as did other conventional Protestant religions. People who had once turned to their minister or priest for moral guidance, sought refuge in psychiatry, Eastern religions, gurus, or drugs. Divorce, abortion, adultery, living together outside of marriage, and out-of-wedlock births—all things that up to a decade before had been considered shameful—were now "acceptable" to many and even preferable, leading psychiatric pioneer Karl Menninger of the Menninger Brothers Foundation to write his book *Whatever Became of Sin?*

Films of the Seventies

The films of the early 1970s were a continuation of the films released in the last few years of the 1960s with the advent of a number of innovative younger directors (dubbed "Movie Brats" by some and "auteurs" by others) joining already established directors: Martin Scorsese, Steven Spielberg, George Lucas, Brian DePalma, Alan Pakula, Robert Altman, Francis Ford Coppola, William Friedkin, Woody Allen, Peter Bogdonavich, George Roy Hill, and Paul Mazursky. As a result, many memorable films were made: *Five Easy Pieces, The Last Picture Show, The French Connection, The Godfather, American Graffiti, Jaws, Star Wars, Rocky, Patton, Chinatown, The Sting, Network, The Day of the Jackal, One Flew over the Cuckoo's Nest, Taxi Driver, Kramer vs. Kramer, Annie Hall, Manhattan,* and *Dirty Harry.* With directors being given a freer hand after the removal of the Hays Code restrictions, many of the films were countercultural and very violent, such as *Mean Streets*, *A Clockwork Orange,* and *Apocalypse Now.*

Christian Themes in the "Me" Decade Films

Very few films with Christian themes were produced during the 1970s, which is why this is the shortest chapter in the book. In those that were, the lifting of the Hays Code's prohibition against casting religion in an unfavorable light allowed filmmakers to go as far as they wished in satirizing the Last Supper and portraying Jesus Christ and John the Baptist in modern dress. This chapter begins with one of the most anti-institutional films ever made, *M*A*S*H*.* Directed by Robert Altman, himself disaffected by both his Jesuit schooling and his Army service, the film ridiculed both the military and Christianity, especially in the famous scene parodying the Last Supper. That same spirit of ridicule may be found, although in a much less vitriolic way, at the end of the decade in *Monty Python's Life of Brian* and in the crude Burt Reynolds flick *The End.* Jacques Barzun, in *From Dawn to Decadence* (2000), called "irreverence" the spirit of this era and said it was "the monopoly of the clever and the bold. They saw through everything and spoke out with an amused smile. Their skill was always mentioned in obituaries and in articles introducing those freshly in the news. It was rarely noticed that when nothing is revered, irreverence ceases to indicate critical thought."

Other Christian-themed films offered adolescent takes on Bible stories that said more about the young adults of the 1970s than they did about Christian philosophy. They were best characterized by two films that portrayed flower children following a singing and dancing Christ in *Jesus Christ Superstar* and *Godspell,* as well as Franco Zeffirelli's *Brother Sun, Sister Moon,* in which Saint Francis and his followers are transmogrified into "hippies" and the dialogue is clearly aimed at the Vietnam War. By contrast, what many, including myself, believe is the best portrayal of Jesus Christ's life was not a feature film but a television miniseries, Franco Zeffirelli's *Jesus of Nazareth.* Ironically, one of the best Christian-themed films of the period was *The Exorcist,* a movie that was written off by many at the time as simply a horror film, but in fact it displays a religious depth that can now be best appreciated in the DVD of the director's cut, featuring additional footage and an excellent commentary by director William Friedkin. Another film that stood out is *In This House of Brede,* which stars Diana Rigg as a Benedictine nun.

M*A*S*H (1970)

*M*A*S*H*, an acronym for "Mobile Army Surgical Hospital," has no central plot; instead it consists of a collection of loosely linked vignettes. Episodically throughout the film, helicopters bring wounded soldiers into the MASH unit, leading to frantic operating room scenes full of blood, gore, and sawed-off limbs. The main focus is on two hotshot surgeons, Hawkeye Pierce (Donald Sutherland) and Trapper John McIntyre (Elliot Gould), whose main preoccupations, when they are not cutting, are womanizing, consuming alcohol, and tormenting Major Frank Burns (Robert Duvall), a self-righteous, pharisaic fraud. Burns, an incompetent doctor, is supposedly a happily married man but is having an affair with the head nurse, Major "Hot Lips" Houlihan (Sally Kellerman). Other important characters include an inept but presumably well-meaning commanding officer, Colonel Henry Blake (Roger Bowen); Radar O'Reilly (Gary Burghoff), the Colonel's aide; and Captain Duke Forrest (Tom Skerritt), a redneck surgeon cut from the same cloth as Hawkeye and Trapper John, who resents the recruiting of Oliver Harmon (Spearchucker) Jones (ex-NFL star Fred "the Hammer" Williamson), a black neurosurgeon to help the unit win a football game.

The film is celebrated for several comic scenes. Perhaps the most famous involves Hawkeye and Trapper John arranging to broadcast Frank Burns and Hot Lips having sex over the camp loudspeaker so that all can hear, ultimately causing Frank to be taken away in a straitjacket. After Frank is gone, the two pranksters continue to torture Hot Lips, exposing her as she is taking a shower in an effort to determine if she is a "natural" blonde.

The unit's priest Father Mulcahy, known as "Dago Red" (Rene Auberjonois), a simple-minded pious ninny, breaks the secret of the Confessional and reveals that one of his "flock," the dentist Captain Walter Waldowski (John Schuck), known as Painless Pole, has "confessed" that he is impotent. Reputed to have "the biggest equipment in the U.S. army," Painless decides to commit suicide. Hawkeye plans a "Last Supper" for Painless before his suicide, a scene that satirizes Leonard DaVinci's famous painting of "The Last Supper," positioning Painless at the center in Christ's seat. Dago Red hears Painless's final Confession and gives him absolution in advance of his "suicide." Then, Painless is wrapped and put on a gurney and given something to drink (presumably poison) while the film's theme "Suicide is Painless" is played in the background. Then, a beautiful lieutenant, known as

"Dish" (Jo Ann Pflug), comes to give him the "treatment," which "miraculously" restores his potency.

Commentary

M*A*S*H was one of the most popular films of the 1970s, in large part because it was released at a moment in history when "anti-institutionalism" was the name of the game. *M*A*S*H* not only ridicules the nobility of war and the military, but, especially with its famous "Last Supper" scene, skewers Christian doctrine as well. It is for this reason that I've included it in this book. *M*A*S*H*, despite its qualities as a work of art, was one of the first post–Hays Code films to seriously mock Christian principles and ethics, marking a sea change in how religious topics were presented in film.

Based on a novel by Korean War doctor H. Richard Hornberger and sportswriter Bill Heinz, who jointly used the pseudonym Richard Hooker, *M*A*S*H* was Altman's second Hollywood feature film and his most commercially successful. Altman brought a fresh and unique style of direction to the film—a style that is fast-moving and episodic, with overlapping of dialogue and action. The outlandish sex scenes and practical jokes were unfamiliar to audiences used to movies made before the jettisoning of the Hays Code in 1967. Because of its timeliness, humor, and creativity, the film garnered almost unanimous critical praise. It won the Grand Prix at the 1970 Cannes Film Festival and was nominated for five Academy Awards with Ring Lardner, Jr., who had been blacklisted as a member of the Hollywood 10 during the 1940s, winning for Best Adapted Screenplay. Interestingly, the Oscar for Best Picture that year was awarded to *Patton*, a more traditional and accurate portrayal of the military, which has retained its power with the passing of time.

I must admit that the film was a favorite of mine when it first came out, but on reviewing it three decades later, it seemed to me to be a distillate of angry, sadistic, and anti-institutional humor. As a doctor, I saw no sense of the patients as persons, nor are they ever followed out of the operating room except to die. They are simply raw meat and that's the point, to convey the horrors of war and the stupidity of the military at a time when many of us were protesting at being misled by our leaders about the Vietnam War. It's meant to be cruel and angry, emotions that were perfectly conveyed by those masters of cinematic cynicism, Sutherland and Gould.

As a Christian, I saw many highly disrespectful jabs at clergymen and the most profound elements of Catholic dogma, particularly Confession and the Eucharistic feast/Last Supper. The sole doctor who professes to be religious, Major Frank Burns, is an incompetent, mean-spirited hypocrite. The priest, irreverently named Dago Red, is a nebbish who breaks faith by revealing the secret of the dentist's confession and dithers over whether to give absolution to him in advance of his suicide. Altman's profound dislike of the Catholic Church and the military comes out forcefully in this film (see p. 196).

So, why does it not strike me in the same way as it did in 1970? Clearly, I have changed; I was younger and given the prevailing cultural influences of the 1960s, I found the satire very funny. But probably more importantly, the context for the film has changed. In 1970, the film which was set in the Korean War, provided a lightning rod for all the pent-up rage and iconoclasm engendered by opposition to the Vietnam War, the assassinations of the Kennedys and Martin Luther King, Jr., and the Civil Rights Movement. Without that context and having seen the price American society paid for the prevailing "sex, drugs, and rock and roll" and anti-institutional culture that the film celebrated, it now seems as bereft of a welcoming port as the proverbial Flying Dutchman.

I am not alone in my judgment, as I discovered in the 2006 anthology of outstanding film reviews *American Movie Critics* edited by Phillip Lopate. Richard Corliss, *Time* magazine's film critic wrote of *M*A*S*H*: "As the vehicle of Ring Lardner's return to the top of his profession—and as a film that received almost unanimous critical praise—*M*A*S*H** deserves two viewings, or none. At first sight, this comedy about a group of medics just behind the lines in Korea may seem cruel but very funny. The second time *M*A*S*H** seems funny but very cruel. Granted that the surprise of a joke is part of its appeal; but *M*A*S*H** has, in its writing and direction, a style so relaxed and assured that it isn't lost on second viewing. What does become obvious is that this smooth style disguises a bludgeon, which the main characters in the film employ on anyone who disagrees with them."

Interestingly, the television series started by mimicking the film's acerbic tenor and was almost canceled until the cast was transformed by softening and humanizing Hawkeye while playing down his womanizing. The patients' stories were put front and center such that Alan Alda, who played Hawkeye, was invited to give the commencement speech at Columbia University Medical School. Trapper John and Colonel Blake were replaced by two officers who were faithful to their wives. In addition, the antireligious

Figure 7.1. *M*A*S*H*. The parody of the Last Supper.

messages were dropped. Dago Red was replaced by Father Mulcahy, a priest who cares for orphans and who, while naïve, is never ridiculed. Radar's role was expanded and a cross-dressing Max Klinger (Jamie Farr), eager to be discharged, was added. As a result, the much-loved ensemble series lasted for twelve seasons and is continually shown in reruns throughout the world.

The Godfather (1972)

The Godfather, based on the novel by Mario Puzo, opens at a festive Italian wedding where the five Mafia families gather to celebrate the wedding of Connie (Talia Shire), the daughter of Godfather Don Vito Corleone (Marlon Brando). It's quite authentic, showing the *poste* (the bag the bride holds at the reception to collect gifts, in this case thousands of dollars, a fortune in those days). There's Mama Corleone (Morgana King) leading the tarantella, a grandfather dancing with his granddaughter standing on his shoes, and someone at the buffet table throwing a sandwich to his friend in the back of the crowd, the reason these receptions were sometimes called "football weddings." Finally, there's an added Hollywood touch I must have missed growing up—when the Don's hothead son Sonny (James Caan) excuses himself from his wife for a little tryst with a bridesmaid while the women discuss his "manhood." Meanwhile the Don holds court as petitioners, including his godson Johnny Fontane (singer Al Martino), beg favors after kissing his hand saying "baciamo la mano" to show respect. In one case, he chastises an undertaker who went to the police rather than the Don when his daughter was raped and did not receive satisfaction. The Don takes on his case in the spirit of his daughter's wedding, saying he may ask him for a return favor some day, which he does.

Brando is marvelous as the Don, who makes offers people can't refuse. One is to a movie director who obstinately refuses to give a plum part to Fontane who "ruined" one of his favored starlets and wakes up to find the head of his prize stallion in his bed. The Don's son Michael (Al Pacino) is a returning war hero whom the Don hopes will go straight and become a United States senator. As a sign of his break with the past, Michael attends the wedding with his WASP girlfriend Kay (Diane Keaton). One of the rival gangs almost kills the Don who had refused, against the advice of his "consigliere" (Robert Duvall), to use his political and judicial connections to help the other families move into the lucrative narcotics trade. The Don considers this to be evil, unlike gambling, prostitution, and bootlegging, but the other families say it's okay if it's restricted to the black and Hispanic communities.

As a result of the attempted assassination, Michael feels compelled to join the family business as he is the only one who is a "civilian" and wouldn't be suspected at a "peace" meeting where he can exact retribution on the would-be assassins. After he kills their enemies, Michael is hustled to Sicily (which allows the film to introduce lovely scenery), an "Old World" chaperoned romance with Apollonia Vitelli (Simonetta Steffanelli) and another Italian wedding before another hit occurs, and Michael's bride is killed. After the hotheaded Sonny, who has taken over as Don, is set up and killed, his now recovered father brokers a peace deal with the other families. Michael returns to America and takes over the family's "olive oil business" when the Don dies of a heart attack after a wonderfully playful scene with his grandson in a garden. Michael cements his position as the new Don by engineering the killing of his adversaries while he stands as godfather for his nephew at Baptism, after which his trusted lieutenant Clemenza (Richard Castellano) garrots the child's father who had set up Sonny.

Commentary

The film is about family loyalty and meting out justice according to its rules; as the participants say, "it's not personal, it's business." The film captured the public imagination with its signature line "I'll make him an offer he can't refuse" that remains widely used. There is no question that the film is a masterpiece, ranking second behind *Citizen Kane* on the AFI top 100 Greatest Films. It garnered three Oscars (Best Picture, Actor, and Adapted Screenplay) and deserved more, being nominated for Best Director, Music, Sound, Film Editing, and Costume Design as well as receiving three nominations for Best Supporting Actor (Caan, Duvall, and Pacino). The threesome split the vote, which probably allowed Joel Grey to win for *Cabaret*.

While extraordinary, it is also troubling, beginning with its cold-blooded violence. There are about 30 killings by people who are otherwise portrayed as sympathetic figures. As Mario Puzo said in an interview, "this is a novel about family not about crime. I made them all to be good guys except they committed murder once in a while." Disturbingly, as Coppola stated in a video extra, the decapitation of the stallion engendered more complaints than the many ruthless shootings and garrotings. Another troubling factor is the ethnic stereotyping. Italian-Americans had been portrayed in films through the 1930s as knife-wielding, wine-drinking, babymakers. Given that they accounted for the highest ethnic representation in servicemen during World War II, prejudice such as occurred at Ivy League and other elite schools (like Columbia medical school where I graduated) began to be acknowledged and to dissipate during the late 1950s and early 1960s. This film was so compelling that it not only spawned sequels but also many more well-crafted films like *Goodfellas* and television programs like *The Sopranos*, which was the highest-rated HBO show into the new millennium. Not surprisingly in a recent survey, 75 percent of respondents said that the first thing that came to mind when asked about Italian-Americans was the Mafia, and the second was "pasta." It's worth noting, however, that these negative stereotypes were created or fostered by Italian-Americans themselves, specifically Mario Puzo, Francis Ford Coppola, Martin Scorsese, David Chase, Al Pacino, Robert DeNiro, Joe Pesci, and others.

As for the portrayal of Christians, *The Godfather* is relatively straightforward. The Corleones follow what admittedly some Catholics do, that is, a disconnect between their ostentatious celebration of religious rituals and their daily life. The negative allusions are few in this picture and its successor but would dominate the last one in the series. Nonetheless, one of the most powerful scenes is the Baptism scene at the end when Michael is renouncing Satan on behalf of his newborn godson while the camera flashes to the killings that he has ordered. This technique of interweaving ritual Catholicism and murder continues in the other films.

The Godfather Part II (1974)

Both a prequel and a sequel, this film begins in 1959 a few years after Michael and the family have moved to a new compound in Lake Tahoe to consolidate its Nevada gambling empire. Like its predecessor, this film opens with a party, this time celebrating Michael's son Anthony at his First Communion. At the party Michael (Al Pacino) receives visitors requesting favors as his father did at Connie's wedding reception. This includes a corrupt Nevada United States senator, Pat Geary (G. D. Spradlin), who despises Italians and vows to terminate dealings with Michael (an ironic reminder that Don Vito wanted Michael to go "straight" and become a senator).

The film then flashes back to 1901 and the town of Corleone in Sicily and the assassination of Vito's father by Don Ciccio (Giuseppe Sillato) for a presumed slight. To make sure there is no reprisal, the Don kills Vito's brother and his mother, but Vito escapes to America, landing at Ellis Island where his name is changed from Andolini to Corleone. The scene shifts to 1917, showing Vito (Robert De Niro) as a young married man with three children. He is working hard and skimming money on the side without paying the requisite protection to the head of the Black Hand (as the Mafia was then called). When the ostentatious Don Fanucci (Gastone Moschin) threatens Vito and his friends, Vito offers to take care of the situation. During the Feast of Saint Rocco, Vito stalks the Don and

Figure 7.2. *The Godfather Part II*. Saint Rocco's statue is paraded through Little Italy while Vito Corleone stalks and then murders the local Mafia Don.

brutally murders him. Later in a flashback to 1925, he is shown as the respected Don meting out his brand of "justice" and "protection" from his olive oil company.

The film returns to 1959 where Michael is almost assassinated in his own compound on orders of his would-be partner in Miami, Hyman Roth (Lee Strasberg), after being set up by his brother Fredo (John Cazale). Michael feigns lack of knowledge of the perpetrator when he travels to Havana to meet Roth, presumably to consummate a deal to take over the gambling casinos there. Instead he orchestrates Roth's assassination and escapes just as Fidel Castro is taking over. Roth survives and gets one of Michael's pals, Frankie Pantangeli (Michael V. Gazzo), to spill his guts to the Kefauver Commission on organized crime. Michael perjures himself and is saved by bringing over Frankie's brother from Sicily to make sure that Frankie obeys the rule of omerta (silence). Senator Geary, whom Michael has saved from his involvement in the sadomasochistic death of a prostitute, gives an impassioned defense of Italian-Americans before leaving the hearing. The film ends with Michael's marriage having dissolved and his getting rid of his enemies, including Fredo, whose murder he only permits after their mother has died. Michael is left brooding alone at Lake Tahoe with brief reflections of his enlisting in the Marines the day after Pearl Harbor when his future seemed so different.

Commentary

The screenplay for this long and confusing film, which cuts back and forth to Nevada, Sicily, New York, Los Angeles, Washington, D.C., Miami, and Cuba, was mainly the handiwork of Coppola rather than Puzo, whose mastery as a storyteller and his authentic knowledge of the Italian-American community, permeated the first film. Coppola tried to substitute a lot of Italian dialogue, even in the American scenes, which come off as Italian dialect poorly mouthed by nonnative speakers such as Bruno Kirby as the young Clemenza. As Coppola notes in the video extras, the early reviewers panned it, but along the way, it began to get better reviews with some saying that it defied the truism that sequels are never as good as the original. Indeed, some thought it better than the first. Put me firmly in the first group of reviewers.

How then to explain the fact that it was awarded six Oscars including Best Picture, Best Supporting Actor (De Niro), Best Art and Set Direction,

Best Music, and Best Screenplay as well as five more nominations Best Actor (Pacino), Best Supporting Actors (Strasberg and Gazzo), Best Supporting Actress (Shire), and Best Costume Design? My answer is that it's like a referee making up for a bad call which the Motion Picture Academy is wont to do when it messed up the first time, especially when it involves people they like. An oft-cited example is giving Elizabeth Taylor a Best Actress Oscar for *Butterfield 8* in 1960 instead of for *Suddenly Last Summer* in 1959 or *Cat on a Hot Tin Roof* in 1958 in which she was far more deserving. *The Godfather* became a legend in the intervening two years; so, to my mind, they made up for it in the awards for a film that even its supporters called bloated, unfocused, and tedious for long stretches.

As for the Christian scenes, there are few, but Coppola again intercuts the murders with Catholic rituals as when the young Vito's stalking of Don Fanucci parallels the procession of the statue of Saint Rocco loaded with money and people kissing the relic during the August 16th feast. This point-counterpoint approach paradoxically both heightens and softens the effects of the ruthless murders on the viewers. There is also a scene where Fredo teaches his young nephew Anthony how to fish and recounts how he went fishing with his father and other relatives and was the only one to catch any fish. His secret was that he said a Hail Mary before each casting of the line. Coppola said that this was based on his own life. Later Fredo is ready to take Anthony fishing, but Michael calls his son back because it's time to pay back Fredo for his disloyalty. Fredo tells Anthony as he leaves the dock that he will use the trick to catch him a fish and later as Fredo says the Hail Mary, he is assassinated. Finally, Father Carmelo, who presided over the First Communion was a real priest, Father Joseph Medaglia, who also presided over the Baptism at the end of *The Godfather*.

The Exorcist (1973)

After a brief view of a tony Georgetown party to set the scene, the film then cuts to Mosul, Iraq, in 1972 to set up the underlying mythology. Father Merrin (Max von Sydow), a Jesuit priest who is both an archeologist and an exorcist, is excavating near the walls of Nineveh across from where Nebuchednezzar ruled. He becomes aware of the demon Pazuzu, who reputedly unleashed the dogs of war and chaos setting up the clash of good and evil. The story returns to Georgetown where Regan MacNeil (Linda Blair) lives with her mother Chris (Ellen Burstyn), a Hollywood actress who is making a movie about the student riots. She meets Father Karras (Jason Miller), a Jesuit priest and counselor who trained at Harvard, Bellevue, and Johns Hopkins. Karras is disillusioned with God and his calling, ostensibly because of the suffering around him; yet he refuses to give money to a homeless man who begs for his help and only infrequently visits his mother who lives alone in New York pining for his visits. When his mother is admitted to Bellevue, Karras laments that he could have helped her if he had become a psychiatrist instead of a priest. At this point, the movie's tone changes as a strong wind blows across Georgetown.

Regan shows a Captain Howdy doll to her mother, not knowing that Pazuzu is hiding in the doll. Regan slowly becomes possessed after she hears her mother curse her estranged father who refuses to come from Los Angeles for the child's birthday. When Regan spouts obscenities, Chris thinks it's her fault. Pazuzu causes Regan to shake the bed violently, crawl downstairs like a dog, and vomit profusely. After undergoing many invasive medical tests and an intense psychiatric evaluation, Regan is given Ritalin without success. Finally, a psychiatrist hypnotizes her and reveals that someone has taken possession of her. After the demon engineers the death of the movie director who, Regan fears, is becoming her mother's lover, everyone is convinced that Regan is possessed by the devil.

Father Merrin is called back from Iraq and asks Father Karras, the counselor, whose life is spiraling out of control into depression, to assist him. They confront the demon armed only with a bottle of Holy Water, a small crucifix, the Roman exorcism ritual, and their own belief in the ability to face down the devil. The battle with the demon inhabiting the possessed girl and the two priests is stunning, and in the end the priests perish but the child is reclaimed.

Commentary

The Exorcist grossed over $400 million worldwide. It won Oscars for Best Screenplay and Sound (particularly for the voicing of the devil by actress Mercedes McCambridge) and received eight other nominations for Best Picture, Director, Actress, Supporting Actor, Supporting Actress, Cinematography, Art Direction, and Film Editing. I did not see it when it first came out because of my busy schedule as a doctor and father (as well as the hype about it being a horror-and-special-effects movie, neither genre being a favorite of mine). I'm glad I waited 32 years to see the director's cut with

10 minutes added as well as the commentary track by the director, William Friedkin. I came away impressed by Friedkin's inherent understanding of what he refers to as "the constant struggle within all of us, minute by minute between good and evil, a struggle going on in humanity from the beginning of time." He started the film in a very idyllic way to set up the question "What did this girl or her family do to warrant the invasion of her mind and body by the devil?" The answer, of course, is "nothing." The only response to this invasion is that the power of Christ must "compel the demon to leave, otherwise he will prevail."

When asked by Brian Kellow about movie critic Pauline Kael's contention that the film was "the biggest recruiting poster the Catholic Church had had since the sunnier days of *Going My Way* and *The Bells of Saint Mary's*," Friedkin, a non-Catholic, called it "wrong-headed" at the time. Later, however, he allowed that he knew "many people who went into the priesthood because of that." He went on to recount a story about Jimmy Cagney telling him, "Young man, I've got a bone to pick with you. I had a barber for twenty years, and he saw the movie and he left being a barber to enter the priesthood." All Friedkin could say was "I'm sorry, sir," and that it was unintended.

The film is based on a novel by William Peter Blatty, which in turn was based on a true story of a normal 14-year-old boy in Mount Rainier, Maryland, who was possessed and underwent exorcism. The last surviving Jesuit

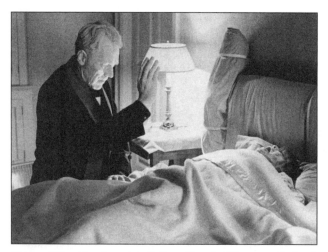

Figure 7.3. *The Exorcist*. Father Merrin (Max von Sydow) blesses Regan (Linda Blair) as he attempts to exorcise her demon.

priest who was present at the exorcism in 1949, Father Walter H. Halloran, died March 4, 2005. The exorcism was performed at a St. Louis Hospital by Jesuits at St. Louis University with the approval of Cardinal Lawrence Ritter of St. Louis. Halloran was assigned to hold down the boy, whose pseudonym was "Douglas Deen," while Father William Bowdern performed the exorcism with the assistance of Father William van Roo. Father Halloran told the *Catholic News Service* that he observed streaks and arrows and words like "hell" rise on the boy's skin. He added, "The little boy would go into a seizure and get quite violent and so Father Bowdern asked me to hold him. Yes, he did break my nose."

Interestingly, according to *Los Angeles Times* reporter Tracy Wilkins, in February 2005, the Vatican set up a training program for 100 priests to combat the shortage of exorcists, especially in the United States. There are hundreds of claims of possession worldwide, but only a few are considered to need exorcism. Only three to four cases of demonic possession were certified by the Catholic Church in the 20th century (see *The Exorcism of Emily Rose* [2005], p. 347).

Jesus Christ Superstar (1973)

Directed by Norman Jewison, this rock opera has no spoken lines and is essentially a play-within-a-play. It begins with a youthful cast of largely unknown actors disembarking from a bus on location in Israel and setting up to give a performance of *Jesus Christ Superstar*. The intent of the play is to portray Jesus as a man, not a divinity, and it is told from Judas's point of view, although it follows the canonical Gospel of Matthew.

The disciples try to learn what Jesus (Ted Neeley) has planned in the aria, "What's the Buzz?" Judas (Carl Anderson) is essentially the main character as he begins to become disillusioned with Jesus for talking too much about heaven and not about alleviating poverty on earth or defeating the Romans and other oppressors to establish an earthly kingdom. Mary Magdalene (Yvonne Elliman) consoles Jesus, massaging his feet with oil to soothe his irritability at Judas's constant criticism to the tune of "Everything's Alright." In the song "I Don't Know How to Love Him," she admits her love for Jesus the man.

The story covers the last weeks of Jesus's life, from his entrance into Jerusalem up to his Crucifixion, and focuses to a large extent on the Last Supper and the subsequent events, particularly Peter's denials and Judas's betrayal. It also portrays King Herod and Pontius Pilate sending Jesus to die to the aria "Crucifiction."

Commentary

The film was nominated for one Oscar (for the music) and was the eighth highest grossing film of 1973, earning $13 million. Tim Rice, who wrote the lyrics, and Andrew Lloyd Webber, who wrote the music, had also collaborated on the highly successful play *Joseph and the Amazing Technicolor Dreamcoat*. They toyed with the idea of producing a "rock opera" and released a "concept" album that became a best seller. They then transformed it into an acclaimed Broadway (and West End) musical and ultimately into this, the first rock opera on film. The score and the theatrical presentation are quintessential representations of the 1970s. For me, this film is like opening a 1970s time capsule and seeing the hair, clothes, and other detritus of that era. The lyrics reference contemporary patois, and the costumes (bell-bottoms, platform shoes, psychedelic colors) are 1970s styles (never wonderful anyway) taken to the nth degree.

The play was the target of protests by orthodox Christians who decried the emphasis on Jesus's humanity and the failure to portray his Resurrection and Ascension to highlight his divine nature. Oddly enough, it was also called anti-Semitic because of the prominence of Caiaphas and Herod in

Figure 7.4. *Jesus Christ Superstar.* **A disillusioned Judas (Carl Anderson) lectures Jesus (Ted Neeley) about talking too much about heaven.**

Jesus's condemnation and death on the cross. Over the years, it has become less controversial and continues to be produced as a secular play that happens to feature Jesus.

Godspell (1973)

Like *Jesus Christ Superstar*, *Godspell* is a film adaptation of a popular off-Broadway musical, this one created and produced by Stephen Schwartz and John-Michael Tebelak, who wrote it as his master's thesis at Carnegie Mellon University. It was filmed at the Cherry Lane Theater, where it opened in 1970, and Andrew Carnegie's Manhattan mansion on 91st Street. Based on parables from the Gospel of Saint Matthew, much of the lyrics come from the Episcopal hymnal. The film opens with God speaking as John the Baptist (David Haskell) crosses the Brooklyn Bridge into Manhattan showing contrasting views of the ubiquitous seventies graffiti and the World Trade Center. People are shouting at one another, and their diversity is displayed with quick shots of a black man with an Afro, a black girl off to a ballet rehearsal, a waitress reading *Ulysses* in a diner, a girl entering a casting studio where everyone looks like her, and a black girl Xeroxing her face. John proclaims to the people, "Prepare ye the way of the Lord," and the group heads to the Bethesda Terrace in Central Park. Christ (Victor Garber) appears in the form of a dopey-looking guy with a heart on his forehead and clown makeup. He turns into Superman and sings "God Save the People." There's a lot of frolicking and false jollity and cavorting down Manhattan streets. The gang goes into a junkyard, and they romp around like children.

Christ tells them, "I did not come to abolish the law and the prophets but to complete it." The group moves on to the Soldiers and Sailors Monument on Riverside Drive where He tells them, "If someone hits you on the right cheek, offer him the left." There's a lot of clown and Keystone cops comedy with vintage clips as well as Barbara Stanwyck and Mae West impersonations. Back in Central Park, the group dances around the Angel Fountain where Christ is baptized and then goes back to the junkyard. Jesus wipes the paint off His forehead, washes the apostles' feet, blesses the bread and wine in Jewish, and distributes the Bread, saying "Take and eat, this is my Body." Then He says farewell and sits on fender to pray while all go to sleep. He says, "Father, if it is possible, let this cross pass me by. Not as I will but as You will." The Temptations of Christ are inserted here. Judas (Carl Anderson) arrives in a police car. Jesus is crucified on a wire fence accompanied by a lot of psychedelic light and shaking, saying, "O God, I'm dead." The chorus sings, "Long Live God," and Jesus is taken up Park Avenue to the strains of "Day by Day."

Commentary

Roger Ebert gave the film four stars; he liked its simplicity, unpretentiousness, and its use of New York settings, calling it "strangely irreverent, wacky, and endearing." This begged the question, "Was he watching the same movie I was?" Even allowing for its good intentions, this seems completely overboard. He said that he almost had to be dragged to see the play and found it so relaxing that the good feelings carried over to the movie. As they say, "You had to be there." I'd be interested in his take now since in my estimation, the film has not stood the test of time like true four-star classics. Admittedly, this silly pastiche has a wholesomeness about it, but it is mainly an anachronism and historical relic of the 1970s. Still, there's no question that the play had an impact. "Day by Day," whose lyrics are "To see Thee more clearly; Love Thee more dearly; Follow Thee more nearly, Day by Day" became a standard hymn in Catholic Churches at guitar masses for decades. So did two other songs: "Whatever You Do for the Least of My Brothers" and "All Good Gifts Around Us Come from Heaven Above."

Like *Jesus Christ Superstar*, the film's goal appears to be an attempt to adapt religion to reach young people with the Christian message even though it is unnecessarily watered down and for some Christians "blasphemous." In

Figure 7.5. *Godspell.* John the Baptist (David Haskell) baptizes Christ (Victor Garber) attired in a Superman costume.

my opinion, both films are tedious and eminently forgettable except as 1970s artifacts. On the plus side, however, interspersed among the frolicking are parables (the Unworthy Servant, the Sower and the Seed, the Lilies of the Fields, and the Prodigal Son) as well as the Beatitudes. The moral of the Good Samaritan story is said to be, "Don't trumpet your charity. Your left hand must not know what your right hand does. Your heavenly father sees what you do in secret and rewards you." All things considered, those messages are better than those of the many films that followed it.

In This House of Brede (1975)

Phillipa Tolbert (Diana Rigg), a successful businesswoman and widow, leaves her London office for the last time, unbeknownst to her staff. She hails a taxi for a posh restaurant to have dinner with Sir Richard (Denis Quilley), her lover who is married with children. He orders her a stiff drink and lights her cigarette as he tries for the last time to dissuade her from entering a Benedictine convent. She assures him that she is not running away from him, but toward something else. The next day, she boards her cat with a neighbor and takes a train to the abbey, the "House of Brede." On the way, Phillipa stops at a nearby pub where she consumes three whiskeys and smokes a pack of cigarettes. After settling the bill, she knocks at the abbey door and answers the ritual question of why she is there: "To try for my vocation as a Benedictine in this House of Brede." She is welcomed by the wise, now dying abbess who has been counseling her as she has struggled with her decision.

Much of the film involves rituals as she and others progress from postulants to novices and finally to taking final vows. As Dame Phillipa, she has some marvelous interactions with a young postulant, Joanna (Judi Bowker), who considers her the loving mother she never had, which awakens in Phillipa painful memories of her daughter who died in a car accident. Some excellently limned relationships include one with the new level-headed, spiritually caring abbess Dame Catherine (Gwen Watford) and another with Dame Agnes (Pamela Brown), a nun from the nearby village who entered the abbey at 18. From the time of Phillipa's arrival, Agnes is, as she later admits, consumed with envy of the 40-year-old Oxford graduate who has seen the world, knows Japanese, has been married, and been a successful businesswoman.

In an interesting subplot, a Japanese Christian asks the abbess to accept five Japanese postulants and train them to start an abbey in Japan. Phillipa, by virtue of her fluency in Japanese, is given the assignment of training them, much to the dismay of Agnes who is mistress of the novices. The self-abnegation, as the worldly, sophisticated Phillipa throws herself into such chores as scrubbing floors and taking care of the sick, is well shown. In this respect, one comes away with a feeling that, despite the inevitable pettiness and human frailty, the abbey is permeated with peace, prayer, and caring, wrapped in a sublime Gregorian chant.

Commentary

Blessed with an excellent script based on Rumer Godden's (see the following Backstory) novel of the same name and an outstanding performance by Diana Rigg, this is one of the most balanced and affirming movies about nuns ever produced. Like many films based on books, however, it may be best to see the film first to appreciate it fully because it is only a distillate of what is more richly conveyed in the novel. Godden took as her model the

---

BACKSTORY

Rumer Godden: From *Black Narcissus* to *In This House of Brede*

Margaret Rumer Godden (1907–1998) was taken, when she was nine months old, to colonial India where her father ran a shipping line. After returning to England in her twenties, she studied dance and then resettled in Calcutta in 1930 and opened a mixed-race dancing school. She also began writing poetry, adult fiction, and children's books. Her husband of eight years abandoned her and their two children in 1941, and she moved to Kashmir where she continued writing and teaching dance. Her first autobiography, titled *A Time to Dance, No Time to Weep*, dealt with this period of her life. She remarried in 1949, this time much more happily, and she and her husband returned to England where she continued to write books that ultimately totaled over 60.

Her conversion to Catholicism explains the change in setting from an Anglican monastery in her book *Black Narcissus* (1939) to a Catholic abbey in *In This House of Brede* (1969). In both she examined the conflict between the religious devotion of individual women and their submission to the Benedictine rules of discipline. Also worthy of note is *The River* (1951), directed by Jean Renoir and for which she wrote the screenplay based on her 1946 book. An undisputed classic, it captures her adolescent love affair with India.

Her second autobiography was called *A House with Four Rooms* based on her favorite Indian proverb: "Everyone is a house with four rooms, physical, mental, emotional, and spiritual. Most of us tend to live in one room most of the time, but unless we go into every room every day, if only to keep it aired, we are not a complete person." Written when she was 82, she went on to say, "My house is, of course, slightly worn now, but I still hope to go on living quietly in all of it, finding treasures old and new, until the time comes when I shall have, finally, to shut its door." Awarded the Order of the British Empire in 1993, her door finally closed in Scotland at age 90, ending a very rich life.

Stanbrook Abbey at Callow End near Worcester, England, which has an interesting backstory, as documented in the Catholic Encyclopedia. The site of a Priory before the Reformation, Stanbrook Abbey was seized by the Crown and given to a nobleman's family. In 1625, a Benedictine abbey was founded at Cambria in Spanish Flanders (later part of France) by Thomas More's great-great-granddaughter. In 1793, the abbey's 22 nuns were imprisoned by French Revolutionaries. A number of nuns and a priest were killed, and only Robespierre's assassination saved others from the guillotine.

After being rescued, they escaped to England and settled in Stanbrook Hall, which was purchased by a priest disguised as a country squire because of the rampant anti-Catholicism. Later a landmark church was built, and the monastery became known for its liturgy, singing, and private printing press. In 2002, with only 28 professed nuns (average age 65) and two postulants, the Abbess decided to sell the 21-acre property and relocate to Yorkshire. This raised concerns that the historic property would be converted into a gated community with luxury condos, resulting in a fierce debate that reached to the House of Commons.

Monty Python's Life of Brian (1979)

After the huge success of *Monty Python and the Holy Grail,* which took on the Arthurian legends, the acclaimed British comedy ensemble Monty Python's Flying Circus (consisting of John Cleese, Terry Gilliam, Michael Palin, Graham Chapman, Terry Jones, and Eric Idle) searched for another subject to parody. Kicking around such ideas as "Jesus Christ–Lust for Glory," they finally arrived at a spoof involving someone mistaken for Jesus. The film starts with a star guiding Three Wise Men to the Messiah through the narrow streets of Bethlehem to a stable where Mandy Cohen (Terry Jones) has given birth after being raped by a Roman soldier Naughtius Maximus. She says that they are in the wrong place and tries to get rid of them until she learns that they have gold, frankincense, and myrrh and she tells them to stay. "What's his name?" the kings ask. They are told that it is "Brian," and they say "We worship you, O Brian." When they realize that Jesus is in the next stable, they leave, then return to take back the gifts meant for Jesus.

Fast forward to Judea in AD 33 on a Saturday afternoon when Brian (Chapman) follows a crowd and a pretty activist, Judith (Sue Jones-Davies), to hear Jesus give the Sermon on the Mount. Those on the periphery think Jesus is saying "Blessed are the Cheese makers" and "Blessed are the Greeks who shall inherit the earth." Insults are traded and a fight breaks out. Brian then joins the People's Front of Judea and is assigned to write "Romans Go Home" on a wall. Aghast at the poor Latin, a Roman soldier makes him write it correctly 100 times. Later, Brian gives an impassioned speech and is mistaken for the Messiah. He runs away, but the people keep following him and telling him that he is the real Messiah. They talk about his miracles. After spending the night with Judith, he confronts the crowd and agrees that he is the Messiah and tells them, "Now F— off."

Brian's mother Mandy says that he is not the Messiah. Then the crowd calls her Blessed Mother and says variation of the Hail Mary. Brian tells them, "You don't have to follow anyone. You are all individuals." They reply in unison that they are all individuals. The crowd asks Mandy if she is a virgin. Captured by the Romans, Brian is sent to be crucified, but Pontius Pilate pardons him and then reverses himself. Pilate lisps, which occasions many laughs from the crowd. Later, stuttering brings a lot of laughs. The film ends with a dozen or more being crucified, all calling themselves Brian.

Commentary

This puerile (think of the stuttering and lisping scenes) but highly popular film (rated the top British comedy in 2006) was banned in many parts of Britain, Ireland, Norway, Italy, and some states in the United States. It was the subject of debates on British television with such heavyweights as Sir Malcolm Muggeridge, which pleased Cleese and Gilliam, the major creative forces of the group. Gilliam said it was meant to be heretical as a criticism of organized religion and such things as beliefs in signs. Director Terry Jones in another interview made no bones of his disdain for Christianity, especially Catholicism when he said, "Any religion that makes a form of torture into an icon that they worship seems to me to be a pretty sick sort of religion." Idle also thought it was heresy because "It's attacking the Church." Interestingly, Jones did cut out scenes offensive to Jews before its release, although they remain in the published script. He left in a scene of the mass suicide of Jews at the crucifixion, which led rabbis to join nuns on picket lines outside the theater where it opened in New York City.

To my mind, it's not worth getting offended over. It's like an extended Saturday Night Live send-up or a very British prep school spoof of an epic movie. Call it satire or ridicule, it's certainly tasteless, but that's the point with the "nothing's sacred" crowd. Indeed, the most tasteless scene of the crucifixion is paradoxically the most accessible and optimistically upbeat because of the catchy music. One of those being crucified tells the others to purse your lips and whistle "Always Look on the Bright Side of Life." As everyone joins in, the lyric changes to "Look on the Bright Side of Death" and then back to "Look on the Bright Side of Life" as the camera pans over those being crucified. The film's last message is "if you enjoyed this film, why not go and see *La Notte,*" an inside joke presumably because that film is the second of an impenetrable trilogy by Michelangelo Antonioni about alienation that was all the rage among cineastes in the 1960s. In short, you're either in the mood for this inanity and it cracks you up, or you find it to be juvenile and a waste of the limited time we have on earth.

Wise Blood (1979)

This bizarre movie was directed by John Huston (billed as Jhon Huston). Korean War veteran Hazel Motes (Brad Dourif) returns to rural Georgia on the C T Lord Highway lined with billboards about repentance, forgiveness of sin, and Jesus Christ. His intensity and his black garb result in his being called a preacher by the hooker he beds down with after seeing her telephone number on a dirty train station bathroom wall. He is followed around by a mixed-up young man, Enoch Emory (Dan Shor), who says "I know things I ain't never learned." He calls it "wise blood," a gift of the prophets.

Hazel, who was told by his preacher grandfather (Huston) that Jesus would never leave him, begins railing against street corner preachers like Asa Hawks (Harry Dean Stanton), a phony blind man, and his over-sexed daughter Sabbath Lily (Amy Wright). Hazel starts preaching about the "Church of truth without Christ where the blind don't see, the lame don't walk, and the dead stay that way." Hazel tools around in an old dilapidated Ford Fairlane trying to get away from Jesus, believing that "A man with a good car don't need to be justified." But it's to no avail. There are a number of weird twists and turns, including him blinding himself with lime and putting stones in his shoe to cause bleeding. The most entertaining scene involves Hoover Shoates (Ned Beatty) as a huckster who wants Hazel to exploit the money-making potential of his ministry and when he refuses, sets up a competing "Holy Church of Jesus Christ Without Christ."

Commentary
Wise Blood, which has a lot of N words in lines such as "Jesus is a trick on n— s," became a cult film on college campuses. It is based on a novel by Flannery

O'Connor, a devout Catholic who died young from lupus. Her "Southern Gothic" novels are set in the South and populated by strange and eccentric characters. This is the story of someone who was raised with the concept of a fire-and-brimstone-punishing God and tries to shake that Jesus who "will always be with him." He tries to convince himself and others that we don't need Jesus, whom he calls a liar, and that there's no such thing as the fall of man and consequently no need for redemption. Since there's no judgment, one can live one's life the way one wishes. Still, he can't escape the "Hound of Heaven" (p. 157) because deep down, he is a martyr in atheist clothing. Other targets in the film are those who appropriate Christ and use him for their own ends by emphasizing sin and damnation rather than love. To my mind, the film is not entertaining but at many points frustratingly weird; however, it might serve well in a college discussion of O'Connor's works.

Short Subjects

Brother Sun, Sister Moon (1973)

Scored by the popular 1970s rock singer Donovan, this well-meaning but rather lightweight film is director Franco Zeffirelli's attempt to tell a modern version of the life of St. Francis of Assisi. Thinking war is beautiful, Francesco (Graham Faulkner) joins a crusade to enrich himself and to gain glory and indulgences. Returning home ill, he rises from his sickbed, climbs onto the roof, and returns a bird's song. Appreciating nature opens his eyes to the world around him. Seeing how badly his father treats the dyers in his factories, he cries for them and renounces his father's aspirations to the nobility, and becoming a flower child, entering into a trance-like state for most of the film.

Leaving the town church singing "Brother Sun, Sister Moon," he goes off to resurrect the ruined church of San Damiano. He gives away his garments and goes naked into the public square and visits a richly accoutered Bishop who won't interrupt his post-Lenten meal to talk to him. When his pal Bernando (Leigh Lawson) returns from the Crusades dispirited, his friends excitedly say, "You must have slaughtered thousands of Muslims." Instead, Bernando talks about the horror of war and the deterioration of our ideals that sounds more like a commentary on the Vietnam War than the Crusades. Zeffirelli goes back and forth in time and place, interpolating scenes of Francesco's naked friends bathing with the sick in the river as they sing seventies songs about peace, love, and friendship. Francesco goes to

Rome to appear before Pope Innocent III (Alec Guinness). The Pope and cardinals are all bejeweled and richly caparisoned. Francesco lectures them on the lilies of the field. He gets thrown out by the cardinals. The Pope in a trance calls him back and tells him that he started the same idealistic way, but then the Church governance took over. "You in your poverty put us to shame." The Pope kisses Francesco's feet ,and the film ends with "Gloria in Excelsis Deo" as Francesco is permitted to start his order. The film's best assets are the Oscar-nominated art/set direction (it was filmed on location in Assisi) and Alec Guinness.

Jesus of Nazareth (1977)

This is not a Hollywood feature film, but a 371-minute, two-part miniseries made for television in Italy and the United Kingdom. It deserves a brief mention because it is the most coherent and accurate narrative of Jesus's story on film. In our fast-paced world, it takes commitment to devote the six hours of viewing that this series requires, but the episodes lend themselves to interrupted viewing or as discussion starters. It has an outstanding cast, beautiful cinematography, and remarkable faithfulness to the New Testament story of Jesus.

The film opens with Joseph in the temple and proceeds to Anna coming to see him to agree to a contract to marry Mary. It ends with Mary Magdalene coming to the upper room where the apostles are afraid and cowering. She tells them, "I have seen the master. He is risen." They don't believe her. "I denied Him," Peter says, "because I was a coward." She responds, "We are all cowards; He's forgiven all of us." Peter heeds Christ's mandate, sending them forth to all nations and, as he turns to the audience, the words "Don't be afraid. I will be with you all days to the end of time," echo in the background.

Saturday Night Fever (1977)

Based on Nik Cohn's magazine article, "The Tribal Rites of the New Saturday Night," this crude portrait of a dysfunctional Italian-American family stars John Travolta as Tony Manero, a swaggering 19-year-old paint store clerk. Manero lives for Saturday night disco dancing, cruising with other losers, drinking, and sex in the backseats of cars. The film launched Travolta's movie career, and he exudes sexual and animal energy in his dance numbers. It's included here because his brother Frank Jr. (Martin Shakar) is a priest who has made Tony appear to be the "black sheep."

Figure 7.6. *Saturday Night Fever.*
Tony Manero (John Travolta) takes the
Roman collar his brother Frank left
behind after quitting the priesthood, and
fashions it as a noose.

When Frank quits the priesthood, his parents are broken-hearted. Tony questions his brother as to whether they asked why. Father Frank replies, "No, they were afraid that I might say 'celibacy.'" He continues, "One day, you look at a crucifix and it's only a man on a cross. Mama and Papa's dream of pious glory—I can't defend their fantasy. All I had was their belief in the image of me as a priest." Unable to continue living at home, Frank heads for a settlement house, leaving his Roman collar for Tony as a gift. Tony puts it on and feigns hanging himself.

There are two sad subplots. One involves the girlfriend of Tony's friend who loves Communion wafers and is pregnant but won't have an abortion which leads to her boyfriend's death. The other involves the virginal girl Annette (Donna Pescow), who tries so hard to have Tony love and marry her that she agrees to have sex with him, but he stops when he learns she is "unprotected." Having found another girl, Tony rejects Annette when she brings him condoms, and she allows herself to be raped by Tony's buddy while Tony sits in the front seat of the car. Tony asks her if she's happy because now she's not a "nice girl" any more, illustrating the false double standard whereby he is lionized for his sexual exploits as a "stud," but the girl is a "whore" if she is sexually active. Travolta's character became a seventies disco icon, but to me, the film is a prolonged Bee Gees VH-1 music video, overwhelmed by crudeness and ignorant messages, that deserves to be buried in a 1970s time capsule.

CHAPTER EIGHT
HEAVEN HELP US: THE 1980s

T he 1980s has been labeled the "Decade of Greed" as epitomized in Oliver Stone's 1985 film *Wall Street*, when the "hero," Gordon Gekko, proclaims with great assurance: "Greed is good." However, as Dinesh D'Souza points out, the label is not only inaccurate but trivializes this important decade. Actually, contributions to charity by corporations and the affluent more than outstripped inflation, and the top 5 percent of earners were responsible for 46 percent of the taxes collected while the tax burden of those with lower incomes declined. Indeed, it is probably more accurate to affix that label to the nineties at which time much of the economy was fueled by the tech boom before it went bust, and corporate corruption such as at Enron flourished.

On the other hand, geopolitically the 1980s was a decade of profound change. Particularly noteworthy events in 1980 were President Carter's failed attempt to rescue the American hostages followed by the resignation of his Secretary of State Cyrus Vance, who had opposed the mission, and Carter's decision to boycott the Moscow Summer Olympics because of Russia's invasion of Afghanistan. Due to the considerable efforts of Deputy Secretary of State Warren Christopher, the 444-day captivity of the remaining 52 Iranian hostages ended minutes after the inauguration of Carter's successor, Ronald Reagan. The latter took a confrontational position vis-à-vis the Soviets with his decision to fund a missile defense shield and his challenge to Gorbachev in 1987 at the Brandenburg Gate on the 750th Anniversary of Berlin to tear down the Berlin Wall, which ultimately was dismantled in 1989 leading to the reunification of Germany in 1990. Gorbachev's initiation of Perestroika, along with Reagan's joint efforts with England's Prime Minister Margaret Thatcher and Pope John Paul II have been widely credited for the subsequent collapse of the Soviet Union and the development of democracies in former Eastern bloc states like Poland and Czechoslovakia (see Fund, O'Sullivan).

As a result of the accident at a nuclear facility at Three Mile Island in Pennsylvania in 1979, followed in 1986 by the damage to the nuclear power plant in Chernobyl, Russia, which caused widespread devastation, the building of nuclear power plants was halted in the United States but not in France and Japan which depend heavily on them for energy. In addition to the increase in ecosensitivity, there was a rise in health consciousness especially with respect to the use of tobacco. Another major medical development was the discovery of AIDS and the identification of the causative AIDS virus that Patient X, a Canadian airline steward, had transmitted to a large number of men in a gay bathhouse in San Francisco. By the mid 1980s, it was recognized to be pandemic in many areas of the world, especially Africa, and much emphasis was placed on prevention and curbing of unprotected sexual activity.

Computers began to be widely available in homes initially mainly for video games featuring ninja mutant turtles, Nintendo, and PacMan, and later for e-mail, as a replacement for typewriters, and later for news and blogging. In addition, the notion of "political correctness" emerged with a vengeance. Any political speech, news report, book, or article with the slightest scent of racism or sexism was condemned, while such concepts as "affirmative action" and "sexual harassment" took on much greater import in the business, academic, and political worlds. The barriers to women in the workplace and especially in the professions of law and medicine began to disappear, and as a result, more women entered the workforce, deferring marriage and childbearing. Concepts of the family changed dramatically as rates of divorce, cohabitation, abortion, and single motherhood increased. At the same time, homosexual rights became a more dominant theme and homosexuality, a more widely accepted lifestyle. The outing of Rock Hudson, who had been an icon of heterosexuality in his many film and television roles, and his death from AIDS in 1985, put a face to the disease.

Films of the 1980s

Films had always played an important role in America, but they were not widely available once they had been shown in theaters except in film retrospectives. I remember hosting film series for adults and children at the University of Colorado Medical Center in the 1970s, using 16 mm prints to show films that were either noteworthy or which had not even been shown in Denver. This all changed with the development of Betamax and later VHS players that allowed films to be seen when convenient and in the home. The most popular films of the 1980s were such blockbusters as *E.T.: The Extra Terrestrial*; the sequels to the 1977 George Lucas film *Star Wars (The Empire Strikes Back* and *Return of the Jedi); Conan the Barbarian*;

and Steven Spielberg's Indiana Jones films, beginning with *Raiders of the Lost Ark* (1981), followed by *Indiana Jones and the Temple of Doom* (1984), and *Indiana Jones and the Last Crusade* (1989). Although the "lost ark" refers to the lost "ark of the Covenant," *Raiders of the Lost Ark* is hardly a religious film. Instead, these films were all about fantasy, science fiction, and "magic," sometimes expressed in a humorous, tongue in cheek manner as in *Back to the Future*. In addition to the series of "sci fi" and fantasy films, some hugely popular films of the 1980s were comedies. In many cases, these were extremely well-made and well-acted, such as *Ghostbusters*, *Tootsie*, and *Working Girl*.

Christian Themes in 1980s Films

A few excellent Christian-themed films were released in the first half of the 1980s, including *Chariots of Fire, Witness, Babette's Feast*, and *Places in the Heart*. Although none placed among the top 50 grossing films, they all were financially successful by Hollywood standards, and several achieved critical acclaim as well, most particularly *Chariots of Fire* and *Babette's Feast*, which won the Academy Award for Best Picture and Best Foreign Film, respectively. However, during this decade, anti-Christian (principally anti-Catholic) films began to proliferate. These ranged from the juvenile caricatures of religious themes, such as *History of the World Part I* and *Heaven Help Us* (originally titled *Catholic Boys*) to much more serious and confrontational films such as *Mass Appeal, Agnes of God*, and *The Mission*. The 1980s ended with the production of two of the most controversial Christian-themed films, *The Last Temptation of Christ* and *Jesus of Montreal*. In the former, Martin Scorsese, another major director and disaffected Catholic, filmed Nikos Kazantzakis's version of Jesus, who dreams of being married and having a child with Mary Magdalene or of its possibility. *Jesus of Montreal* centers on a reenactment of the *Passion Play* in which Jesus is the illegitimate son of a Roman soldier, and the actor becomes a Christ figure. Both won plaudits from the critics, although neither did well with the public. However, protests by the Catholic League (p. 239), an analogue of the Jewish Anti-Defamation League, did increase the visibility and box office of *The Last Temptation of Christ*. In short, these films and others covered briefly in the Short Subjects of this chapter and the Back Story (p. 227) illustrate the steep downturn in respect for organized religion (particularly the Roman Catholic Church) and for the sensitivities of practicing Christians by Hollywood filmmakers.

Chariots of Fire (1981)

Chariots of Fire interweaves the stories of two gold medal winners at the 1924 Paris Olympics: Harold Abrahams (Ben Cross), who channels his energy to overcome anti-Semitism, and Eric Liddell (Ian Charleson), who runs for God's glory. It opens in 1979 at a memorial service held for Abrahams in a crowded English cathedral, where the choir sings the hymn "Jerusalem" and then cuts back to the arrival of this son of a Jewish financier as an entering student at Cambridge. A porter says, "One thing for sure with a name like Abrahams, he won't be in the chapel choir," but, as it turns out, he becomes an outstanding choir member. Abrahams says that his father, who emigrated from Lithuania, loved England and wanted nothing but that his sons become Englishmen. He goes on to say that his father "forgot that this country is Christian and so are its corridors of power." Running is Abraham's way to take them on and show he's the best. For him, winning at the Olympics would confer immortality as the fastest man on earth. In short, it's a matter of life and death.

Abraham's most formidable opponent is Eric Liddell, called the "Flying Scotsman" (like the famous train). The son of a Presbyterian minister, who is destined with his sister to be missioners in China, he also loves running but does it for God's glory. When his sister Jennie (Cheryl Campbell) says that competing and racing are sacrilegious, he responds, "We need a muscular Christianity to make people sit up and take notice. I run in God's name and let the world sit back and wonder." Liddell compares running in a race to faith. "It requires concentration and will, energy of soul. When a runner breaks the tape, he experiences elation. How long does that last? Where does the power come from, to see the race to the end? From within! Jesus said the power of God is within you." Later he says, "I believe that God made me for a purpose but he also made me fast. When I run I feel his pleasure. To win is to honor him" (Screenwriter: Colin Welland).

After arriving at Cambridge, Abrahams wins the inaugural freshman run by circling the Great Court at Trinity College at Cambridge in 60 seconds, presumably the first one to do so in 700 years. Though this is historical fiction, it does allow the filmmakers to illustrate the casual prejudices of the British upper classes when the supercilious Master of Trinity College (Sir John Gielgud) remarks to the Master of Caius (Lindsay Anderson): "Maybe they are God's chosen people." Still, when it's clear that he must improve greatly to beat Liddell, Abrahams hires a private tutor named Sam Mussabini (Ian Holm). This occasions another bigoted remark by the Master of Trinity, on learning that Mussabini is half-Italian and half-Arab.

The twist in the story is that the qualifying heat for the 100-meter dash, in which Liddell is favored over Abrahams, is held on the Sabbath. Saying it's against God's law for him to run, Liddell gives up a chance at the Gold medal, which goes to Abrahams, even resisting the entreaties of the Prince of Wales (David Yelland). He is called a true man of principle for putting God before king and country. His Anglican teammate Lord Andrew Lindsay (Nigel Havers), who has already won a gold medal in hurdles, gives up his starting position in the 400 meters relay to Liddell, passing up a chance at a second medal. His American opponent slips Liddell a note before the race, "it says in the good book, 'He who honors me, I will honor.'"

Commentary

The title is taken from William Blake's poem, "And Did Those Feet in Ancient Time" which was set to music by Hubert Parry in 1916 as the hymn "Jerusalem" sung at the movie's beginning. It postulates that Christ visited England with Joseph of Arimathea to build the new Jerusalem. In so doing, Jesus calls for his bow of burning gold, his Arrows of Desire, and his spear and, commanding the clouds to unfold, he says, "Bring me my Chariot of Fire."

The film was made for $5 million in two months and was rejected by many distributors, with one film agent reported to have said, "Who wants to watch a film about two young men running around in their underwear." It is considered the most improbable Oscar winner of all time having beaten out *Reds*, which was made for $35 million and had three bankable stars. It is on many lists of the greatest films of all time. It also won Oscars for Best Screen Writing, Costume Design, and Music Scoring, and garnered nominations for Best Director, Supporting Actor (Holm), and Film Editing. The score by Vangelis Papathanassiou played on a piano and a synthesizer is extraordinary. It fits the film, like the *The Third Man* theme did for that film, and became just as popular worldwide as an instrumental recording. There are great running scenes, but the most evocative one is the scene of the athletes running through the surf on the beach in slow motion to Vangelis's main theme.

While fairly faithful to the story, there are a number of inaccuracies, in addition to the fact that Abrahams did not beat the clock in the race around

Figure 8.1. *Chariots of Fire.* **After he helps win the Olympic Gold medal, Eric Liddell (Ian Charleson) is carried on his teammates' shoulders.**

the courtyard. Actually, the first to do it (in 1927) was Lord Burghley, who is the model for Lord Lindsay. He didn't allow his name to be used in the film because he did not give up his place for Liddell and didn't win the gold medal in the hurdles but was eliminated in the heats. The most important alteration involved depicting Liddell as first learning that the qualifying heat for the 100-meter dash would be on the Sabbath when he is boarding the boat for Paris. In reality, Liddell knew months before and had already decided to forego that race and to train for the 400 meter relay. Still, none of the changes substantially alter the truth, and they make for a better story. Finally, it's worth noting that Liddell did go to China as a missionary and died there in 1945 under the Japanese occupation.

True Confessions (1981)

A detective, Tom Spellacy (Robert Duvall), investigating the death of a priest in a whorehouse while in bed with a prostitute, brings the priest's rosary to his brother, the Bishop's secretary Monsignor Des Spellacy (Robert De Niro) in his elegant archdiocesan office. Des flippantly says that the priest might have been on a house call. Spellacy asks when was the last time he hung his pants over the bed when making a house call, and Des admits with a smile that it wasn't how he was taught at the seminary. Shortly afterwards, the prostitute, a porn movie actress whose favorite film was *Going My*

Way, is murdered. Tom finds her cut in half in the field and notes that she had an abortion before dying.

Monsignor Des is shown piously leading children in recitation of the rosary over the radio, hearing confession, and giving communion in the Latin rite. At the same time, he turns a blind eye to the rigging of lucrative awards to Jack Amsterdam (Charles Durning), an ex-pimp and corrupt construction company owner, who is awarded the highest Catholic layman honor by the Los Angeles archdiocese. He also fixes the church raffle to allow a city councilman's daughter to win so that the Church can get his vote on the planning board for a building permit. Des's confessor, Father Seamus Fargo (Burgess Meredith), the only good priest, tells him that his problem is that he loves power and using it.

Finally, Des is shamed into action by his less than saintly policeman brother who had been a police bagman protecting Amsterdam in the old days. Speaking out against Amsterdam destroys Des's career (he was on his way to being a Bishop), and he is sent to the parish equivalent of "Siberia" where, as the Cardinal's secretary, he had once been ordered to send his mentor Father Fargo. Des finds happiness in "Siberia" following in the footsteps of Father Fargo who taught him "the meaning of being a priest."

Commentary

The screenplay with its oh-so-hip profanity-laced dialogue was written by the husband and wife team of John Gregory Dunne and Joan Didion (from Dunne's novel) and based on an unsolved murder case that was given the nickname "Black Dahlia." It involved a woman whose severed body and mutilated face was found in a Los Angeles park in January 1947. Probably because of its gruesomeness, it generated widespread press coverage and a phalanx of law enforcement officers worked on the case, which was never officially solved. It has been the subject of at least two other films, *Who is the Black Dahlia* (1975) and Brian De Palma's 2006 *The Black Dahlia*, as well as a computer game. Other than the bizarreness of the murder, there was no evidence of prostitution or religious connections that are made in this film.

Religion is handled with much flippancy as when Detective Spellacy, on visiting his mother, pushes aside a nursing home nun who tells him to wait because she's receiving communion, telling her, "May all your sons be Jesuits." The Catholic hierarchy does not come off well, giving awards to the powerful and corrupt while banishing truth-tellers to parishes in "Siberia." This is not a new theme; for example, in the 1954 film *On The Waterfront*

(p. 117), Father Barry is threatened with being sent to the diocesan equivalent of Abyssinia if he creates a stir by confronting the corrupt union.

The Scarlet and the Black (1983)

It's 1943 in German-occupied Rome and the Gestapo, under the command of Colonel Herbert Kappler (Christopher Plummer), initiates a crackdown on Jews and the Italian resistance. An Irish priest in the Holy Office of the Inquisition, Father Hugh O'Flaherty (Gregory Peck), with the approval of Pope Pius XII (Sir John Gielgud), takes the central role in the Vatican's attempt to hide Jews and escaped POWs. Posing as a nun, postman, street sweeper, and even a Nazi officer, O'Flaherty leaves the Vatican to guide his charges to safety. Kappler complains to the Pope who says that the Vatican is a neutral and sacrosanct jurisdiction. Knowing that O'Flaherty cannot be arrested when he is in the Vatican, Kappler has a white line drawn around Vatican City and keeps surveillance on O'Flaherty with the intention of killing him if he steps outside to rescue someone. As the Monsignor plays a cat and mouse game with him, the film has its lighthearted moments, but it also shows Gestapo brutality as they round up Jews and those hiding them, including a priest who is tortured and dies.

Commentary

Based on J. P. Gallagher's book *The Scarlet Pimpernel of the Vatican*, this little-known gem features excellent acting by both Gregory Peck and Christopher Plummer. A made-for-television film, it recounts the true story of Monsignor O'Flaherty who was well-known in social circles in Rome before World War II, where he became friendly with many Jews and members of the nobility. His rescue efforts really began in late 1942 when some of his Jewish and anti-Fascist friends were rounded up. He began rescuing them and hiding them in monasteries, convents, and his residence in the German College in the Vatican. In September 1943, when Germany occupied Italy, Hitler sent SS Obergruppenfuhrer Karl Wolff (General Max Helm in the film) to crack down on the "lax" attitudes of the Italians in rounding up and deporting the Jews to Auschwitz. O'Flaherty intensified his efforts and also broadened them to include Allied POWs including British pilots. He hid people in a cluster of apartments, in Castel Gandolfo, and in the Vatican, using various disguises for his escapees including monsignor's robes and Swiss guard uniforms.

Figure 8.2. *The Scarlet and the Black.* Father O'Flaherty (Gregory Peck) reads his breviary while taunting the Nazi Commandant by staying just inside the lines of Vatican City.

It is true that O'Flaherty was warned that he would be arrested if he left the Vatican and that Kappler almost caught him a few times. Once he charged football-like through Gestapo soldiers to reach sanctuary in the Church of St. Mary Major, and another time he escaped through a coal chute into a delivery truck. It is estimated that of 9,700 Roman Jews, 1,000 were sent to Auschwitz, and the rest were hidden—5,000 under Church auspices. Israeli scholar Pinchas Lapide estimated that in other parts of Italy 40,000 were saved. After the war, Kappler was sentenced to

---

BACKSTORY

Pope Pius and the Jews

Pope Pius XII's efforts to hide Jews started in 1938, and the elaborate apparatus set up to rescue Jews in Italy could not have been possible without his direct involvement. Indeed, Rabbi Lapide estimated that the Catholic Church under Pius XII saved as many as 860,000 Jews from certain death, which he said exceeded those saved by all other churches and rescue missions combined. The chief rabbi of Rome, Israel Zolli, who was a personal observer of Pius's work, called him a Righteous Gentile for his efforts and later converted to Catholicism taking the Pope's given name Eugenio as his own. The *New York Times* in its Christmas editorial of 1941 praised the Pope for being "a lonely voice crying out of the silence of a continent." As noted by Rabbi Dalen and Sister Marchione, these feelings were seconded by Golda Meir at the time of the Pope's death. The most striking commentary was a 1944 statement by Albert Einstein who said that "Only the [Catholic] Church stood squarely across Hitler's campaign for suppressing the truth." He added that he never had any interest in the Church but now felt great affection and admiration, adding "and am forced to confess that what I once despised. I now praise unreservedly."

life imprisonment in a jail outside of Rome. His only visitor was O'Flaherty who came monthly and in 1959, he baptized Kappler. My only cavil is the seemingly rather tepid support given O'Flaherty by Pope Pius XII, which is unfair (see Backstory).

Mass Appeal (1984)

Father Farley (Jack Lemmon) is a middle-aged parish priest whose dialogue sermons are popular and whose parish is thriving. Portrayed as comfortable and driving a Mercedes, he is challenged by a typical 1970s activist radical, Mark Dolson (Zeljko Ivanek), who is sent to his church as a deacon by seminary director Monsignor Burke (Charles Durning). The latter comes across as an orthodox homophobic Neanderthal who wants Dolson straightened out. Dolson admits to having been in a homosexual relationship with another seminarian and questions Church dogmas. Farley ultimately accepts the criticisms of the younger man (not unlike what professors were doing in response to campus takeovers) and covers for his homosexuality.

Commentary

This movie, with a bankable star like Jack Lemmon, did not—justifiably—live up to its title, grossing only $1.9 million in the United States in 22 years. Tendentious and tiresome, the film's main utility may be as a historical artifact for discussion purposes in that it embodies the mentality that enabled the Catholic Church's sexual abuse scandal which peaked in the 1980s, 80 percent or more of which involved overt homosexuality. The development of so-called lavender or pink seminaries in many American cities. This transformation in the seminaries had been fostered or at least tolerated by the local Bishops and seminary rectors beginning in the 1960s and especially in the 1970s and early 1980s. It also coincided with the decline in applications for seminaries by heterosexuals and a more liberal approach to dogma as opposed to strict orthodoxy in the wake of Vatican II, as documented in Michael Rose's book *Goodbye, Good Men*.

As these seminarians were ordained and continued their practices in their dioceses, their behavior was covered up by Bishops who quietly reassigned offending priests who practiced pedophilia to other parishes on the advice of lawyers and psychiatrists. As documented in an excellent *Time* magazine article by Amanda Ripley, appropriately titled "In Plain Sight," the most egregious examples were in Boston where the serial abusers Father John J. Geoghan and Father Paul Shanley were shunted around by Cardinal Law and his auxiliary Bishops. Shanley, whose archdiocesan rap sheet went back 30 years and was known to two or three cardinals and a number of their subordinates, was especially overt, being a member of the North American Man/Boy Association. Known as the "hippie priest," Shanley was "a media darling" because of his outspoken challenge to orthodox beliefs about homosexuality and even pedophilia. Shanley managed until his retirement in 1996 to "charm" all he encountered, if that word can be used in any sentence referencing that heinous devil. He was even praised by Cardinal Law for his 30 years of service. Law who was pressured to resign had a brief period of mortification for his behavior and then was given a plum assignment in Rome and participated in the ceremonies at the death of Pope John Paul II. So much for accountability, especially given the great price these events and the politicization of the Church had exacted in Boston, as documented by Lawler in his book, *The Faithful Departed: The Collapse of Boston's Catholic Culture.*

Agnes of God (1985)

Sister Agnes (Meg Tilly), a disturbed nun at the cloistered Montreal convent of Les Petites Soeurs de Marie Magdalene, gives birth and seemingly murders the baby. As screams ring out, Mother Superior Miriam Ruth (Anne Bancroft) is closing the convent gates while the nuns are processing around a cross in the courtyard saying the rosary. Miriam finds Agnes covered in blood. When the ambulance arrives, Miriam is crying over the wastebasket where presumably the strangled baby lies. Her attempt to cover it up is thwarted when a chain-smoking psychiatrist, Doctor Martha Livingston (Jane Fonda), arrives to investigate, saying, "I am not from the Inquisition and I am not from the Middle Ages."

They go to see Agnes who says that the only man she has been alone with is her elderly confessor, Father Martineau. Agnes denies seeing the baby, leading Dr. Livingston to ask, "Is she totally bananas, only slightly off center or just a good liar?" The Superior tells Dr. Livingston that Agnes stopped eating on orders from God. She was getting fat, had vaginal bleeding, and thought it was stigmata, but Miriam did not send her to a doctor. Livingston tells Mother Miriam that their life is one of poverty, chastity, and ignorance and gets a court order to hypnotize Agnes. She learns of a secret passage from the convent to a nearby barn that Agnes's nun friend, now dead, told her about. It turns out that Agnes is Miriam's niece and that Miriam knew about the baby. Agnes told her God did it, and she wanted to believe Agnes was "blessed" and had a Virgin Birth!

Commentary

This is one weird film, or as Roger Ebert said in giving it one star, it is "a badly confused movie"; yet it garnered Oscar nominations for Best Actress (Bancroft) and Best Supporting Actress (Tilly). Besides being confusing, it drips with anti-Catholicism. The nuns are either certifiable nutcases, hypocritical liars, or simple-minded naïfs. Livingston explains why she hates the Church, saying it has "no corner on morality." She relates the story of her best friend in fifth grade being run over by a car, and the nun saying that it happened because she didn't say her morning prayers. The Mother Superior agrees that some of the saints were crazy and that there are no saints anymore.

Today's PC Police would probably not have much problem with the trashing of Catholics and nuns just described, but I'm afraid that they would get freaked out by the fact that Livingston is a chain-smoker and that she and the Mother Superior, who used to be a two-pack-a-day smoker, share a smoke as they exchange confidences. They joke about how they could see Saint Peter smoking a pipe, Saint Joan chewing tobacco, the

Figure 8.3. *Agnes of God.* **Mother Superior (Anne Bancroft) comforts her niece Sister Agnes (Meg Tilly).**

Apostles rolling their own, Saint Ignatius and Mary Magdalene smoking a cigar, and even Christ smoking socially. All I can say is "Not in front of the children, please!"

Heaven Help Us (1985)

Set in 1965 in St. Basil's, a Brooklyn parochial school for boys, this tale centers on a straight arrow, Michael Dunn (Andrew McCarthy), who is alienated by his sadistic and perverted teachers. It opens with a standard Catholic school movie "joke" when a solemn service turns chaotic as a student rapidly sounds a clicker (one that nuns used to signal when the children should stand or kneel). Later in class, a Franciscan Brother orders a boy to put his chewing gum on the tip of his nose all day. He knocks a boy's head against the blackboard and orders another to eat the paper that's passing around the class. In the cafeteria, a Brother carries one boy out after catching him "playing with himself."

When Dunn remarks at the teachers' behavior, the haughty principal (Donald Sutherland), who insists on being addressed in every exchange as "Brother Thaddeus" tells him, "Brothers know their business. They will turn you into a man, better yet a priest, and won't your parents be proud? They'll be smiling down from heaven." When a prank is played on the class nerd Caesar (Malcolm Danare), the sadistic Brother Constance (Jay Patterson) has the students remain on their knees until "the joker steps forward." Saying he doesn't enjoy violence, he slaps a student and hits Dunn on the hands with a ruler. The one good Brother, Timothy (John Heard), tells Brother Thaddeus, "I thought I would learn a lesson in running a class but saw a demonstration in brutality." Thaddeus's response is "Brother Constance is an effective teacher, one of the best we have. We all come to the order with ideals, but authority must never be undermined."

The obligatory confessional scene involves the class wise guy Rooney (Kevin Dillon) advising a boy who says he jerked off 168 times in the month to change it to three times and make it "impure thoughts and wet dreams." The priest is Father Abruzzi (Wallace Shawn), known as the "Pervert" who gets excited by the discussion of masturbation and runs out of the confessional. Rooney takes the priest's place (another favorite of Catholic school movies) and fools Caesar into believing that his failure to footnote references is plagiarism and will keep him out of Harvard.

A lame subplot involves an affair between Dunn and the underage daughter of the local candy store owner. When the Brothers succeed in having Social Services take her away from her father, the store is closed. In retaliation, the students decapitate St. Basil's statue. The sadistic Brother puts four boys in the closet and then whips them, prompting the good Brother Timothy to deck the sadist. The students cheer, the sadist is transferred, and the good guy replaces him. Dunn, thoroughly turned off by the Catholic Church, goes off to Woodstock after graduation.

Commentary

Originally titled *Catholic Boys*, there is little commendable about Catholicism or Catholic education in this film. Its heroes are the wise guys who smoke, obsess about sex and masturbation, drink Jack Daniels, go on joy rides, play jokes on everyone, and flout authority. The big scene is the annual dance with the girls from Virgin Martyrs School. With the boys on one side of the gym and girls on the other, Father Abruzzi, the "Pervert," gives a lecture on the evils of lust beforehand: "The church is here to guard you. Never confuse love with the deadliest of the deadly sins." He writes "LUST" on the blackboard and continues:

> There is a beast living within each and every one of you and that beast is LUST. The beast wants to consume you and spit you out into the eternal fires of hell where for all eternity your flesh will be ripped from your body by grotesque serpents with razor sharp teeth. Your blood will boil. Your bones will burn and your marrow will be reduced to putrid slime. Any questions? Have a nice time. Enjoy the dance. (Screenwriter: Charles Purpura)

The Brothers then go around separating the couples during slow dances.

There's also the obligatory Papal visit. As the Pope passes to the strains of "Largo Factotum," the hypocritical Brothers beam and make the Sign of the Cross. Brother Thaddeus is so overwhelmed that he cries. Rooney tells his classmates, "If the Pope waves to you, you can have sex without sin." His punishment is cleaning St. Basil with a toothbrush. In short, any resemblance of this self-indulgent conceit to the Catholic schools I knew is, as the movie disclaimers used to say, "purely coincidental."

The Mission (1986)

The introduction proclaims, "The historical events represented in this film are true and occurred in 1750 around the borders of Paraguay." The Guarani natives are about to be "enslaved by the Spanish," while their "noble souls incline toward the mission," although they are not above crucifying a Jesuit and setting him adrift in the rapids. A new missionary, Father Gabriel (Jeremy Irons), goes up the river and is allowed to proceed when he transfixes the natives with his hornpipe. He meets Captain Mendoza (Robert De Niro), a Portuguese slaver and tells him, "We're going to make Christians of these people." Mendoza answers, "If you have the time." Gabriel responds, "Are you laughing at me? You're a mercenary, a slave trader, you killed your brother." Mendoza admits killing his brother Felipe (Aidan Quinn) in a fit of rage over a woman and believes that he cannot be redeemed. As penance, he carries Christ's cross in the Passion reenactment. He starts reading St. Paul about charity. He then resolves to do a major penance involving dragging a net full of armor up a steep waterfall. Unsuccessful and completely wiped out, he is suicidal but is saved by Gabriel and decides to become a Jesuit. Gabriel tells him that if he becomes a Jesuit, he will have to accept his orders as the commander-in-chief.

They set up an idyllic communal mission where the natives make instruments and music as well as farm. Sums of money—120,000 escudos—are distributed among all. Altamirano (Ray McAnally), an emissary from Rome, tells them that the Jesuits, who have separated themselves from the Spanish authorities, are thought to have too much power, and the Church must show its authority over them. According to a treaty between Spain and Portugal and blessed by the Vatican, this part of Jesuit Paraguay had been turned over to the Portuguese. Altamirano says, "I speak for the Church which is God's instrument on earth. If the Jesuits resist, they will be expelled from Portugal, then Spain, then the other countries." Gabriel counsels peaceful resistance, but Mendoza and another priest, Father Fielding (Liam Neeson), disobey. They fight the combined Spanish and Portuguese soldiers while Gabriel prays and parades with a monstrance bearing the Eucharist and says mass among the women and children. Neither prayer nor muskets work and, as the mission burns, the three priests and many natives die while others run off into the wilderness. Gabriel has the last word, "The Light shines in the darkness and the dark shall not overcome it."

Commentary

The film's director was Roland Joffe, who directed the much better *City of Joy* and *The Killing Fields,* and the screenwriter was Robert Bolt who wrote the marvelous *A Man for All Seasons.* The film was nominated for seven Academy

Figure 8.4. *The Mission.* **Father Gabriel (Jeremy Irons) carries the monstrance bearing the Eucharistic host in a procession through the native compound.**

Awards (Picture, Director, Cinematography, Editing, Art Direction, Costume Design, and Musical Score). It deservedly won for the exquisite cinematography and should have won for Ennio Morricone's brilliantly evocative musical score. However, my wife and I found the story to be a completely confusing mishmash. Roger Ebert put it well in saying that he would have preferred to see the documentary of how the movie was made to learn "why so many talented people went to such incredible lengths to make a difficult and beautiful movie—without any of them, on the basis of the available evidence, having the slightest notion of what the movie was about."

In researching the film, I learned that in accord with the "Treaty of Madrid" in 1750, a Spanish Jesuit named Altamirano was sent to Paraguay to transfer seven Jesuit missions to the Portuguese. Still, the confusing nature of the narrative and the farfetched penance Mendoza inflicts on himself in attempting to carry the net filled with armor up the waterfall led me to stop suspending disbelief. As far as I could discern from watching the film twice, the following were the take-home messages:

1. The natives are noble savages who live an idyllic existence but are about to be enslaved and their land plundered in turn by the brutal Spaniards and Portuguese with the collusion of the institutional Church.

2. The Church hierarchy is involved in an internecine conflict with the Jesuits who are setting up missions to convert the natives and better their lives, but who are being threatened with destruction by the Church's Spanish and Portuguese civil and military partners.

3. The film's hero is an obsessively fanatic Jesuit who is fighting the institutional Church, the Spanish, and the Portuguese.

4. Captain Mendoza, the other sort-of good guy, is a Portuguese slaver and killer who has a conversion experience and joins forces for most of the movie with the fanatic Jesuit before the latter finally spins completely out of control.

5. Everything ends badly for everybody as "The Mission" is burned to the ground, but the CD of the soundtrack remains a worthy relic.

Babette's Feast (1987)

As the camera sweeps over the barren, desolate landscape of 19th-century Jutland, Denmark, the narrator (Ghita Norby) says, "In this remote spot lived two sisters with both parents and in the flush of youth." Their father, a minister, had christened them Martina (Vibeke Hastrup) and Filippa (Hanne Stensgaard) after Martin Luther and Philip Melanchthon. The sisters spent all their days and income on good works, taking food to the poor and the elderly. Their father had been a priest and prophet and founder of a Protestant sect. Each year, they gathered to sing "Jerusalem, my heart's true home. Your name is forever dear to me. Your kindness is second to none" (Screenwriter: Stephane Audrane). They were said to be beautiful once but never went to parties or dances and now live with their servant Babette.

The scene shifts to their youth when a dissolute lieutenant, Lorens Lowenhelm (Gudmar Wivesson), who has been banished to their village, falls in love with Martina and attends the minister's prayer sessions. He reforms his ways, but she refuses to leave her parents to return with him to Stockholm once his banishment is over. On returning to Stockholm, he marries Queen Sophie's lady-in-waiting but retains his love for Martina. Next, Achille Papin (Jean-Philippe Lafont), a famous opera singer comes to the town in search of rest and seclusion. He is a "Papist" and makes the sign of the cross but joins the Protestant faithful in hymn singing, which surprises the minister. He recognizes Filippa's marvelous voice and gives her singing lessons and falls in love with her. He wishes her to come to Paris with him, but her father nixes that relationship with a Roman Catholic, and Filippa stops taking lessons from him. When Papin returns to France, the minister is happy.

Years later on a stormy night, Babette appears. She had to leave France, and Papin, who never married and still loves Filippa, arranges for her to go to Jutland. There she is appalled at the grim food (salted cod, bread soaked in brine, etc.). Fourteen years pass as she works for the daughters. After the minister's death, small schisms begin to occur among the faithful. Recognizing that the 100th anniversary of their beloved minister's birth is looming, Babette makes a plea for peace and brotherhood. Having won 10,000 francs in a lottery, she decides to make a dinner. Instead of the modest supper the sisters request, she orders quail, turtle, and expensive glasses for wine; one sister has a nightmare of a drunken orgy. The lieutenant (now a general) comes to the feast and comments on the fine amontillado, the real turtle soup, the blinis demidoff, the Veuve Clicquot 1860 champagne, and especially the caille en sarcophagi which he remembers having in Paris. Only then is it revealed that Babette was the head chef at the Café Anglais in Paris where he had had the delicacy.

Commentary

Director and screenwriter Gabriel Axel adapted this bittersweet Danish classic by Isak Dinesen about religious fidelity, familial loyalty, foregone dreams, and good works, as well as good food acting as a communal cement. It deservedly won the Academy Award for Best Foreign Film. My late wife, an excellent French chef, loved this movie with its message that good food, bonhomie, and Christian feelings of peace and harmony are part of striving to be what Christ urged us to be. The religious overtones are subtle but unmistakable. The reference to the New Jerusalem as their ultimate home holds out the promise that despite the lack of fulfillment of foregone loves, as well as a career as a singer, the sisters will ultimately arise in glory. The same is true of Babette, whose brilliance as a chef is sublimated in making the simplest and most primitive of dishes. She not only gets a chance to revel in her artistry but to use it to good effect. The feast echoes the Last Supper where Christ broke bread with his disciples. The power of that feast to break down barriers and erase old enmities reminds one of Christ's message, "Do this in memory of me."

Broken Vows (1987)

The clueless and celibate Father McMahon (Tommie Lee Jones) is utterly unable to relate to sexuality and the real world. In hearing a boy's confession, he gives "the Church's opinion": "You can't touch the girl and you can't touch yourself." "Then what can you do?" asks the boy. Mc Mahon has a revelation while giving last rites to a gay artist. Before he dies, the man tells him he has to get out more. He learns that one "faithful" parishioner is shacked up with the wife of a guy who cruises gay bars. A gay man confronts him saying that, although he looked up to him, he could never speak to him except in the confessional when he was told not to sin again.

McMahon is called by someone who wants to talk about the "hang-ups of priests and nuns." The priest asks, "You mean celibacy?" "Yes, every time you pick up a paper, a priest is running off to marry his housekeeper," says the respondent. The priest goes off to find the artist's friend Nim (Annette O'Toole) to learn more about why he was murdered. He sits on her bed; candles are lit. They drink brandy, talk things through and have sex as he lets his cincture (the symbol of chastity) drop. He has to be at Church for the 8 o'clock Mass. "Are you going to confess and beg forgiveness?" she asks him. He replies, "I'm ashamed at betraying Christ. The Church said I made a solemn vow to Him." "You're a baby," she tells the priest. They both say they love one another as they say goodbye.

McMahon confesses to Monsignor Casey (Milo O'Shea). "God expects obedience," says Casey. To which McMahon answers, "And I have broken my vows." "You're not the first," Casey acknowledges. McMahon says that "The last 12 years have been too easy. I lost track of what the Church is all about. I'm not going to be a priest unless I can be a good one in whatever context that can be."

Commentary

The film's primary theme is that celibacy is harmful to the priestly vocation. One gets the feeling that breaking the vow of celibacy has redeemed Father McMahon whether he decides to remain a priest or not. In making that case, the film suggests that many priests are running off with their housekeepers. This is not only false but an interesting inversion of the truth in that at least 80 percent of the breaches of the vow of priestly chastity in the sexual abuse scandal involved homosexuality and about 5 percent pedophilia.

The second theme is that the Church should acknowledge practicing gay Catholics and in fact the girl tells him that the artist was more of a Christian than he, the Pope, and the Archbishop of Canterbury. The development of the relationship with the girl and the sudden effect of the dying man on the priest are not believable. As my wife Colette pointed out, there's better character development and a more credible depiction of the "heterosexual priest has an affair" theme in Father Andrew Greeley's books and *The Thorn Birds* TV mini-series, which remains the all-time classic of the genre.

The Last Temptation of Christ (1988)

This film, adapted by Paul Schrader and directed by Martin Scorsese from the novel by Nikos Kazantzakis, is one of the most controversial Christian-themed films of all time. Jesus (Willem Dafoe) is portrayed as a Jewish carpenter who makes crosses for the Romans to use in crucifixions and is beaten up by Judas (Harvey Keitel) for being a collaborator in the death of Jews. Indecisive as to what he should do, he mortifies himself with a silice (a sharp metal band around his leg), flagellation, and fasting, while waiting for God's direction. He goes to a whorehouse where he watches about ten people have sex with Mary Magdalene (Barbara Hershey). He is the last in line, but although he is the only one she loves, he refuses to have sex, for which he apologizes to her. He calls himself a chronic liar and a hypocrite. Saying that he has Lucifer inside of him, he refuses to rebel against God because of fear.

Judas tells him that he has been sent by the Jewish zealots to kill him, but he didn't do so because Jesus might be the Messiah. Jesus responds, "How could I be, when they wanted to stone Mary Magdalene to death, I wanted to kill them but only 'love' came out of my mouth." He meets up with John the Baptist who is whipping a bunch of naked people into a frenzy with fire and brimstone oratory and is baptized (without the appearance of a dove or the Father calling him his "beloved son").

Jesus is told to go to the desert where he is tempted several times by the devil in the form of a snake. He goes back to the apostles and pulls his heart out of his chest and says God is inside of us. He said he believed in love but now "I believe in this," brandishing an axe. He then starts curing people and resurrects Lazarus, but he rejects Mary as not being his mother. He clears the temple of the moneychangers and then asks Judas to betray him. There is a violent scene of his being scourged and getting kicked in the groin by the Roman soldiers, and being crowned with thorns. On the cross, he asks God to release him from the suffering. His guardian angel comes and takes him down from the cross and leads him to Mary Magdalene where they have sex, and she bears a child. When Mary is killed, under the premise that there is only one woman in the world with many faces, he partners with Lazarus's sister Mary and then Martha and has two other children. He is a happy carpenter until the day when the temple burns, and he is an old man and berated by the apostles and Judas for having run away like a coward when his place was on the cross rather than having a family. The guardian angel turns out to have been the devil in disguise. Jesus climbs back on the cross, saying, "I didn't want to be your son. Take me back. I want to be crucified and to be the Messiah." This is followed by "It is accomplished" and psychedelic colors.

Commentary

The film opens with a disclaimer that it is not based on the Gospels but upon Nikos Kazantzakis's fictional exploration of the incessant merciless battle between the spirit and the flesh, played out in the arena of Jesus's soul. One gets the feeling that the novel and the film represent the reflection of the struggles of Kazantzakis, and ex-seminarian Martin Scorsese, with their own personal demons, much as *The Passion of the Christ* was for Mel Gibson. Their point is that if Christ was truly human, he must have experienced all the temptations that beset them and everyone (such as lust,

Figure 8.5. *The Last Temptation of Christ.* **Jesus (Willem Dafoe) marries Mary Magdalene (Barbara Hershey) in a presumed reverie as he hangs on the cross.**

BACKSTORY

The Catholic League

Founded in 1973 by Jesuit Father Virgil C. Blum, the Catholic League for Religious and Civil Rights, commonly known as the "Catholic League," is an organization designed to "defend the rights of Catholics . . . to participate in American public life without defamation or discrimination." Although it is not formally connected to the Catholic Church, its offices are located within the headquarters of the Archdiocese of New York, and many high-ranking Church officials have endorsed the League's positions. In addition, although the League takes stands against movies it considers "anti-Catholic," it is not part of the United States Conference of Catholic Bishops Office of Film and Broadcasting (direct descendant of the National Legion of Decency), which continues to rank the appropriateness of films for Catholics. Through its current president, William A. Donohue, the Catholic League publicly comments on many issues that involve anti-Catholic expressions in politics, the arts, and the media. Not surprisingly, certain films—*The Last Temptation of Christ* and *Dogma*, for example—have incurred his wrath, and he has been vocal about their anti-Catholic content.

craving for power, vengeance, etc.). However, they seem to have forgotten that he was also God. Consequently, they picture Christ as a tortured soul, making crosses for executions, being a liar, as well as an indecisive and clueless wimp most of the time. His relationships with God, as well as Mary Magdalene, his mother Mary, and Lazarus's sisters are also confusing. The result is that he is overshadowed by Judas, who is the real star of the picture. So what is meant to be deep and philosophical comes off as largely incoherent and banal.

Many Christian groups picketed the film, which only gave it more visibility and notoriety than it deserved. Despite the publicity, this boring and excruciatingly long film sank under the weight of being neither entertaining nor, for most viewers, thought provoking. At times, it is unwatchable, which pretty much explains why it has not surfaced much in the past 20 years, although it remains a favorite of cineastes and critics. Peter Gabriel's score and David Bowie as Pilate serve as 1980's date stamps.

Jesus of Montreal (1989)

Daniel Coulombe (Lothaire Bluteau), the best student in his acting school class, returns to Montreal from a spiritual quest in India and Nepal. He is recruited to play Jesus in a new staging of the annual Passion play, whose overly dramatic and conventionally orthodox nature no longer attracts patrons. He assembles some of his old drama school buddies, beginning with Mirielle

(Catherine Wilkening), who works in a soup kitchen and sleeps with Father Leclerc (Gilles Pelletier), the priest who recruited him. She is naturally cast as Mary Magdalene. Martin (Rémy Girard) dubs porno films that feature threesome sex. Constance (Johanne-Marie Tremblay), who appears in provocative perfume ads and whose acting talent is said by her director/lover to be all in her rear end, is cast as the Virgin Mary. Finally, Rene (Robert Lepage) does a voice-over for a documentary on the Big Bang theory as explaining creation.

Daniel pores over texts in the library and "updates" the Passion story using recently discovered noncanonical Gnostic gospels to make it more relevant as well as catering to 1980s theatrical audiences with a nude Jesus on the Cross. Stating that we know little about Christ's birth or death and that what we know was written years later by his disciples, who may have embellished the story or lied, this version challenges the existence of Jesus or at least His importance. No longer considered to be the Messiah and "son of God" but the "son of man," Jesus is called Yeshua Ben Panthera, the illegitimate son of a Jewish mother and Panthera, a Roman soldier. He is likened to the many magicians like Simon who performed so-called miracles at a time when the world was believed to be flat, and there was much ignorance abroad. In true postmodern fashion, Daniel, as Jesus, encourages the people to beware of priests and look within themselves not to churches and other institutions for salvation.

The production is well received except by the Catholic clergy. Meanwhile, Daniel begins to turn Christ-like. After disrupting a commercial audition during which Constance is humiliated (driving the money-changers from the temple), the police arrest Daniel. He refuses help from a lawyer and pleads guilty to charges of vandalism and aggravated assault. A psychiatrist pronounces him saner than most judges. Having become an instant celebrity, he resists the various schemes of fame and fortune proposed by a slick lawyer (the temptation of the Devil) and takes up the cause of the poor and the needy.

Father Leclerc's clerical superiors send him to demand script modifications, or the performances will be canceled on the grounds that the play is being performed on private church property. This is met with ridicule by the actors, who almost complete one more performance when the police arrive to halt the play, and a riot ensues. One protestor inadvertently knocks over the Cross, and Daniel is severely injured. He is brought to a crowded Catholic hospital emergency room where he is ignored, and his companions are treated rudely. Daniel temporarily recovers and walks out of the hospital and begins preaching like Christ in the Montreal subway before collapsing. He is taken to an uncrowded Jewish hospital where he is given immediate attention, and his companions are treated caringly. Unfortunately, it's too late. His tragic death (as a Christ-figure) only adds to his legend and accomplishes what he resisted in life, memorialization by a theater in his name to perpetuate his message. In addition, the transplantation of his corneas and heart suggests that he will be resurrected, like Christ.

Commentary

While not agreeing with Adele Reinhartz's praise for this movie in her book *Jesus of Hollywood*, I do agree with her statement that this reconstruction of the Passion and the Jesus story from noncanonical sources is "anti-history." She goes on to say that it "serves as a powerful vehicle for the major themes of his (Denys Arcand's) film: the hypocrisy of the Catholic Church in Quebec and the degradation of art where bottom line means all." It is not coincidental that much of the story centers on the St. Joseph's Oratory on Mount Royal, a major pilgrimage site where the faithful ascend its steep steps on their knees. Arcand is one of the many Quebecois who, in the last 40 years, have rejected the Church and the piety of their presumably ignorant and easily led forebears. He personifies the hypocrisy in a Father Leclerc, who came from a poor family and entered the priesthood at 19 where he found comfort and status and, as a theater buff, was able to see all the great theatrical personages. Despite breaking his vow of chastity, he refuses to send his resignation to Rome to marry his lover because, bereft of skills, all he'll get is $50, some clothes, and a "bye-bye." He also refuses to alienate his superiors by defending his friends who created a new version of the Passion using writings "suppressed by the Church." His order to shut down the play ultimately leads to the death of Daniel (Jesus).

To my mind, the film is as much about the theater and the price of celebrity as it is about Jesus or religious institutions and their representatives. The latter, none of whom are praiseworthy, are subjected to ridicule and one-sided polemics with no recognition that belief in Christ and his message has more to do with faith than scientific or literary proofs. It's true that we don't know what Christ looked like, nor do we have much solid information about his birth and much of his life. That's why those who have faith are called "believers," but that does not mean that those who call themselves Christian are free from sin. One is tempted to say, "Ye of little faith protesteth too much." Why bother tearing down and ridiculing the beliefs of others? Rather seek a belief system that fits you better.

Figure 8.6. *Jesus of Montreal.* **Daniel Coulombe (Lothaire Bluteau) takes on Christ's persona and chases the Materialists out of the studio.**

The film is far from entertaining. It will appeal to those who like avant-garde films or enjoy seeing the Catholic Church getting its comeuppance. Others should skip it unless they want to use it as a springboard to discuss Gnostic gospels and Christology or whether hypocrisy, licentiousness, and venality by clerics and even Popes vitiate the Catholic Church's claim to being a "divine institution in human hands." One thing in the film's favor is that if an actor is going to become his character, then I would much prefer that he become Christ-like rather than the character played by Ronald Colman in *A Double Life* who becomes Othello offstage and murders a woman.

Short Subjects

Tender Mercies (1983)

Though episodic, this gentle, song-filled film became a popular favorite on the strength of an Academy Award–winning screenplay by Horton Foote and a bravura performance by Robert Duvall who won the Oscar for Best Actor. It opens with Mac Sledge (Duvall), a legendary country singer but now a penniless has-been, hitting alcoholic rock bottom in an isolated Texas motel. The owner, a beautiful Vietnam War widow and devout Christian, Rosa Lee (Tess Harper), puts him to work for room and board and $2 an hour if he forswears alcohol. She and her precocious ten-year-old son Sonny (Allan Hubbard) help him to overcome his demons including two failed marriages, spouse abuse, and alienation from his teenaged daughter, Sue Ann (Ellen Barkin). In so doing, he learns how to love, not just be loved, and the three become family.

The title comes from Rosa Lee telling him, "When I say my prayers, I thank the Lord for his blessings and tender mercies, and you and Sonny head the list." The scenes surrounding the double baptism by immersion of Sonny and Mac are especially touching. Despite Mac's redemption, the film, though uplifting, ends on a sober note when, after Sue Ann is killed in a car accident, Mac questions why God has done this to him and says, "I don't trust happiness; never have, never will." In short, the message is to enjoy the present because one never knows what the future may bring.

Places in the Heart (1984)

Though farfetched, this story of a sheriff's widow, Edna Spalding (Sally Field), who saves her farm during the Depression with the help of an itinerant black farm worker, Moze (Danny Glover), and a blind boarder, Mr. Will (John Malkovich), is heartwarming. Field (who won an Oscar for Best Actress in a Leading Role) and Glover are outstanding. However, the film would have been stronger without the interweaving of an irrelevant and annoying subplot of an adulterous affair involving Spalding's brother-in-law Wayne Lomax (Ed Harris). The film is included because of the religious elements that occur at the beginning and end. During the opening credits, the director pans a church and then numerous instances of people saying grace before meals. Thereafter, God is only referred to sporadically, usually by Moze, but reenters in force at the end with a fantasy service at a Protestant church. Here the dead and living, who have been enemies, reconcile saying "Peace of God" as they receive the Eucharist under both forms of bread and wine with the latter being distributed in tiny containers, a way that was not yet in use in the 1930s. While the sentiment is worthy and many were touched by it, I found it somewhat incongruous given that in the prior scene KKK members in the congregation savagely beat Moze and ran him out of town. I was left wondering what had occasioned this sudden change of heart.

Witness (1985)

John Book (Harrison Ford,) a detective investigating a murder in the men's room at the 30th Street train station in Philadelphia, discovers that a young Amish boy (Lukas Haas) witnessed the crime and quick-wittedly escaped detection. Although the boy is unable to identify the murderer in lineups, Book begins to suspect police involvement. He, the boy, and his widowed mother (Kelly McGillis) become targets, and after Book is seriously wounded, they escape to Amish country in Pennsylvania. The movie takes on spiritual and romantic elements that elevate it from a procedural thriller to the first rank. The spiritual elements include a respectful portrayal of the Amish way of life, not just focusing on their eschewing technology, but on their sense of family and community. They help one another build barns and houses and rush to one another's aid in times of danger and need. They welcome the hard-boiled detective whom they call "English." As the widow nurses Book back to health, they fall in love. This is conveyed in a tasteful and memorable series of romantic scenes, culminating in their dancing to Sam Cooke's "What A Wonderful World" before the screen fades to black. Despite the love between them, as well as between Book and the child, the fact that they live in irreconcilable worlds adds poignancy to the story.

The Assisi Underground (1985)

This film is included because, like *The Scarlet and the Black*, it recounts the true story of Catholic clergy and laymen rescuing Italian Jews during World War II. Unfortunately, it is neither as entertaining nor as well acted as the former. Based on *The Assisi Underground: The Priests Who Rescued Jews* by Alexander Ramati, the film describes the Catholic underground network that helped Jewish refugees escape the Nazis after the Germans occupied Italy in September 1943. A nun, Madre Giuseppina (Irene Papas), works with a Franciscan Friar, Padre Rufino (Ben Cross), and Bishop Nicolini (James Mason in his last role), to hide 15 Jews, including a nuclear scientist and his wife (Professor Rieti [Roberto Boccardo] and Eva Rieti [Didi Ramati]). They vouch that the Jews are Christian pilgrims and hide them in the Chapel of St. Francis and the Cloister of St. Clare in Assisi. They smuggle in insulin for the wife, but when they are prevented from doing so, she dies. Commandant Muller (Maximilian Schell), a devout Catholic, seemingly unwittingly aids the priests. When the SS Commandant in nearby Perugia captures some of the Jews and their helpers, Muller asks that he spare them. The other replies, "We have shot 3,000 priests in Europe. Do you think we will hesitate to shoot one more?" He does spare the priest but kills some of the others, and releases the rest.

On June 17, 1944, the Allies entered Assisi, and the closing credits state that 80 percent of the 40,000 Italian Jews were saved. Padre Rufino was named a Righteous Gentile. Bishop Nicolini and Madre Giuseppina were praised for their efforts. Commandant Muller was absolved of war crimes and returned to Assisi in 1950. Mario Rieti rose to be the head of a department at a New York university and another refugee, Gino Bartali, became a championship cyclist and won the Tour de France.

The Name of the Rose (1986)

Despite having good actors, the confusing plot and the unrelievedly dark atmospheric setting make it more frustrating than entertaining. Set in the Middle Ages, its protagonist is a monk/investigator, William (Sean Connery), who tries to solve murders that are occurring in a gloomy monastery with a forbidding tower and a labyrinth at the bottom. Unlike the down-to-earth William, the monks at this place are a bunch of weirdos typified by Bernardo Gui played by F. Murray Abraham at his most saturnine. William tells us what's going on using his protégé, trusty novice Adso of Melk (Christian Slater), as a sounding board. One monk is found dead at the base of the tower; another drowns in a barrel of wine. The Grand Inquisitor makes an appearance, and things really get confused as ancient secrets are revealed. William and Adso are in dire peril and escape, leaving us as much in the dark as ever. All we are left with in this long slow-moving film is the memory of those weirdo monks. It must be celibacy that's responsible.

Au Revoir Les Enfants (1987)

The title of Louis Malle's recollections of his boarding school days during the last years of World War II, "Goodbye Children," can be taken on at least four levels. The most literal is at the beginning, when a wealthy mother (Francine Racette) is saying good-bye to her two sons at the train station after Christmas vacation for their return to school. The younger brother Julien Quentin (Gaspard Manesse) is the smart-aleck class leader, always making fun of the teachers and playing pranks and inflicting petty cruelties on classmates, including a new student Jean Bonnet (Raphael Fejtö). The second level involves much of the early part of the film that focuses on the coming of age of adolescent boys saying good-bye to childhood.

The third level represents a true good-bye to childhood innocence for Julien, who is blissfully unaware of the war going on around him and doesn't know what a Jew is. He comes to realize that Jean, whom he has disliked as a competitor but slowly bonds with, is one of four Jewish boys being hidden by the priest director Père Jean (Philippe Morier-Genoud). The fourth level occurs when a disgruntled ex-employee betrays the Jewish students, and the local Gestapo enters the classroom asking for Jean. Julien instinctively looks back at him, inadvertently giving him away. As the priest and the children are rounded up and marched away, Julien must truly say good-bye to the children, leaving an indelible mark on his psyche.

The boys were sent to Auschwitz and were executed immediately. Père Jean was shipped to Compeigne, Neue Bremm, and Mauthausen where he shared his sparse rations and ministered to the prisoners. He died of tuberculosis three weeks after liberation. This remarkable film, one of my wife's favorites and one she used in her middle school French immersion classes, lost the Oscar to *Babette's Feast* as best foreign film of the year. It is included because it illustrates how French clergy and laypersons hid Jewish children at great peril to themselves.

Romero (1989)

Produced by Paulist Father Ellwood Kieser known as the "Hollywood Priest," this is the first feature film financed by the Catholic Church. *Romero* tells the true story of Archbishop Oscar Arnulfo Romero y Galdamez (Raul Julia). He was named Archbishop of El Salvador in the late 1970s with the approval of the government leaders. They were convinced that he was a conservative bookworm who wouldn't make any waves and, because of his delicate health, wouldn't live long. However, he becomes increasingly aware of massive human rights violations, such as the killing of an activist priest, who advocated land reform and better wages, and the "disappearance" of political opponents by the corrupt government.

BACKSTORY

The Worst of the 1980s

This decade, especially the last half, saw the acceleration of the downward trend in reverence to Christianity in the movies. The following films are mentioned briefly only to illustrate their irreverence and tastelessness. Oddly enough, many featured well-known movie stars, but almost all bombed at the box office. Mel Brooks's *History of the World-Part I* (1981), narrated by Orson Welles, is a pastiche of prolonged and generally tasteless skits parodying, among other things, the Ten Commandments, the Inquisition, and the Last Supper. *Monsignor* (1982) stars Christopher Reeves as a priest who connives with a Mafioso to control the Vatican Bank with the aid of a corrupt Cardinal and is brought down after seducing an idealistic nun (Genevieve Bujold) and being complicit in her death. Tom Berenger in *Last Rites* (1988) plays a priest and son of a Mafioso, who gets involved with a Mexican woman, the mob, and murder. In *The Penitent* (1988), Raul Julia is the penitent who becomes involved in a New Mexican primitive and brutal Catholic cult that graphically reenacts the Crucifixion. Two escaped convicts (Robert De Niro and Sean Penn) in *We're No Angels* (1989) are welcomed as distinguished Church scholars at a monastery where they sell souvenirs with the Weeping Virgin on one side and a thermometer on the other. Don't mistake it for the incomparably better 1956 film of the same name, which has nothing to do with religion.

When Romero confronts the president-elect, he is told to stay out of politics. He responds that he will write the American president to halt the arms being shipped to El Salvador that are being used to kill the people and becomes a "revolutionary," along the lines of Gandhi. A government-sponsored sign is shown that reads, "Be a patriot, kill a priest" as government sponsored "death squads" begin to murder priests and destroy churches. In 1980, while Romero is saying mass, he is assassinated in a manner that echoes *Becket* (p. 169). The movie ends with the declaration that "The Bishop may die but the Church of God will never perish." Though this film is not great art, being more like a human rights documentary than a traditional feature film, it makes up for this with the star power of Raul Julia. It is compelling as a depiction of the life of the Catholic Church in a Latin American country and of a martyr worthy of sainthood. In 1997, Pope John Paul II bestowed upon Romero the title of Servant of God as a step in the process of canonization as a saint, and he is one of only ten 20th-century martyrs depicted above the Great West Door of Westminster Abbey, London.

Cinema Paradiso (1989)

Set in postwar Sicily, Giuseppe Tornatore's warm-hearted, nostalgic, partially autobiographical film is a testament to how much movies meant to the populace in transporting them out of their poverty-stricken, war-torn surroundings to other worlds. This is especially true for a young boy named Salvatore Di Vita or "Toto" (Salvatore Cascio) whose father died on the Russian front and who hangs around the theater pestering the projectionist Alfredo (Philippe Noiret). Their relationship as surrogate father and son deepens when Toto, whose full name means "lifesaver" in Italian, pulls Alfredo from the burning theater after the nitrate film catches fire. Toto becomes essential as an assistant to the now blinded projectionist. The film follows them into Toto's young adulthood (Jacques Perrin) and his first love that is unrequited. Alfredo urges him to leave his hometown for Rome and never to return. The reason for including this Oscar-winning foreign film is because of the early scenes where the parish priest previews all the movies and orders all the scenes of kissing cut. The well-meaning but narrow-minded priest is portrayed sympathetically and even comically. Tornatore ingeniously uses the clips to bring the movie full circle at the end, as Alfredo had spliced them together to be given as his posthumous gift to Toto, now a big-time movie director.

DOGMA: THE 1990s

T he 1990s in the United States was an era of economic prosperity, dominated by President William Jefferson Clinton, especially the last half of the decade. He was impeached but was not removed from office, although later he was disbarred for lying under oath about his relationship with a White House intern. Nonetheless, his popularity was such that, had he been permitted to seek a third term, it is likely that he would have been reelected. Although the decade was generally peaceful, there were some major occurrences. The first bombing of the World Trade Center by Islamic terrorists occurred in 1993, although its portent was not recognized until September 11, 2001. In December 1998, President Clinton ordered four days of bombing in Iraq to destroy a facility thought to be manufacturing weapons of mass destruction. He also sent troops to Bosnia and Kosovo. Finally, the suicide bombing of the USS *Cole* at its berth in Yemen during the run-up to the 2000 presidential election was another omen for what would occur in the millennium. On the domestic front, the failed health care reform effort and a tax increase early in the Clinton presidency helped Republicans capture Congress in 1994. To the credit of all concerned, this resulted in genuine bipartisanship in enacting important legislation in such matters as welfare reform, tax policy, and education.

During this decade, computer technology boomed, making many people—most stunningly many very *young* people—incredibly rich. As Ben Mezrich says in *Bringing Down the House*, his book about the six MIT students who took Las Vegas casinos for millions, "If the 80s made greed more acceptable, the 90s elevated it to an art form." The general affluence of the age continued to foster self-indulgence and a sense that rules were meant to be broken. It was also a decade when the national consensus about mores and morals, once seemingly apparent or at least taken for granted, generally eroded. This was abetted by the rapidity with which often diametrically opposed beliefs could be transmitted via the Internet. The philosophy that "the end justifies the means" gained greater currency during the decade in different walks of life, including government, business, and sports. One flagrant illustration was the widespread use of steroids and other performance-enhancing drugs by baseball players in defiance of laws, with the complicity of owners and baseball's management. This led to players breaking longstanding records cherished by diehard fans as well as big paydays for the players involved.

Cell phones and e-mail became ubiquitous, fostering instantaneous communication and altering how, when, and what we communicated. They came to be used for good (for emergencies) as well as bad (drug traffickers and terrorists). Increasingly, people, especially the young, spent more time with computers and less time in personal interaction and communication. For the most part, quiet reflection and the ability to make oneself blissfully unavailable were lost.

Films of the 1990s

Cinematic blockbusters continued to be produced, most notably *Titanic* (which not only won 11 Oscars in 1997—the same number that *Ben-Hur* won 40 years earlier—but became the biggest grossing film of all time). Other popular films included *Star Wars: Episode 1* (1997), *Jurassic Park* (1993), *Forrest Gump* (1994), *Men in Black* (1997), and Disney's *The Lion King* (1994). All these films, with the exception of *Titanic*, were fantasies and/or science fiction and were enhanced by truly astonishing special effects, again as a result of the enormous advancements in computer technology. More traditional films were also critical and financial successes, including *The English Patient, Life is Beautiful, Schindler's List, The Cider House Rules*, and *Saving Private Ryan*.

Christians in 1990s Films

More Christian-themed films were produced during the 1990s, most of which reflected the continuing lack of respect for the Christian faith. Of the films discussed in this chapter, two-thirds are critical of Christians, including several that contain a high degree of vitriol and obscenity aimed at the Catholic Church (for example, *The Basketball Diaries* and *Dogma*). Movies such as *The Pope Must Die, Nuns on the Run, Sleepers, Primal Fear, Stigmata, The Godfather Part III*, and *The Cider House Rules* were also part of this trend. We'd come a long way from the priests played by Bing Crosby and Spencer Tracy! The times had indeed changed. Parishioners, whether Catholic or Protestant, were much better educated (at least generally, if not in their religions). Priests and ministers couldn't automatically command respect because of their station, presumed erudition, or collar. Indeed, many religious stopped wearing such outward signs of their office.

As this chapter's title highlights, the movies of this decade were, on average, the most antagonistic to orthodox dogma and institutional religion, especially Catholicism, and were a major impetus for the creation of this book. The sexual revolution of the 1960s and 1970s had led many congregants to challenge orthodox dogma with regard to birth control, abortion, divorce, and homosexuality. As a result, the number of so-called "lapsed Catholics" grew (said to be 10 percent of Americans in a 2007 survey of the Pew Forum on Religion and Public Life). The memberships in traditional Presbyterian, Episcopal, and other Protestant denominations declined even more sharply as their faithful drifted to more Evangelical and Pentecostal congregations. Trying to stem this tide, the mainstream Protestant denominations modified their stances about these contentious subjects, especially divorce, abortion, and homosexuality. As they did, they became less threatening to secularists. Nevertheless, Orthodox Catholics, Fundamentalists, and Evangelicals continued to hold fast to traditional dogmas and Biblical precepts, and, as a result, became the target-of-choice by moviemakers. The latter came in for some hits in such films as *Misery*, *Rapture*, and *The Shawshank Redemption*.

Films like *Priest* continued to focus on clerics' breaking of the vows of celibacy and one, *The Boys of St. Vincent*, was particularly prescient in that its appearance predated the explosion on the national scene of the subject of pedophilia, in this case by lay brothers. According to the report of the John Jay College of Criminal Justice to the National Catholic Conference of Bishops issued in 2005 and supplemented in 2008, the abuse involved 4 to 5 percent of priests, 80 percent of which were homosexual encounters and about 5 percent of which involved pedophilia.

Despite this spate of negative films, some noteworthy films were released in the 1990's, including an undisputed classic (*Schindler's List*), and three (*Sister Act, Rudy, Dead Man Walking*) which treated the Catholic religious in an affectionate style more reminiscent of films of the 1940s and 1950s. Another, *The Apostle*, honored the Christian belief in redemption and was the product—at his own personal expense—of respected actor Robert Duvall. The emergence of these films, not to mention their acclaim and popularity, gave some hope that positive Christian references were still possible in American film.

The Godfather Part III (1990)

The film opens in 1979 in New York City where Michael Corleone (Al Pacino) has resettled. Divorced from his wife and estranged from his children, he invites them to attend a solemn ceremony in which he will receive one of the highest papal honors, in recognition of his charitable contributions. At the party afterwards, he announces a gift of $100 million for the poor in Sicily and the resurrection of the church there to be administered through the Corleone Foundation headed by his daughter Mary (Sofia Coppola).

Craving legitimacy, Michael tries to put his life of crime behind him and distributes large sums at his "farewell" meeting with the heads of the five families. However, he is sucked back into the gang warfare when Joey Zasa (Joe Mantegna) and his mentor, the head of the Altobello family (Eli Wallach), engineer an attempt to kill him and the others. Egged on by his sister Connie (Talia Shire), who wants the old ways to continue, Michael reluctantly agrees to avenge the assassination attempt. He employs Vincent Mancini (Andy Garcia), his brother Sonny's illegitimate son who is a hothead and a Lothario like his father. Vincent, dressed as a mounted policeman, kills Zasa during a festive procession through New York's Little Italy.

The major subplot involves Michael's pledge to help bail out the Vatican Bank, which has been looted and mismanaged out of $700 million by the venal Archbishop Gilday (Donal Donnelly), his compatriot Frederick Keinszig (Helmut Berger), known as "God's banker," and an Italian Mafioso, Don Licio Lucchesi (Enzo Robutti). In exchange, he will gain control of a legitimate Italian institution allied to the Bank and to the Vatican. Ratification of the deal is delayed by the death of Pope Paul VI. When Michael's friend Cardinal Lamberto (Raf Vallone), "a true priest" and reformer, ascends the papal throne as Pope John Paul I, the deal is approved, and everything looks good. But then, the Archbishop poisons the Pope, and Keinszig absconds to London with millions.

Other subplots involve Mary Corleone falling in love with her first cousin Vincent against Michael's wishes, and his son Tony (Franc D'Ambrosio) becoming an opera singer instead of a lawyer, as the Don had wished. Everything comes to a head when all go to Sicily for Tony's debut in *Cavalleria Rusticana*, and Vincent and Connie orchestrate the assassinations of the Archbishop, Keinszig, Lucchesi, and Altobello interwoven into the opera performance. After the performance, on the steps of the Opera House, an assassin that Altobello had hired to kill Michael only wounds him and instead kills Mary. Michael's loud scream is the last sound heard, and he dies alone in his garden years later.

Commentary

Bloated at 161 minutes, this film is really a Coppola home movie, which is how he described it in *Newsweek* at the time of the film's release, a story of a family using his family. The movie is also a reunion of the original *Godfather* cast survivors except for Tom Hagen, the Godfather's *consigliere* in the first two films, because Robert Duvall balked when they offered him less money than Pacino. Daughter Sofia gives a totally unconvincing performance in the pivotal role of the Godfather's daughter Mary. Coppola's sister Talia Shire, who was excellent in the original *Rocky* and tolerable in the previous *Godfather* films, overacts, as do the acclaimed actors Joe Mantegna and Eli Wallach. The perpetually suntanned George Hamilton, who replaced Robert Duvall as the consigliere, looks like a fish out of water. The film received Oscar nominations for Best Picture, Best Director, Best Supporting Actor (Andy Garcia), Best Direction and Best Editing, Art Direction, Cinematography, and Original Song, but won none.

As with the other films in the series, violence is omnipresent and is often juxtaposed with religious ceremony and spectacle. This one involves a Mafia-infiltrated Vatican with a ruthless Archbishop, a corrupt Vatican banker, and the presumed poisoning of a would-be reformer Pope. This led movie critic Michael Medved to note that by Michael's unwillingness to deal drugs and his desire for legitimacy, "the leaders of organized crime display more scruples and human emotion than the leaders of organized religion." Still, to be fair to Coppola, the script was based on unproven conspiracy theories about Pope John Paul I's death 33 days after his elevation and corrupt practices by the Vatican bankers with ties to the Mafia in a book by Yallop, later refuted by Cornwell. By lending intrigue and grand visuals, these theories were a godsend to Coppola, who had originally not wanted to make a sequel, and who had discarded various scripts involving the drug trade over the years.

There are novel touches in this new crop of assassinations, such as the Archbishop having a rosary stuffed in his mouth before being suffocated, and my favorite, death-by-cannoli during an opera performance. Although there is one estimable clergyman in Cardinal Lamberto, for the most part, religion is used as a morbid, superstitious, and hypocritical prop, inviting

Figure 9.1. *The Godfather Part III.* Two killers dressed as priests murder the local Mafia boss.

ridicule. In short, one can be mesmerized by the Godfather saga's sense of detail and yet be turned off by its distortion of the concept of family, of an ethnic group, and of a religion.

Black Robe (1991)

Based on a novel by Brian Moore, this is the story of an idealistic Jesuit, Father Laforgue (Lothaire Bluteau), who wants to convert the Indians in New France (Quebec) in the 17th century. As an altar boy in Rouen, his idol was a Jesuit who had returned after having his fingers severed by the Iroquois but vowed to go back saying, "What is more glorious than converting the savages?" After two Jesuits are massacred at a mission among the Hurons, Father Laforgue embarks on a 1,500-mile trip up the Saint Lawrence River as winter approaches. His only companions are Algonquins, whose leader Chomina (August Schellenberg) vows to protect him, and a young Frenchman, Daniel (Aden Young), who idolizes him and wants to become a priest.

On the trip upriver, the Indians blame the Jesuit or "Black Robe" for their misfortunes. After inadvertently witnessing Daniel having sex with Chomina's daughter Annuka (Sandrine Holt), Father LaForgue flagellates himself as penance. The Indians and Daniel desert him, but Chomina orders them back. The Iroquois capture them and plan to skin the survivors alive, but Annuka seduces and kills a guard, allowing them to escape. Arriving at a place that Chomina had dreamt would be his last resting place, he dies.

Laforgue wonders why Chomina, who was better than many Christians, would not see God and asks himself, "What can we say to people who feel that their dreams are the real world and that this world is only an illusion?" Then he answers, "Perhaps they are right?"

Laforgue goes alone to the Huron mission, as predicted in Chomina's dream, and finds a Jesuit killed by the Hurons for being "responsible" for an epidemic of fever. The Hurons are initially hostile, saying, "The Black Robes want us to give up our dreams, have only one wife, and stop killing our enemies. If we do, we will no longer be Hurons." However, they agree to be baptized if it will end the fever, and LaForgue baptizes them en masse. The film ends with a visual of the sun gleaming on a cross. The epilogue says, "Fifteen years later, the Hurons, having accepted Christianity, were routed and killed by their enemies, the Iroquois."

Commentary

This morality play tells a more realistic story of the culture clash between Native Americans and the "white man" than the acclaimed 1990 film *Dances with Wolves*. Beautifully photographed with a very evocative sound track, it is very slow moving and lacks *Dances'* humor. Seeing it with a storm raging outside the theater made me better appreciate the privations suffered by the dour and intense black-robed priest bent on "converting the savages" and

Figure 9.2. *Black Robe.* **Father Laforgue (Lothaire Bluteau) sets off with the Hurons on a 1,500- mile trip to a mission where the previous priest was killed.**

BACKSTORY

Isaac Jogues: The Black Robe

Born in Orleans, France, in 1607, Isaac was the fifth of nine children. He entered the Jesuit novitiate at Rouen and trained to be a missionary in New France where he was sent in 1636. Arriving at Trois Rivieres and not knowing the language, he was sent upriver in a canoe with five Hurons to the Huron mission. After six years of relative peace and harmony, he was sent to Quebec to get supplies and on the return was ambushed on August 3, 1642, by the Iroquois. Most of the Hurons fled, and he and his two companions were captured. He was serially tortured or "caressed" by running the gauntlet while being savagely beaten, as well as having his fingernails and fingers removed except for his right thumb. He was enslaved for 13 months while the Iroquois refused ransom by the Dutch Calvinists. Finally, when he was destined to be burnt at the stake, the Calvinists induced him to escape, and he was sent back to France via New Amsterdam.

Arriving in a state of destitution, he was received by the Rector at Rennes who, not recognizing him, asked news of Jogues, who was said to be dead, and was told that he was speaking to Jogues. He was welcomed at Court and allowed by Pope Urban IV to celebrate Mass, which was canonically forbidden because of his mutilated hands. Sent back to New France at his request in 1644, he negotiated peace with his former Iroquois captors in early June 1646. Giving up safety in Quebec and returning to New York, he was blamed for illness and crop blight. Beaten and slashed with knives, near what is now Lake George, he was taken to the Iroquois village (now Auriesville) where he was tomahawked. His head was placed on the fort's palisade, and his body thrown into the Mohawk River. In 1930, Jogues and his seven companions (the North American martyrs) were canonized by the Catholic Church.

the small Algonquin band on their 1,500-mile journey. It very sensitively portrays the clash in beliefs and the challenge to the Jesuit's certainty of his vision. The film with its episodes of violence, interspersed among images of utter tranquility, will turn off some, and mesmerize others, especially those with a fondness for Native Americans, French Canada, Jesuits, philosophy, and the Adirondacks/St. Lawrence region. Even so, the seeming futility may leave many like *Chicago Sun-Times* reviewer Roger Ebert "in a state of depressed suspension, wondering if that could possibly be all there was." That there was is evident from the story of Saint Isaac Jogues (see above).

Sister Act (1992)

Deloris van Cartier (Whoopi Goldberg), a lounge singer in Reno, Nevada, is having an affair with a gangster, casino owner Vince LaRocca (Harvey Keitel). Refusing to divorce his wife and marry her, he tells her that he went to confession and told Father Antonelli that theirs was a special love, and the priest said that if he got a divorce, he would burn in hell for all eternity.

He asks her, "You want me to go against a priest and get ex-communicated?" When she inadvertently witnesses a murder, she realizes that her boyfriend "kills people" and that she is now in danger. Given refuge in the Witness Protection Program, she is assigned to a sympathetic cop, Eddie Souther (Bill Nunn), who places her in a San Francisco convent, figuring nobody would look for her there. That the nuns are all white seems hardly optimal, but the role was originally designed for Bette Midler.

The rest of the film is a genial comedy as Sister "Mary Clarence" gets the nun's choir to stop singing "Hail Holy Queen Enthroned Above" off-key while adding a little bounce. She fills the pews as they do a version of "My Guy" which becomes "My God" about Jesus. The Mother Superior (Maggie Smith) is the only one aware that "Mary Clarence" has not taken the vows and is reluctant to let this potentially bad actor into her convent, which has withdrawn from the surrounding neighborhood as it changed demographically. With some misgivings, she allows her to proselytize and reach out to the poor, which leads to her being discovered and kidnapped, only to be saved in a rather silly chase through Reno. Fortunately, the movie ends rousingly as the now de-frocked Sister Mary Clarence leads the choir in a take-off on "I Will Follow Him" in a command performance for the Pope during his visit to San Francisco. The Pope claps in rhythm and then initiates a standing O.

Commentary

Reminiscent of comedies of the 1940s and 1950s, this well-written, well-directed, and well-acted film is pure entertainment as films were once meant to be. Viewers need only suspend disbelief and simply enjoy it. Actually, many critics, including Roger Ebert, were not impressed with it, but the public, including my family, loved it. It earned over $230 million at the box office worldwide and over $60 million in DVD rentals. A sequel, *Sister Act 2: Back in the Habit,* was rushed out the following year with Goldberg as a Vegas star being asked to put on her habit again to save a Catholic school from closing. The cliché-ridden and derivative script was terrible, and the film fell flat.

While the nuns in *Sister Act* come off as overly naïve and simple, they are not portrayed as idiots. Maggie Smith is especially good as the Mother Superior, who has the strength to stand up to Sister Mary Clarence, yet is wise enough (sometimes against her will) to give her enough rope to pull off her feats with the choir and the public. Mary Wickes is also very good as the inept choir director, Sister Mary Lazarus, who is displeased at being displaced but comes around. Finally, Kathy Najimy adds life to the movie

Figure 9.3. *Sister Act*. Hiding out in a convent, lounge singer Deloris van Cartier (Whoopi Goldberg) leads the choir in a religious version of "My Guy."

as the portly, ebullient Sister Mary Patrick who buys into the change in the choir's direction from the outset.

As for the film itself, what is most interesting is that it portrays the Catholic Church in a respectful and sympathetic way. While light and unrealistic, it calls attention to the plight of inner city parishes, many of which have closed as their traditional ethnic flocks moved to the suburbs. In this case, the parish is impoverished, and the church is mainly empty. The nuns remain behind their walls, having withdrawn from the community until Sister Mary Clarence gets them to mingle with their neighbors and alters the liturgy, thus filling the church. While the liturgical transformation makes for successful cinema, it misses the reality about those parishes which have been able to survive and even thrive in the inner city. They have done so principally by offering an alternative to failed public schools by educating the children of the neighborhood, even when the majority of the families do not profess Catholicism. Maybe that's why the sequel focused on rescuing the school but turned out to be just too weak a copy of *The Bells of St. Mary's* and its predecessor.

Rudy (1993)

Rudy (Sean Astin), one of 14 children growing up in a devout Catholic family in Joliet, Illinois, dreams of going to Notre Dame, but his father (Ned Beatty) tells him the school is only for rich kids, smart kids, and great athletes. His high school coach encourages him, as does his best friend and coworker Pete (Christopher Reed), who tells him that "dreams are what makes life tolerable." He joins his father and brother working in a steel mill. After Pete's accidental death, Rudy visits Notre Dame where he is fortunate to meet the school's past president, Father John Cavanaugh (Robert Prosky). Cavanaugh is supportive without promising Rudy anything. He says two things are incontrovertible in this world, "There is a God and I'm not Him." He says that he will get Rudy into nearby Holy Cross Junior College and that semester by semester, he can continue if his grades are good.

Rudy also starts working with Fortune (Charles S. Dutton), Notre Dame's black janitor/groundskeeper who is supportive of his dream one day to wear a Notre Dame football uniform, even while telling him: "Look at you. You're five foot nuthin' and you weigh a hundred and nuthin' and with hardly a speck of athletic ability." At Holy Cross Junior College, he is diagnosed with Attention Deficit Disorder (ADD) and dyslexia and improves with counseling. In 1974, after two years of hard work, Rudy is admitted to Notre Dame, and his proud father is ecstatic. Football Coach Ara Parseghian (Jason Miller) allows Rudy to play on the practice squad despite his small size, and he uncomplainingly takes a bruising and a battering from his much larger teammates. Two days before the final game with Georgia Tech in Rudy's senior year, the captain and the other players go to the office of Coach Dan Devine (Chelcie Ross), who had replaced Parseghian, and ask that Rudy be one of the 60 players allowed by NCAA rules to dress for the game. The student body finds out through the newspaper that Rudy will suit up.

After a priest says the Hail Mary in the locker room, Rudy leads the team onto the field. Then they pray "Our Lady of Victory" and the response "Pray for us." Devine doesn't want to put Rudy in the game, but the players start a "Rudy" chant which fills the stadium. The coach reluctantly puts him in on the last play, and Rudy is triumphantly carried off the field.

Commentary

This is the quintessential feel-good movie and is one of the few recent films to show Catholicism and priests in a favorable light. It also portrays a very warm relationship of Rudy with the black groundskeeper, who lets Rudy sleep on the premises because of his financial straits and who encourages him, ultimately sharing in his glorious moment. As noted on the DVD, the film is very faithful to the true story of Daniel E. "Rudy" Ruettiger, who says that his story's real message is "Hope is the most powerful thing you can give people." The first movie filmed on the Notre Dame campus since *Knute Rockne All-American,* it was directed by David Anspaugh, who along with screenwriter Angelo Pizzo, was responsible for the 1986 film *Hoosiers* that is considered one of the best sports movies of all-time. In 2005, *Rudy* was cited as one of the best sports films of the past 25 years.

Shadowlands (1993)

In 1950s England, C. S. "Jack" Lewis (Anthony Hopkins), a noted author, lives a safe cloistered existence as an Oxford Don. Once an atheist, he has undergone a conversion and writes and talks on Christian themes. He is portrayed as having all the answers, whether teaching or on the lecture circuit. Early on in the story, he reads a letter about a bus veering off course and killing 24 royal cadets. The letter's author asks: "Where was God?" and "Why didn't he prevent it?" and "Does God not love us?" Lewis's answer is: "It's because God loves us that he makes us the gift of suffering. Or to put it another way, pain is God's megaphone to rouse a deaf world."

This somewhat facile answer will be challenged when he meets poet Joy Davidman Gresham (Debra Winger) and her son Douglas (Joseph Mazzello). Described as a "Jewish, Communist American," Joy has also converted to Christianity and as a fan of Lewis's writings, has begun a long-distance correspondence with him. She visits him at Oxford and shakes up both his life and the very intellectual Donnish environment.

The Greshams are invited to spend Christmas with Lewis and his brother Warnie (Edward Hardwicke), with whom he lives. Douglas asks to see the wardrobe from Lewis's childhood that inspired his famous novel *The Lion, the Witch, and the Wardrobe,* and is disappointed when there is no magical gateway behind the clothes. After the Greshams return home, Joy divorces her alcoholic, abusive husband. She then returns to England and asks Lewis to marry her so that she and her son can remain in England. He does so in a civil ceremony but bolts after the ceremony, and they live apart, he in Oxford and she in London. However, he continues to be drawn to her and finally, when she fractures her femur, which is rotten with cancer, their relationship begins to deepen into love.

Lewis then starts to question his long-held beliefs saying, "If you love someone, you don't want them to suffer. You want to take the suffering on to yourself. I feel like that. Why doesn't God?" They remarry at her bedside in an Anglican ceremony. After an idyllic period during her remission, she relapses and comes home to die. Both Lewis and Douglas are devastated when she is gone. When Lewis shows up at a university get-together, he says, "Maybe suffering has no purpose. I've just come up with a bit of experience. Experience is a brutal teacher." The Dean says, "Only God knows." Lewis responds, "God knows but does he care?"

Commentary

This well-made and well-acted film, directed by Richard Attenborough, about a very private Oxford Don who falls in love with a New York intellectual activist was adapted from a play by William Nicholson. It is entertaining mainly because of the performances by Winger and Hopkins and is definitely for those who like romantic dramas. Some of the dialogue is clipped and not easily intelligible; so using the English subtitles on the DVD may be advantageous. Although said to be "a true story" of the relationship between Lewis and Gresham, Dr. Bruce L. Edwards, a C. S. Lewis scholar, noted that their 10-year correspondence, meetings, courtship, and marriage were "compressed into two years," and Joy's two sons conflated into one. As a feature film, some license is warranted, but he faulted the film for not conveying that their relationship was fueled by his writings in defense of Christianity. Ignoring "the centrality of Christ to their lives," he believes, is "analogous to scripting the life of Michael Jordan with little reference to basketball."

Figure 9.4. *Shadowlands.* **C. S. Lewis (Anthony Hopkins) hugs his cancer-stricken wife Joy (Debra Winger).**

BACKSTORY

C. S. Lewis: Chronicle of a Christian

Clive Staples "Jack" Lewis (known as C. S. Lewis), is perhaps the best-known Anglican "apologist" for his works, particularly *Surprised by Joy*, *Mere Christianity* (based on radio broadcasts he made in the 1940s), and his children's series, *The Chronicles of Narnia*, which have been in print for over 50 years and have sold millions of copies worldwide. Interestingly, Lewis was also a very close friend of J. R. R. Tolkien, the Catholic author of *The Lord of the Rings*, and both were popular "Dons" at Oxford. Lewis also taught at Cambridge.

Lewis was born in Belfast, Ireland, in 1898, and he was educated at home by tutors, at boarding school, and later at University College, Oxford. Although he was baptized an Anglican (Church of Ireland), he declared himself an atheist as an adolescent and became very interested in fantasy and pagan mythology. However, by age 31, he had returned to Christianity "kicking and screaming," as he recounts in his memoirs of his early life, *Surprised by Joy*, which many believe is about his marriage to Joy Gresham, but it was written well before he met her. On the other hand, his book *A Grief Observed* poignantly relates his sadness over Joy's death. Lewis's death on November 22, 1963, was overshadowed by the assassination of President John F. Kennedy. He remains an important voice to Christians and others around the world.

As Edwards notes, "suffering," Lewis's major preoccupation in the film, was something he dealt with in 1940, but by the 1950s, he was on to other topics and writing *The Chronicles of Narnia*. There is no question that he grieved after Joy's death and that it challenged his faith as is evident in his *A Grief Observed*, but Edwards calls the last climactic scene which depicts a "hopeless Lewis inconsolable and bereft of any nurture or comfort from his Christian faith, weeping uncontrollably" as being "regrettable." Although such a scene might have occurred, he disagrees with its portrayal as "the final statement about Lewis's life with Joy and faith in God." He points to Lewis's last book *Letters to Malcolm; Chiefly on Prayer* as evidence of his emergence "from the shadowlands of grief and despair to a restored and invigorated faith." In short, Lewis grew. By risking love, he learned that with the joy of it comes the pain of loss. As his wife Joy says: "That's the deal."

Schindler's List (1993)

Based on a 1982 book by Australian novelist Thomas Keneally, this is the story of a Catholic playboy and master con man, Oskar Schindler (Liam Neeson), who collaborates with the Nazis. He agrees to hire Jewish workers in his ceramics factory because they cost him less. His accountant and factory manager, Itzhak Stern (Ben Kingsley), scours the Krakow ghetto to hire them, and they are excluded from the concentration camps as necessary workers. Under Stern's guidance, Schindler becomes bonded to his workers as if they are the children he never had, and he slowly evolves into a heroic figure.

When the crackdown occurs, and they are moved to the concentration camp, Schindler bribes the Commandant Amon Goeth (Ralph Fiennes) to continue the factory on the premises. Goeth is a weak, shallow, vicious man given to outbursts of senseless sadistic violence, shooting Jews from his balcony for target practice. His cold detachment is appallingly shown when he plays Mozart on the piano as Jews are rousted from the ghetto and wantonly shot. When the Nazis close the camp and transfer the prisoners for extermination at Auschwitz, Schindler uses his connections to move his workers to Czechoslovakia where he sets up a munitions factory that never turns out workable shells. Finally, as the Red Army closes in and the Nazis surrender, he spends the rest of his wealth to get the 1,100 Jews to safety.

Commentary

Rarely does one encounter a film that is so powerful, well acted, and engrossing that it leaves viewers both awed and teary-eyed. The film deservedly won seven Oscars, including for Best Picture, Best Director (Steven Spielberg), Best Screenplay (Steven Zaillian), Best Cinematography (Janusz Kaminski), Best Art and Set Direction (Alan Starski), and Best Film Editing (Michael Kahn). The Oscar- and Grammy-winning Musical Score (John Williams) was performed by Itzhak Perlman. There were five additional nominations for Best Actor (Neeson), Supporting Actor (Fiennes), Costume Design, Makeup, and Sound. It also won many other awards, including Golden Globes for Best Motion Picture (Drama), Best Director, and Best Screenplay.

As good as it is, the viewer must be prepared, as was demonstrated by the unfortunate occurrence described by Lorant involving Oakland California's Castlemont High School students. They laughed and heckled as one of the victims was killed early in the film, offending audience members who had lost relatives in the Holocaust. Even those who appreciate the magnitude of the subject have been reluctant to see the film because it would be depressing. Actually, it would be depressing not to revisit this incomprehensible event regularly to see how close the Nazi campaign of sheer evil came to succeeding. Yes, the tragedy is overwhelming. How could the slaughter of six million Jews along with priests, ministers, homosexuals, and those considered to be "feeble-minded" not be? Although there are harrowing scenes, the film is much less graphic than some television documentaries. Paradoxically, the film is uplifting, showing that the story of the survivors is the true "triumph of the will," which ironically is the title Hitler's publicist Leni Reifenstein gave to her celebration of Nazism.

Spielberg exercises a profound effect on the audience through the use of black and white, giving the film a documentary feel, and the judicious use of color, which occur in four instances. Color appears at the beginning as the candles glow orange while the family celebrates Shabbat. It disappears as they are harassed and then rounded up. It reappears in the Warsaw Ghetto when a young girl in a bright red coat is about to be killed. In actuality, the girl in the red coat, Roma Ligocka, who was conspicuous in the Ghetto, survived. The third use of color again involves candles when Schindler and the prisoners are about to be liberated and they celebrate Shabbat. This hopeful sign is affirmed at the end of the film when the *Schindler's List* survivors put a stone on his grave—a Jewish symbol of honor and the black and white turns to color. One is engulfed with the feeling that despite the killing, life prevails. Poland which had, under Casimir the Great, welcomed Jews six centuries before, had been left with fewer than 4,000 survivors. In contrast, the Jewish descendants of the Schindler's list survivors alone number 6,000.

Figure 9.5. *Schindler's List.* **Oskar Schindler (Liam Neeson) relies on his factory manager Itzhak Stern (Ben Kingsley) to select the Jewish workers who will comprise his List.**

I include *Schindler's List* in a book about Christians in the movies not because Schindler was a saint, which he definitely was not, but because he was a hero, and a Christian one at that. To be a saint requires consistent goodness whereas, as Eva Fogelman describes in her excellent book *Conscience and Courage* about other heroic rescuers of Jews, great evildoers may become heroes through a single action. Schindler was a Nazi spy in the Sudetenland and instrumental in the overthrow of Poland. Most survivors knew his dark side but thought him to be a lovable and heroic opportunist. One survivor said, "He was not a Jew lover," and nothing in the film suggests that he was. He was a man given to spontaneous emotions, one who loved pretty women, gambling, drink, and the high life. Still, his activities were so perilous that he was jailed three times for a week at a time. When 300 women on his list were brought to Auschwitz by mistake, he brazenly visited the camp to save them. His postwar life was characterized by failures in business and in marriage. After years of trying, the Schindler survivors, especially Poldek (Leopold)

BACKSTORY

Righteous Gentiles: Christians Rescuing Jews during the Holocaust

This designation, formally known as "Righteous among the Nations," has been conferred since 1963 by the State of Israel on those who have been found to have substantially risked their lives to save Jews during the Holocaust. A commission, headed by a Supreme Court justice, accords the title under the authority granted by the Knesset, the Israeli parliament, to Yad Vashem, the Holocaust Martyrs and Remembrance Authority established in 1953 to keep the Holocaust's memory alive. The honor consists of a medal, a certificate, memorialization in the Garden at Yad Vashem, and a ceremony in Israel or the awardee's country of origin.

Of the over 20,000 who have been recognized, most have been Polish and Dutch. Notable awardees include Oskar Schindler (*Schindler's List*); Monsignor Hugh O'Flaherty (*The Scarlet and the Black*); Raoul Wallenberg, the Swedish diplomat credited with saving 15,000 Jews; Chiune Sugihara, the Japanese envoy who granted 3,400 transit visas to Jews living in Japan; and Aristides de Souza Mendes, who helped 30,000 Jews to escape to neutral Portugal.

Controversy about the criteria used to confer the designation has arisen over the case of Lutheran pastor Dietrich Bonhoeffer, who spoke out against Hitler beginning in 1933. He was jailed in 1943 and executed in 1945 as a supporter of the plot to overthrow the Fuhrer. Their reasoning was that Bonhoeffer spoke out as a matter of Church/State policies and that he was not directly involved in saving Jews, although evidence suggests that he did help three Jewish converts to Christianity to escape. Some believe that their real concern may be that his designation would open the door to many others, such as the Bishop of Muenster Clemens August von Galen who condemned Hitler's policy of euthanasia in 1941 and even Pope Pius XII, who was nominated by the Chief Rabbi of Rome for his role in facilitating the rescue of Jews by O'Flaherty and others.

Pfefferberg, were able to bring his story to light. They convinced Israel to invite the down-and-out Schindler for a month each year to Jerusalem where he was welcomed as a hero. He was the third person to be given the revered designation of "Righteous Gentile" (see Backstory). When he died in 1974 at the age of 66, he was buried in the Catholic cemetery in Jerusalem. If he had not done what he did, Schindler would have died a lonely and forgotten man. One is reminded of the fate of the two sinners in John Greenleaf Whittier's poem "The Two Rabbins": "Heaven's gate is shut to him who comes alone; save thou a soul and it shall save thy own."

Boys of St. Vincent (1993)

This two-part television film is about pedophilia perpetrated by lay brothers in the Mount Cashel orphanage in Newfoundland, run by the Congregation of Christian Brothers or Irish Christian Brothers (not to be confused with the De la Salle Christian Brothers). Closed in 1989 after over 300 allegations of sexual abuse (principally in the 1970s and early 1980s), the institution represents the worst of the Catholic sexual abuse scandal, including the cover-up before it exploded into universal consciousness. The film has many powerful scenes picturing a Brother Peter Lavin (Henry Czerny), who repeatedly calls Kevin Reevey (Johnny Morina), a 10-year-old boy, to his room after lights out to kiss and fondle him. The boy escapes but is returned to the orphanage where Lavin says he loves the child even though he "lied" to the police.

The abuse continues, and the school's handyman tips off a detective who gets confirmation from the brother of an orphan who is being sexually molested by another Brother. Kevin refuses to testify because of his fear of crossing Lavin. The statement is shown to the Archbishop who tells Lavin to get the place in order. Lavin tells the kids not to talk, or they will be left homeless. The investigation is hushed up in order to assure that a million-dollar grant will be awarded to the institution. Lavin is finally caught *in flagrante delicto* with Kevin. and he is dismissed as head of the orphanage. All reference to sex abuse is removed from the dismissal record at the request of the Archbishop. The institution gets its grant, and the sexual abuse continues.

Commentary

The second part of the film covers the events that took place 15 years later when Lavin, now married with two children, is arrested and, along with other perpetrators, is brought to trial. Lavin's wife begins to wonder if he molested their children, which he does not deny. The film is relentless and depressing, as all involved wind up broken to various degrees. It is very hard to take it all in at one sitting, not just because of its length (210 minutes) but because of the tawdriness of the behavior of people who are supposedly committed to God and are in a position of trust. However, if watched in parts, it can serve as an excellent catalyst for discussion of the sex abuse scandal that rocked the Catholic Church and of the particular ethos of the time when it flourished. What is most disturbing was the cover-up by bishops and others in authority because of legal and financial concerns rather than acting as the moral leaders they were supposed to be. All their attempts to keep a lid on the sexual abuse only caused it to flourish. In the end, it not only proved more costly financially and to their institutional credibility but more importantly to the mental and physical health of the victims.

Priest (1994)

This Miramax-distributed BBC production begins with an old priest, Father Ellerton (James Ellis), praying in St. Mary's, a Catholic church serving a hardscrabble Liverpool neighborhood. Angered at having been transferred abruptly and without gratitude, he takes down the church crucifix and after a long walk and bus trip, uses it as a battering ram to attack the Bishop's residence. His replacement is Father Greg Pilkington (Linus Roache), a recent seminary graduate described as "orthodox" in comparison to the other resident priest, Father Matthew Thomas (Tom Wilkinson), who gives rousing sermons that Greg describes as Labor Party speeches. Matthew emphasizes compassion and assuring people reach their potential rather than following Church rules. Greg calls this social work and stresses accountability rather than scapegoating others for one's fate, which Matthew finds offensive. Against Matthew's advice, Greg insists on their making home visits, and they are turned away harshly by Catholics with the only ones opening their door being Jehovah's Witnesses.

Greg is appalled to find that Matthew is having sex with the housekeeper, Maria Kerrigan (Cathy Tyson). Matthew explains that when he was stationed in a South American village for four years, he found that if he didn't have a woman, the people ignored him. Maria says that she seduced Matthew and that Matthew wanted to marry her, but she refused because he would have to give up the priesthood for which he is presumably best suited.

Greg attends a wake where it's clear that he is out of sync with his earthy parishioners. He has some drinks, returns to the rectory, takes off his Roman collar, puts on a leather jacket, goes to a gay bar, and hooks up with Graham (Robert Carlyle), a fellow Catholic. After a bout of explicit and vigorous sex, Greg returns to his priestly duties. When Graham realizes that he is a priest, he visits Greg and gives him his telephone number, and they have sex again, after which Graham attends Mass. Greg is shown going through the consecration and seeing Graham, reflects on their sexual encounters as he blesses the bread and wine. Refused communion by Greg, Graham storms out of the church. Father Ellerton, who is concelebrating the Mass, is incredulous, saying he never refused anyone communion.

The other theme involves a schoolgirl, Lisa (Christine Tremarco), confessing incest with her father. Greg advises her to tell her father to stop it. At a school play, the father tells Greg to keep his nose out of his business. Later, the father enters the confessional where he makes no pretense of confessing to Father Greg but defends incest saying that Pope Alexander VI once sold a man the right to commit incest for 24,000 pieces of silver. He leaves the confessional with the clear intent to continue the incest and without absolution. Greg tells Matthew that he can't intervene without breaking the seal of the confessional. Later while praying for guidance, Greg shouts at Christ on the crucifix: "Do something. Don't just lie there you smug idle bastard." He says that Christ wouldn't give a damn about the Church's rules and regulations, like not breaking the seal of confessional that allows evil to thrive. Eventually, the mother, who works at the rectory learns of the abuse and is enraged that Greg kept the secret. She denounces him in front of children whom he is teaching about the Stations of the Cross.

Greg seeks refuge with Graham who has a new partner. Greg splits, but Graham overtakes him, and they make up and make out in Graham's car and are busted by a policeman. When the arrest hits the front pages, Greg takes an overdose of seconal and is hospitalized. The Bishop (Rio Fanning) visits him, and Greg says that he believes that being gay makes him more compassionate and a better priest. The Bishop tells him to "Piss off out of my diocese." Matthew tells Greg to "Bugger the Bishop" and calls the hierarchy, careerists, hypocrites, and Pharisees who love trappings of power more than the teachings of Christ, love, and compassion. Greg is sent to a remote church where Matthew visits and tells him that celibacy is not God's rule but man-made and that those who believe homosexual acts to be sinful are bigots. He suggests they say Mass together at St. Mary's where most of the parishioners walk out when they see Greg. The remaining few refuse to receive the Eucharist from him, except for Lisa with whom he offers a tearful embrace and apology.

Commentary

The U.S. Catholic Conference Department of Communication gave *Priest* an A-IV, that is, films that "while not wholly morally offensive in themselves, require caution and some analysis and explanation." This reflects the less traditional and more liberal approach to movie reviews by the Catholic Conference since the demise of the Legion of Decency. By contrast, *Priest* was ranked ninth in a 2005 poll of the top 10 anti-Catholic films. Cardinal O'Connor called it "as viciously anti-Catholic as anything that ever rotted on the silver screen." Two prominent critics agreed. Michael Medved said it displayed "the most profound hostility to the Catholic Church that I have seen in the last 15 years of reviewing films." Roger Ebert, who gave it one star, called it "shallow and exploitative" and went on to say, "For this movie to be described as a moral statement about anything other than the filmmaker's prejudices is beyond belief."

I agree with the above statements and include this film because it serves as the quintessential example of the lack of respect or understanding of Catholic dogma in this generation of filmmakers, as well as the encouragement given to them in flouting orthodoxy by some in well-placed "intellectual" Catholic circles. Not only are tendentious issues not put into context, but the arguments are one-sided and self-righteous polemics against orthodox Church teaching by a priest who is openly living with his housekeeper. Maybe, as my wife suggested, the film can serve as a discussion starter for its three major contentions. First, priestly celibacy should be abandoned since heterosexual and homosexual sex by priests is okay and may even be beneficial with respect to identifying with the folks. Second, ignoring Catholic dogma is all right as long as one's heart is in the right place on social justice issues, but don't mention abortion, please. Third, the seal of the confessional should be broken when circumstances dictate. In discussing the third point, it's well to keep in mind that the idea that Father Greg would have broken the seal of the confessional by revealing the incest is bogus. Not only did the girl's father discuss this with him outside the confessional, but the exchange in the confessional was not a valid confession since he neither expressed remorse nor intended to stop the behavior.

Dead Man Walking (1995)

Based on the book by Sister Helen Prejean, this film documents her transformation into the most famous advocate against the death penalty. Prejean (Susan Sarandon) is appointed spiritual advisor for Matthew Poncelet (Sean Penn), a death row inmate convicted of brutally killing a young couple in a lover's lane. Prejean visits the father of the slain boy and offers to provide counseling but is shown the door. Contrasting scenes show a Protestant minister defending the death penalty and a Catholic candlelight vigil against it. Prejean visits the parents of the girl whose body is shown nude, spread-eagled with the opening to the vagina turned up. The mother tells her that the girl, who was entering the air force, was proud of her "Class of '88 making a difference" pin, which was embedded deep into her body due to the ferocity of the stabbing. Sister tells her that "Every person is better than their worst act." Seeing that Prejean has not changed her mind about abolishing the death penalty, the mother says, "Sister, you have to leave this house. You can't befriend a murderer and be our friend."

Poncelet finally admits his responsibility for the killings and thanks the nun for loving him. They sing the hymn, "Be Not Afraid," and the nun holds his shoulder and reads from the Bible. After the priest blesses him, his last words are: "A terrible thing I done taking your son from you. I hope my death gives you relief. Killing is wrong whether done by me, y'all or the government," and he is executed. The film ends at the cemetery with Prejean and a parent praying together as Bruce Springsteen's song *Dead Man Walking* plays over the credits.

Commentary

This film was written and directed by Tim Robbins and stars his partner Susan Sarandon (a graduate of Catholic University), who are both well-known liberal activists. Sarandon won an Oscar for Best Actress, and Robbins, Penn, and Springsteen won Oscar nominations. Though well acted, I found the film slow-moving and distractingly full of cuts back and forth. Still, it is the most favorable portrayal of a nun in decades, probably because the campaign to abolish the death penalty is very popular with the mainstream media and increasingly in liberal Catholic circles.

There is never any doubt where the moviemakers stand. Yet, to their credit, Poncelet is never whitewashed. He is portrayed as a Holocaust-denier and white supremacist who admires Hitler and says that if he had his life to do it over again, he would come back as a terrorist, bombing government buildings. However, given the absoluteness of the filmmakers' stance, I was disappointed that no one raised the question in the film, nor has Sister Prejean, as to whether Goebbels, Eichmann, Hussein, Jeffrey Dahmer, and convicted murderers who kill guards and inmates or others after they are released should get the death penalty. This is not a matter of revenge or simply as punishment, but to keep them from further victimization of innocents or by continuing to influence their followers to perform heinous acts.

The filmmakers admit that it is a dramatization and not a faithful rendition of Prejean's book. Two death row inmates, Elmo Patrick Sonnier and Robert Lee Willie, were conflated into the character of Matthew Poncelet. Both were executed in 1984 by the electric chair instead of lethal injection as shown in the film. The latter method, which Louisiana instituted in 1993, was used in the film because, as noted in the film's official press production notes, Prejean and Robbins didn't want to "give people the moral out (of the most humane death), whereby people could say, 'Oh well, we used to do electrocution but that's too barbaric so now we are humane and inject them." These are not the only objections to the story. Recent books by the victims' families, *Dead Family Walking* and *Victims of Dead Man Walking*, have cast doubt on the veracity of depictions of the killers and events in Prejean's book. As of 2008, there has been no counter to their challenges by Sister Prejean.

Figure 9.6. *Dead Man Walking.* **Sister Helen Prejean (Susan Sarandon) and another nun accompany Matthew Poncelet (Sean Penn) on his march to execution.**

CHAPTER NINE

Entertaining Angels: The Dorothy Day Story (1996)

Produced by the Paulists, this story of liberal Catholic icon Dorothy Day (Moira Kelly) opens with her being incarcerated for protesting against the hydrogen bomb and flashes back to her early life as a Greenwich Village habitué, hanging with Eugene O'Neill and other Bohemian artists, Communists, anarchists, and socialists. She drinks, chain smokes, advocates free love, and champions women's suffrage and other causes in rallies and marches while writing for the Socialist newspaper *The Call*. She says, "I want to do something no one has ever done before." O'Neill replies, "Eat, drink, and make love. I'll even throw in free poetry," but she wants much more. She becomes pregnant by Lionel Moise (Boyd Kestner), a handsome Lothario, who, after promising to stand by her when he drops her off at an abortionist, flees. She slashes her wrists, but her roommate saves her.

Day moves to rural Staten Island where she hooks up with another Bohemian atheist who also eschews commitment and refuses to marry her when she becomes pregnant again. This time she has the child and converts to Catholicism through the influence of Sister Aloysius (Melinda Dillon), a practical, down-to-earth, and gently disarming nun who runs a communal soup kitchen. Returning in 1933 to a Manhattan beset by misery and poverty, she prays to the Lord, asking Him to tell her what He wants and what she is supposed to do.

Enter Peter Maurin (Martin Sheen), a Canadian ex-Christian Brother who talks a mile a minute and is all ideas with little practicality. Day turns her brother and sister-in-law's apartment, where she and her daughter are staying, into a homeless shelter (Hospitality House) at his instigation. The movie shows her founding the *Catholic Worker* newspaper, whose stands earn it a comparison to the Communist-run *Daily Worker*. Living hand-to-mouth in crowded quarters, they can't help many people. Accused of running a flophouse, her staff confronts her after a very disturbed resident commits suicide by slashing her wrist in the bathtub and another, a prostitute, steals money to buy liquor. They say, "We're tired of your ego, your arrogance. Even your own daughter doesn't have a bed. No more bedbugs, prostitutes, and mental patients." Peter falls silent and wanders off, saying "he's lost." After communing with God, Day agrees that much of what she was doing was egocentric and based on her desire to change the world. She promises to listen to her staff. The film's epilogue says: Day "continued to feed the hungry, clothe the naked, and shelter the homeless until her death in 1980. A champion of nonviolence, she was jailed repeatedly for opposing the nuclear arms race and the Vietnam War. More than a hundred Catholic Worker soup kitchens and hostels for the homeless carry on her struggle for peace and justice."

Commentary

The obscure title comes from the idea that in hosting guests, one should treat the poor as one would the rich, as if one were entertaining angels. The film features a radiant performance by Moira Kelly and an absorbing first 45 minutes in which we learn about Day's life before her conversion. The second part of her life that the filmmakers wished to celebrate falls flat cinematically, partly because of an unconvincing performance by Martin Sheen and an air of earnestness and self-righteousness. Jim Forest, a former managing editor of the *Catholic Worker* and a Day biographer, called the film disappointing in his "Entertaining Angels" article and pointed out many inaccuracies. For example, Sister Aloysius was not the upbeat post–Vatican II nun who ran a soup kitchen and gave Day some books to read, but "a tough old bird" who insisted, as was customary at that time, that she memorize the Baltimore Catechism. The visit by Cardinal Spellman (Brian Keith) to shut down her newspaper and shelter in which he capitulates and praises her, never happened; it is a typical cinematic ploy to show the heroic protagonist standing up to the hierarchy. Forest says that Spellman occasionally made life difficult for her but largely ignored her. Interestingly, Cardinal O'Connor, a successor of Spellman as New York's Archbishop, later proposed her for sainthood. Forest also calls into question the cinematic crisis device at the end.

What struck me particularly was how Day seemed to love the world generally but sorely neglected her own daughter. I would have liked to have heard what happened to her. Furthermore, it would have been interesting to learn that Day, once a proponent of free love, opposed the sexual revolution. As Beth Randall notes in her brief biography of Day, she complained that "this whole crowd goes to extremes in sex and drugs. . . . Also it is a complete rebellion against authority, natural and supernatural even, against the body and its needs, its natural functions of childbearing." Finally, the filmmakers might have acknowledged the many charitable Church institutions that predated Day's, such as those founded in Manhattan and elsewhere by Mother Frances Cabrini, the first American citizen to be declared a saint by the Catholic Church.

Sleepers (1996)

Based on a memoir by Lorenzo Carcaterra, who, as Shakes (Jason Patric), tells us at the outset that Hell's Kitchen was dominated by the Catholic Church and that spouse abuse was a cottage industry, that the police were all on the take, and everyone knew everybody and everything. An early scene ridicules nuns as they tell children to be "Soldiers of Christ and defenders of the Faith." Even the priest Father Bobby (Robert De Niro) joins in the fun as he disrupts the Mass by manipulating the clickers the nuns used to signal when the children should stand and kneel (a standard Catholic movie joke). The sacrament of confession also is ridiculed, as the boys go into the priest's area to hear the confession of the local prostitute as she recounts her exploits without any intention of changing her lifestyle. On leaving she thanks the boys for listening (chortle, chortle).

Father Bobby is a reformed hoodlum whose best friend is in Attica for killing three people. He confesses to having thought "about becoming a cop and leaving the good guys"—a throwaway line that honest cops must have loved. The local Mafioso King Benny (Vittorio Gassman) says that Father Bobby would have made a good hit man and laments his loss to the "dark side." The presumably well-meaning but mischievous boys spend much of their time doing petty crimes. When their harassment of a Greek hot dog cart owner results in the maiming of a 67-year-old, they are sent to a reform school populated by sadistic guards, four of whom repeatedly sexually abuse them. One of the guards later becomes a Catholic lay minister.

The film fast forwards to 10 years later with the boys officially classified as "sleepers," juveniles who have been sentenced for nine months or more in a correctional facility. Two are cold-blooded killers with no redeeming virtues. Their behavior is presumably attributable to their upbringing and especially the sexual abuse. They get their revenge by lightheartedly killing the most sadistic guard in a restaurant to the tune of "Walk Like a Man." They calmly pay the check and leave. They are defended by a down-and-out lawyer (Dustin Hoffman), who colludes with the prosecutor, an old buddy (Brad Pitt), and gets the killers off when Father Bobby perjures himself on the stand, saying that they were at a Yankee game with him when the murder occurred.

Commentary

This star-studded Barry Levinson film, featuring DeNiro in one of his many flawed priest roles, was one of the films that led to this book. I was extremely upset that so many talented megastars, which also included Kevin Bacon and Minnie Driver, would make such a powerful but patently false film that wantonly discredits people and institutions. Janet Maslin, the *New York Times* film reviewer, said of *Sleepers,* while it's possible that the story is true as author Carcaterra says, "It's also possible that Santa and the elves spend all year at the North Pole, making a list and checking it twice." Ann Sjoerdsma, book reviewer of the *Virginian-Pilot,* called the book "the most preposterous memoir since *Gulliver's Travels,* but, alas without Swiftian wit." John McPhee once said that nonfiction should be just that, not fictionalized, or filled up with made-up quotes. His beliefs seem to be regarded as quaint by people with far less talent. Carcaterra, a journalist and later producer/writer of television's *Law and Order,* said the story is true, but he admitted changing the names, dates, identifying characteristics of people and institutions, location of the trial, and where people lived and worked.

Like Maslin and Sjoerdsma, I don't buy it. Having lived and worked not too far from the locale from the 1940s to the 1960s, the memoir seemed bogus to me. It smacked of Carcaterra having watched *Angels with Dirty Faces* and *Boys Town* in reverse too many times. Both movies are mentioned early in the book. Indeed, because no evidence about similar events or perpetrators could be found in the Manhattan District Attorney's files or Carcaterra's school records, a disclaimer was added when the film was shown on cable. Given the repeated trashing of law enforcement officials as well as Catholic rituals, clergy, and laymen, as far as I could see, the only hit man in this story is Carcaterra. The victims were hard-working correctional officers and the Catholic Church.

The Spitfire Grill (1996)

The Spitfire Grill tells the story of Percy Talbot (Alison Elliott), a woman who after serving five years in a Maine penitentiary for manslaughter, decides to spend her parole in rural Gilead, Maine, a town that has fallen on hard times since the quarry closed. The local Protestant church stands empty because the inhabitants can no longer afford a minister and must travel to Bethel for church services. The sheriff gets Percy a job in a diner, the Spitfire Grill, run by Hannah Ferguson (Ellen Burstyn), who has difficulty with mobility, and her niece in-law Shelby (Marcia Gay Harden), who befriends Percy. Although she can't cook, Percy becomes indispensable, especially after Hannah sustains a serious injury. Hannah decides to sell the Grill and Percy sets up a magazine essay contest to bring in money, with the diner going to the winner. Meanwhile, Percy must cope with the scorn of local busybodies who learn that she is on parole.

Actually, both Hannah and Percy have dark stories. Hannah's son Eli (John M. Jackson) was a very accomplished young man who returned from the Vietnam war a mental cripple. Hannah tells Percy that she "lost" her son. Percy tells her that at least she didn't kill her boy. "You didn't let him die." Then Percy tells Hannah how her stepfather had sexually abused her since she was nine. At 16, she got pregnant; she hated what her stepfather had done to her, but loved the life in her. She swore to protect the baby when it came. One night her stepfather beat her in a drunken rage, and the baby died. She believed God would never forgive her for not protecting her baby, but her stepfather said it was good that the baby died. He went after her with a knife, and she killed him. Rather than reveal the ending, it is sufficient to say that the town is resurrected, the lost son is found, and the Spitfire Grill survives under the ownership of a Percy look-alike and her child.

Commentary

This slow-moving, atmospheric, gentle, and heartwarming film appealed to Sundance Film Festival goers who voted it the Festival's audience award. Conversely, it held little appeal for *New York Times* film critic Caryn James, who raised a hullabaloo about it having been financed by a company "owned by an order of Catholic priests." This led her to suspect it of "indoctrination," of what, one wonders. She quoted an anonymous potential buyer of the distribution rights as saying: "Once you know the context of the financing, a religious agenda does emerge from the film." Not the film itself but the financing.

Yet, this simple film is much less indoctrinating than many secular and politically correct agenda films that flood theaters. Take *The Cider House Rules*, which was lavishly praised by mainstream media critics. None accused it of indoctrination when abortion was not just promoted in the movie but also at the Academy Awards ceremony as John Irving accepted the Oscar for Best Screenplay. There's also the false assumption that films without values are value free, which they are not. Affirming no value (nihilism) or saying all values are equal (moral equivalency/cultural relativism) is a value. James was also upset that Castle Rock bought the rights for $10 million and stood to make $30 million. Isn't that what film producers and distributors are in business for, to make a profit? As it turned out, because of limited distribution and lack of critics' support, the film which cost $6 million to make earned about $13 million, a far cry from her estimate but a small profit nonetheless.

The film was indeed produced by Gregory Productions, the for-profit arm of the Sacred Heart League, whose mission is to promote Judeo-Christian values, especially reverence for God. Interestingly enough, though, the writer and director, Lee David Zlotoff, is not Catholic but Jewish, and the religious affiliation of the characters in the film is Protestant. The film's dominant theme is set forth in the two lines from the hymn, "There is a Balm in Gilead to heal the worried soul. There is a Balm in Gilead to make the wounded whole." Percy is made whole in Gilead and finds redemption in laying down her life for a friend. It's hard to see how these messages can offend anyone, except possibly if one finds the idea that a victim of incest wants to keep her innocent child as being offensive.

The Apostle (1997)

It's 1939 in New Boston, Texas, when a little white boy is brought into a predominantly black Holiness church by a black woman waving her fan with Christ's face on it, while she responds to the preacher "Praise the Lord." The movie flashes forward to the present when Euliss "Sonny" Dewey (Robert Duvall) and his mother (June Carter Cash) stop at the scene of an accident, and he rushes down to minister to a young couple trapped in the car, telling them the Lord loves them. When he gets a response from the boy, he returns to the car elated saying, "Momma we made news in heaven this morning." Momma sings one of the film's many hymns, while Sonny drives and recites psalms. Sonny is an itinerant preacher who is sincerely religious but is always traveling away from home and his wife (Farrah Fawcett) and two children and admits he has a wandering eye and wicked ways. When he catches his wife in bed with their church's youth minister, he hits the young man in the head with a baseball bat, and the man later dies.

Sonny escapes to Louisiana where he is befriended by a black ex-preacher who has lost a leg and spends his days fishing. After a period of fasting, as well as angry and confused raging at the Lord, he reimmerses himself in the river and is reborn as the Apostle EF. He then travels to Bayou Boutee where he again is befriended by a dignified black ex-preacher, Brother C. Charles Blackwell (John Beasley), who lets him use his old church. Sonny refurbishes the building with the help of neighbors and children, and they turn it into a Pentecostal Holiness church named the "One Way Road to Heaven." He uses the radio to give fiery sermons saying, "I'm a genuine, Holy Ghost, Jesus-filled preachin' machine this mornin'!" in a successful effort to bring blacks and whites together. There's a subplot that "lightens" the movie, involving his dating a lovely young lady, Toosie (Miranda Richardson), who turns out to be married. His past catches up with him and he is brought to justice, but not before he preaches a powerful farewell. The movie ends with him leading his prison chain gang in singing praise to the Lord as they swing their picks.

Commentary

Robert Duvall was deservedly nominated for a Best Actor Oscar for his portrayal of a complex man given to outbursts of emotion. On the one hand, he is a womanizing hustler and, on the other, a committed Christian trying to help the poor and fostering the emotional side of Christianity which his congregants crave. The film, which is filled with gospel singing and witnessing to the Lord, was a labor of love for Duvall, who wrote the script and tried for 15 years to get it made, finally financing $5 million himself. He had wandered into a Holiness Church in Arkansas and wanted to show the good side of these evangelicals—the bad side, he said, having been amply shown on film. Many Holiness Church members felt they couldn't trust a Hollywood denizen because they had always been made fun of, but Duvall convinced them that he would not.

He used real preachers in the tag-team preaching scene, at the end of which a black preacher is shown coming down from a frenetic spiritual excitement and others are shown falling down and being genuinely overcome. The two black women who are central to the scenes involving the "One Way Road to Heaven" church were nonactor congregants at Holiness churches. The neon sign was patterned on a real church sign. His radio sermons were based on those of J. Charles Jessup and the fistfight scene with the troublemaker (Billy Bob Thornton), who wanted to bulldoze the church and who later converted, was based on a real episode involving a Reverend Len Baggot.

The actor, who breaks down at the end, had been "saved" as a child but was reportedly turned off to religion by "a preacher who went bad." His emotional reaction in the film represented a genuine catharsis. Indeed, the

Figure 9.7. *The Apostle.* Sonny Dewey (Robert Duvall) immerses himself after the savage beating of his wife's lover and is born again.

film was criticized for painting too rosy a picture of Pentecostalism and for fostering a relativistic approach as when Apostle EF looks at the Catholic priest blessing the Louisiana fishing boats and says, "You do it your way. I do it mine, but we get it done, don't we?" In the end, though, this story about an earthy flawed man gives a welcome window into a form of Christianity that is too often distorted.

Elizabeth (1998)

Loosely based on the life of Queen Elizabeth I of England, the film begins during the reign of her half-sister, Mary Tudor (Kathy Burke), known as "Bloody Mary." The first scene shows a prelate intoning, "By order of their gracious majesties Queen Mary and King Philip, we are come to witness the burning of these Protestant heretics who have denied the authority of the one true Catholic Church and his Holiness the Pope. Let them burn for all eternity in the flames of hell." A dumpy and apparently mentally disturbed Queen Mary sits next to her corpse-like consort shrieking to the Duke of Norfolk (Christopher Eccleston), "My sister was born of that whore Anne Boleyn. She will never rule England." She is assured that proof of Elizabeth's disloyalty and treachery will be found. The beautiful Elizabeth (Cate Blanchett) is first seen dancing with her attendants and flirting with her lover, Robert Dudley (Joseph Fiennes). Then Norfolk and his fellow Catholics come to arrest and imprison her in the Tower of London. Mary spares her life and keeps her under house arrest, even though Elizabeth refuses to promise not to reinstate the Church of England if she ascends the throne.

When Mary dies, Elizabeth becomes queen, and the rest of the movie consists of her advisor Sir William Cecil (Richard Attenborough) parading suitors for her approval with a silly distraction involving a French suitor, the Duke of Anjou (Vincent Cassel), who turns out to be a bisexual transvestite. There are innumerable intrigues involving the Spanish, the French, Mary of Guise (Fanny Ardant), the Duke of Norfolk, and Sir Francis Walsingham (Geoffrey Rush) from whom Elizabeth learns statecraft and ruthlessness. After a disastrous attack on Scotland, Walsingham presumably kills Mary of Guise and imprisons six vocal Catholic bishops, allowing Elizabeth to get passage of the Act of Uniformity that reinstates the Church of England. She argues that it is better to have a single Church with a common prayer book and a common purpose. The Bishops accuse her of forcing them to give up allegiance to Rome.

The Pope (Sir John Gielgud) presumably issues a Papal Bull that deprives Elizabeth of her throne and releases her subjects of any allegiance. It also declares that "any man who will undertake her assassination will be welcomed by angels into the Kingdom of Heaven." Elizabeth's maidservant is mistaken for her and killed. This unleashes a wave of killings and torture of conspirators and Catholics with their heads exhibited on spikes of the Traitor's gate. The film ends with Elizabeth kneeling before the Blessed Virgin as a maid cuts off all her hair. She declares: "I have become a Virgin. I am married to England" and she places thick, white makeup on her face, assuming an almost-Kabuki appearance and her role as "bride of England." The epilogue says, "She reigned for 40 more years, a period considered England's Golden Age and that Walsingham remained her most trusted advisor."

Commentary

The film received seven Oscar nominations including Best Picture, Best Actress (Blanchett), Best Art/Set Direction (John Myhre and Peter Howitt); Best Costume Design (Alexandra Byrne), Best Cinematography (Remi Adefarasin), and Best Original Dramatic Score (David Hirschfelder) but won only for Best Make-up (Jenny Shircore). Nevertheless, David Denby in the *New Yorker* called it "a horror film masquerading as an historical pageant." And much pageantry there is! As Janet Maslin said in her *New York Times* review, "This is indeed historical drama for anyone whose idea of history is back issues of *Vogue*." It has been called more fiction than history what with the fact that the Duke of Anjou was one of the few suitors not to go to England and the transvestite scenes are made up; Mary de Guise wasn't killed by Walsingham but died of "dropsy." The Pope did not issue a Catholic version of what apparently awaits Jihadist suicide bombers, and Elizabeth, far from being a nervous naïf, was a multilingual "hardened and practiced politician who was not afraid of her power" when she ascended the throne. Whatever is accurate occurred not in the brief period of the film but over a thirty-year period.

The commentary on the DVD claims it is not an interpretation of history, but a portrait of the personality of Elizabeth as a modern feminist who "slouches on the throne" as she rejects suitors and wonders why she needs a man. She tells her lover Robert "I am no man's Elizabeth. I will have one mistress and no master." When told that she's only a woman, she answers, "I may be a woman but if I choose it, I can have the heart of a man. I am my father's daughter and I am not afraid of anything."

The main thrust of the drama, which Maslin called "resolutely anti-Catholic," is given in the prologue: It's "England 1554, Henry VIII is dead. Henry's oldest daughter [Mary Tudor], a fervent Catholic, is on the throne. The Catholics' greatest fear is that Elizabeth will succeed her." The Catholic monarch Mary is portrayed as a shrew whereas the Protestant Elizabeth exudes beauty and grace. The dour Catholics, including the Pope, are constantly scheming to kill Elizabeth and Walsingham, while the Anglicans are shown in a sunnier light. As the Catholic League noted, one comes away from the film believing that the blame for the Catholic-Protestant conflict lay principally with Catholics, ignoring the beheading of Thomas More; the Catholic suppression, and the confiscation of Church properties by Henry VIII and his successor Edward. For these reasons, the film was ranked in the top 10 anti-Catholic films in 2004 but the anti-Catholicism in the 2007 sequel *Elizabeth: The Golden Age* (see chapter 10) far surpassed it in that category.

The Cider House Rules (1999)

Based on a novel and screenplay by John Irving, *The Cider House Rules* is set during World War II, at St. Cloud, a Maine orphanage in which the children are unbelievably neat, clean, and well-behaved. Doctor Wilbur Larch (Michael Caine) is a selfless physician who cares for the children and also provides abortions on request. Larch's favorite child is Homer Wells (Tobey Maguire), a *wunderkind* without any formal education. Homer is destined to remain at the orphanage when his various adoptions fall through; in one case, he is removed from a home for parental abuse where his crib has a picture of Saint Theresa of the Little Flower over it.

Under Larch's tutelage, Homer becomes an adept obstetrician and surgeon at age 16. The doctor and his protégé are remarkably in tune, clashing only over the issue of abortion. Larch argues passionately for his obligation to perform abortions for anyone who requests one. Homer is just as adamantly against the practice because he and his fellow orphans wouldn't be around if their mothers had elected it.

When Wally Worthington (Paul Rudd), an Air Force pilot on leave, drives his pregnant fiancée, Candy Kendall (Charlize Theron), to St. Cloud for an abortion, Homer's refusal to participate engenders an impassioned speech by Larch as to why abortions are necessary. After the procedure, as the very handsome couple is ready to tool away in their convertible, Homer, much to Doc's dismay, asks if he can join them so that he can see the world. Homer takes a job with a group of itinerant African-American migrant workers on Wally's father's apple orchard. He easily becomes a member of the family and is taken under the wing of the group's patriarch, Mr. Rose (Delroy Lindo), an honest, hard-working, and wise man. Homer lives with the migrants in the cider house, where a set of rather stupid and insulting rules are displayed.

Meanwhile, Doc writes letters to Homer trying to convince him to replace him. He forges Homer's name on his college degree from Bowdoin and his medical school degree from Harvard. Telling the nurses that he will introduce Homer's candidacy at the orphanage's annual board meeting, he goes on to rail at the board's bigotry and narrow-mindedness about religion. Disparaging them as Christians with missionary zeal, he attempts to use reverse psychology by telling the board that they won't want Homer because he's "too Christian" for them to hire as his replacement sight unseen. Of course, they do. Larch had also perpetrated another fraud by wanting Homer to be free from military service and switching Homer's records with those of Homer's best friend Fuzzy (Erik Sullivan), who had heart disease and died.

When the migrant band returns for the second summer of picking apples, Homer discovers that the respected Mr. Rose has impregnated his daughter. Now Homer is faced with a dilemma. Does he or doesn't he perform an abortion? The answer is pretty clear; of course, he does. When

Candy rejects his love upon the return of her pilot fiancé, who was partially paralyzed by enemy gunfire, Homer, now 17, returns to take up the work of Doc, who has died from an ether overdose.

Commentary

The Cider House Rules is well made, engrossing, and well acted (especially by Michael Caine—who won an Oscar for Best Actor in a Supporting Role—and Tobey Maguire). It also received an Oscar for Best Adapted Screenplay (John Irving), and Oscar nominations for Best Picture, Best Director (Lasse Hallström), Best Editing (Lis Zeno Churgin), Best Art Direction (David Gropman and Beth A. Rubino), and Best Original Score (Rachel Portman).

Despite the quality of the film, its basic premise is troubling. The title comes from a series of oppressive rules for migrant workers about not going on the roof to cool off, eat lunch, or look at the stars. As one worker says, "they think we are dumb niggers and need dumb rules." In effect, as we shall see, the author's and director's purpose is that rules are meant to be broken, when necessary. Lovingly and gauzily filmed, the movie subtly draws the viewer into rooting for the well-acted central characters. What lies just below the pretty veneer are incest, fraud, deceit, a druggie-doctor, betrayal, parricide, and abortion. John Irving, in accepting the film's Oscar for Best Adapted Screenplay, made no bones in his acceptance speech about its advocacy of abortion. As he said in the film's official press production notes, "Homer learns a harsh lesson, that the demands of that then-illegal procedure were such that anyone who knew how to perform an abortion, had to perform it . . ."

Hallström, who directed *What's Eating Gilbert Grape*, as well as *My Life as a Dog*, also makes his intent clear in the press production notes: "The concept of the rules intrigued me, too, rules made by people who know too little about the circumstances under which people live. The movie plays around with the rule concept in many areas. The rules about relations, marriage, race, abortion, and sexuality. *The Cider House Rules*, to me, is about breaking those rules that don't make sense or are not adjusted to reality." Charlize Theron echoed him, saying that the characters "all break rules, we all break rules. We're all human and society's standards don't always relate to real life."

As someone who taught medical ethics for over 10 years, I found Irving's, Hallström's, and Theron's thesis about moral decision-making in general and abortion in particular to be much too facile. The word *dilemma* is often carelessly used to describe difficult decisions involving incomplete information, but abortion is a true dilemma. The potential actions are irreconcilable, just as are the diverging horns from which the word is derived. The issue is divisive because the contrary positions are bolstered by similarly nonconvergent arguments principally related to beliefs as to when life begins and whether the fetus is a "person" as well as how commensurate its autonomy or "personhood" rights are with the mother's. Auxiliary arguments such as the "wantedness" of the child are also invoked.

Regardless of the intellectual and moral arguments advanced, national polls and my own anonymous medical student surveys reveal logical inconsistencies and cognitive dissonance on both sides of this issue. For example, some who believe that the fetus is a person at conception and that abortion is taking a human life, will support an abortion in the case of rape and incest, not just when the mother's life is in danger. Similarly, some who doubt that the fetus is a person will not support abortion on demand and will admit to showing off ultrasound pictures of their "babies" or argue for inheritance rights of frozen embryos. In the end, how we act is not simply a product of our beliefs, but how and why we act when those beliefs are called into question. The old concept of breaking a rule being a sin (deontology), a moral theory that once prevailed, has been more and more replaced by one that asserts that the end justifies the means (consequentialism or utilitarianism). In sum, *The Cider House Rules*, is well worth seeing. It can serve as a useful trigger for a rigorous discussion of abortion in particular and ethics in general.

Stigmata (1999)

Father Andrew Kiernan (Gabriel Byrne), a papal investigator of miracles, visits a crowded church in Belo Quinto, Brazil, where a statue of the Virgin Mary is bleeding from its eyes. The "miracle" began at the death of the pastor Father Almeida, who lies in state. Suddenly a strong wind blows out all the candles, and doves fly through the nave. Just as suddenly everything returns to normal. The investigator returns to Rome and is solicited on his way to the Vatican by prostitutes who offer a "Vatican discount." He laughingly refuses and reports his findings to Cardinal Daniel Houseman (Jonathan Pryce), who refuses permission to investigate it and sends him off to Pittsburgh to investigate reports of a woman with Stigmata.

A boy had stolen Father Almeida's rosary out of his coffin and sold it to a tourist who sent it to her self-confessed atheist, party girl, and licensed cosmetologist daughter Frankie (Patricia Arquette). After touching the rosary, she gets Stigmata on her wrists and begins speaking and writing in Aramaic as well as developing an odor of sanctity (jasmine). Kiernan begins to believe that these are real but is puzzled because only people who deeply believe in God develop Stigmata as they grow closer to God.

The mystery begins to unravel when Father Kiernan learns that his Vatican friend Father Delmonico (Dick Latessa), along with Father Almeida and a Father Petrocelli, was assigned to translate every third page of a new Gospel. Presumably this is standard operating procedure when the Vatican is worried that only a select few can know the whole truth. Delmonico tells him that there are 35 gospels, not four, and that "the Vatican only lets out what it wants to." Indeed, this explosive new gospel could undermine the institutional church. It professes that, "The Kingdom of God is inside you, and all around you, not in mansions of wood and stone. Split a piece of wood and I am there. Lift a stone and you will find me." In other words, you don't need an institution between you and Jesus. Almeida and Petrocelli were excommunicated and escaped. The girl has become Father Almeida's messenger through his rosary. Houseman comes to Pittsburgh and tries to strangle her to "save the Church." Kiernan stops him and then goes to Belo Quinto to find the gospel.

Commentary

Long pauses, loud music, and special effects are used to try to make the film seem portentous and scary, but it never rises above weird. Like *The Da Vinci Code*, this film also qualifies as another account of a malevolent and deceitful Catholic hierarchy. The epilogue explains why *Stigmata* made the top 10 anti-Catholic film list (see Backstory, p. 348): "In 1945, a scroll was discovered in Nag Hamadi which is described as 'The Secret Sayings of the Living Jesus.' The scroll, the Gospel of St. Thomas, has been claimed by scholars around the world to be the closest record we have of the words of the historical Jesus. The Vatican refuses to recognize the Gospel and has described it as heresy." Actually, no Christian denomination accepts this as a canonical New Testament gospel, and it is generally believed to be an example of Gnostic gospels written by people who were challenging the beliefs of the early church. Still, I found this film to be much less offensive than others because it is noisy, violent, and farfetched, making it less accessible and less capable of penetrating the viewer's brain than some of the more hip and flip films like *Dogma*. Its best attribute is the acting of Gabriel Byrne.

The Third Miracle (1999)

Allied bombers appear over a town in Slovakia where Nazis have conscripted Jews and gypsies to work in the factories. A gypsy girl grabs her statue of the Virgin Mary and runs to the church gate where she kneels and prays. A wounded German soldier looks on in wonder from a cart as bombs turn into doves and all are saved. Fast forward to 1979 in a Chicago ghetto where Father Frank Shore (Ed Harris), an alcoholic priest, hangs out and patronizes the soup kitchen. He is on leave for eight months as the diocesan postulator who checks out purported miracles. His depression resulted from his discrediting of a beloved priest who turned out to be a devil worshipper who committed suicide. Halting the beatification process demoralized a whole group of Catholics, including an idealistic Franciscan who called Shore "a miracle killer." His buddy Father Leone (Michael Rispoli) comes to get him because the Bishop wants him on a case since he has always found such claims to be hoaxes.

The statue of the Blessed Virgin at the Polish parish of St. Stan's started weeping blood when a very devout congregant, Helen O'Leary, died and has continued to weep blood only when it rains and only in November, the month Helen died. Doves also appear in the sky. At Helen's funeral Mass, a young girl with terminal lupus walked in the rain to the church, stopped by the Virgin's statue, became covered in blood, and was cured. Shore interviews Helen's daughter Roxane (Anne Heche), a lapsed Catholic who disputes the idea that her mother was a saint. Later, he tracks down the girl with lupus (now a prostitute), who admits that she did pray to Helen before the cure, but her prayer was that she be allowed to die.

The subplot involves an infatuation between Shore and Roxane. The weakest scene occurs at Helen's gravesite where they drink vodka and pour some on her mother's grave. Then he tells her he's not a virgin, and they start dancing until they are interrupted by a funeral cortege. They go to a bar and then to her apartment where their lovemaking is interrupted by a phone call that the statue is weeping blood, which turns out to be Helen's blood type. Shore completes the report recommending that Helen be put forward for sainthood. He then returns to see Roxane who tells him of a friend who wants to become a Catholic because they can do anything they want and go to confession and say a few Hail Marys and everything is fine. She tells him not to go. They kiss, he leaves, and she's devastated.

The devil's advocate, Archbishop Werner (Armin Mueller-Stahl), who turns out to be the Nazi soldier at the film's beginning, comes to speak against Helen's sainthood before a Vatican panel convened in Chicago. Werner says the obstacle between Helen's soul and God is that she was married. Shore points to many married saints and says, "We have many saints who spent their lives in chastity and prayer. Helen is a saint of the people who live in an ordinary world." There are a few twists before the end, which includes the third miracle. I won't spoil it because the film on balance is worth seeing.

Commentary

Like *Stigmata*, this film, by *Europa Europa* director Agnieszka Holland, also features the Blessed Virgin weeping blood, but it's much better. The principal reason is the acting of Ed Harris and Anne Heche and an interesting story despite the weak subplot; however, it wouldn't be Hollywood without some faux Hollywood theology and history. Roxane's friend's conception of being absolved of one's sins misses the point that one must be contrite and have a sincere desire to amend one's life. Also, when she says her mother was not a saint, she cites her mother's abandoning her when she was 16 to move into a convent as a housekeeper saying, "She cared more about the Church and that priest than she did about me." Shore responds with a story about a woman whose husband died: "St. Jane Frances de Chantal wanted to become a nun. Her 10-year-old cried and didn't want her to go, lying down in front of the convent. Chantal stepped right over the child and a hundred years later, she was declared a saint." As it turns out, Chantal was widowed with four children at 28 when her husband was killed in a hunting accident. The record shows that she stayed with the children for 10 years and continued to supervise their education and placement in society. When she did found the Convent of the Visitation for widows and laypersons who did not want full orders, it was with the understanding that she could leave when necessary to take care of her personal business.

The best lines are when the troubled Shore goes to confession to Father Leone, who is genuinely happy in his ministry, and confesses that he is troubled and struggling with his faith. In the end, Shore cites Tertullian's rule of faith as to why he still believes in God, "I believe because it is absurd." In other words, he accepts it because "it is an impossibility in an impossible world." There's a little bit of erudition that can provoke hours of post-film discussion.

Dogma (1999)

The rousing opening shows Cardinal Ignatius Glick (George Carlin) standing in front of his cathedral in New Jersey kicking off a new campaign. He says: "Now we all know how the majority of the media in this country view the Catholic Church. They think of us as a passé, archaic institution. People find the Bible obtuse . . . even hokey." He then says that he is retiring the crucifix which he calls a time-honored Catholic symbol that gives people "the willies" in favor of a more modern symbol. "The Buddy Christ" is one of the many revamps he plans as part of the "Catholicism WOW" campaign being unveiled over the next year. He also offers plenary indulgences, which absolve all their sins, to those who pass through an arch on the way to the cathedral.

Two fallen angels, Bartleby and Loki (Ben Affleck and Matt Damon), plan to travel to New Jersey to bring down the Church by passing through the gates and being redeemed, thus negating God's power and destroying the Church. God's avenging angel Metatron (Alan Rickman) must stop them. He gives the task to Bethany Sloane (Linda Fiorentino), who is a descendant of Mary and Joseph (the great-great-great-great-great-grand-niece of Jesus Christ) and works in an abortion clinic. She is helped by the 13th and 14th apostles who were left out of the Bible because one was black, Rufus (played by a foul-mouthed Chris Rock), and the other, a woman named Serendipity (Salma Hayek), who is a stripper. God is a woman portrayed by singer Alanis Morrissette.

Rufus gives out such wisdom about God as in this dialogue with Bethany. Rufus says, "He still digs humanity, but it bothers Him to see the S— that gets carried out in His name—wars, bigotry, televangelism, but especially the factioning of all the religions . . ." As noted in the preface, Rufus disdains "beliefs" which are trickier to change and limit growth as opposed to "ideas" which can be easily changed, making life more malleable and progressive.

Commentary

This film's title highlights the problem of contemporary filmmakers with orthodox religion, namely the need to accept certain dogma. Loaded with big-name stars, it is essentially a profane, angry, offensive, and sometimes funny *Saturday Night Live* skit blown up into a feature-length movie. After the Catholic League and other groups threatened the Disney Studio, the parent of Miramax, with boycotts, the film was screened by Joe Roth, the studio president who was said to have told Harvey and Bob Weinstein (the chiefs of Miramax) that it was the most subversive film he ever saw and that he would be afraid to have his name attached to it. The film was sold to Lion's Gate Films, which released it theatrically, and Miramax distributed it internationally. Later Disney and Miramax parted ways.

The film is a product of Kevin Smith who was described by Ann Hornaday, then a *Baltimore Sun* film critic, as a 29-year-old "man of huge appetites whether for food, cigarettes or swearing" but serious about religion. She said he is "a lifelong devout Catholic who takes his faith seriously—even if he doesn't buy many of its institutional trappings." He apparently became convinced in his twenties that "his views on homosexuality and abortion made it impossible for him to be a Catholic." Then, he decided that it wasn't him who was wrong but the Church. "I realized that faith being a very personal thing, it doesn't matter what issues I don't see eye-to-eye on the church with, because I'm not there for their benefit. I'm there for God. And I see eye-to-eye pretty much on everything with God." The Bible, he said, is more often than not used as a tool of misinformation or as a weapon. People wield it saying, "'This is why we hate blacks' [or] 'This is why God hates gays.' And it's not the case. That's why *you* hate gays. I think God loves everyone."

Richard Alleva, the film critic for *Commonweal*, nailed the mentality behind the film as reminiscent of "sitting around dormitory rooms or cafeteria tables during my years at Catholic U. I encountered countless wiseacres who might have ceased going to mass but were satirically obsessed with Catholic dogma, hierarchy, mores, and style. They were always forthcoming with fantasy scenarios featuring such situations as God coming down to earth and . . . God's a woman! a pro-abortion feminist woman! who's . . . uh, black and no . . . wait, I've got it, a black lesbian with a leather fetish. Now guess what happens when she calls the Pope on the carpet!"

Interestingly enough, writing for a liberal Catholic periodical, he felt compelled to praise the film especially in contrast to the other terrible film he reviewed that issue (see *The Messenger*, p. 294). Admitting that the

Figure 9.8. *Dogma*. Ben Affleck and Matt Damon play fallen angels who try to sneak back into heaven, thereby negating God's power and destroying the universe.

storytelling is a mess, Alleva praised its insolence and occasionally eloquent dialogue and special effects and couldn't resist adding a jab at the end at the conservative head of the Catholic League who had protested the film, "And a very Merry Christmas to The Catholic League." This illustrates the split within the Catholic Church where people try to score points against fellow Catholics along ideological divides, making it easier for anti-Catholicism to flourish.

Father Gene Phillips, a noted Catholic film critic and author of several books on film, defended *Dogma* as a discussion-starter for young people who were drawn to the film to explore what they believe and why. He contrasted this with *Stigmata*, which he found to be blasphemous and anticlerical. The problem is that it would take a syllabus to correct the inaccuracies and outright stupidity in *Dogma*. Even the IMDb website, a respected independent movie database, listed many goofs made in *Dogma* under the heading "errors made by characters (possibly deliberate errors by the filmmakers)" which at one time included a defense of Pope Pius XII who was vilified in the film. The sad thing is that too many people get their history and theology from the movies. So while I'm not in favor of boycotts, I also don't countenance making light of such travesties as *Dogma*, whose cool hipness makes them worse than films like *Stigmata* whose appeal is limited and whose anti-Catholicism is decidedly heavy-handed.

Short Subjects

Misery (1990)

A deranged "nurse from hell" (Kathy Bates), responsible for many Intensive Care Unit deaths and living in secluded Maine, rescues her favorite romance novelist Paul Sheldon (James Caan), injured nearby during a snowstorm. Always shown with a cross hanging from her neck, she locks him up and says that God chose her to save him so he could finish the last book in the series. She kills the local sheriff and puts two bullets in her gun, one for Sheldon and one for her, once he finishes. Bates's Academy Award–winning performance makes this film worth watching, despite the annoying metamessages, most particularly that devout Christians are gun-toting crazies.

Nuns on the Run (1990)

As in the 1989 film *We're No Angels,* Robbie Coltrane and Eric Idle play gangsters, except they impersonate nuns rather than priests and hide out in a convent where they get to see such sights as nuns naked in the shower, a cranky old nun, and an alcoholic who hides whiskey in her habit. Roger Ebert, who said that he was taught by nuns for eight years and found them to be "dedicated teachers and kind women" as I did in my seven years with the nuns, said, "The movie has the air of a gang of adolescents who think they're getting away with something—writing nasty words on the blackboard when sister's out of the room."

The Pope Must Die (1991)

This title was altered to *The Pope Must Diet* for American distribution after complaints by Catholics. It stars Robbie Coltrane as an overweight Italian parish priest fond of women, cars, and food. In his youth, he fathered an out-of-wedlock child, now a famous rock star. He accidentally becomes pope (Pope Dave) and gorges on Communion wafers in private. He slowly discovers the corruption in the Mafia-controlled Vatican, including a private harem of seductive nuns, illicit arms deals, and a Vatican bank run by a corrupt cardinal, and springs into action. In the words of the Miramax press release, the film "urges an end to the corruption that threatens the Catholic Church. And its hero is a priest who cares enough about the Church to risk his life to save it." Who knew that the real intention of the Weinstein brothers, as they turned out so many anti-Catholic films at Miramax, was to save the Church?

291

The Rapture (1991)

Sharon (Mimi Rogers), a call-center worker by day and a wild sexpot by night, is visited by two evangelists who tell her to accept Jesus to be saved. She finds God, who her live-in boyfriend Randy (David Duchovny) says "is like a drug." At work, she starts asking callers if they have met Jesus. Her supervisor takes her aside, and she tells him, "God made me an information specialist for a reason. We have to prepare for His return." Seeing that she has "the rapture," she is allowed to join an office Fundamentalist group who seek "the pearl of great price" with the help of an African-American boy (DeVaughn Nixon) who communicates with God. The "Boy" tells her that her dreams and spouting of apocalyptic prophecies mean that she must go to the desert and await God. She takes her 10-year-old daughter Mary, who wants to go to heaven to see her deceased daddy. After two weeks, starving and half-mad, Sharon shoots her daughter to send her to God. Unable to shoot herself, she is rescued by a friendly policeman. Renouncing a God who would make her kill her daughter, she is taken to the River Styx where she sees Mary, who tells her to come to the other side. This film is included to show the depths Hollywood is plumbing in portraying believers.

The Shawshank Redemption (1994)

Leonard Maltin called this acclaimed, well-crafted film "hollow and predictable," and I agree. The protagonists are charismatic convicted murderers Andy (Tim Robbins), who says he was railroaded, and "Red" (Morgan Freeman), in a Maine penitentiary. Except for the sadistic rapist Bogs Diamond and his gang of perverts called "The Sisters," the rest of the convicts are good guys, almost all, except Red professing innocence. By contrast, the evildoers are the guards and a particularly despicable warden, a self-righteous Bible-quoting hypocrite who embezzles state funds with Andy's help. Over the safe where he keeps his ill-gotten gains is a supposed Biblical quote in needlepoint: "His judgment cometh and that right soon." The closest to that saying in the Bible is in Proverbs 29:26: "Many seek the ruler's favor, but every man's judgment cometh from the Lord." This portrait of Fundamentalist Christians as hypocrites has become the Hollywood norm.

The Basketball Diaries (1995)

This story of poet Jim Carroll's (Leonardo DiCaprio) descent into drugs and hustling his body is based on his book he wrote at 17. Carroll gained fame at

22 despite his limited vocabulary (F— is the operative word) and worldview (masturbation and taking drugs are the major activities by Carroll and his crowd, all of whom wear crucifixes). The movie starts with his seemingly demented mother shouting at Carroll, "Go F— Yourself, you SOB bastard" and never reaches those heights again. At school, a priest paddles him and when the bell rings, Carroll says, "Too bad, Father, I was just getting to enjoy myself." The priest, true sadist that he is, replies, "I can do it again tomorrow." When his best friend dies of leukemia, one of the gang suggests that the despondent Carroll talk to a priest. He responds, "I wouldn't ask one of those co———s for directions. S—F— happens."

Still, Carroll has a picture of the Sacred Heart over his bed. When he goes to confession for mugging a woman, he questions his penance of 10 Hail Marys and 5 Our Fathers: "That's my punishment? It sucks." As he reminisces about being an altar boy and helping the priest with incense, he dopes up. He's stoned through most of the movie and robs to feed his habit until Reggie, a black ex-junkie, gets him to go cold turkey. This vulgar, self-indulgent, execrable movie is included to show the depth that some films with major stars have sunk. Ironically, DiCaprio, two years shy of his career-making role in *Titanic*, accepted the role after the original lead actor, River Phoenix, died of a drug overdose.

The Preacher's Wife (1996)

This misbegotten remake of *The Bishop's Wife* (see chapter 4) stars Denzel Washington as Dudley the angel who returns to earth to help out a selfless, workaholic minister (Courtney B. Vance) whose dedication is estranging his wife (Whitney Houston). Despite Washington's good looks and charm, he never exhibits Cary Grant's wit in the original version; nor is Houston in the same acting league as Loretta Young; nor is the earnest Vance able to carry off his side of the triangle as David Niven did. While the filmmakers deal reverently with religion, Whitney Houston and her music, which was nominated for an Academy Award, overshadow the story.

Primal Fear (1996)

Based on a novel by William Diehl, this film recounts the brutal murder of a widely respected archbishop of Chicago, presumably by Aaron/Roy (Edward Norton), a homeless altar boy at the cathedral, after he is found blood-covered and hiding in a confessional. A hotshot, publicity-seeking lawyer,

Martin Vail (Richard Gere), takes on the case. He finds pornographic videos in the Archbishop's plush apartment that show him getting his jollies as he videotapes two altar boys and an altar girl having sex. The Archbishop had threatened to stop housing the homeless youths if they didn't cooperate in his sexual abuse. It turns out that the Archdiocese was also involved in shady real estate ventures. Aaron confesses to the murder to Vail but feigns a split personality which is confirmed by psychiatrist Dr. Molly Arrington (Frances McDormand). His alter ego, Roy, tries to break the neck of the prosecutor, Ms. Venable (Laura Linney), and is reprimanded by the Judge (Alfre Woodard). Still, he is acquitted because of the mental instability, memory loss, and sexual abuse. As he walks free, he laughs at his lawyer saying there never was a meek Aaron, but only the violent Roy.

This profane, violent, and manipulative film is made memorable by Edward Norton's debut performance as a brutal killer with seemingly confused split personalities playing off Richard Gere as an arrogant know-it-all. The complete trashing of the Catholic Church in a powerful star-studded film with excellent supporting actors John Mahoney and Andre Braugher troubled me, especially given the string of such movies for over a decade.

Extreme Measures (1996)

A brilliant neurosurgeon (Gene Hackman), who transects the spinal cords of homeless men to find the cure for paraplegia and quadriplegia, hires ex-FBI agent Frank Hare (David Morse) to kill a young medical resident (Hugh Grant) who is on to him. Before doing so, he lovingly strokes a picture of the Sacred Heart of Jesus, then turning the picture upside down, straps on his gun, says good-bye to his family, and blows away his colleague who has second thoughts about their assignment. The religious affiliation of this cold-blooded killer seemed utterly gratuitous. Following on the heels of the much-acclaimed *Pulp Fiction*, where a killer quotes the Bible as he wastes his victims, this film's negative Christian allusions (along with those in *Shawshank Redemption*, *Primal Fear*, and *Sleepers*) provided the impetus for this book.

The Messenger: The Story of Joan of Arc (1999)

Unlike the previous two Joan of Arc films (see pp. 30 and 97), which hewed closely to the trial documents and other historical records, this film took considerable liberties with her story. The most egregious, besides the bizarre portrayal of Joan (Milla Jovovich), is the addition of a sister who gets killed and raped—in that order—by an English soldier as Joan hides directly behind the closet door her sister is being pushed against. This gives a revenge motive for her leading the army against the English. Joan is so scrupulous that she goes to confession two to three times a day. Fortunately, she has a benign, avuncular priest who tells her to stop being so scrupulous. She hungers for Christ so much that she breaks into the sacristy and drinks the wine. Much of her day is spent running through the fields and then going ecstatic as she hears loud sounds and sees swirling clouds just before Christ appears on a garden chair or a sword falls from the sky. One is impelled to shout out, "Get thee to a psychiatrist," only they didn't have any in those days.

John Malkovich plays the Dauphin Charles VII, and Faye Dunaway plays his wife as Yolande of Aragon. Joan leads the French in battle with the help of some trustworthy lieutenants. The French soldiers forswear swearing, but the English more than make up for any profanity deficit in the film with their use of the F word. The French are victorious, and Joan wins the loyalty of the troops with her courage. The Dauphin prances about complaining that his coronation at Rheims is being rushed because he says he needs more pomp and circumstance. After he is crowned, he agrees with his advisors that Joan's usefulness is at an end, and he fails to give her reinforcements to complete the assault on Paris. When she raises an army to attack the Duke of Burgundy at Campeigne, he again fails to help her. Joan is captured and brought before a clerical court overseen by Bishop Cauchon, who, in this version, is portrayed as trying to help Joan (never mind the historical record). The film reaches its most ludicrous point when Joan is jailed, and an apparition in the form of Dustin Hoffman, billed as her "conscience," begins harassing her. He pushes her to acknowledge that it was all about pride and delight at bloodletting, not doing God's will. Hoffman uses his typical combination of Buddha-like silences, halting speech, and repetitions of what Joan says, accompanied by badgering when the moment is propitious. In a word, he's obnoxious, and the film is too. It's recommended for those who like their saints deconstructed by psychoanalysis and enjoy battle melees and gore.

AMAZING GRACE: 2000 TO THE PRESENT

T he new millennium began, in effect, with the stunning terrorist attack on the United States on September 11, 2001. Initially,
Americans bonded with one another putting on a front of solidar-
ity and patriotism. There was also an outpouring of religiosity, with people
who hadn't been to a religious service in years flooding churches and syna-
gogues. Yet, these feelings receded relatively quickly. Within 18 months,
President George W. Bush, whose 2000 election had been contested all
the way to the United States Supreme Court, retaliated against Al Qaeda
in Afghanistan and then launched war on Iraq, which rapidly toppled the
despot Saddam Hussein.

After the initial successes, the war dragged on due to a terrorist insur-
gency fueled by Iran and recruits from other Muslim countries and it became
increasingly unpopular. Further polarization of the country occurred over the
narrow reelection of President Bush in 2004. In 2007 President Bush altered
the U.S. strategy into a counterinsurgency and a surge in troops. The resulting dramatic reduction in violence and the decision by Sunnis to support
U.S. efforts coupled with the establishment of a democratically elected Iraqi
regime turned the tide. The war, which had been declared "lost" by Senate
Majority Leader Reid and others, was being won, such that American troops
began being withdrawn. Interestingly, the good news removed the war from
the front pages of major newspapers and television screens such that the
polarization over the war remained. This and a downturn in the housing
market and the economy set the stage for one of the most momentous presidential elections in the nation's history.

Films of the New Millennium

Just as society was in a state of uncertainty and profound change at the beginning of the new millennium, so too the films of the first years seemed to
reflect a wide range of tastes and influences. Films that won the Oscars during the first decade mirrored society's curiosity about such disparate topics
as Chinese culture and martial arts (*Crouching Tiger, Hidden Dragon,* 2000,

directed by Ang Lee); old musicals (*Chicago,* 2002); feminism (*Million Dollar Baby,* 2004); and homosexuality among cowboys (*Brokeback Mountain,* 2005). Epic fantasy films also remained popular, particularly Peter Jackson's *Lord of the Rings* trilogy, *Spider-Man,* and *Star Wars* "prequels." Technology also made great strides, particularly the use of CGI (computer-generated imagery), and several animated films enjoyed great popularity, including *Finding Nemo* (2003), *Shrek, Shrek 2, The Incredibles,* and *Ratatouille.*

Hollywood, which has been dominated by liberal actors and filmmakers since the 1970s turned out a number of documentaries critical of the president and of his policies, including Michael Moore's prize-winning films *Bowling for Columbine* (2002) and *Fahrenheit 9/11* (2004), and Al Gore's Oscar-winning *An Inconvenient Truth* (2006). However, despite the disillusionment with the war on all sides of the political spectrum, a spate of anti-Iraq War films starring A-list actors (*In the Valley of Elah, Redacted, Rendition, StopLoss,* and *Lions for Lambs*) all fared poorly at the domestic box office; only *The Kingdom,* which was a more positive take, did well.

Most puzzling, as Andrew Klavan noted, was the unwillingness in Hollywood to make film portraying the terrorist attacks in the past two decades that have been perpetrated by Middle Eastern Muslims, for fear of being accused of racial profiling. Two films in which Middle Eastern Muslims were the bad guys were produced in the 1990s (1994's *True Lies* and 1998's *The Siege*), but after 2001, portraying Muslims as potential enemies was curtailed. Only writer and director Paul Greengrass bucked the trend with his superb film *United 93* (2006), which told the story of the fourth hijacked plane that crashed in Shanksville, Pennsylvania. Indeed, the reverse happened in Ridley Scott's *Kingdom of Heaven* (2005), which presents a fictional account of the Third Crusade, in which Christians, especially the clergy or those committed to the Pope, were the bad guys, and Saladin and the Muslims were the good guys. This was quite different from Cecil B. DeMille's 1933 epic *The Crusades,* which was much more even-handed in its portrayal.

Christian Films of the New Millennium

In the new millennium, there was a continuation of legal challenges to the placement of crèches and other Christian symbols as well as the politically correct hesitancy to say "Merry Christmas" or to refer to Christmas in stores, calendars, and festive events. Institutions which had been founded by Christian denominations altered their crests; for example, Columbia University removed the three crosses but not the crown from its insignia, distancing itself from its Anglican but not its royal antecedent. Brown University parted ways from its predominantly Baptist and congregational origins by removing its motto "In Deo Speramus" from its crest. Some Catholic institutions gave up their Catholic identity and became secular, in part to assure federal funding. Like many prominent "Catholic" politicians, other universities became Catholic in name only as key faculty rejected dogma about abortion, homosexuality, embryonic stem cell research, etc. At the same time, new orthodox Catholic universities began to proliferate and gain prominence.

As Michelle Malkin documents, the most extreme example of political correctness run amok was when simulated terrorist attacks were conducted to train students in two New Jersey schools in the event of a recurrence, and Fundamentalist Christians were made the presumed perpetrators. Not surprisingly in this social climate, the savaging of Christians, especially Catholics, continued into the first decade of the new millennium with such films as *Chocolat, Sister Mary Explains It All, The Dangerous Lives of Altar Boys, Amen, The Magdalene Sisters*, and *Saved*. Still, just when all seemed lost, Mel Gibson's *The Passion of the Christ* appeared.

The film was attacked viciously by Frank Rich of the *New York Times* and others for almost a year before it opened, and the ability to secure wide distribution was delayed until after it garnered record opening-day box office receipts. Made for $30 million and hampered by the initial unwillingness of distributors to show the film widely, it still managed to gross $370 million domestically and an equivalent amount from foreign distribution and DVD sales. Its success has sparked interest in how to reach committed Christians, who have been turned off by their portrayal in films. Along with other moviegoers, they are beginning to rebel against the explicit sexuality, gratuitous violence, and preadolescent grossness of many current films. The filmmakers who produced *The Nativity Story* (2006), about the birth of Jesus, said that without *The Passion of the Christ*, their film would probably not have had wide distribution, let alone be made.

The success of *The Passion of the Christ* was followed by 2007's *Amazing Grace*, another film congenial to Christianity, which tells the story of William Wilberforce, a born-again Christian, who has been credited as the driving force behind England's abolition of the slave trade in 1807. Nevertheless, during the film's production, the original director Hugh Hudson, who had been responsible for the religiously sensitive *Chariots of Fire*, was replaced. When the film was released, Michael Apted, the new director, gave many interviews indicating that he had altered the original script to play down Wilberforce's Christian motives and instead emphasized secular and political motivations.

In short, we are at a major crossroads in the portrayal of Christians by Hollywood filmmakers. As a result of the success of *The Passion of the Christ*, they recognize that the market they have alienated is large. At the same time, it seems difficult for them to go against the secular dogma of the reigning cultural elites about Christians and Christianity, as witnessed by *Kingdom of Heaven*, *The Da Vinci Code*, *Breach*, *Elizabeth: The Golden Age*, and *Doubt*. For Christians to be dealt with more fairly in the years ahead, devout Christians will have to speak out against false and unjust portrayals and, in addition, as Spike Lee once urged blacks, to play a more active role in filmmaking, other media, journalism, the internet, and the law that are so influential in molding public opinion.

Keeping the Faith (2000)

Father Brian Kilkenny Finn (Edward Norton) forlornly nurses a beer in a bar where the bartender is a "Sikh Catholic Muslim with Jewish in-laws." Acknowledging that it's very complicated in that he's also reading *Dianetics*, the bartender puts on his towel like a stole and prepares to listen to the priest's confession, saying, "How long has it been since your last drink?" The movie flashes back to P.S. 84 introducing "2 Micks and a Yid." The "Yid" will grow up to be Rabbi Jake Schram (Ben Stiller); the "Micks" will become Father Finn and Anna Riley (Jenna Elfman), with whom both are infatuated.

Finn and Schram are both bumbling New Age clergymen. Finn's cassock catches fire, and he hits a parishioner with the thurifer (incense holder). Schram farts during a circumcision. They do stand-up comedy to packed houses, go to a gay disco, and wear combat pilot shades as they strut down the street. When the Rabbi's congregation doesn't get into singing, he invites a Harlem choir to do a calypso routine with bongos. Jewish mothers fax résumés and videos of their daughters to the Rabbi who must marry to become a Head Rabbi. Asked if he misses sex, Finn answers, "No, it's not an issue for me. I'm completely committed to what I do. That particular sacrifice is a symbol of my commitment."

Then, Anna, who has become a high-powered executive, returns from California. She tells Finn that "Your faith is a large part of why I love you."

He takes her comment as reciprocation of his love and is upset when she falls for Schram. He gets drunk and, in his clerical garb, crashes a Bar Mitzvah service and shouts, "I'm not drunk. I'm Irish. This is mother's milk. He stole my girlfriend." The scene is embarrassing to watch. Later, he tells his buddy, "You're lucky I'm a priest. Forgiveness comes with the job." He tells Anna, "I thought you loved me and that affected me. I began to doubt myself." The film ends with interfaith dancing after the Rabbi gives a Yom Kippur sermon saying, "No Rabbi can save anyone. He can only offer himself as a guide to other fearful beings."

Commentary

This lightweight movie is about two clergymen who want to "kick the dust" off their faiths and bring an Old World God into a New Age. The bartender's familial religious mix personifies both moral confusion and moral equivalency. The difficulty of sustaining consistent beliefs in any organized religion is illustrated when the Rabbi says, "Jews want their Rabbi to be the person they don't have time to be," and the priest replies that "Catholics want their priests to be the persons they don't have the discipline to be." In their stand-up routine, they pointedly affirm a subjective sense of religion free from dogma when they say, "The difference between faith and religion is that faith is not about having the right answers; it's a feeling, a hunch, it's God."

Figure 10.1. *Keeping the Faith.* Rabbi Jake Schram (Ben Stiller) and Father Brian Kilkenny Finn (Edward Norton) bring a decidedly unorthodox sensibility to their ministries.

To my mind, the most interesting dialogue is between Father Finn and his spiritual director, Father Havel (Czech director Milos Forman), whose name is an apparent homage to Vaclav Havel, the first president of the post–Soviet Czech Republic. Finn says, "I keep thinking about what you said in seminary, that the life of a priest is hard and if you can see yourself being happy doing anything else you should do that." Havel responds:

> That was my recruitment pitch, which is not bad when you're starting out because it makes you feel like a marine. The truth is you can never tell yourself there is only one thing you could be. If you are a priest or if you marry a woman it's the same challenge. You cannot make a real commitment unless you accept that it's a choice that you keep making again and again and again. (Screenwriter: Stuart Blumberg)

This exchange, at least, hits the right note.

Chocolat (2000)

Vianne Rocher (Juliette Binoche), an itinerant blithe spirit, literally blows into Lansquenet, a poor town in post–World War II France, on the strength of the north wind, with a duffel bag and her daughter Anouk (Victoire Thivisol). Vianne proceeds to transform an abandoned store into a well-stocked *bonbonnière* and presides over it with elegant low-cut outfits. Her main aim is to disturb the *tranquility* of a town that is proud of its "hard work, modesty, and discipline" and "where everyone knows his place." She is just in time to rescue the poor benighted Catholic populace during a pre–Vatican II Lent by seducing them with her aphrodisiac Mexican chocolate. Comte de Reynaud (Alfred Molina), who runs the town as a rigid moralist with the requisite off-putting expressions and attitudes, decides to declare war over her chocolate.

Vianne's landlady Armande (Judi Dench), an elderly diabetic, eats the chocolate, upsetting her daughter Caroline (Carrie-Anne Moss), another moralistic prude, who is angry at Mom for not being willing to go to a nursing home. In this extremely small town, Caroline manages to prevent Mom from seeing her grandson, a hurt which Vianne remedies. Vianne also diagnoses "spouse abuse" as the root cause of a seemingly psychotic kleptomaniac's problem and counsels Josephine (Lena Olin) to leave her husband and to work and live with her in the shop. As Josephine transforms herself, the movie makes disparaging comments about the Comte, the Catholic Church, and Frenchmen. The film becomes even less believable when Roux (Johnny Depp), an Irish guitar-playing "river rat" and his good-hearted itinerant companions, camp at the end of town and are vilified by the intolerant Count and his priest mouthpiece as "godless drifters." Never fear, all ends well when the Comte capitulates to Vianne.

Commentary

This is an admittedly well-done and well-acted movie. It was nominated for five Oscars: Best Picture, Best Actress (Juliette Binoche), Best Supporting Actress (Judi Dench), Best Original Music (Rachel Portman), and Best Adapted Screenplay (Robert Nelson Jacobs), as well as many other awards. Indeed, what most troubled me were its excellent atmospherics and star power that sucked in and seduced the viewer. However, beneath its gooey veneer, *Chocolat* is another Lasse Hallström/Harvey Weinstein pastiche of bigotry and half-baked philosophy like their other well-crafted movie, *The Cider House Rules*. Vianne's expressions and manner are characterized by a smarminess that confirms her possession of the truth. Indeed, as Jennet Conant, *New York Times* reporter, noted, Binoche infuses Vianne with so much supernatural strength that she "unflinchingly takes on a whole French village to prove a point or two—about single motherhood, sensuality and what the right blend of chili peppers and cocoa can do."

Figure 10.2. *Chocolat.* **A traditionalist French Count and a naïve young priest are no match for a New Age chocolatier.**

Named one of the top 10 anti-Catholic films in 2004, it ridicules the Church's "old-fashioned concept" of giving up something (like chocolate) for Lent. The Church is represented by a moralistic prude and a rather inane, easily led priest who sings "You Ain't Nothing But a Hound Dog" while sweeping the outside of the church and who allows the Comte to edit and rewrite his Sunday sermons. Its adherents are "sheep," who attend Mass and listen to the jejune priest and must be rescued by Vianne. The moral of this heavy-handed "fantasy" is announced straightforwardly at the movie's end: "It's not what we don't do or what we exclude, but what we embrace and whom we include." In short, one simply needs an attitude of inclusiveness and acceptance of people doing their own thing. This is 1960s philosophy redux, courtesy of aging Boomers.

Sister Mary Explains It All (2001)

Introduced with chant, holy pictures, a Bible, a rosary, and stained glass windows, this made-for-cable film begins with a traditional third-grade Nativity pageant set in the 1960s and then shifts to 20 years later. Sister Mary Ignatius (Diane Keaton), a certifiable nutcase, alternately preaches a fire-and-brimstone sermon on heaven, hell, and limbo while quizzing her favorite seven-year-old student on the Baltimore Catechism. She has invited the now-grown children to recreate the original pageant. The disaffected foursome egg on Sister Mary with lines like, "Unbaptized babies who died before the Second Vatican Council are in Limbo," and "the entire Catholic religion is based on low blood sugar."

Philomena Rostovich (Jennifer Tilly) rails against the Church because her mother had 26 children without birth control, and she and most of the children were institutionalized. Gary Sullivan (Brian Benben), who is gay, says he was seduced when he was in the seminary. Aloysius Benheim (Wallace Langham) says that Sister used to hit his head against the blackboard. Angela Di Marco (Laura San Giacomo) talks about being raped and having two abortions because she was clueless about sex as a result of the Church's teaching. Their satiric tableau ends with baby Jesus on the cross. Then Angela pulls a gun on Sister Mary Ignatius and asks her to admit that there is no God. Sister wrestles the gun away. Angela comes at her with the Cross, and Sister shoots her and holds the gun on the other three. When she learns that Gary went to confession that morning and didn't have sex with his partner afterward, she shoots him so that he can go straight to heaven. She lets the unwed mother/prostitute go when she promises to marry the father. She also excuses the suicidal alcoholic spouse abuser because he at least married and had children. It ends with the choir singing a hymn to the glory of God and Sister Mary praying the rosary.

Commentary

The screenplay for this vitriolically anti-Catholic film was written by a lapsed-Catholic playwright, Christopher Durang, and is based on his off-Broadway one-act, Obie Award–winning play *Sister Mary Ignatius Explains It All for You.* As quoted by O'Malley from a Durang essay, he explained his motivation: "Looking back, I realized that the Catholicism of my childhood had an answer for absolutely everything—it was extremely thorough. I had this impulse to write a play in which a nun came out and explained everything—the nature and purpose of the universe, if you will, but as told through the prism of Catholic dogma" (at least as Durang learned it). While legitimate questions may be posed about the Catholic beliefs and rituals altered after Vatican II, they are overwhelmed by the sheer nastiness, ridicule, and out-of-control ending. Why well-known stars would be parties to this mess is beyond me.

The Magdalene Sisters (2002)

This fictional "factually-based" film begins in Dublin with a priest singing an Irish song at a wedding while Margaret (Anne-Marie Duff) brings her friend Bernadette (Nora-Jane Noone) upstairs to her cousin Kevin (Sean McDonagh). He rapes her as the camera focuses on a rosary hanging from a chair. Bernadette is sent brusquely by the priest to a House run by the Magdalene Sisters whose philosophy is, "Through the power of prayer, cleanliness, and hard work, the fallen may find their way back to Jesus Christ."

The film is filled with a lot of angry nuns walking the girls down long corridors when they aren't working them hard in the laundry, which is said to be a way of cleansing their immortal souls. When a girl answers back, a nun replies, "Don't ever interrupt me. Were you too busy whoring with the boys to learn that?" One girl escapes to be with her child, but the parents' side with the nuns and priests, and she is returned. A sadistic nun loves cutting the girls' hair and is delighted when she is brought two more disobedient girls. In an attempt to escape, a girl flashes a boy who works there. She is caught and gets beaten by a nun who is applauded by a priest. A nun lines up naked girls and picks out ones with the littlest breasts, the biggest breasts, and the biggest bottom. That leaves only the hairiest, which is awarded to Christine, who cries and later hangs herself.

One girl enters the convent. She is lauded as "a young penitent who has turned her back on the evils of the world. The transformation of what she once was, should be noted by you all." The clincher is the priest exposing himself during Mass. The film ends by declaring that "It's estimated that 30,000 women were in Magdalene asylums throughout Ireland. The last one closed in 1996."

Commentary

The DVD contains a "documentary" entitled *Sex in a Cold Climate* in which two women recount their experiences. It ends with a victim saying, "What remains is a lasting antipathy to the Church." However, filmmaker Peter Mullan admitted that many of the Magdalene girls remained lifelong devout Catholics, suggesting that he, and the maker of the documentary on which it was based, may have chosen selectively from the survivors of the 30,000 young women. It's not surprising that this film was produced and released by Miramax and the Weinstein Brothers who have made a number of anti-Catholic films or that the critics loved this film. The *Baltimore Sun* critic Michael Sragow's review was headlined, "Religious Disorder: Gripping, searing *Magdalene Sisters* confronts the hypocrisy of a church that victimized the fallen women it purported to save." An issue of the *New York Times,* which the same day also ran one of Frank Rich's many articles against *The Passion of the Christ,* contained an article by novelist Mary Gordon entitled "How Ireland Hid Its Own Dirty Laundry" which accepted everything in the film as the whole truth.

I found the most cogent commentary to be by film critic Steven Greydanus on his website www.decentfilms.com. He noted that, although the work is fiction, "tragically, there may indeed be truth to the charges and some might have been worse." However, he faulted the filmmaker for not exploring the social or cultural pathology of the perpetrators and of Ireland itself that fostered such behavior as well as the fact that such institutions were not solely Catholic. Most telling was his citation that director Peter Mullan, who compared the nuns to the Taliban, "was raised Catholic but in interviews has stated that he has considered himself a Marxist from his teenaged years, and has described belief in heaven and hell as 'nonsense' and 'the whole notion of celibacy' as 'nuts' and 'perverse.'" Mullan claimed that his film isn't meant to be anti-Catholic but acknowledged, as Greydanus notes, "his animosity toward his Catholic upbringing and admits that he brought his prejudices and sympathies to the project."

As Greydanus notes, no character in a Roman collar or wimple manifests a shred of kindness, decency, or spirituality, and none evinces guilt or regret. Their only humanizing aspects are introduced to show their hypocrisy, as with the Irish song opener followed by the priest helping to institutionalize the victim. Another example is when the sadistic Sister Bridget (Geraldine McEwan) becomes teary-eyed watching the scene in *The Bells of St. Mary's* where Ingrid Bergman's character discusses why she chose to be a nun and asks God to take the bitterness from her heart and to be able to do God's will.

Amen (2002)

Based on Rolf Hochhuth's controversial 1963 play *The Deputy*, nuns are shown shepherding Jewish handicapped children into the gas chambers. An SS lieutenant, Kurt Gerstein (Ulrich Tukur), sees families being exterminated and tries to alert Americans and British through the Swedish ambassador. He is told that only the Vatican can doing anything about it. A sympathetic priest brings him to see a Cardinal who says that the Pope is too afraid of Communists to confront the Nazis and that's why he signed a Concordat with Hitler. The Church also doesn't want to pay taxes. The papal nuncio says that he is "weary of the whining of the Jews."

The film alternates between churchmen turning a blind eye to the Holocaust and Germans simultaneously worrying that they are running out of chemicals for the gas chambers, while joining in singing "Silent Night." The Pope is shown giving a vague Christmas address that does not mention the concentration camps. A priest from Berlin gives documentary evidence of Polish and Hungarian concentration camps to Papal nuncio. The Pope counsels "moderation," saying that he worries about endangering Catholics in Germany and Austria by speaking out but that "at the right time, we will speak." Gerstein hangs himself when accused, as a devout Christian, of not doing everything in his power to stop the atrocities. The epilogue states that he was "rehabilitated 20 years later."

Commentary

This hateful anti-Catholic movie about the complicity of Pope Pius XII in the Holocaust has about as much validity as *The Protocols of the Elders of Zion* about Jews. Despite having been proven thoroughly baseless by Jewish and Catholic scholars of the Holocaust, like the "protocols" which continues to have legs in anti-Semitic writings, this canard has been kept alive by James Carroll, author of "Hitler's Pope," and others because it sells. The film's self-serving justification is stated at the end: "*The Deputy* is a massive morality play that examines the question of Pope Pius XII's failure." The filmmakers go on to say, "Also as the film is made with the advantage of increased historical knowledge, *Amen* is less critical of the Church than is Hochhuth's original work," and they show their corrections of some of Hochhuth's errors. Too bad they didn't wait a few more years as they could have dispensed with the film entirely. The recent unsealing of the Vatican archives has provided more evidence to show the thesis of the Pope's complicity to be fiction. Indeed, Rome's Chief Rabbi Elio Toaff proposed giving Pope Pius the title of "Righteous Gentile," reserved for non-Jews who risked their lives to save Jews during the Holocaust. The final unmasking of the lie occurred on January 25, 2007, when a Russian KGB defector, Lt. General Ion Mihai Pacepa, revealed that he was in charge of disinformation campaign "Seat-12" in Romania in the late 1950s and early 1960s to picture Pope Pius XII as an anti-Semite who encouraged Hitler's Holocaust. When Rolf Hochhuth's play appeared in 1963, Pacepa received a congratulatory visit by General Ivan Agayants, the head of KGB's disinformation department for a job well done. Sadly, the lie endures.

Luther (2003)

As the film opens, a storm rages mirroring Luther's (Joseph Fiennes) mental state as he confesses that he is "too full of sin to be a priest" and calls God "a self-righteous judge." The confessor tells him that none of what he confesses is sinful and that God is not angry with him but that he is angry with God. Luther responds that he is looking for a God who will love him. The confessor thinks it's best for Luther to get out of the cloister and to see the world, so Luther travels to Rome, which he finds to be a circus, a running sewer where one can buy sex *and* salvation.

Sent by the abbot to Wittenburg to teach theology, Luther challenges the notion that there is no salvation outside the Holy Roman Church and the rule that suicides can't be buried in holy ground. He challenges the selling of relics saying that there are enough nails from Christ's cross to shoe every horse in Saxony, even though his patron Frederick the Wise of Saxony (Sir Peter Ustinov) has a prized collection of relics. He despairs of the dissolute Popes like Alexander VI, who had three mistresses and five children. He has hope for the next Pope, Leo X, who was made a cardinal at 13, but the Pope, needing money to build St. Peter's, offers the Bishopric of Mainz for 10,000 ducats. The Pope recruits John Tetzel to sell indulgences to support St. Peter's. Tetzel is quoted as saying, "When a coin in the coffer rings, a soul from Purgatory springs." Luther publishes the 95 Theses on the cathedral door at Wittenburg, including condemnation of the sale of indulgences, and the sales decline 80 percent. The Pope fumes, saying, "That damn heretic, he will burn in hell. This drunken monk is intoxicated with himself. Sober him." Luther is summoned to appear at Augsburg and threatened with excommunication but refuses to recant. His confessor releases him from his Augustinian vows and sends him to the protection of Frederick, who also refuses to release him.

The Pope orders that Luther's books be burned and issues a Papal Bull excommunicating him. Luther publicly burns the Papal Bull and his books of canon law. Frederick enlists the help of the Holy Roman Emperor to protect Luther. His confessor visits him in Worms and says, "I hoped you would reform the Church, not destroy it. You are tearing the world apart." Luther responds, "When you sent me out to boldly change the world, did you not think there would be such a cost?" Luther translates the New Testament into German and tells the people to learn to despise the cross and pretense. The peasants rise up against their lords and overrun monasteries and kill monks in what was later called the Peasants War. Luther supports the nobles against the peasants whose revolt he had helped instigate.

When nuns escape from the convents, Luther marries a nun, Katrina von Bohr. Journeying to Augsburg in 1530, he tells the princes to challenge the Holy Roman Emperor and draws up a new confession of faith, called the Confession of Augsburg. The film ends with the following epilogue: "What happened at Augsburg pushed open the door of religious freedom. Martin Luther lived for another 16 years preaching and teaching the Word. He and Katrina von Bohr enjoyed a happy marriage and 6 children. Luther's influence extended into economics, politics, education and music and his translation of the Bible became a foundation stone of the German language. Today over 540 million worship in churches inspired by his Reformation."

Commentary

This film, produced by various Lutheran groups, has two excellent stars in Fiennes and Ustinov. It is appropriately critical of the Catholic Church at the time and portrays Luther very favorably, albeit as a tormented soul for much of the picture. His main adversary was Johann Tetzel, a Dominican monk who started selling indulgences in 1503. While selling them in Germany in 1517, he declared that anyone who bought an indulgence could choose a soul to be freed from Purgatory. His claim was considered to be the proximate cause of Martin Luther's drawing up the 95 Theses. It's important to remember that many Catholics criticized Tetzel for his conduct, although he was never repudiated by Rome and indeed, his ability to get money for building St. Peter's was welcomed by Pope Leo X and his cardinal advisers, again showing how an institution presumed to be divine can be subverted by the humans in charge.

More might have been made of how Luther, whose writings had empowered and inflamed the peasants, was so appalled at the extreme reaction of some that he reportedly told the nobles, "Strike them down and stab the rebels like mad dogs. This must be stopped." It's estimated that 50,000 to 100,000 died in the Peasants War in 1524–1525. Though the film loses steam in the last third, it is worth seeing especially as a catalyst for the discussion of the many theological issues raised and the real abuses that led to the Reformation as well as the changes in the Catholic Church as a result of the Counter Reformation. The interviews on the DVD are interesting, especially Ustinov's comment that "Luther was too good a Catholic to remain a

Figure 10.3. *Luther.* **Luther (Joseph Fiennes) nails the 95 Theses on the door of the Castle Church at Wittenberg on October 31, 1517, signaling the beginning of the Reformation.**

Catholic and too good a Catholic to be a good Protestant." This film conveys this paradox exceedingly well.

Thérèse: The Story of Saint Thérèse of Lisieux (2004)

Thérèse (Lindsay Younce), who wrote in her diary that she wanted to be a saint but felt helpless, was born into a well-to-do and devout family. Her mother had wanted to be a nun and a saint and her father, a monk. When they married, they vowed to be celibate, but a priest told them that this was contrary to the sacrament of marriage, so they went on to have nine children (five daughters survived). Born in 1873, Thérèse was the youngest and most pampered. When she was four, her mother died of breast cancer, and Pauline (Linda Hayden), the eldest, became her surrogate mother. Thérèse is pictured as very scrupulous and confessing trivial things as being sinful. With no friends at school, she convinces her father to have Pauline homeschool her. When Pauline leaves to join the Carmelites, Thérèse becomes ill and is delirious for two weeks, recovering only after looking at a statue of the Virgin. Her other sisters, Marie (Maggie Rose Fleck) and Leonie (Mandy Rimer), leave to join the Carmelites and Poor Clares, respectively, and Thérèse remains the spoiled child, crying and throwing tantrums when things don't go her way until the Christmas when she is 14. She apparently has a revelation that it's not all about her and begins to care about others, including an unrepentant assassin named Pranzini (Brian Shields) who had killed three women in Paris. Not wanting him to go to hell, she prays earnestly for him and is rewarded by the news that he embraced the crucifix on his way to the guillotine. She also begins praying for priests whom she believes to be "weak and fragile men, despite their holy vocation."

Thérèse campaigns to enter the Carmelites at 15, a year before it's allowed, but the local Bishop declines her request. On a trip to Rome, she petitions the Pope against protocol and has to be physically removed by the Swiss Guards. However, she gets her wish and finds that the convent is not all she expected. She is rather frail for the arduous duties, and she is clumsy and not used to hard work. She runs into petty opposition from one nun but again she has a revelation about doing little sacrifices rather than grand deeds for people without getting praised and in effect creates her Little Way to sainthood. Thérèse develops tuberculosis and dies after telling Pauline that her mission is about to begin and that she will spend her time in heaven by doing good on earth. Her sister Pauline released an edited version of

Thérèse's autobiography, which had such an impact that she was canonized 28 years after her death in 1897 and named one of the 33 Doctors of the Catholic Church.

Commentary

This independent film funded by many Catholic groups and donors, is a throwback to *The Song of Bernadette*. Though gentle and beautifully photographed, it suffers from the fact that almost all the participants are first-time filmmakers. Earnest and well-meaning, it will appeal to those who are sick of films with profanity, violence, and gratuitous sex and are searching for films about someone who takes religion seriously.

The film probably is best suited to discussing the meaning of sainthood and canonization. There are countless saints not canonized by the Catholic Church. The recognition is meant to celebrate a life or life's work that might inspire the faithful. For example, Mother Teresa said she was inspired by Thérèse's Little Way, noting that being a saint was not being perfect but accepting one's weaknesses and the feeling that God will not abandon you. On the other end of the spectrum was the famed chanteuse Edith Piaf, who, despite a sordid life (chronicled in *La Vie en Rose)*, had a deep devotion to Saint Thérèse whom she credited with restoring her eyesight after a severe infection.

The 1986 French film *Thérèse* by Alain Cavalier is a less glossy version of Thérèse's story and more convincingly depicts why she was declared a saint. However, it is harder to watch because it is so slow-moving and disjointed, consisting mainly of tableaux, most of which occur in the convent. Still, the lead actress, Catherine Mouchet, radiates a childlike simplicity and saintliness that seems to capture Thérèse's spirit. There is also much more emphasis on the Carmelites' austere life and arduous work, which Thérèse accentuates by eschewing bedcovers when it is cold, as well as fasting and pushing herself to work in the laundry when sick.

There is also a scene where a young doctor (Joel LeFrancois) tells the Mother Superior (Clemence Massart-Weit) that Thérèse has tuberculosis, and she rejects his diagnosis. After Thérèse dies, the Mother Superior asks to be flagellated by her sister Pauline (Sylvie Habault) for having lied about how sick Thérèse was. Another interesting facet involves a nun, Lucie (Hélène Alexandridis), who has a crush on Thérèse and is banned from seeing her when she is sick. Lucie is shown talking about cleaning lepers' stumps with

Figure 10.4. *Thérèse.* Thérèse of Lisieux (Lindsay Younce) works hard and mortifies herself despite suffering from widespread tuberculosis.

water and then drinking it. She also sneaks up to Thérèse's bed and after leaving her a note, tastes her spittle at the bedside. She ultimately leaves the order as she had threatened to do if Thérèse died.

As a very old nun tells Thérèse, "Don't worry, for a Carmelite, the first thirty years are the hardest." In short, this film shows a side of saintliness which most will see as daunting. That may be why the more recent film emphasizes Saint Thérèse's Little Way or doing the little things, something many who aspire to do good may consider less onerous, except for the fact that it comes with a string attached, that is, doing those things for others anonymously.

The Passion of the Christ (2004)

The film spans the time from Christ's agony in the Garden of Gethsemane to the Resurrection. As Christ prays, He is beset by the devil, in the guise of a woman to give up His burden. A snake slithers out from under the woman to bite Him, but Christ steps on the snake and crushes it. This is followed by Judas's betrayal, Peter cutting off the soldier's ear, Christ's healing the wound, and telling Peter to put the sword away. At the Court of the High Priest Caiaphas, there is a flashback to Christ's childhood. After Jesus says He is the Messiah, Caiaphas shouts "Death!" and strikes Jesus. Pilate the Roman governor then challenges the Jews saying, "He is the prophet you welcomed into Jerusalem five days ago, now you want Him put to death." He sends Christ to Herod who mocks Him and returns Him to Pilate, who has

Him scourged, thinking that this will satisfy the crowd. This scene is very graphic and prolonged. The Roman soldiers mock Jesus by putting a crown of thorns on Him. Pilate shows Christ to the crowd saying, "Behold the Man," and offers to release Him, but the people prefer Barabbas and shout, "Crucify Him!" Pilate washes his hands of Him literally and figuratively, and Christ begins the carrying of the Cross. As He falls the second time, Mary runs to Him, saying, "I am here." Simon of Cyrene, recruited to help Jesus carry the cross, tells the Romans to stop beating Christ, and a Roman calls Simon "Jew" for standing up to them. Veronica wipes his face with her veil.

Simon and Jesus look up at Golgotha, and the film flashes back to Christ preaching the Sermon on the Mount. "Love your enemies and pray for those who persecute you. For if you only love those who love you, what reward is there . . . I am the Good Shepherd, I lay down my life for the flock. No one takes my life from Me." There are flashbacks from the crucifixion to the breaking of the bread at the Last Supper as Christ says, "This is My Body which I give for you." As the Romans hammer nails in Christ's hands and feet (which is not sugar-coated and pretty upsetting), He says, "Father, forgive them for they know not what they do." Every jarring move in the nailing is portrayed, as are faces of the sadistic Romans. Caiaphas says, "You said you could destroy the temple and rebuild it in three days. Prove yourself and come down from the Cross."

The good thief asks Christ to remember him when he enters his kingdom, and Christ responds, "I tell you this day you shall be with me in Paradise." He is beaten by a Roman soldier. Then, the sky darkens as the Romans play dice for his garment. One soldier is afraid, as are the chief priest and the elders. Mary and John go to the base of the Cross. After kissing Christ's feet, Mary says, "Flesh of my flesh, heart of my heart, my son, let me die with you." He says to Mary, "Behold your son," and to John, "Behold your Mother." Then, "My God, My God, why have you forsaken me. It is accomplished. Father into your hands I commend my spirit." The ground shakes. The Romans break Christ's bones and put a spear in His side; out runs water mixed with blood. Caiaphas sees the Temple being destroyed. Christ is taken down from the Cross into the arms of His mother. The last scene shows the stone being removed from the tomb and the resurrected Christ walking out.

Commentary

This film faithfully tells the New Testament biblical story according to Matthew (and for the most part, in Aramaic in which it was first written).

Whether people want to accept its message is a different issue. Although the film was vilified for being anti-Semitic in a yearlong media campaign before it was released, any fair-minded person would not call the film anti-Semitic. It is the Romans who scourge Christ mercilessly, crown Him with thorns, beat Him as He carries the cross, nail Him to the cross, and break His bones. As noted in Lopate's *American Movie Critics*, the *New York Times* critic A. O. Scott said, "To my eyes it did not traffic explicitly or egregiously in the toxic iconography of Jew hatred. . . . and the onscreen villainy does not exceed what can be found in the source material" (Matthew's Gospel). He points out that Gibson excised the Gospel's attribution to the Jews of the words "His blood be upon us and upon our children." Ironically, a far more faithful 1964 film version of St. Matthew's Gospel by Pasolini (p. 171), in which the Jews do say those words has been critically acclaimed without any outcry, let alone a campaign such as was launched against Gibson. For a more detailed treatment of the controversy, consult Mark Royden Mitchell's *God, Man & Hollywood*.

To my mind, what Gibson was trying to do had nothing to do with the Jews and everything to do with getting at the essence of Jesus's sacrifice for mankind. In fact, the purpose is stated at the film's beginning with the introductory crawl: "He was wounded for our transgressions, crushed by our iniquities; by His wounds, we are healed. Isaiah 53." Jim Caviezel, in an Academy Award–deserving performance (although the Academy gave no major nominations to the film), portrays Christ as a tortured soul who fulfills His destiny by undergoing unspeakable suffering to redeem man. *The Passion*

**Figure 10.5. *The Passion of the Christ*.
Jesus (James Caviezel) is crowned with thorns.**

BACKSTORY

Playing Jesus

The life of Jesus Christ has been an important subject since the inception of film. Jesus's life story itself is a difficult one to portray, sure to offend someone no matter how careful the filmmaker plans. Furthermore, playing the part of Jesus presents enormous challenges because of the duality of His nature and the absence of any images taken in life. We have no idea what He looked like but to some extent, it doesn't matter. Without real models, filmmakers, like artists, have been given free rein, which has resulted in various portrayals. Early films about Jesus often avoided showing His face by photographing an actor from behind, or simply represented Him symbolically by showing only His hands.

In the age of the religious epic, even an actor of the stature of Charlton Heston, who made his fame playing such religious icons as Moses (*The Ten Commandments*), John the Baptist (*The Greatest Story Ever Told*), and Ben-Hur (*Ben-Hur*) never played Jesus. Those who did were often unknowns or foreign actors like Max von Sydow in George Stevens's *The Greatest Story Ever Told*, who had starred in Swedish films but not yet in Hollywood. Jeffrey Hunter, who played Jesus in Nicholas Ray's version of *King of Kings* in 1961, was Jesus's age at the time of His public life but looked much younger. This led some to call the film, "I Was a Teenage Jesus."

In the 1970s through the 1990s, filmmakers began to present Jesus from a human rather than a divine perspective. Noteworthy representations include a flower child (Victor Garber in *Godspell*); a weak Jesus (Ted Neeley) overshadowed by Judas in *Jesus Christ Superstar*; an indecisive Jesus coping with temptations of the flesh as well as marriage and parenthood (Willem Dafoe in *The Last Temptation of Christ*); and an actor asked who achieves celebrity by creating a revisionist Passion play box office hit (Lothaire Bluteau in *Jesus of Montreal*). The new millennium brought back a film showing the duality of Christ's nature while highlighting the enormity of his human suffering (James Caviezel in *The Passion of the Christ*).

Whether traditional or offbeat, how we react to the filmmakers' depiction often depends on how closely the representation squares with our religious views. In the past few decades, critics have been more likely to applaud films that show a Jesus reduced to a human rather than a dual God/Man nature. This may be a greater comfort to secularists more interested in a personal God or to those who wish to be free of dogma and the confines of an institutional church. Still, the success of Mel Gibson's relatively traditional *The Passion of the Christ* underscores that many potential moviegoers are more moved by the classic portrayal of Jesus.

---

of the Christ, like *The Passion of Joan of Arc*, does not qualify as entertainment. It is barely watchable at times because of the brutality, an aspect commented on by most critics as one of the reasons they hated it. Yet, the public flocked to it, and it earned over $700 million worldwide (over a billion dollars counting DVD sales and rentals). Picturing brutality is an inevitable part of filming the reality of the crucifixion (unlike the many gratuitous portrayals of violence as in *Pulp Fiction*, *Kill Bill*, and *The Matrix*, lauded by the same critics). Gibson acknowledged the violence by releasing an edited version for those who wanted something less graphic.

I believe that one can understand the film by considering it in two dimensions: the first being Gibson's attempt to show the enormity of Christ's sacrifice for us and the second, on a more personal level, his desire to exorcise his own demons and in the process encourage the audience to do the same. There is substantial evidence that Gibson was successful in the latter, as it was anecdotally reported that some viewers turned themselves in for crimes they committed after seeing the film. Finally, it is a film that is best taken in small doses, and my recommendation is that those who are concerned about being overwhelmed by watching it in its totality should break the film into segments. Given that it only focuses on Christ's last days, the film can serve as an excellent supplement to Franco Zeffirelli's more comprehensive miniseries, *Jesus of Nazareth*.

The Ninth Day (2004)

This powerful German film opens with a Luxembourgian priest Henri Kremer (Ulrich Matthes), who has been helping Jews escape, being herded with others to Dachau prison in a cellblock devoted to the clergy. The priests secretly concelebrate Mass and are interrupted by a brutal SS officer who forces them to sing a song about death and then beats and crucifies someone who sings off key. The Bishop of Luxembourg has refused to leave his residence to meet with the Nazi gauleiter after the German invasion and instead has had the church bells rung daily. Kremer, who was a protégé of the Bishop, is given a nine-day leave to return to Luxembourg to persuade him to sign a decree of cooperation with the Nazis. The Bishop refuses to meet with Kremer, and each day tension grows between Kremer and his handler Gebhardt (August Diehl), a young Gestapo officer who has some commonalities with Kremer. They both were strongly influenced by their mothers, and Gebhardt had studied for the priesthood, but two days before ordination had left to join the Nazis. In one of their philosophic discussions, Gebhardt says, "You're right, Jesus was a Jew. That's what he wanted to overcome. He showed us the way. That's what we Aryans have to thank him for. By defeating the Jew in me, I am doing the work of the Lord." In another exchange, Gebhardt talks about his dissertation on the mutual dependence of Jesus and Judas. "No Judas, no crucifixion. No Judas, no universal Church," he declares. Having given up on the Bishop, he asks Kremer to sign the document of cooperation in his stead, postulating that Kremer will be saving the Church from Communism by allying with the Nazis and in effect being Judas to the Church.

There are numerous flashbacks to the camp and how Kremer's thirst led him not to tell his compatriots about a faucet that he found that leaked very small drips. He feels guilty when a fellow cleric tries to escape because of thirst and is electrocuted at the fence. Finally, he meets the Bishop who tells him that the Luxembourgians know what it means when he rings the bell. The churches remain filled. He tells Kremer that the Pope's silence to that point is based on what happened in the Netherlands when the Bishop of Utrecht wrote a pastoral letter condemning the Nazis for deporting the Jews and 40,000 "non-Aryan" Catholics (Jewish converts) were sent to concentration camps in retaliation. He asks, "What would be the result if the Pope lodged a protest, 200,000? 300,000?" The rest of the film is very tense as Henri tries to make a decision about whether to sign, while beset by concerns for his family, his fellow priests, and the Church.

Commentary

In an interview included on the DVD, director Volker Schlöndorff remembers seeing *The Passion of Joan of Arc* (see p. 30) at a Jesuit boarding school and wanting Joan to say one word so that she wouldn't burn. He said, "I could never understand why some people have such certainty within them about certain things that they would rather die than betray them or themselves." That's what intrigued him about this story of Jean Bernard who was one of about 3,000 Catholic clergy, 100 Protestant pastors, and 30 Orthodox priests in "the priests' block," almost half of whom died. Bernard was imprisoned for writing an article for a Resistance newsletter saying Jesus was a Jew while attacking Nazi racial theories as well as helping Luxembourgians escape the Nazis in 1941. His nine-day release occurred in January 1942; he was released later in 1942 through the help of his brother who was a Nazi collaborator. In 1962 he published his diary, much of which related to the events described in the camp. The film's accounts of the events in Luxembourg were invented from sketchy diary entries. One major difference between the film and the diary is the powerful tap water nightmare story that actually came from author Primo Levi, who was incarcerated in Auschwitz, and who in his memoir also noted that a prisoner's overwhelming object was to survive.

Another deviation relates to Kremer's statement of frustration about the Pope's "silence" on the Nazis and feeling abandoned in the concentration camps. Actually, as Bernard wrote in his diary, *Priestblock 25487,* every protest by a religious authority was accompanied by more brutal treatment by the guards to the point where the Protestant pastors said to the priests, "Again, your big naïve Pope and those simpletons, your bishops, are shooting their mouths off. Why don't they get the idea once and for all, and shut up? They play the heroes and we pay the price." Schlöndorff does mention the tragic effect of the pastoral letter in Utrecht, but the timing is off; the deportations occurred six months afterwards in July 1942. What he does not mention is that far from being silent, Pope Pius condemned totalitarianism and racism and atrocities against noncombatants in his first encyclical in 1939 as well as his Christmas broadcasts of 1939 through 1941. These pronouncements were widely praised at the time, including by the *New York Times.*

Despite Schlöndorff's failure to relate much of this, the film is a very nuanced approach to a controversial subject and is an excellent antidote to the highly prejudicial one Hochhuth took in *Amen* (see p. 307). Finally, the film is worth seeing for the intense portrayal of Kremer by the gaunt hollow-cheeked Matthes whose burning eyes not only sear all they gaze upon but are truly the portals to his tormented soul until his decision creates a sense of relief and almost joy.

Figure 10.6. *The Ninth Day.* Father Kremer (Ulrich Matthes) argues with his Nazi handler Gebhardt (August Diehl), who is trying to obtain Church support for the invasion of Luxembourg.

Saved! (2004)

Set in an evangelical Christian high school, the film opens with Mary (Jena Malone) saying:

> I've been born again my whole life. Accepting Jesus into my life is a big decision especially for a three year old. Jesus became the center of my life. I was a member of the Christian Jewels. I was anti-abortion. My mother was the "best Christian interior decorator." I had the perfect Christian boy friend. I went to a Christian school. (Screenwriters: Brian Dannelly, Michael Urban)

Then everything goes south when her boyfriend Dean (Chad Faust) and she go to the bottom of a swimming pool, and he tells her he is gay. On the way up she hits her head, and a nearby carpenter morphs into Jesus who tells her that Dean needs her now more than ever and that she must do everything to help him. She wonders how he can be gay when "he's the best Christian I know"; maybe he's afflicted by a toxin. Her overbearing friend Hilary Faye (Mandy Moore), who always drops Jesus's name, shoots the penis on the target at a shooting range and says that this is a sign that Mary must give up her virginity. Mary has sex with Dean, who is then sent by his parents to Mercy House, a Christian treatment facility for "drug addiction, alcoholism, degayification, and unwed mothers."

Hilary Faye is intent on "saving" a Jewish girl, Cassandra Edelstein (Eva Amurri), a chain-smoker and a stripper who has "Jesus Loves You" with a gefilte fish instead of the Christian fish sign on her license plate. Mary's mother (Mary Louise Parker) goes off with married Pastor Skip (Martin Donovan) to a Christian conference. We see Skip shouting out, "Give it up for Jesus. Get your Christ on. Who wants to get saved?" Cassandra says she does, to the delight of all. Mary becomes pregnant but doesn't get an abortion and is ostracized by her friends. Dean finds a male life partner at Mercy House and takes him to the prom. Told that the prohibition on gays is black and white in the Bible, Dean says "I know in my heart that God still loves me." Mary asks, "Why would God make us all different if he wanted us to be the same?" Hilary Faye, the fanatic Christian, has a crisis of faith and goes nuts running her car into a statue of Jesus, decapitating him. Mary has a baby. The film ends with "There has to be a God or something out there. You just have to feel it. When you think about what Jesus would do, I don't know, but in the meantime, we'll try to figure it out."

Commentary

Not surprisingly, this example of juvenile moviemaking is the first film for Brian Dannelly, a 40-year-old who, in an interview with Frank Langfitt, said, "I think a person's faith changes and grows throughout his life." He attended a Catholic elementary school, a Jewish summer camp, and Arlington Baptist High School, which forbade dancing and held record burnings. The entertainment for the prom was a puppet show. The school no longer burns records, but there were no strapless gowns, music or dancing, or a puppet show at the 2004 prom.

This film is included not only because of the trashing of evangelicals but also because of the critical praise it received which showed that I was in a distinct minority. This included comments, such as "wickedly funny" (*Wall Street Journal*), "irreverent take on phony reverence is refreshing" (*USA Today*), "acutely perceptive and boldly hilarious satire" (*Rolling Stone*), and finally "two thumbs up" from Ebert and Roeper with the added comment, "People are going to think this movie is an attack on Christianity and what it is basically is an attack on intolerance."

In a sense, the film is a Rorschach for the belief systems of the film critics, as Jonathan Last pointed out in the *Wall Street Journal* article. He noted that one critic called it, "A sweet and funny movie that starts off with a bite but settles into an honest feeling of happiness and acceptance for all types of people and their choices." However as Last noted, the critic didn't mean all types of people as he went on to call the movie "a gentle exploration of why the judgments of the Catholic Church are so screwed up." As Last pointed out, "*Saved* is about evangelical Christians, not Catholics, but you know how it is. They all look alike." Last quoted another critic who complained that the filmmakers "chickened out by not delivering a good steel-tipped whipping" that the evangelicals, whom he called "warmongers praying for corpse-heaped victory," deserved. Others were disturbed that the abortion option was given short shrift. In short, the critics are as responsible for the fare Hollywood turns out as are the filmmakers.

Kingdom of Heaven (2005)

The film opens in a remote town in France in 1187 with the proclamation that "It's almost a hundred years since Christian armies seized Jerusalem. Europe is in the midst of repression and poverty. Peasant and lord alike flee to the Holy Land to seek fortune and salvation." As a woman who committed suicide after her baby was stillborn is being buried, the cross is snatched from her neck by a priest (Michael Sheen). Her husband, Balian de Ibelin (Orlando Bloom), a blacksmith, is visited by a knight, Godfrey de Ibelin (Liam Neeson), his illegitimate father, who begs forgiveness for abandoning him and asks that he accompany him to Jerusalem. After rejecting his offer, Balian encounters the priest who tells him that his wife's head was cut off as was customary for suicides and that she can't enter the Kingdom of Heaven anyway. Balian murders the priest, grabs his wife's cross, and heads for Jerusalem to try to obtain forgiveness for himself and his wife even though he is no longer a believer. After joining his father's party, a local posse tries to capture Balian, and Godfrey is seriously wounded.

When they reach Messina, the Crusaders' embarkation point for Jerusalem, a Pilgrim intones: "To kill an infidel is not murder, it's a path to heaven." This is followed by a lot of talk about how the Muslims created an idyllic society among Christians, Jews, and Muslims and that they allowed others to worship in Jerusalem when they held Jerusalem for 300 years. By contrast, the Templars, an elite army reporting to the Pope, slaughtered the Muslims when they regained Jerusalem and that the Crusaders started the wars. Before dying, Godfrey, a friend of the Muslims, knights his son and tells him to support the enlightened king of Jerusalem, Baldwin IV (a leper played by Edward Norton in a mask to hide his face), in his attempt to establish a Kingdom of conscience.

Balian is the only survivor of a shipwreck when a Muslim and his servant accost him. He fights fairly against the Muslim lord and kills him but spares the servant. When he later releases him, he learns that the servant was the real Muslim Lord, earning him lifelong Muslim gratitude. On his arrival in Jerusalem, he finds the benign Baldwin dying, though still trying to make peace with Saladin through his trusty adviser Tiberias (Jeremy Irons). Balian falls in love with the king's sister Sibylla (Eva Green). Her husband is the ruthless Christian Guy de Lusignan, who, along with the bloodthirsty Knight Templar, Reynald de Chatillon, wants all-out war.

When Balian refuses to kill Guy as the price for winning Sibylla's hand (it's his conscience), Guy becomes king and provokes war by killing Saladin's sister. The Christians and Muslims fight, and Balian is saved by his Muslim friend. Saladin (Ghassan Massoud) sends his physician to take care of the wounded. He beheads Raymond but spares Guy because a king can't kill a king. Balian says, "I thought we were fighting for God until I realized that we were fighting for wealth and land." The craven Bishop of Jerusalem wants to leave and when asked about the people who will remain, he says it's unfortunate but it's God's will. Balian uses his blacksmith skills to build siege engines, and he tries to defend Jerusalem. Saladin surrounds the city. He says the "Christians butchered every Muslim when they took the city. I'm not like those Christians. All will be safely escorted to the sea." Saladin picks the cross up from the floor and sets it on the altar. Balian and the now widowed Sibylla go back to France where he returns his wife's cross to her grave. Meanwhile, Pope Urban II and Pope Leo IV call for a new Crusade, saying, "We hope no one will be slain but those who die are promised the Kingdom of Heaven." Balian refuses Richard the Lionheart's request to return to capture Jerusalem, saying he's just a simple blacksmith.

Commentary

If you like endless, noisy battle scenes and don't mind sitting through a convoluted, historically inaccurate film, this one is for you. To see how far the pendulum has swung in filmmaker attitudes since 1933, you might want to compare this with the other historically inaccurate—but closer to the truth—Cecil B. DeMille film, *The Crusades*. It might make you want to learn more about the complex truth of the Crusades and Islamic Christian history than this biased account or the distorted sound bites of today (see Madden, Riley-Smith, and Spencer).

Any resemblance between this film and either the life of the real Balian of Ibelin or the real story of the Crusades is, as they used to say in the movies, purely coincidental. Balian was not a blacksmith but a French nobleman. There was no romance with Sibylla, who actually was devoted to Guy; indeed, Balian married Sibylla's stepmother—nor was he the idealist pictured in the film. Guy did not succeed Baldwin, Sibylla's son by a previous marriage. Guy and Reynauld were not Knight Templars. The latter were essentially military monks who took a vow of celibacy and were committed to freeing Jerusalem, which had been captured 300 years before by the Muslims. The Bishop of Jerusalem was not craven as pictured nor was Tiberias (based on Raymond of Tripoli) the faithful and wise confidant. Not only was he not present at the crowning of Guy, but he was busy engineering a coup. Saladin's sister was not killed. After capturing Jerusalem, Saladin did sell the thousands who couldn't pay a ransom into slavery.

What's worse than the myriad inaccuracies is the so-called creative license that applies a modern sensibility and cast to events that occurred in a very different time and place. On the DVD, director Ridley Scott and his consultants excuse the liberties under the premise that Christians and Islam are not just equally culpable, but Christians are more at fault. They ignore the fact that Christianity prevailed in Syria, Egypt, Constantinople (now Istanbul), and other Middle Eastern locales until the Moors led by Mohammed conquered them. The Moorish advance into Europe was halted in 732 by Charles Martel at the battle of Tours in France. Later the Moors gained control over parts of Spain, only to be expelled by Ferdinand and Isabella. As Novak reminds us other attempts at Moorish conquests by the Ottoman Turks were turned back in 1571 near Greece at the Battle of Lepanto, a "miraculous" victory ascribed to "Our Lady of the Rosary" and by the Jan Sobieski's Polish cavalry outside the gates of Vienna in 1683. These and other historical events are cited by Osama bin Laden and other extremists and deserve to be well-known by Christians.

Furthermore, the evidence for tolerance to Christians and Jews in Islamic-dominated societies was as scarce then as it is today. It's important not to sugarcoat the history, especially because of the recent slaughter of Christians in Muslim countries that continues to this day from Armenia to Sudan, East Timor, Lebanon, and even the persecution of Coptic and Kurdish Christians, all of which seem to fly below the radar of the mainstream press and Hollywood.

The film bombed in the United States and Canada, earning only $47 million compared to its cost of $130 million. It made $164 million in secular Europe, Arab countries, and the rest of the world. Indeed, Muslims cheered the fictional placement of the cross on the altar as evidence of their tolerance. Too bad those Christians who have been slaughtered didn't have Ridley Scott's fictional Saladin to appeal to.

The Da Vinci Code (2006)

Robert Langdon (Tom Hanks), a professor of religious symbology at Harvard, is giving a talk in Paris on his book, *The Sacred Feminine*, while, Silas (Paul Bettany), a crazed albino monk, is killing a curator at the Louvre. Before he dies, the curator has time to scrawl Langdon's name in blood, stagger over to a painting and leave a cryptic message, draw a pentagram in blood on his chest, and collapse spread-eagled in Da Vinci's famous Vitruvian Man position.

The curator turns out to be one of the four Grandmasters of the Priory of Sion, a group that opposed the Knight Templars who sought the Holy Grail, the chalice Christ used at the Last Supper. The members of the Priory of Sion believe that the Holy Grail was not the literal cup, but instead was Mary Magdalene's womb, and that she married Jesus and bore his child before escaping to France where their seed started the line of Merovingian Kings. Apparently the Catholic Church perpetuated the myth that Mary Magdalene was a prostitute in order to discredit her. The Priory, which included such illustrious members as Isaac Newton and Leonardo Da Vinci, has served as the guardian of Mary Magdalene's sarcophagus.

The Priory is opposed by the Catholic order of Opus Dei, which secretly works for the Vatican to suppress the potentially explosive revelation that Christ was just a man, as set forth in the Gnostic Gospels of Philip and Mary Magdalene. The Priory holds that, for political reasons, the Emperor Constantine helped the Church orchestrate the adoption of the Nicene Creed that affirmed Jesus as both man and God at the Council of Nicaea in AD 325. Bishop Manuel Aringarosa (Alfred Molina) of Opus Dei controls Silas by cell phone. When not on a murder mission, Silas is shown praying, making the sign of the Cross, flagellating himself, and tightening the jagged metal band (a cilice) around his thigh to cause bleeding.

Back at the Louvre, Langdon has been called by the police to the murder site. The curator's granddaughter Sophie (Audrey Tautou), a cryptographer on the Paris police force, joins Langdon, and they escape police Captain Fache (Jean Reno), who is in cahoots with Opus Dei, in a frantic car chase that leads to a Swiss bank, churches, and a chateau. Enter Sir Leigh Teabing (Ian McKellen), the foremost expert on the Holy Grail, who relates how the Vatican has engineered the greatest cover-up in history. If people knew that Mary Magdalene was the real disciple who Christ meant to carry on for Him, Peter would be discredited, the Vatican and the Pope would lose power, and the Church would have to stop suppressing women. Langdon, who was raised a Catholic, begins to see the light and, being a student of feminine symbols, he starts piecing things together.

Finally, Langdon and Sophie reach a church in Britain with a secret crypt where the Priory has kept its records. Alas, Mary Magdalene's sarcophagus is gone. It turns out that Sophie is none other than the descendant of Mary Magdalene, and if only they had found the sarcophagus, DNA testing would have proved it. They speculate that the Church stole the sarcophagus. Langdon says, "What does it matter if Jesus was God or just an extraordinary man who was a father?" They part as Sophie joins her new Priory of Sion friends and protectors. Langdon goes to the Ritz but inexplicably leaves the hotel and climbs on I. M. Pei's Louvre pyramid (a feminine symbol) to pray over what could be Mary Magdalene's sarcophagus.

Commentary

The film, like the megabestseller on which it is based, is profoundly anti-Catholic. The bad guys are Silas, the very devout, garden-variety weird Hollywood monk (see *History of the World Part 1*, *The Name of the Rose*, *Elizabeth: The Golden Age*), and the Catholic Bishop (Alfred Molina) on a murder mission from the Pope. Parenthetically, Molina is getting typecast as the go-to hateful conservative Catholic (see *Chocolat* and *Luther*). It also reduces Jesus to a man and thus dispenses with all that Christian dogma.

Although the book's author Dan Brown cited copious "documentation," the story of the secret society was shown to be a hoax perpetrated by Pierre Plantard and three friends who made up the Priory of Sion in 1956, not 1099. Plantard, who had been convicted of fraud and embezzlement in 1953, "planted" the Priory's so-called secret dossiers in the Bibliotheque Nationale in the 1970s where they were later "discovered." The dossiers, which cited Isaac Newton, Leonardo Da Vinci, and Victor Hugo as members, were later found to be fraudulent. When confronted with this, Brown replied that the book was only a novel. In this way, he used "documentation" to appeal to those who wanted to believe the conspiratorial worst of Catholics, while laughing all the way to the bank.

There's no doubt that Brown's novel is a page-turner that captivated hundreds of millions of readers, with many making pilgrimages to Code sites, but it's full of errors (see Ehrman, Olson and Miesel, Welborn), including easily correctable mistakes about Paris, and it unfairly characterizes Opus Dei. This lay order of conservative Catholics, founded in 1928 and aimed at deepening their faith and combating secularism, has become a favorite media whipping boy, coming in for another hit in the 2007 film *Breach*. However, the main problem with the *Da Vinci Code* is that, in contrast to the book, it commits the unpardonable sin of moviemaking: it's boring. The normally brilliant but totally miscast Tom Hanks has never looked more uncomfortable in a film. To call his acting "wooden" would be to insult a lot of my furniture. The chemistry between him and Tautou suggests that much of the movie was filmed with them on separate continents. They try to

Figure 10.7. _The Da Vinci Code_. A crazed albino monk (Paul Bettany), controlled by an evil Bishop, threatens to kill Sophie (Audrey Tautou), reputed to be a descendant of the liaison between Mary Magdalene and Jesus.

convey a gravitas, but manage only to look seriously unhappy until the next-to-last scene when they actually smile, maybe knowing the film is almost over. That's certainly how I felt.

The Nativity Story (2006)

Heralded by Jeremiah's prophecy of a Messiah, the first of the film's four story threads shows the slaughter of the "innocents" (all male children under two years in Bethlehem) as Herod (Ciarán Hinds) and his son Herod Antipas (Alessandro Giuggioli) attempt to stamp out this supposed challenger to their earthly rule over Israel. The second chronological thread portrays Zechariah (Stanley Townsend) being struck dumb for not believing that his elderly barren wife Elizabeth (Shohreh Aghdashloo) will bear a son who will herald the Messiah's coming. His muteness is ended when he proclaims what the angel foretold, that the boy be named John despite their having no family antecedents with that name. The third thread involves the Three Wise Men recognizing that the alignment of the stars has signaled the Messiah's birth is about to occur. After some internal squabbling, which provides welcome comic relief, they proceed on their long journey and, after being detained to have dinner with Herod, reach their destination.

The major story follows Mary (Keisha Castle-Hughes), a spirited teenager who helps her poor family make ends meet while still playing with her girlfriends and flirting with the boys. Her carefree adolescence ends abruptly when she is betrothed to Joseph (Oscar Isaac), a carpenter who can provide a dowry and a secure home. Unhappy at being promised to someone she doesn't know and doesn't love, Mary retreats into an olive grove where Gabriel appears to her and announces the Virgin Birth. She then visits Elizabeth, whom Mary has been told is with child. Unfortunately, the filmmakers decided not to include the lovely Magnificat response to Elizabeth's questioning as to why the mother of her Lord should come to her.

The scenes of Mary's return, obviously pregnant, her condemnation by the townspeople, Joseph's consternation, and his steadfast refusal to accuse Mary of adultery are beautifully rendered. The arduous trip to Bethlehem for the census culminates in the birth of Jesus; as with the earlier scene of Elizabeth giving birth to John, the delivery is replete with painful straining and perspiring. This may have been done to counter the beatific portrait of the birth of Jesus but is soon replaced by the more pacific scenes of the visiting shepherds and the Wise Men who return home by another route to avoid Herod. The film then flashes back to the opening scene of the slaughter of the innocents, as the Holy Family flees to Egypt to escape Herod's wrath.

Commentary

This rather unpretentious film ends where most Jesus films begin and thus breaks new ground. The first feature film to premiere at the Vatican, it should become a Christmas staple. It clearly owes a great debt to the financial success of *The Passion of the Christ* for getting a distributor like New Line Cinema to allow it to open in about 3,800 theaters. While not a blockbuster like *Passion*, its $45 million box office gross exceeded production costs by $10 million.

The film's many assets include, first and foremost, its look and feel. The locales (Morocco and rural Southern Italy where *The Passion of the Christ* and *The Gospel According to St. Matthew* were filmed) look authentically poor and remote from the seat of power. The characters look like they belong there as well. The major innovation is the large part given Joseph who is finally accorded his due on film. There are many poignant moments as when he stands by Mary and when he ruminates about whether he, as a father, will be able to teach Jesus anything. Most special is the scene after he has walked

Figure 10.8. *The Nativity Story.* **Christ is born.**

on the rocky terrain guiding Mary on the donkey. As he rests, Mary washes his bloody feet and tells the child in her womb, "My child, you will have a good and decent man to raise you—a man who will give of himself before anyone else."

Amazing Grace (2006)

Amazing Grace chronicles in flashbacks the story of William Wilberforce (Ioan Gruffudd) who had an evangelical Christian conversion in 1794 at age 25. He is dissuaded by his friend William Pitt the Younger (Benedict Cumberbatch) from becoming a man of the cloth and using his beautiful voice to praise the Lord but instead to use his considerable gifts to "change the world." Saying, "Surely the principles of Christianity lead to action as well as meditation," Pitt urges Wilberforce to remain in Parliament as the representative from Hull and to champion the cause of abolishing the slave trade. He is tutored in the issues by Thomas Clarkson (Rufus Sewell), an abolitionist evangelical Anglican preacher who suggests that he learn about the treatment of slaves en route to Jamaica where only 200 of the 600 slaves who leave Africa arrive alive. Wilberforce boards a slave ship with a freed slave, Olaudah Equiano (Youssou N'Dour), who authored an influential book about his life as a slave. His mentor is a preacher, John Newton (Albert Finney), who repented his 20 years as a slave trader and penned the autobiographical confessional words which later became the text of the hymn "Amazing Grace."

In 1789, Wilberforce makes a memorable four-hour speech on the floor of the House of Commons for the abolition of the slave trade but is shouted down by many Parliament members who, along with their constituents, are benefited by the slave trade. Dejectedly, he goes to Bath for rest and recuperation from the colitis that plagued him, seeking refuge from the pain with the opiate laudanum. There he meets Barbara Ann Spooner (Romola Garai), almost 29 years his junior and an ardent abolitionist, through a bit of matchmaking by his cousin Henry Thornton (Nicholas Farrell) and his wife Marianne (Sylvestra Le Touzel). The rest of the film is devoted to their marriage, his repeated submission of antislave trade legislation, with the help of Lord Charles Fox (Michael Gambon) and Pitt. In 1807, after 18 years, he is finally successful, and Fox praises him while the parliamentary members stand and applaud in unison. The movie ends with a wonderful rendition of "Amazing Grace" by a bagpiper and a marching band at Westminster Abbey where Wilberforce is buried next to Pitt. The epilogue notes that he founded the first Bible Society, animal welfare group, free education movement, and national gallery of art in England, as well as worked for prison reform and child labor protection.

Commentary

The backstory of this film is particularly pertinent to the thesis of this book. In numerous interviews on its release, director Michael Apted made the point capsuled in a *Baltimore Sun* headline, "For 'Grace' Director Apted, Politics Were Paramount" (by Joe Burris). In an interview with *Christianity Today*, Apted said that when he was brought in to replace Hugh Hudson, the director of *Chariots of Fire*, the project was a straight "biopic" and that early scripts were too much the story of man's "finding, losing, and finding Christianity." He asked Steven Knight, who replaced *Chariots* screenwriter Colin Welland, to focus on the antislave trade law because he "wanted the film to be a testament to the political process, how outcries for justice can alter the course of history," harking back more, as he said, to JFK and Camelot. He also wanted it to have diverse appeal and "didn't want to put people off" with Wilberforce's faith and risk being "preachy." When asked about his own spirituality, Apted said he was an "agnostic" but that "oddly enough" his brother was a priest and that he "grew up in a fairly Christian environment" which he didn't pursue as an adult.

With the script changes and the numerous confusing flashbacks, we learn little of the mentoring that Newton gave Wilberforce or what led to his conversion from being a dissolute wealthy young man into a committed evangelical Christian. All we see is him rolling around in the grass saying in effect that he found Christ. Indeed, as critic Keith Aaron Harris said, mention of Christ is kept to a minimum "with Wilberforce looking merely like a decent, if ambitious, chap who would be out canvassing for Greenpeace if he were around today." Harris wondered if *Malcolm X* could have been made without showing his pilgrimage to Mecca. Yet, Harris admitted that in minimizing the Christian motive which energized Wilberforce's 18-year struggle, Apted might have dodged "excess criticism—or worse, indifference—from film critics and moviegoers in a cultural marketplace with segregated slots for 'Christian' or 'family' entertainment." So, in that regard, it may have managed to reach a wider audience which, if so motivated, could learn about the real Wilberforce.

The fictional parts of the film are many and range from the trivial to the very important. The match with Barbara Ann Spooner who, although not mentioned, was a very committed evangelical Christian, was actually opposed by the Thorntons. Also made up is the king's son, the Duke of Clarence (Toby Jones), who is shown giving Wilberforce an IOU for a slave to continue a poker game. Wilberforce rejects it and after forfeiting a big pot, retaliates by singing "Amazing Grace," an impossibility since the hymn's tune was not composed until 50 years later. Furthermore, Charles Fox wasn't a lord and would have been unable to praise Wilberforce had he even been alive when the bill was passed.

Of greater importance is that almost all of Wilberforce's political life was motivated by his evangelical Christianity. His antislave activism was part of a continuum that stretched back to St. Paul, St. Vincent De Paul, Popes, Quakers, New England Protestants, and Methodists, including John Wesley, whose last letter before his death was to Wilberforce encouraging him to persevere. Wilberforce belonged to the Clapham sect which, as Richard John Neuhaus notes, was thought, even in its day to be a bunch of "pietistic prudes." Indeed, his two aims were to end slavery and to improve manners (morals), not "to change the world" as the film would have it. To that end, he founded the "Society for the Suppression of Vice" and successfully appended a rider to the bill authorizing the British East India Company to allow Christian missioners to set up schools in India. Two of Wilberforce's sons

Figure 10.9. *Amazing Grace.* **Evangelical Christian William Wilberforce (Ioan Gruffud) gives an impassioned speech in Parliament against slavery.**

became Catholics, and one was an Anglican Bishop who decried Darwin's *The Origin of Species.*

Many have wondered how a sickly small man could have achieved so much. By all accounts he was an incredible orator. As James Boswell, Johnson's biographer, put it, "I saw what seemed a mere shrimp mount upon the table; but as I listened, he grew and grew until the shrimp became a whale." A Christian might say that he had a "divine spark" and that his earthly reward was to learn three days before his death in 1833 that the bill abolishing slavery in the British Empire had passed the House of Commons and was soon to become law.

Bella (2006)

The premise of this unassuming gem of a film is articulated early when Jose (Eduardo Verástegui), a scruffily bearded line chef at his brother Manny's (Manny Perez) restaurant, says, "My grandmother used to say, 'If you want to make God laugh, tell him your plans.'" It opens at the seashore where Jose is watching little children at play. Rather than being the pervert that their parents seem to think he might be, a flashback shows Jose four years before to have been a handsome rising soccer superstar. With a cigar in his mouth and on his way to a big payday in his flashy convertible, he inadvertently runs over a little girl who has darted into the street between two parked cars. Convicted of involuntary manslaughter and sent to jail, his career is ruined. He is tormented daily by the vision of the despondent single mother (Ali Landry) carrying the dead child in her arms and screaming to God to give her child back.

Fast forward to the present when Nina (Tammy Blanchard), a repeatedly tardy single coworker, learns she is pregnant and is fired by the impulsive Manny. Jose leaves the restaurant to console Nina, and Manny fires him too, setting up a brotherly conflict. As they travel in New York City and then to Long Island, Jose listens sympathetically to Nina as she advances all the arguments for abortion. Broke and jobless, she tells him of her unfitness to raise a child and of her own unhappy family life. Her father died when she was 12, and her grief-stricken mother became a reclusive couch potato leading to Nina's leaving home, never to return. Jose takes Nina to his family's home where she is welcomed by his Mexican mother (Angélica Aragón) and Puerto Rican father (Jaime Tirelli). They share a feast, featuring food, music, and dancing, which reminded me of my growing up in a home with a Spanish father and Italian mother. Nina is struck by the warmth and love of his family and she tells him as they return to the city that, though she wouldn't trust herself, she would trust him with the child

In a touching scene, Jose makes breakfast for Manny and himself and they are reconciled, recalling a similar rapprochement of the fraternal chefs in the wonderful film *Big Night*. When Jose whispers his plans in Manny's ear, he is told that he's crazy. The film then dissolves to the beach where Jose is playing with a happy four year-old Bella (Sophie Nyweide), as they await the return of Nina, who has gotten her act together, and whom Bella recognizes as her mother. The result is the healing of two wounded souls and the indirect giving back to the world of the lost, happy little girl.

Commentary

Although *Bella* has only three overt manifestations of Christianity, two involving saying grace before meals and another of praying the rosary in an abortion clinic waiting room, it is included because it has a powerfully Christian message. It also illustrates how the deck is stacked against the production and distribution of "wholesome" films, free of profanity and gratuitous violence or sex, and which challenge the prevailing secular and politically correct dogma. Still, in what may represent a change in attitudes, it is the classiest and most thoughtful of five feature films about abortion between 2004–2007 where the single mother opted to either keep the child or give it up for adoption. The others were the remake of *Alfie* (2004), where the mother chose to keep the baby rather than abort it as in the 1966 original; *Waitress* (2007); *Juno* (2007); and *Knocked Up* (2007).

Like *The Princess Bride*, *Amélie*, *Hotel Rwanda*, *Life Is Beautiful*, *American Beauty*, and *Chariots of Fire*, *Bella* won the "People's Choice" award at the Toronto Film Festival. However, unlike the others, it did not attract a distributor, despite having a very positive message about Latinos and their sense of faith and family. The film's star Eduardo Verástegui, a Mexican model, singer, and soap opera actor, decided in 2002 to abandon his playboy lifestyle because of his rediscovered Catholic faith. He turned down lucrative acting roles to concentrate on countering the trashy portrayal of Latinos as thieves, druggies, prostitutes, profane criminals, and predatory Don Juans. As he says on the DVD special feature, his intent was to elevate the dignity of Latinos in the eyes of America and the world.

He joined director/writer Alejandro Monteverde, a graduate of the film program at the University of Texas, Austin and writer/producer Leo Severino to form Metanoia films, whose first venture was *Bella*. When the film failed to attract a distributor, they decided, along with financier Sean Wolfington, to take it across the country for a year. Through support from Catholics and other Christians, they showed it to enthusiastic crowds in churches, auditoriums, the Smithsonian Institution, and at the Heartland Festival where it won the top award. The family that runs Goya Foods got behind the film and bought tickets for indigents. The DVD recounts this journey and contains an extensive list of "Thank Yous" to people who helped the film finally garner Lions Gate and Roadside Attractions as its distributors. On its release, few theaters initially carried the film, but it quickly shot up to number one in revenue per screen and got further visibility.

However, *Bella* was dismissed by the few mainstream media critics who chose to review it. The *Variety* critic called it "a mediocre film that wows crowds" and got appropriately slammed by bloggers to his site. The 23-day whirlwind filming in and around New York City led one snide reviewer to say that the surroundings upstaged the story. I don't agree. Actually, it's a heartwarming story of compassion, selflessness, and redemption. The film's impact has been chronicled in Tim Drake's book *Behind Bella: The Amazing Stories of Bella and the Lives It Changed*. One story involves Verástegui's befriending of a Mexican couple while researching the film at an abortion clinic. Months later, they called to say that they had decided to have the child and asked permission to name him Eduardo. How much better is that than inciting violence as some films do!

Breach (2007)

The use of actual footage gives the movie a documentary feel as Attorney General John Ashcroft announces the arrest of master spy Robert Hanssen on February 20, 2001. The film then cuts to two months earlier, showing Hanssen (Chris Cooper) saying the rosary in an empty Catholic Church. This is the first of many indications that Hanssen is a devout Catholic. The scene shifts to Eric O'Neill (Ryan Phillippe), a young ambitious FBI surveillance operative, who gets a call on Sunday, December 24 from his superior (Laura Linney). She directs him to go to FBI headquarters where he is assigned to spy on Hanssen to get incriminating information about sexual perversion. Although O'Neill was told of the evidence against Hanssen, the filmmakers choose to show him being kept in the dark.

Instead they weave a story showing Hanssen being obnoxious to Eric and repeatedly testing him to see if he has been assigned to spy on him. All the while, Hanssen tries to get O'Neill, a lapsed Catholic graduate of a Jesuit high school, and his wife, a "lapsed Protestant," to embrace the Catholic faith and pray the rosary. He has a crucifix on his office wall, a statue of the Blessed Virgin, and the catechism of the Catholic Church on his desk. There is a scene in the Catholic Information Center where he tries to get O'Neill interested in reading doctrinal books and another when they enter a church and both dip their hands in holy water. However, O'Neill crosses himself left to right in the eastern Orthodox fashion. If that had actually happened, his cover would have been blown. Later they go to a traditional Latin Mass together and then Hanssen's wife, played like a stereotypic 1950s throwback, tries to get O'Neill's wife to convert to Catholicism and to have babies.

Hanssen takes swipes at Planned Parenthood, homosexuals, and Hillary Clinton, and stops by to lecture O'Neill's wife about Opus Dei. When O'Neill reports that he has found no evidence of sexual perversion or anything incriminating, he is told the full story of the man's perfidy. Later, Hanssen tells O'Neill to mail a package to someone in West Germany and finds that it contains a videotape secretly made of Hanssen and his wife having "rough sex." In another scene, O'Neill is almost caught downloading Hanssen's palm pilot but fools him by dropping on his knees and praying before the crucifix in Hanssen's office. The nervous Hanssen sends a letter to his Russian handler saying that his usefulness is over. This scene is intercut with him breaking down in a confessional. Finally, he is caught on his last spy drop and while being led away he says to O'Neill, "Pray for me."

Commentary

The film is filled with disconcerting gaffes such as the two banks of 30 votive candles all lit in an empty church in the opening shot. Later, Hanssen will pray in another empty church with five banks of votive candles lit. As he exits the D.C. church, there's a Toronto store on his left and no pedestrians, but then he melds into a crowded Washington sidewalk. The only thing that makes this film worth seeing is the outstanding performance by Chris Cooper, who manages to convey Hanssen's paradoxical and enigmatic personality through his facial expressions and the terse delivery of his lines. While the film has some basis in truth, a number of the characters and incidents have been fictionalized. Hanssen's real story is actually more interesting and is told in part in an excellent March 5, 2001, NBC Dateline segment which, interestingly, never mentions his Catholicism that is so central to the movie. It describes some of the clever tactics he used in communicating with his "control" and notes that his wife Bonnie wasn't as clueless as portrayed in the film. In fact, she got wind of his treachery at the beginning in 1985. She made him give the money he received to charity and asked him to go to confession and never do it again. He stopped for a while but then resumed, this time making the drops more carefully, at a park near his home where he could go unsuspected to walk the dog or for evening exercise.

Contrary to the film, the agent knew from the outset that the FBI had the goods on Hanssen through a partial fingerprint. They even had a stakeout on him from a house across the street (not mentioned in the film). O'Neill was simply brought in as a closer to illuminate the porn issue. Actually, Hanssen never videotaped their sex but actually transmitted it live to his friend in West Germany. Viewers might wonder how such a minor character like O'Neill became the hero who took down Hanssen. The reason is simple. O'Neill quit the bureau three months after Hanssen was captured and got permission to shop the story in Hollywood that became the basis of the screenplay. The issue of the Catholicism was chosen to sustain the visuals and incidents of what was a thin two-month story rather than a rich 15-year saga. As the director says on the DVD, if they had disclosed all this at the beginning, there would have been no film. The director avows that he tried to be careful not to convey a direct connection between traditional Catholicism and Hanssen's sexual repression, perversion, hypocrisy, and treachery. That would be more believable if his Catholicism was not evident in so many scenes.

It's too bad because Hanssen's complete story is perversely fascinating. In interviews on the DVD, his colleagues say they were unaware of his treachery and that he was "boring," for example, never talking about football around the water cooler but instead focusing on ethics, morality, religion, and computer terminology. Indeed, this and his presumably devout Catholicism were the perfect cover in that he was a walking FBI agent cliché. Still, his brother-in-law, who worked for the FBI, told them to investigate him in 1990, but Hanssen managed to get control of the investigation. His treachery cost the U.S. billions as well as an estimated 50 covert agents, some of whom were executed. He didn't do it for the money, which he could not spend without arousing suspicion. One colleague said that he must have relished the high wire act in which he fooled everyone in his attempt to pull off the perfect crime.

Elizabeth: The Golden Age (2007)

According to the prologue, it's 1585 and "Philip of Spain, a devout Catholic, had plunged Europe into a Holy War. Only England and its Protestant Queen stand in his way." Bald-pated monks, severely dressed in black, process in Spain's cathedral followed by the gimpy black-accoutered Philip II (Jordi Molla) saying his rosary and proclaiming that God has spoken to him. He says, "England is ruled by the devil and we must set it free." He devastates the forests to build the Armada. Meanwhile Sir Francis Walsingham (Geoffrey Rush) tells Elizabeth (Cate Blanchett) that "every Catholic is a potential assassin" and that she must destroy them. She answers that half her country is Catholic and she will only punish those who conspire against her.

Meanwhile in Scotland, the Catholic Mary Queen of Scots (Samantha Morton), the next in line for England's throne, plots to assassinate Elizabeth. Her devout followers are either shown praying or working on some homicidal venture. Although portrayed as hideous, she has one poignant moment when she forgives her executioner before being beheaded on orders from Elizabeth. The bulk of the film involves Elizabeth in sumptuous costumes and pageantry, as she sails the Thames or receives yet another royal mismatch, this time a prince from Austria. There's a dalliance with Sir Walter Raleigh (Clive Owen), who ultimately incurs her wrath for getting her lady-in-waiting, Bess Throckmorton (Abbie Cornish), pregnant. Finally, there's the launching of the Spanish Armada with Christ's picture on the sails as Philip tells his sailors that God wills this. As usual, he is trailed by his mute little daughter Isabella, who carries her Elizabeth doll. After the Armada's defeat, Philip is shown despairing while Elizabeth comes to terms with Raleigh and Bess, and cuddles their baby.

Commentary

This slow-moving, glossy production is like a Madame Tussauds wax museum production. The protagonists are stick figures rather than flesh and blood, substituting speeches for dialogue. Elizabeth's many scenes seem to be orchestrated poses, although Blanchett was nominated for a Best Actress Oscar. The filmmaker Shekhar Kapur tells us who the bad guys are and, in using the term "holy war," seems to be saying that Catholics are like the Jihadists, while at the same time, playing to environmentalists as she shows Philip ordering deforestation to build his ships. As for its historical accuracy, there are so many fictions, such as the mute little Infanta with her Elizabeth doll (she was 21 at the time), that film critic Colin Colvert said in noting its "bogus history" and "ugly anti-Catholic imagery," "This isn't historical fabrication, it's mutilation."

While the original *Elizabeth* made the top-10 list of anti-Catholic films (see Backstory, p. 348), this clearly surpasses it in that respect. In every scene the Catholics are shown with rosaries or other religious imagery, while pledging or plotting to kill someone. The most outlandish scene involves the Spanish sailors kneeling on deck praying the rosary as the storm, which will destroy them, rages about them, before they finally take action. Can anyone believe that this is what happened? Then, as the fleet sinks, a rosary that must have been the size of a garden hose flutters on screen as it heads for the bottom of the ocean. There are 15 more years left in Elizabeth's reign, so there may be a sequel. The only possible deterrent is that the majority of reviewers panned the film, although few mentioned the central anti-Catholic theme. One wonders if the villains had been Islamic or Jewish rather than

Catholic whether this film would have been made, found a distributor, or escaped critical obloquy on that score.

Doubt (2008)

Based on the Pulitzer Prize– and Tony Award–winning play *Doubt: A Parable* by John Patrick Shanley, who also wrote and directed the screenplay, the film is set in the St. Nicholas parish and school in the Bronx in 1964. It focuses on the conflict between the principal Sister Aloysius Beauvier (Meryl Streep) and the associate pastor Father Flynn (Philip Seymour Hoffman) who, she believes, has an inappropriate relationship with the school's first black student, Donald Miller (Joseph Foster II). After Miller tells Flynn, whom he idolizes, that he wants to be a priest, Flynn gives the boy a toy ballerina powered by magnets.

Flynn gives three sermons during the film. In the first, he recalls the sense of loss and doubt about the future that many felt after the assassination of JFK. Telling the parishioners that they were not alone in feeling lost, he says that "doubt can be a bond as powerful and sustaining as certainty." During his sermon, Sister Aloysius walks down the left aisle banging a talking student on the head and waking another. She is unremittingly harsh to the students, leading Flynn to tell the young innocent Sister James Marie (Amy Adams) that the "dragon is hungry this morning." Seeing Flynn grab a troublemaker by the wrist, Sister Aloysius warns Sister James to report anything where Flynn appears out of line. Later, Sister James reports that Donald was called out of class to the rectory by Flynn and returned frightened and with alcohol (the communion wine) on his breath. Afterwards, she saw Flynn put Donald's undershirt in the boy's locker. Sister Aloysius tells her that it was just like another priest at her previous school. She had thought the problem would be with the Irish and Italian boys beating Donald up, but this hadn't happened because Flynn was his protector.

When the three meet to plan the Christmas pageant, Flynn says that it is getting stale and recommends adding a secular song. Sister James suggests "Frosty the Snowman," which Sister Aloysius calls a pagan song that should be banned from the airwaves. This prompts Flynn to argue that the "Church needs to change. It's a new time. We have to be friendlier. The parents and children should see us as part of their families." Sister Aloysius, who believes that they must maintain their distance and is happy that the students fear her, is even more determined to "bring him down." Flynn's next sermon on the power of gossip to destroy lives, and the inability to rein it in once let loose, is well illustrated by a story about cutting a pillow and watching the wind take the feathers in all directions.

Sister Aloysius meets with Mrs. Miller (Viola Davis), who has used her salary as a cleaning woman to send Donald to St. Nicholas against the wishes of his father who beats the child, as he did after the Communion wine incident. She says that she thought the public school students might kill him. She says that it was because of "his nature" (implying that her son is gay, something she can't account for or understand). She says that this doesn't excuse the priest. Sister Aloysius agrees, saying that she wants to get rid of him. Mrs. Miller defends the priest as the only male figure who tried to protect Donald and expresses her belief that if her son is implicated in such an affair, her husband will kill him. Further, she wants nothing to jeopardize his ability to complete eighth grade in June, so he can get into a good high school and then college. A subsequent meeting between Flynn and Sister Aloysius devolves into an improbable shouting match after she confronts him with the fact that it's his third parish in five years and that she checked with a nun in the last one about him. She admits that she doesn't have "proof" of molestation, but she has "certainty."

Flynn's last sermon is at Christmastime when he bids the congregation farewell and then goes into the pews where he wishes a parishioner "Happy Holidays." Sister James returns from a Christmas visit to her sick brother in Maryland and tells Sister Aloysius, "You did it; you got him out" and adds that Donald Miller is heartbroken. Sister Aloysius says that, despite telling the Monsignor about her suspicions, Flynn was made pastor of a parish with a large school, which is a step up. She tells Sister James that her call to the nun was a lie and then breaks down, sobbing and reveals that she has doubts.

Commentary

Shanley's writing credits are impeccable, having written numerous plays and the Academy Award–winning screenplay for the marvelous *Moonstruck*, but his only venture into directing was the failed *Joe Versus the Volcano*. He would have been better served by turning the project over to a director with experience and stature commensurate with those of his A-list stars. The film belies its origins as a play by being slow-moving and talky. It's filled with long pan shots and silences as well as three storms and sudden risings of the wind through open windows meant to represent the "winds of change" and the storms that beset the Catholic Church after the Vatican II council (1962–1965).

Drawing on memories of his boyhood in a Bronx Catholic neighborhood, Shanley reproduces many liturgical rituals such as altar boys filling cruets with wine and water, and censors with incense, as well as the ringing of the bells at the consecration that will be familiar to older Catholics. He also had the help of his kindergarten teacher to whom the film is dedicated, the nuns at Mount Saint Vincent College in the Bronx (where some filming was done), and informal advice given to Hoffman by a priest friend.

Nonetheless, there are some noteworthy gaffes. The most glaring is when Father Flynn wishes "Happy Holidays" to a parishioner as he says his good-byes, rather than "Blessed Christmas" or "Merry Christmas" as would have been common in 1964. The second involves Flynn saying that the Christmas pageant is "stale" despite this being his first Christmas at Saint Nicholas and the nonsense about Sister Aloysius calling "Frosty the Snowman" a "pagan" song. Ironically, it serves to highlight the reversal of fortune four decades later when the mention of Christmas is being systematically erased from the public square in favor of the generic "Happy Holidays" presumably so as not to give offense to non-Christians.

Minor discordant notes were the accents, seemingly more reminiscent of New England than the Bronx, and that of the non-Italian man (Haklar Dezso) who plays Reginella Campagnola (a personal favorite) on the zither (not an accordion) at the movie's opening. The few classroom scenes focus mainly on history as Sister James gives a lecture about FDR's admonition that we have nothing to fear but fear itself and saying that the three greatest presidents were Lincoln, FDR, and JFK, hardly a general consensus. There's also a brief shot of a blackboard showing a diagrammed sentence. The absence of the mandatory religion class is odd since it is a Catholic School, after all.

The film's production notes clearly state how the audience should feel about the protagonists. Father Flynn is described as a "vibrant charismatic priest trying to upend the school's strict customs which have long been fiercely guarded by Sister Aloysius Beauvier, the iron-gloved principal who believes in the power of fear and discipline." With this and the director's stated purpose to highlight the 1960s challenge to institutions like organized religion and the military, the actors become stick figures freighted with messages rather than being well-rounded, flesh-and-blood individuals. Little is learned about Father Flynn's past except in innuendo, presumably to keep the audience in doubt. In passing, we learn that Sister Aloysius was married and her husband died 20 years before in World War II. One is left to wonder if that is what turned her into a cold and rigid sourpuss. Meryl Streep's wickedly gleeful overacting, as she plays the cat intent on catching the mouse, makes Sister Aloysius's breakdown at the end rather implausible.

The central question is whether Flynn is a victim of slander or is a homosexual priest who engages in pedophilia. Putting the boy's undershirt in the locker, calling him from class to the rectory, finding alcohol on the boy's breath on his return, and hugging Donald in the school corridor when a classmate spills his books are all suggestive. One thinks back to the gift of the toy ballerina and wonders if it is a Freudian reference to the boy's playing the feminine role in their relationship.

Hoffman is excellent in maintaining the strong persona of an injured party until two-thirds through the picture when Sister Aloysius confronts him. He then becomes uncharacteristically strident, taking refuge in the nun's failing to follow the lines of authority rather than challenging the allegations. Is it because she's right about his abusing the child and her unwillingness to accept that it's between his confessor and himself, as his rapid removal and frequent previous transfers suggest? What are we to make of the mother's conflicted thoughts as she suggests that her son is gay and that, although this does not excuse the priest, to let matters stand until June because Flynn is compassionate and protective of Donald, whose ability to graduate is of paramount concern? Does the end justify the means?

One can question whether Flynn would have been transferred on such flimsy evidence as the film presents. Still, this would be his fourth parish in five years at a time when priests were at a parish for at least seven years and often more. This suggests that the allegations are true and raises the important issue of negligence by the Bishops in sending priests who were sexually abusive to other parishes without specifying why, and who, after the sexual abuse scandal exploded into public consciousness, failed to censure their own. Shanley said that he only told Hoffman the "truth" and that his play "celebrated the fact that you can never know anything for certain." Now it's one thing to say we live with uncertainty. Doctors do all the time. David Seegal, my medical school mentor, said that when we graduated that if we didn't say "I don't know" at least ten times a day when caring for our patients, we would be fooling ourselves and cheating the patients. However, he said that it shouldn't end there in that we needed to strive mightily to get

---

BACKSTORY

The Transformation of Nuns from Beautiful and Serene to Weird and Nasty

Non-Catholic moviegoers from the 1940s through the 1970s could be forgiven for believing that all nuns are stunning. Some of Hollywood's most beautiful women played nuns, including Ingrid Bergman (*The Bells of St. Mary's*), Jennifer Jones (*The Song of Bernadette*), Loretta Young (*Come to the Stable*), Audrey Hepburn (*The Nun's Story*), Julie Andrews (*The Sound of Music*), Debbie Reynolds (*The Singing Nun*), Diana Rigg (*In this House of Brede*), and last but not least Deborah Kerr. In contrast to the others who, for the most part were the picture of serenity, Kerr, in each of her "nun" roles portrayed a woman committed to her religion but torn by more earthly desires. In *Black Narcissus*, as Sister Clodagh, prioress of a convent in the forbidding Himalayas, she is attracted to the local British agent (David Farrar). In *Heaven Knows, Mr. Allison,* she plays Sister Angela, the lone survivor on an island bombed by the Japanese. When a hard-bitten marine (Robert Mitchum) washes ashore, it creates a closeness that leads the marine to propose, which sends the devout nun reeling. Her ability to create and maintain her inner conflict and the resulting tension in a believable way requires extraordinary talent.

As for serene nuns, they virtually disappeared in the 1980s with the appearance of the disturbed *Agnes of God* (Meg Tilly) and her protector, the ex-chain-smoking Mother Superior (Anne Bancroft); the activist Sister Prejean (Susan Sarandon) in *Dead Man Walking*; Eric Idle and Robbie Coltrane as thieves hiding in a convent in *Nuns on the Run*; Diane Keaton as the crazed nun from hell in *Sister Mary Ignatius Explains It All*; Jodie Foster as Sister Assumpta (alias Nunzilla) in *The Dangerous Lives of Altar Boys*; the unrelievedly cruel nuns in *The Magdalene Sisters*; and the harsh and devious Sister Aloysius (Meryl Streep) in "Doubt." The last of the beautiful and serene breed, Maggie Smith made an appearance as the Mother Superior in *Sister Act* in which Whoopi Goldberg plays a lounge singer who assumes a nun's identity under the witness protection program. What a transformation in thirty years!

---

at the truth. Clearly there are many times we do know the truth, whether it be cancer or pedophilia; how we go about acting on that knowledge is quite another matter entirely.

Short Subjects

Lost Souls (2000)

A chain-smoking French teacher (Winona Ryder) lives in a Catholic retreat house and attends exorcisms performed by the strange priest (John Hurt) who exorcised her. By deciphering a secret code, she learns that Satan plans to inhabit a crime writer (Ben Chaplin) on his 33rd birthday, figuring that Christ became man 2,000 years ago and now it's his turn. What could have possessed Meg Ryan to coproduce it and Janusz Kaminski the cinematographer of *Saving Private Ryan* to codirect it, is hard to fathom.

Diary of a City Priest (2001)

Father John McNamee (David Morse), pastor of a North Philadel-phia parish in a once Catholic working-class neighborhood, now a poor African-American ghetto, thinks his parishioners see him as "a pathetic, lonely man on his way out." He looks down on suburban Catholics who give him a car that won't last long in his neighborhood. He resents the money spent in making Philadelphia's Archbishop a Cardinal and remembers the good old days when he was "running with the Berrigans" (the anti–Vietnam War priests who were jailed for destruction at military sites and other politi-cal activism). He ruminates on celibacy, saying that "The Church is almost cruel in asking this of otherwise ordinary human beings" and has running dialogues with various people he calls "saints" including St. Malachy, St. Thérèse, Simone Weil, Thomas Merton, Dorothy Day, St. John of the Cross, and St. Francis. People drop in for handouts, but there's no sense of community. The movie ends with his hope that he will do what he does more generously and patiently.

Full of self-pity with no comic relief, the film is dedicated to Robert Bresson, director of *Diary of a Country Priest*, (see p. 138), also a depressing depiction of a lugubrious, self-absorbed priest. In this case, the priest is a product of the Vietnam War era when the notion was that peace and love would reign if people would come together and sing "Kumbaya." The film may have value in picturing the burnout and loneliness that affects priests in this era of dwindling vocations when faced with the lack of priests in the rectory for companionship and work-sharing, the changing nature of inner city parishes, and the constant attacks on the priesthood.

Evelyn (2002)

After his wife runs off with a lover to Australia, a jobless alcoholic, Desmond (Pierce Brosnan), attempts to raise Evelyn (Sophie Vavasseur) and her two brothers. The maternal grandmother reports them to the social services agency, and he loses custody because Irish law mandates that, in the absence of a mother figure, children must be sent to an institution overseen by the Catholic Church (said to be involved in a "cozy conspiracy" with the Irish state). The boys are sent to a Christian Brothers school, a seemingly nurtur-ing environment. Evelyn, however, is greeted by Sister "Frigid Brigid" (An-drea Irvine), who treats the children harshly and metes out severe corporal punishment. She insists that Evelyn sleep with her arms crossed, not on her stomach, so as not to tempt the devil. Desmond will later nearly choke the nun to death for striking Evelyn, and the nun will lie on the stand under oath. Evelyn then comes under the care of a kindly nun, Sister Theresa (Marian Quinn), and blossoms into a very thoughtful and articulate youngster.

Desmond's friend Bernadette (Julianna Margulies) reforms him, and he gains media and public support for his campaign to gain parental rights for fathers. The courtroom scene, the film's high point, hinges on Evelyn's grandfather (Frank Kelly) having told her that sunbeams are "angel rays." While on the stand, Evelyn is bathed in sun that she believes is sent by her dead grandfather. She takes courage and becomes an outstanding witness. Her reflections are suffused with a wisdom and understanding of the true nature of Christianity that contrast sharply with those of many adults. The case is won, and the law is overturned. The portrait of a lone man prevailing over the government and the Catholic Church occasioned applause from some audience members at the screening I attended. Unfortunately, director Beresford leaves viewers with the misleading impression that the orphan-ages at the time (a very different one from today) were essentially detention camps that would rapidly empty, so that the children could return to happy homes. It reminded me of similar campaigns to empty mental institutions in America, which mainly resulted in hordes of homeless. So, my advice is to consider the film, in the screenwriter's words, "a fable inspired by true events" and simply enjoy it.

The Road to Perdition (2002)

This dark, slow-moving film chronicles six weeks in the life of an Irish Mafia hitman, Michael Sullivan (Tom Hanks), and his son. Like *The Godfather*, it intersperses killing with religious symbolism. For example, upon arriving home for dinner, Sullivan pulls out his rosary and then a gun, before saying grace. The Sacred Heart of Jesus and the Sacred Heart of Mary are shown as he goes off to kill mob boss Rooney (Paul Newman), whom he mistakenly thinks was responsible for the killings of his wife and other son. He cautions his son that if he is not back shortly, to go to the First Methodist minister, not their parish priest who is in on the whole business. I include mention of this depressing box office dud because of its self-conscious religious imagery.

We Were Soldiers (2002)

Like World War II movies, this movie makes passing reverential references to religion. The central character is Lieutenant Colonel Hal Moore (Mel Gibson), a devout Catholic and the commanding officer of the 1st and 7th

Cavalry, who led the first major battle of the Vietnam War into the "Valley of Death." He says night prayers with his children and before his unit moves out, meets with a soldier in the chapel to discuss the danger of not returning and its implications, especially for someone with a family. Indeed, the film shows the toll taken on families. Many critics slammed the film, which stuck close to the facts (based on the book by Moore and Joseph Galloway), probably because of its positive take on Vietnam fighters as well as their pervasive hatred for Mel Gibson. Yet, it is the best film about Vietnam (see almost 400 Amazon reviews) in the minds of those who were there. It praises those who served the country with honor. The message, according to Moore, is "Hate War, Honor the Warriors," something that was not done by too many Americans.

The Dangerous Lives of Altar Boys (2002)

This film "recounts" the daily lives of four boys and their female friend in a Catholic high school in 1970s South Carolina. They create a superhero comic book featuring the perpetually angry Sister Assumpta (Jodie Foster) as the evil "Nunzilla" who has a prosthesis and is called "Pegleg." She rides a motorcycle and has sex with Father Casey (Vincent D'Onofrio). One of the boys, whom she calls stupid, is "Captain Asshole" (who kicks the s— out of Sister). Sister Assumpta discovers the comic book and punishes them. They get back at her by stealing a cougar from the zoo to put in her room.

Meantime the boys are shown acting as altar boys holding a paten, saying grace, praying to St. Agatha (the school's patron) while holding their crotches, and singing "Kumbaya" on the bus ride to the zoo. Mixed in are smoking, drinking, a haunted house, and discovery of incest involving the artist's (Emile Hirsch) sweet girlfriend, Margie Flynn (Jena Malone). The filmmaker tries unsuccessfully to inject a highbrow element into this juvenilia by quoting from poet William Blake's "Songs of Innocence and Songs of Experience." Regardless, nothing can dress up this turkey which is yet another ridiculing of Catholicism involving an A-list star.

The Order (2003)

Father Alex Bernier (Heath Ledger), a member of the Carolingens, a secret Catholic order that specializes in the paranormal, says Mass only in Latin and with his back to the faithful "as if Vatican II never happened." The Cardinal of New York, who wants to be Pope, sends him to Rome to investigate the mysterious death of his excommunicated mentor. His girlfriend Mara (Shannyn Sossamon), a mentally disturbed artist whom he once exorcised and who tried to kill him, has escaped from the asylum and walks into his sacristy. She promises not to kill him, and they go off as lovers to Rome. They meet up with another wacko priest, Father Thomas (Mark Addy). Alex is being sought by "The Sin Eater," who absolves unforgivable sins by the unrepentant. They are then allowed to get into heaven by the backdoor. The latter is very tired and is ready to pass on the mantle to someone else in whom he must dump all those terrible sins. Along the way a fake Pope appears. *Boston Globe* film critic Wesley Morris said that the director "beats up on the Catholic Church with the same brainless and pointless histrionics as such Grade F noisemakers as *Lost Souls* and *Stigmata*." Others have called it the worst movie ever made. Unfortunately, there are too many candidates, like *Amen*, for that award.

The Exorcism of Emily Rose (2005)

The film is loosely based on a true story of a priest who was charged with negligent homicide in the death of Anneliese Michel, a devout German college student, whom the Catholic Church said was possessed and who died after a failed exorcism in 1976. The presumed reason behind her willingness to continue to battle the demons was that through her sacrifice, the world would know that demons are real, that God is not dead, and that good will triumph over evil. I missed the logic in that, but others have not in that her gravesite has become a pilgrimage destination.

As for the film, the horror scenes are kept to a minimum and the main action takes place in a courtroom, which provides more drama. It also has excellent performances by Tom Wilkinson as a priest, Laura Linney as the agnostic, hard-drinking defense lawyer who is trying to make partner, and Campbell Scott as the devout Methodist prosecutor.

BACKSTORY

Top Pro-Catholic and Top Anti-Catholic Films

In 2004, The *National Catholic Register* and *Faith and Family* magazine conducted a poll of over 1,000 readers in an effort to designate the 100 movies that most effectively celebrate Catholic life. Also, together with a distinguished ecumenical panel that included film critic Michael Medved and author Philip Jenkins, the poll selected the 10 most "pro-Catholic films" and the 10 most "anti-Catholic films" ever made. It is interesting to note that the majority of the pro-Catholic films were produced before 1968 when the Legion of Decency was disbanded and the Hays Code was lifted. What's more, the anti-Catholic films were all made in 1985 and after.

The top 10 pro-Catholic films:

1. *The Passion of the Christ (2004)*
2. *The Sound of Music (1965)*
3. *A Man for All Seasons (1966)*
4. *The Song of Bernadette (1943)*
5. *It's a Wonderful Life (1946)*
6. *The Ten Commandments (1956)*
7. *The Scarlet and the Black (1983)*
8. *Jesus of Nazareth (1977)*
9. *Schindler's List (1993)*
10. *The Bells of St. Mary's (1945)*

The top 10 anti-Catholic films:

1. *The Order (2003)*
2. *The Magdalene Sisters (2002)*
3. *Sister Mary Explains It All (2001)*
4. *Chocolat (2000)*
5. *Stigmata (1999)*
6. *Dogma (1999)*
7. *Elizabeth (1998)*
8. *The Last Temptation of Christ (1988)*
9. *Priest (1994)*
10. *Agnes of God (1985)*

FILMOGRAPHY

Films are in English unless otherwise noted. DVD and VHS availability based on U.S. releases. Note that most VHS titles are out of print but can be purchased through vendors who specialize in secondhand tapes. New DVDs are released regularly, so check with Amazon and other retailers for titles shown as Not Available on this list.

Agnes of God (1985, Columbia Pictures)
Director: Norman Jewison
Screenplay: John Pielmeier, based on his play
Cinematography: Sven Nykvist; Music: Georges Delerue
Cast: Jane Fonda, Anne Bancroft, Meg Tilly
98 minutes / Color / Rated PG-13 / DVD and VHS: Sony Pictures

The Agony and the Ecstasy (1965, International Classics)
Director: Carol Reed
Screenplay: Philip Dunne, based on the novel by Irving Stone
Cinematography: Leon Shamroy; Music: Alex North
Cast: Charlton Heston, Rex Harrison, Diane Cilento, Harry Andrews, Alberto Lupo
138 minutes / Color / Not Rated / DVD and VHS: 20th Century Fox

Amazing Grace (2006, Samuel Goldwyn Films)
Director: Michael Apted
Screenplay: Steven Knight
Cinematography: Remi Adefarasin; Music: David Arnold
Cast: Ioan Gruffudd, Romola Garai, Benedict Cumberbatch, Albert Finney
118 minutes / Color / Rated PG / DVD: 20th Century Fox; VHS: Not Available

Amen (2002, Canal+)
Director: Costa-Gavras
Screenplay: Costa-Gavras, Jean-Claude Grumberg, based on the play *The Deputy* by Rolf Hochhuth
Cinematography: Patrick Blossier; Music: Armand Amar
Cast: Ulrich Tukur, Mathieu Kassovitz, Ulrich Muhe, Michel Duchaussoy, Ion Caramitru
132 minutes / Color / English, French, Italian, German / Not Rated / DVD: Kino Video; VHS: Not Available

Angels in the Outfield (1952, MGM)
Director: Clarence Brown
Screenplay: Richard Conlin, Dorothy Kingsley, George Wells

Cinematography: Paul C. Vogel; Music: Daniele Amfitheatrof
Cast: Paul Douglas, Janet Leigh, Keenan Wynn, Spring Byington, Ellen Corby
99 minutes / B&W / Not Rated / DVD: Warner Home Video; VHS: Not Available

Angels with Dirty Faces (1938, Warner Bros.)
Director: Michael Curtiz
Screenplay: John Wexley, Warren Duff, Rowland Brown
Cinematography: Sol Polito; Music: Max Steiner
Cast: James Cagney, Pat O'Brien, Humphrey Bogart, Ann Sheridan, Leo Gorcey
97 minutes / B&W / Not Rated / DVD: Warner Home Video; VHS: MGM/UA

The Apostle (1997, Butcher's Run Films)
Director: Robert Duvall
Screenplay: Robert Duvall
Cinematography: Barry Markowitz; Music: David Mansfield
Cast: Robert Duvall, Farrah Fawcett, Billy Bob Thornton, June Carter Cash
134 minutes / Color / Rated PG-13 / DVD and VHS: Universal Home Video

The Assisi Underground (1985, Golan-Globus Productions)
Director: Alexander Ramati
Screenplay: Alexander Ramati, based on his novel
Cinematography: Giuseppe Rotunno; Music: Dov Seltzer
Cast: Ben Cross, James Mason, Maximilian Schell, Irene Papas
115 minutes / Color / Rated PG / DVD: Not Available; VHS: MGM

Au Revoir Les Enfants (1987, MK2 Productions)
Director: Louis Malle
Screenplay: Louis Malle
Cinematography: Renato Berta
Cast: Gaspard Manesse, Raphael Fejtö, Francine Racette, Philippe Morier-Genoud
104 minutes / Color / French / Rated PG / DVD: Criterion Collection; VHS: Orion
    Classics

Babette's Feast (1987, Panorama Films A/S)
Director: Gabriel Axel
Screenplay: Gabriel Axel, based on the novel by Karen Blixen (Isak Dinesen)
Cinematography: Henning Kristiansen
Music: Per Nørgård
Cast: Stephane Audran, Jean-Philippe Lafont, Gudmar Wivesson, Jarl Kulle
102 minutes / Color / Danish, Swedish, French / Rated G / DVD: MGM; VHS: Orion
    Home Video

Barabbas (1962, Dino de Laurentiis Cinematografica)
Director: Richard Fleischer
Screenplay: Christopher Fry, based on the novel by Pär Lagerkvist

Cinematography: Aldo Tonti; Music: Mario Nascimbene
Cast: Anthony Quinn, Arthur Kennedy, Jack Palance, Ernest Borgnine, Katy Jurado
137 minutes / Color / Not Rated / DVD and VHS: Sony Pictures

The Basketball Diaries (1995, New Line Cinema)
Director: Scott Kalvert
Screenplay: Bryan Goluboff, based on the book by Jim Carroll
Cinematography: David Phillips; Music: Graeme Revell
Cast: Leonardo DiCaprio, Lorraine Bracco, Marilyn Sokol, Mark Wahlberg
102 minutes / Color / Rated R / DVD: Palm Pictures; VHS: Polygram Video

Becket (1964, Paramount)
Director: Peter Glenville
Screenplay: Edward Anhalt, based on the play by Jean Anouilh
Cinematography: Geoffrey Unsworth; Music: Laurence Rosenthal
Cast: Peter O'Toole, Richard Burton, John Gielgud, Donald Wolfit, Martita Hunt
148 minutes / Color / Rated PG-13 / DVD and VHS: MPI Home Video

Bella (2006, Metanoia Films)
Director: Alejandro Gomez Monteverde
Screenplay: Alejandro Gomez Monteverde, Patrick Million, Leo Severino
Cinematography: Andrew Cadelago; Music: Stephan Altman
Cast: Eduardo Verástegui, Tammy Blanchard, Manny Perez, Ali Landry
91 minutes / Color / Rated PG-13 / DVD: Lions Gate; VHS: Not Available

The Bells of St. Mary's (1945, Rainbow Productions)
Director: Leo McCarey
Screenplay: Leo McCarey, Dudley Nichols
Cinematography: George Barnes; Music: Robert Emmett Dolan
Cast: Bing Crosby, Ingrid Bergman, Henry Travers, Ruth Donnelly, William Gargan
126 minutes / B&W / Not Rated / DVD and VHS: Republic Pictures

Ben-Hur (1959, MGM)
Director: William Wyler
Screenplay: Karl Tunberg, based on the novel by Lew Wallace
Cinematography: Robert Surtees; Music: Miklós Rózsa
Cast: Charlton Heston, Stephen Boyd, Jack Hawkins, Haya Harareet, Hugh Griffith
214 minutes / Color / Not Rated / DVD and VHS: Warner Home Video

Ben-Hur: A Tale of the Christ (1925, MGM)
Director: Fred Niblo
Screenplay: June Mathis, Katharine Hilliker (titles), H.H. Caldwell (titles), from the novel by Lew Wallace
Cinematography: Clyde DeVinna, René Guissart, Percy Hilburn, Glenn Kirshner, Karl Struss

Cast: Ramon Novarro, Francis X. Bushman, May McAvoy, Betty Bronson, Kathleen Key
148 minutes / B&W / Silent / Not Rated / DVD: Warner Bros. (with 1959 version); VHS: MGM/UA

The Bishop's Wife (1947, Samuel Goldwyn Company)
Director: Henry Koster
Screenplay: Leonardo Bercovici, Robert E. Sherwood, based on the book by Robert Nathan
Cinematography: Gregg Toland; Music: Hugo Friedhofer
Cast: Cary Grant, Loretta Young, David Niven, Monty Woolley, Elsa Lanchester
109 minutes / B&W / Not Rated / DVD and VHS: MGM

The Bitter Tea of General Yen (1933, Columbia Pictures)
Director: Frank Capra
Screenplay: Edward E. Paramore, Jr., Grace Zaring Stone
Cinematography: Joseph Walker; Music: W. Franke Harling
Cast: Barbara Stanwyck, Nils Asther, Walter Connolly, Toshia Mori, Richard Loo
88 minutes / B&W / Not Rated / DVD: Not Available; VHS: Sony Pictures

Black Narcissus (1946, The Archers)
Director: Michael Powell, Emeric Pressburger
Screenplay: Michael Powell, Emeric Pressburger, based on the novel by Rumer Godden
Cinematography: Jack Cardiff; Music: Brian Easdale
Cast: Deborah Kerr, Flora Robson, Jean Simmons, David Farrar, Sabu, Esmond Knight
100 minutes / Color / Not Rated / DVD: Criterion Collection; VHS: MGM

Black Robe (1991, Alliance Communications Corporation)
Director: Bruce Beresford
Screenplay: Brian Moore, based on his novel
Cinematography: Peter James; Music: Georges Delerue
Cast: Lothaire Bluteau, August Schellenberg, Aden Young, Sandrine Holt
101 minutes / Color / Rated R / DVD: Vidmark; VHS: MGM

The Boys of St. Vincent (1993, Canadian Broadcasting Corporation)
Director: John N. Smith
Screenplay: Sam Grana, John N. Smith, Des Walsh
Cinematography: Pierre Letarte; Music: Neil Smolar
Cast: Henry Czerny, Johnny Morina, Brian Dooley, Philip Dinn, Michael Wade
186 minutes / Color / Not Rated (Television Mini-Series) / DVD and VHS: New Yorker Video

Boys Town (1938, MGM)
Director: Norman Taurog
Screenplay: Dore Schary, John Meehan, Eleanore Griffin
Cinematography: Sidney Wagner; Music: Edward Ward

Cast: Spencer Tracy, Mickey Rooney, Henry Hull, Leslie Fenton, Gene Reynolds
96 minutes / B&W / Not Rated / DVD: Warner Home Video; VHS: MGM/UA

Breach (2007, Double Agent Productions)
Director: Billy Ray
Screenplay: Adam Mazer, William Rotko, Billy Ray
Cinematography: Tak Fujimoto; Music: Mychael Danna
Cast: Chris Cooper, Ryan Phillippe, Laura Linney, Gary Cole, Dennis Haysbert
110 minutes / Color / Rated PG-13 / DVD: Universal; VHS: Not Available

Broken Vows (1987, Brademan Self Productions)
Director: Jud Taylor
Screenplay: Ivan Davis, based on the novel *Where the Dark Streets Go* by Dorothy Salisbury
    Davis
Cinematography: Thomas Burstyn; Music: Charles Gross
Cast: Tommy Lee Jones, Annette O'Toole, M. Emmett Walsh, Milo O'Shea
95 minutes / Color / Not Rated / DVD: Platinum Disk; VHS: Cabin Fever

Brother Orchid (1940, Warner Bros.)
Director: Lloyd Bacon
Screenplay: Richard Connell, Earl Baldwin
Cinematography: Tony Gaudio; Music: Heinz Roemheld
Cast: Edward G. Robinson, Ann Sothern, Humphrey Bogart, Donald Crisp
88 minutes / B&W / Not Rated / DVD: Warner Home Video; VHS: MGM (Warner)

Brother Sun, Sister Moon (1973, Euro International Film)
Director: Franco Zeffirelli
Screenplay: Suso Cecchi d'Amico, Kenneth Ross, Lina Wertmuller, Franco Zeffirelli
Cinematography: Ennio Guarnieri; Music: Riz Ortolani
Cast: Graham Faulkner, Judi Bowker, Leigh Lawson, Kenneth Cranham, Lee Montague
121 minutes / Color / Rated PG / DVD and VHS: Paramount

The Cardinal (1963, Otto Preminger Films)
Director: Otto Preminger
Screenplay: Robert Dozier, based on the novel by Henry Morton Robinson
Cinematography: Leon Shamroy; Music: Jerome Moross
Cast: Tom Tryon, John Huston, Burgess Meredith, Ossie Davis, Carol Lynley
175 minutes / Color / Not Rated / DVD and VHS: Warner Home Video

Change of Habit (1969, NBC)
Director: William A. Graham
Screenplay: Eric Bercovici, John Joseph, James Lee, Richard Morris, S.S. Schweitzer
Cinematography: Russell Metty; Music: Billy Goldenberg
Cast: Elvis Presley, Mary Tyler Moore, Barbara McNair, Jane Elliot, Edward Asner
93 minutes / Color / Rated G / DVD: Universal Studios; VHS: Goodtimes Home Video

FILMOGRAPHY

Chariots of Fire (1981, Enigma Productions)
Director: Hugh Hudson
Screenplay: Colin Welland
Cinematography: David Watkin; Music: Vangelis Papathanassiou
Cast: Ian Charleson, Ben Cross, Ian Holm, Nigel Havers, Sir John Gielgud
123 minutes / Color / Rated PG / DVD and VHS: Warner Home Video

Chocolat (2000, Miramax)
Director: Lasse Hallström
Screenplay: Robert Nelson Jacobs, based on the novel by Joanne Harris
Cinematography: Roger Pratt; Music: Rachel Portman
Cast: Juliette Binoche, Alfred Molina, Johnny Depp, Judi Dench, Carrie-Anne Moss
121 minutes / Color / English, French / Rated PG-13 / DVD: Miramax; VHS: Walt Disney
    Video

The Cider House Rules (1999, FilmColony)
Director: Lasse Hallström
Screenplay: John Irving, based on his novel
Cinematography: Oliver Stapleton; Music: Rachel Portman
Cast: Tobey Maguire, Michael Caine, Charlize Theron, Delroy Lindo, Paul Rudd
126 minutes / Color / Rated PG-13 / DVD: Miramax; VHS: Walt Disney Video

Cinema Paradiso (1989, Cristaldifilm)
Director: Guiseppe Tornatore
Screenplay: Guiseppe Tornatore, Vanna Paoli
Cinematography: Blasco Giurato; Music: Ennio Morricone
Cast: Salvatore Cascio, Philippe Noiret, Jacques Perrin, Antonella Attili, Pupella Maggio
155 minutes / Color / Italian / Rated PG / DVD: Weinstein Company; VHS: HBO Home
    Video

Come to the Stable (1949, 20th Century Fox)
Director: Henry Koster
Screenplay: Sally Benson, Clare Boothe Luce
Cinematography: Joseph LaShelle; Music: Cyril J. Mockridge
Cast: Loretta Young, Celeste Holm, Hugh Marlowe, Elsa Lanchester, Thomas Gomez
94 minutes / B&W / Not Rated / DVD: Not Available; VHS: 20th Century Fox

The Crusades (1935, Paramount)
Director: Cecil B. DeMille
Screenplay: Harold Lamb, Waldemar Young, Dudley Nichols
Cinematography: Victor Milnor; Music: Rudolph G. Kopp
Cast: Loretta Young, Henry Wilcoxon, Ian Keith, C. Aubrey Smith, Katherine DeMille
125 minutes / B&W/ Not Rated / DVD: Universal Studios (The Cecil B. DeMille Collec-
    tion); VHS: Universal Studios

The Dangerous Lives of Altar Boys (2002, Egg Pictures)
Director: Peter Care
Screenplay: Jeff Stockwell, Michael Petroni, based on the book by Chris Fuhrman
Cinematography: Lance Acord; Music: Marco Beltrami
Cast: Emile Hirsch, Kieran Culkin, Vincent D'Onofrio, Jena Malone, Jodie Foster
104 minutes / Color / Rated R / DVD and VHS: Sony Pictures

The Da Vinci Code (2006, Columbia Pictures)
Director: Ron Howard
Screenplay: Akiva Goldsman, based on the novel by Dan Brown
Cinematography: Salvatore Totino; Music: Hans Zimmer
Cast: Tom Hanks, Audrey Tautou, Sir Ian McKellen, Paul Bettany, Jean Reno
149 minutes / Color / Rated PG-13 / DVD: Sony Pictures; VHS: Not Available

Dead Man Walking (1995, Havoc)
Director: Tim Robbins
Screenplay: Tim Robbins, based on the book by Sister Helen Prejean
Cinematography: Roger Deakins; Music: David Robbins
Cast: Susan Sarandon, Sean Penn, Robert Prosky, Raymond J. Berry, Celia Weston
122 minutes / Color / Rated R / DVD: MGM; VHS: Polygram Video

Demetrius and the Gladiators (1954, 20th Century Fox)
Director: Delmer Daves
Screenplay: Philip Dunne, based on characters in *The Robe* by Lloyd C. Douglas
Cinematography: Milton R. Krasner; Music: Franz Waxman
Cast: Victor Mature, Susan Hayward, Michael Rennie, Debra Paget, Anne Bancroft
101 minutes / Color / Not Rated / DVD and VHS: 20th Century Fox

The Devil and Daniel Webster (1941, William Dieterle Productions)
Director: William Dieterle
Screenplay: Stephen Vincent Benet, Dan Totheroh, based on Benet's story
Cinematography: Joseph August; Music: Bernard Herrmann
Cast: Edward Arnold, Walter Huston, Jane Darwell, Simone Simon, Gene Lockhart
107 minutes / B&W / Not Rated / DVD: Criterion Collection; VHS: Homevision

The Devil at 4 O'Clock (1961, Columbia Pictures)
Director: Mervyn LeRoy
Screenplay: Liam O'Brien, based on the novel by Max Catto
Cinematography: Joseph F. Biroc; Music: George Duning
Cast: Spencer Tracy, Frank Sinatra, Kerwin Mathews, Jean-Pierre Aumont
126 minutes / Color / Rated PG / DVD and VHS: Sony Pictures

The Devil's Eye (1960, Svensk Filmindustri)
Director: Ingmar Bergman
Screenplay: Ingmar Bergman

Cinematography: Gunnar Fischer; Music: Erik Nordgren
Cast: Jarl Kulle, Bibi Andersson, Stig Järrel, Nils Poppe
87 minutes / B&W / Swedish / Not Rated / DVD: Not Available; VHS: Homevision

Diary of a City Priest (2001, City Story Pictures)
Director: Eugene Martin
Screenplay: Eugene Martin, based on the book by Father Paul McNamee
Cinematography: Michael Perlman; Music: Matthew Levy
Cast: David Morse, Thomas Ryan, Phillip Goodwin, Ana Reader, Robert Sella
77 minutes / Color / Rated PG-13 / DVD and VHS: Heartland Film Festival Video

Diary of a Country Priest (1950, Union Générale Cinématographique)
Director: Robert Bresson
Screenplay: Robert Bresson, based on the novel by Georges Bernanos
Cinematography: Léonce-Henri Burel; Music: Jean-Jacques Grünenwald
Cast: Claude Laydu, Jean Riveyre, Adrien Borel, Rachel Bérendt, Nicole Maurey
110 minutes / B&W / French / Not Rated / DVD: Criterion Collection; VHS: Kino Video

Dogma (1999, View Askew Productions)
Director: Kevin Smith
Screenplay: Kevin Smith
Cinematography: Robert D. Yeoman; Music: Howard Shore
Cast: Linda Fiorentino, Ben Affleck, Matt Damon, Chris Rock, Alan Rickman
130 minutes / Color / Rated R / DVD and VHS: Sony Pictures

Doubt (2008, Scott Rudin Productions)
Director: John Patrick Shanley
Screenplay: John Patrick Shanley, based on his play
Cinematography: Roger Deakins; Music: Howard Shore
Cast: Meryl Steep, Philip Seymour Hoffman, Amy Adams, Viola Davis
104 minutes / Color / Rated PG-13 / DVD: Miramax; VHS: Not Available

El Cid (1961, Rank Organisation)
Director: Anthony Mann
Screenplay: Fredric M. Frank, Philip Yordan, Ben Barzman
Cinematography: Robert Krasker; Music: Miklós Rózsa
Cast: Charlton Heston, Sophia Loren, Raf Vallone, Hurd Hatfield, Geneviève Page
182 minutes / Color / Not Rated / DVD: Miriam Collection; VHS: Best Film and Video

Elizabeth (1998, Polygram Filmed Entertainment)
Director: Shekhar Kapur
Screenplay: Michael Hirst
Cinematography: Remi Adefarasin; Music: David Hirschfelder
Cast: Cate Blanchett, Joseph Fiennes, Geoffrey Rush, Christopher Eccleston
124 minutes / Color / Rated R / DVD: Universal; VHS: Polygram Video

Elizabeth: The Golden Age (2007, Universal Studios)
Director: Shekhar Kapur
Screenplay: William Nicholson, Michael Hirst
Cinematography: Remi Adefarasin; Music: Craig Armstrong, A. R. Rahman
Cast: Cate Blanchett, Clive Owen, Geoffrey Rush, Jordi Mollà, Samantha Morton
114 minutes / Color / Rated PG-13 / DVD: Universal Studios; VHS: Not Available

Elmer Gantry (1960, Elmer Gantry Productions)
Director: Richard Brooks
Screenplay: Richard Brooks, based on the novel by Sinclair Lewis
Cinematography: John Alton; Music: André Previn
Cast: Burt Lancaster, Jean Simmons, Arthur Kennedy, Dean Jagger, Shirley Jones
145 minutes / Color / Not Rated / DVD and VHS: MGM

Entertaining Angels: The Dorothy Day Story (1996, Paulist Pictures)
Director: Michael Ray Rhodes
Screenplay: John Wells
Cinematography: Mike Fash; Music: Bill Conti, Ashley Irwin
Cast: Moira Kelly, Martin Sheen, Melinda Dillon, Heather Graham, Brian Keith
112 minutes / Color / Rated PG-13 / DVD: Vision Video; VHS: Warner Home Video

Evelyn (2002, CinEvelyn)
Director: Bruce Beresford
Screenplay: Paul Pender
Cinematography: Humphrey Dixon; Music: Stephen Endelman
Cast: Pierce Brosnan, Sophie Vavasseur, Andrea Irvine, Julianna Margulies
94 minutes / Color / Rated PG / DVD and VHS: MGM

The Exorcism of Emily Rose (2005, Screen Gems)
Director: Scott Derrickson
Screenplay: Paul Harris Boardman, Scott Derrickson
Cinematography: Tom Stern; Music: Christopher Young
Cast: Laura Linney, Tom Wilkinson, Campbell Scott, Jennifer Carpenter, Colm Feore
    119 minutes / Color / Rated PG-13 / DVD: Sony Pictures; VHS: Screen Gems

The Exorcist (1973, Hoya Productions)
Director: William Friedkin
Screenplay: William Peter Blatty, based on his novel
Cinematography: Owen Roizman
Cast: Ellen Burstyn, Linda Blair, Jason Miller, Max von Sydow, Lee J. Cobb
122 minutes / Color / Rated R / DVD and VHS: Warner Home Video

Extreme Measures (1996, Castle Rock Entertainment)
Director: Michael Apted
Screenplay: Tony Gilroy, based on the novel by Michael Palmer

Cinematography: John Bailey; Music: Danny Elfman
Cast: Hugh Grant, Gene Hackman, Sarah Jessica Parker, David Morse
118 minutes / Color / Rated R / DVD: Turner Home Entertainment; VHS: Sony Pictures

Father Brown (aka *The Detective*) (1954, Columbia Pictures)
Director: Robert Hamer
Screenplay: Thelma Schnee, Maurice Rapf, Robert Hamer, based on the stories of G. K. Chesterton
Cinematography: Harry Waxman; Music: Georges Auric
Cast: Alec Guinness, Peter Finch, Joan Greenwood, Cecil Parker, Bernard Lee
91 minutes / B&W / Not Rated / DVD: Not Available; VHS: Columbia Pictures

The Fighting 69th (1940, Warner Bros.)
Director: William Keighley
Screenplay: Norman Reilly Raine, Fred Niblo, Jr., Dean Riesner
Cinematography: Tony Gaudio; Music: Adolph Deutsch
Cast: James Cagney, Pat O'Brien, George Brent, Jeffrey Lynn, Alan Hale
90 minutes / B&W / Not Rated / DVD: Warner Home Video; VHS: MGM

The Fighting Sullivans (1944, 20th Century Fox)
Director: Lloyd Bacon
Screenplay: Edward Doherty, Jules Schermer, Mary McCall
Cinematography: Lucien N. Andriot; Music: Cyril J. Mockridge
Cast: Thomas Mitchell, Anne Baxter, Selena Royle, Edward Ryan, John Campbell
112 minutes / B&W / Not Rated / DVD: VCI Video; VHS: Ivy Classics Video

The Flowers of St. Francis (1950, Cineriz)
Director: Roberto Rossellini
Screenplay: Federico Fellini, Father Antonio Lisandrini, Father Félix Morlión, Roberto Rossellini
Cinematography: Otello Martelli; Music: Renzo Rossellini
Cast: Aldo Fabrizi, Peparuolo
75 minutes / B&W / Italian / Not Rated / DVD: Criterion Collection; VHS: Not Available

Francis of Assisi (1961, Perseus Productions)
Director: Michael Curtiz
Screenplay: Eugene Vale, James Forsyth, Jack Thomas, based on the novel *The Joyful Beggar* by Louis De Wohl
Cinematography: Piero Portalupi; Music: Mario Nascimbene
Cast: Bradford Dillman, Dolores Hart, Stuart Whitman, Cecil Kellaway, Finlay Currie
105 minutes / Color/ Not Rated / DVD and VHS: 20th Century Fox

Friendly Persuasion (1956, Allied Artists)
Director: William Wyler
Screenplay: Michael Wilson, based on the novel by Jessamyn West

Cinematography: Ellsworth Fredericks; Music: Dimitri Tiomkin
Cast: Gary Cooper, Dorothy McGuire, Anthony Perkins, Richard Eyre, Robert Middleton
137 minutes / Color / Not Rated / DVD and VHS: Warner Home Video

From the Manger to the Cross (1912, Kalem)
Director: Sidney Olcott
Screenplay: Gene Gauntier
Cinematography: George K. Hollister
Cast: Robert Henderson-Bland, Gene Gauntier, Alice Holister, James D. Ainsley
71 minutes / B&W / Silent / Not Rated / DVD: Image Entertainment (with *The Life and Passion of Jesus Christ*); VHS: Kino Video

The Fugitive (1947, Argosy Pictures)
Director: John Ford
Screenplay: Dudley Nichols, based on the novel *The Power and the Glory* by Graham Greene
Cinematography: Gabriel Figueroa; Music: Richard Hageman
Cast: Henry Fonda, Dolores Del Rio, Pedro Armendáriz, J. Carrol Naish, Leo Carillo
104 minutes / B&W / Not Rated / DVD and VHS: Not Available

The Garden of Allah (1936, Selznick International)
Director: Richard Boleslawski
Screenplay: W. P. Lipscomb, Lynn Riggs, based on the novel by Robert Hichens
Cinematography: Virgil Miller; Music: Max Steiner
Cast: Marlene Dietrich, Charles Boyer, Basil Rathbone, C. Aubrey Smith
79 minutes / B&W / Not Rated / DVD: MGM; VHS: Starz / Anchor Bay

God Is My Co-Pilot (1945, Warner Bros.)
Director: Robert Florey
Screenplay: Abem Finkel, Peter Milne, based on the book by Robert Lee Scott, Jr.
Cinematography: Sidney Hickox; Music: Franz Waxman
Cast: Dennis Morgan, Dane Clark, Raymond Massey, Alan Hale, Craig Stevens
90 minutes / B&W / Not Rated / DVD: Not Available; VHS: Warner Home Video

The Godfather (1972, Paramount)
Director: Francis Ford Coppola
Screenplay: Francis Ford Coppola, Mario Puzo, based on Puzo's novel
Cinematography: Gordon Willis; Music: Nino Rota
Cast: Marlon Brando Al Pacino, James Caan, Robert Duvall, John Cazale, Diane Keaton
175 minutes / Color / Rated R / DVD and VHS: Paramount

The Godfather Part II (1974, Paramount)
Director: Francis Ford Coppola
Screenplay: Francis Ford Coppola, Mario Puzo
Cinematography: Gordon Willis; Music: Nino Rota

Cast: Al Pacino, Robert De Niro, Robert Duvall, John Cazale, Diane Keaton, Talia Shire
200 minutes / Color / Rated R / DVD and VHS: Paramount

The Godfather Part III (1990, Paramount)
Director: Francis Ford Coppola
Screenplay: Mario Puzo, Francis Ford Coppola
Cinematography: Gordon Willis; Music: Carmine Coppola
Cast: Al Pacino, Diane Keaton, Andy Garcia, Talia Shire, Sofia Coppola, Eli Wallach
162 minutes / Color / Rated R / DVD and VHS: Paramount Home Video

Godspell (1973, Columbia Pictures)
Director: David Greene
Screenplay: David Greene, John-Michael Tebelak, based on Tebelak's stage musical
Cinematography: Richard G. Heimann; Music: Stephen Schwartz
Cast: Victor Garber, David Haskell, Katie Hanley, Lynne Thigpen, Merrell Jackson
103 minutes / Color / Rated G / DVD: Sony Pictures; VHS: Columbia TriStar Home
    Entertainment

Going My Way (1944, Paramount)
Director: Leo McCarey
Screenplay: Leo McCarey, Frank Butler, Frank Cavett
Cinematography: Lionel Lindon
Cast: Bing Crosby, Barry Fitzgerald, Frank McHugh, Gene Lockhart, Risë Stevens
130 minutes / B&W / Not Rated / DVD and VHS: Universal Studios

The Gospel According to St. Matthew (1964, Arco Film)
Director: Pier Paolo Pasolini
Screenplay: Pier Paolo Pasolini
Cinematography: Tonino Delli Colli; Music: Nino Baragli
Cast: Enrique Irazoqui, Margherita Caruso, Susanna Pasolini, Marcello Morante
135 minutes / B&W / Italian / Not Rated / DVD: Legend; VHS: Water Bearer Films, Inc.

The Greatest Story Ever Told (1965, George Stevens Productions)
Director: George Stevens
Screenplay: James Lee Barrett, George Stevens, based on the book by Fulton Oursler
Cinematography: Loyal Griggs, William C. Mellor; Music: Alfred Newman
Cast: Max von Sydow, Charlton Heston, Carroll Baker, David McCallum, Sidney Poitier
193 minutes / Color / Rated G / DVD and VHS: MGM

Green Light (1937, Cosmopolitan Productions)
Director: Frank Borzage
Screenplay: Milton Krims, based on the novel by Lloyd C. Douglas
Cinematography: Byron Haskin; Music: Max Steiner
Cast: Errol Flynn, Anita Louise, Sir Cedric Hardwicke, Spring Byington
85 minutes / B&W / Not Rated / DVD and VHS: Not Available

The Green Pastures (1936, Warner Bros.)
Directors: Marc Connelly, William Keighley
Screenplay: Marc Connelly, based on his play and on the novel *Ol' Man Adam and His Chillun*
   by Roark Bradford
Cinematography: Hal Mohr; Music: Erich Wolfgang Korngold
Cast: Rex Ingram, Oscar Polk, Eddie Anderson, Edna Mae Harris, Frank Wilson
93 minutes / B&W / Not Rated / DVD: Warner Bros.; VHS: MGM/UA

Guadalcanal Diary (1943, 20th Century Fox)
Director: Lewis Seiler
Screenplay: Lamar Trotti, Jerome Cady, based on the book by Richard Tregaskis
Cinematography: Charles G. Clarke; Music: David Buttolph
Cast: Preston Foster, Lloyd Nolan, William Bendix, Anthony Quinn, Richard Jaeckel
93 minutes / B&W / Not Rated / DVD and VHS: 20th Century Fox

Guess Who's Coming to Dinner (1967, Columbia Pictures)
Director: Stanley Kramer
Screenplay: William Rose
Cinematography: Sam Leavitt; Music: Frank DeVol
Cast: Spencer Tracy, Katharine Hepburn, Sidney Poitier, Katharine Houghton
108 minutes / Color / Not Rated / DVD and VHS: Sony Pictures

Hallelujah! (1929, MGM)
Director: King Vidor
Screenplay: King Vidor, Wanda Tuchock, Ransom Rideout, Richard Schayer
Cinematography: Gordon Avil
Cast: Daniel L. Haynes, Nina Mae McKinney, Harry Gray, Fanny Belle DeKnight
109 minutes / B&W / Not Rated / DVD: Warner Home Video; VHS: MGM/UA

Heaven Help Us (1985, HBO)
Director: Michael Dinner
Screenplay: Charles Purpura
Cinematography: Miroslav Ondricek; Music: James Horner
Cast: Andrew McCarthy, Donald Sutherland, Mary Stuart Masterson, John Heard
104 minutes / Color / Rated R / DVD and VHS: HBO Home Video

Heaven Knows, Mr. Allison (1957, 20th Century Fox)
Director: John Huston
Screenplay: John Huston, John Lee Mahin, based on the novel by Charles Shaw
Cinematography: Oswald Morris; Music: Georges Auric
Cast: Robert Mitchum, Deborah Kerr
108 minutes / Color / Not Rated / DVD and VHS: 20th Century Fox

High Noon (1952, Stanley Kramer Productions)
Director: Fred Zinnemann
Screenplay: Carl Foreman, based on the story "The Tin Star" by John W. Cunningham

Cinematography: Floyd Crosby; Music: Dimitri Tiomkin
Cast: Gary Cooper, Grace Kelly, Thomas Mitchell, Katy Jurado, Lloyd Bridges
85 minutes / B&W / Not Rated / DVD: Lions Gate; VHS: Republic Pictures

The Hoodlum Priest (1961, Murray-Wood Productions)
Director: Irvin Kershner
Screenplay: Joseph Landon, Don Murray
Cinematography: Haskell Wexler; Music: Richard Markowitz
Cast: Don Murray, Larry Gates, Keir Dullea, Logan Ramsey, Cindi Wood, Don Joslyn
101 minutes / B&W / Not Rated / DVD and VHS: MGM

I Confess (1953, Warner Bros.)
Director: Alfred Hitchcock
Screenplay: George Tabori, William Archibald, based on the play by Paul Anthelme
Cinematography: Robert Burks; Music: Dimitri Tiomkin
Cast: Montgomery Clift, Karl Malden, Anne Baxter, Brian Aherne, Roger Dann
95 minutes / B&W / Not Rated / DVD and VHS: Warner Home Video

In This House of Brede (1975, Tomorrow Entertainment)
Director: George Schaefer
Screenplay: James Costigan, based on the novel by Rumer Godden
Cinematography: Christopher Challis; Music: Peter Matz
Cast: Diana Rigg, Pamela Brown, Gwen Watford, Denis Quilley, Judi Bowker, Ann Rye
105 minutes / Color / Not Rated (Made for Television) / DVD and VHS: Ignatius Press

Inherit the Wind (1960, Stanley Kramer Productions)
Director: Stanley Kramer
Screenplay: Nedrick Young, Harold Jacob Smith, based on the play by Jerome Lawrence and
    Robert Lee
Cinematography: Ernest Laszlo; Music: Ernest Gold
Cast: Spencer Tracy, Fredric March, Gene Kelly, Dick York, Harry Morgan
128 minutes / B&W / Not Rated / DVD and VHS: MGM

The Inn of the Sixth Happiness (1958, 20th Century Fox)
Director: Mark Robson
Screenplay: Isobel Lennart, based on the book *The Small Woman* by Alan Burgess
Cinematography: Freddie Young; Music: Malcolm Arnold
Cast: Ingrid Bergman, Curt Jurgens, Robert Donat, Michael David, Athene Seyler
158 minutes / Color / Not Rated / DVD and VHS: 20th Century Fox

Intolerance (1916, Triangle Film Corporation)
Director: D. W. Griffith
Screenplay: D. W. Griffith, Anita Loos
Cinematography: G. W. "Billy" Bitzer

Cast: Lillian Gish, Sam DeGrasse, Mae Marsh, Robert Harron, Constance Talmadge
163 minutes / B&W / Silent/ Not Rated / DVD: Kino Video; VHS: Republic Pictures Home
 Video, Kino

It's a Wonderful Life (1946, Liberty Films)
Director: Frank Capra
Screenplay: Albert Hackett, Francis Goodrich, Frank Capra, Jo Swerling, based on the story
 "The Greatest Gift" by Philip Van Doren Stern
Cinematography: Joseph Walker, Joseph Biroc, Victor Milner; Music: Dimitri Tiomkin
Cast: James Stewart, Donna Reed, Lionel Barrymore, Thomas Mitchell, Henry Travers
130 minutes / B&W / Not Rated / DVD: Paramount; VHS: Republic Pictures

Jesus Christ Superstar (1973, Universal Pictures)
Director: Norman Jewison
Screenplay: Melvin Bragg, Norman Jewison, based on the musical by Andrew Lloyd Webber
 and Tim Rice
Cinematography: Douglas Slocombe; Music: Andrew Lloyd Webber
Cast: Ted Neeley, Carl Anderson, Yvonne Elliman, Barry Dennen, Josh Mostel
108 minutes / Color / Rated G / DVD and VHS: Universal Studios

Jesus of Montreal (1989, Centre National de la Cinématographie)
Director: Denys Arcand
Screenplay: Denys Arcand
Cinematography: Guy Dufaux; Music: Jean-Marie Benoît, Francois Dompierre, Yves
 Laferrière
Cast: Lothaire Bluteau, Catherine Wilkening, Robert Lepage, Rémy Girard
118 minutes / Color / French / Rated R / DVD: Koch Lorber Films; VHS: Orion Home
 Video

Jesus of Nazareth (1977, Incorporated Television Company)
Director: Franco Zeffirelli
Screenplay: Anthony Burgess, Suso Cecchi d'Amico, Franco Zeffirelli, David Butler
Cinematography: Armando Nannuzzi, David Watkin; Music: Maurice Jarre
Cast: Robert Powell, Anne Bancroft, James Farentino, James Earl Jones, Stacy Keach
371 minutes / Color / Not Rated (Television Mini-Series) / DVD: Lion's Gate; VHS:
 Artisan

Joan of Arc (1948, Sierra Pictures)
Director: Victor Fleming
Screenplay: Maxwell Anderson, Andrew Solt, based on Anderson's play, *Joan of Lorraine*
Cinematography: Winton C. Hoch, William V. Skall, Joseph A. Valentine; Music: Hugo
 Friedhofer
Cast: Ingrid Bergman, Francis L. Sullivan, J. Carroll Naish, Gene Lockhart, José Ferrer
145 minutes / Color / Not Rated / DVD: Image Entertainment; VHS: Vid America

FILMOGRAPHY

Joan of Paris (1942, RKO Radio Pictures)
Director: Robert Stevenson
Screenplay: Jacques Théry, Georges Kessel, Charles Bennett, Ellis St. Joseph
Cinematography: Russell Metty; Music: Roy Webb
Cast: Michèle Morgan, Paul Henreid, Thomas Mitchell, Laird Cregar, May Robson
91 minutes / B&W / Not Rated / DVD: Not Available; VHS: Turner Home Entertainment

Keeping the Faith (2000, Miramax)
Director: Edward Norton
Screenplay: Stuart Blumberg
Cinematography: Anastas N. Michos; Music: Elmer Bernstein
Cast: Ben Stiller, Edward Norton, Jenna Elfman, Anne Bancroft, Eli Wallach
128 minutes / Color / Rated PG-13 / DVD: Touchstone; VHS: Touchstone Home Video

The Keys of the Kingdom (1944, 20th Century Fox)
Director: John M. Stahl
Screenplay: Joseph L. Mankiewicz, Nunnally Johnson, based on the novel by A. J. Cronin
Cinematography: Arthur C. Miller; Music: Alfred Newman
Cast: Gregory Peck, Thomas Mitchell, Vincent Price, Roddy McDowell, Edmund Gwenn
137 minutes / B&W / Not Rated / DVD: and VHS: 20th Century Fox)

King of Kings (1961, Samuel Bronston Productions)
Director: Nicholas Ray
Screenplay: Philip Yordan
Cinematography: Manuel Berenguer, Milton R. Krasner, Franz Planer; Music: Miklós Rózsa
Cast: Jeffrey Hunter, Siobhan McKenna, Hurd Hatfield, Carmen Sevilla, Rip Torn
168 minutes / Color / Rated PG-13 / DVD and VHS: Warner Home Video

The King of Kings (1927, DeMille Pictures Corporation)
Director: Cecil B. DeMille
Screenplay: Jeannie Macpherson
Cinematography: J. Peverell Marley; Music: Hugo Riesenfeld
Cast: H. B. Warner, Dorothy Cumming, Ernest Torrence, Joseph Schildkraut, Jacqueline Logan
112 minutes / B&W, Technicolor (two strip) / Silent / Not Rated / DVD: Criterion Collection; VHS: Kino Video

Kingdom of Heaven (2005, 20th Century Fox)
Director: Ridley Scott
Screenplay: William Monahan
Cinematography: John Mathieson; Music: Harry Gregson-Williams
Cast: Orlando Bloom, Eva Green, Jeremy Irons, David Thewlis, Liam Neeson
144 minutes / Color / Rated R / DVD: 20th Century Fox; VHS: Not available

Knute Rockne, All-American (1940, Warner Bros.)
Director: Lloyd Bacon
Screenplay: Robert Buckner
Cinematography: Tony Gaudio; Music: Heinz Roemheld
Cast: Pat O'Brien, Gale Paige, Ronald Reagan, Donald Crisp, Albert Bassermann
98 minutes / B&W / Not Rated / DVD: Warner Home Video; VHS: MGM/UA

The Last Temptation of Christ (1988, Cineplex-Odeon)
Director: Martin Scorsese
Screenplay: Paul Schrader, based on the novel by Nikos Kazantzakis
Cinematography: Michael Ballhaus; Music: Peter Gabriel
Cast: Willem Dafoe, Harvey Keitel, Barbara Hershey, Verna Bloom
164 minutes / Color / Rated R / DVD: Criterion Collection; VHS: Universal Studios

The Left Hand of God (1955, 20th Century Fox)
Director: Edward Dmytryk
Screenplay: Alfred Hayes, based on the novel by William E. Barrett
Cinematography: Franz Planer; Music: Victor Young
Cast: Humphrey Bogart, Gene Tierney, Lee J. Cobb, Agnes Moorehead, E. G. Marshall
87 minutes / Color / Not Rated / DVD: Not Available; VHS: 20th Century Fox

Les Miserables (1935, 20th Century Pictures)
Director: Richard Boleslawski
Screenplay: W. P. Lipscomb, based on the novel by Victor Hugo
Cinematography: Gregg Toland; Music: Alfred Newman
Cast: Fredric March, Charles Laughton, Florence Eldridge, Rochelle Hudson
108 minutes / B&W / Not Rated / DVD and VHS: 20th Century Fox

The Life and Passion of Jesus Christ (1905, Pathé Freres)
Directors: Lucien Nonguet, Ferdinand Zecca
Cast: Madame Moreau, Monsieur Moreau
44 minutes / B&W / Silent / Not Rated / DVD: Passport Video, Image Entertainment (with
    From the Manger to the Cross); VHS: Not Available

Lilies of the Field (1963, Rainbow Productions)
Director: Ralph Nelson
Screenplay: James Poe, based on the novel by William E. Barrett
Cinematography: Ernest Haller; Music: Jerry Goldsmith
Cast: Sidney Poitier, Lilia Skala, Lisa Mann, Isa Crino, Francesca Jarvis, Stanley Adams
94 minutes / B&W / Not Rated / DVD and VHS: MGM

Lost Horizon (1937, Columbia Pictures)
Director: Frank Capra
Screenplay: Robert Riskin, based on the novel by James Hilton

FILMOGRAPHY

Cinematography: Joseph Walker; Music: Dimitri Tiomkin
Cast: Ronald Colman, Jane Wyatt, Thomas Mitchell, H. B. Warner, Sam Jaffe
118 minutes / B&W / Not Rated / DVD and VHS: Columbia Pictures

Lost Souls (2000, Avery Pix)
Director: Janusz Kaminski
Screenplay: Pierce Gardner, Betsy Stahl
Cinematography: Mauro Fiore; Music: Jan A. P. Kaczmarek
Cast: Wynona Ryder, Ben Chaplin, Sarah Wynter, Philip Baker Hall, John Hurt
97 minutes / Color / Rated R / DVD and VHS: New Line Home Video

Luther (2003, MGM)
Director: Eric Till
Screenplay: Camille Thomasson, Bart Gavigan
Cinematography: Robert Fraisse; Music: Richard Harvey
Cast: Joseph Fiennes, Alfred Molina, Jonathan Firth, Claire Cox, Sir Peter Ustinov
128 minutes / Color / Rated PG-13 / DVD and VHS: MGM

The Magdalene Sisters (2002, Magna Pacific)
Director: Peter Mullan
Screenplay: Peter Mullan
Cinematography: Nigel Willoughby; Music: Craig Armstrong
Cast: Anne-Marie Duff, Nora-Jane Noone, Dorothy Duffy, Geraldine McEwan
119 minutes / Color / Rated R / DVD and VHS: Miramax

Magnificent Obsession (1935, Universal)
Director: John M. Stahl
Screenplay: Sarah Y. Mason, Victor Heerman, George O' Neill, based on the novel by Lloyd
    C. Douglas
Cinematography: John J. Mescall; Music: Franz Waxman
Cast: Irene Dunne, Robert Taylor, Charles Butterworth, Betty Furness, Ralph Morgan
98 minutes / B&W / Not Rated / DVD and VHS: Not Available

Magnificent Obsession (1954, Universal International)
Director: Douglas Sirk
Screenplay: Robert Blees, Wells Root, based on the 1935 screenplay and the novel by Lloyd
    C. Douglas
Cinematography: Russell Metty; Music: Frank Skinner
Cast: Jane Wyman, Rock Hudson, Barbara Rush, Agnes Moorehead, Otto Kruger
108 minutes / Color / Not Rated / DVD: Not Available; VHS: Universal Studios

A Man Called Peter (1955, 20th Century Fox)
Director: Henry Koster
Screenplay: Eleanore Griffin, based on the book by Catherine Marshall

Cinematography: Harold Lipstein; Music: Alfred Newman
Cast: Richard Todd, Jean Peters, Marjorie Rambeau, Jill Esmond, Les Tremayne
119 minutes / Color / Not Rated / DVD and VHS: 20th Century Fox

A Man for All Seasons (1966, Highland Films)
Director: Fred Zinnemann
Screenplay: Robert Bolt, based on his play
Cinematography: Ted Moore; Music: Georges Delerue
Cast: Paul Scofield, Robert Shaw, Wendy Hiller, Leo McKern, John Hurt, Orson Welles
120 minutes / Color / Rated G / DVD and VHS: Sony Pictures

Manhattan Melodrama (1934, Cosmopolitan Productions)
Director: W.S. Van Dyke
Screenplay: Arthur Caesar, Oliver H. P. Garrett, Joseph L. Mankiewicz
Cinematography: James Wong Howe; Music: William Axt
Cast: Clark Gable, William Powell, Myrna Loy, Leo Carillo, Mickey Rooney
93 minutes / B&W / Not Rated / DVD: Warner Home Video; VHS: MGM

M*A*S*H (1970, Aspen Productions)
Director: Robert Altman
Screenplay: Ring Lardner, Jr., based on the novel by Richard Hooker (H. Richard Hornberger and Bill Heinz)
Cinematography: Harold E. Stine; Music: Johnny Mande
Cast: Donald Sutherland, Elliott Gould, Robert Duvall, Sally Kellerman, Gary Burghoff
116 minutes / Color / Rated R / DVD and VHS: 20th Century Fox

Mass Appeal (1984, David Foster Productions)
Director: Glenn Jordan
Screenplay: Bill C. Davis, based on his play
Cinematography: Donald Peterman; Music: Bill Conti
Cast: Jack Lemmon, Zeljko Ivanek, Charles Durning, Louise Latham, James Ray
99 minutes / Color / Rated PG / DVD: Not Available; VHS: Universal Studios

Men of Boys Town (1941, MGM)
Director: Norman Taurog
Screenplay: James Kevin McGuinness
Cinematography: Harold Rosson; Music: Herbert Stothart
Cast: Spencer Tracy, Mickey Rooney, Lee J. Cobb, Bobs Watson, Darryl Hickman
106 minutes / B&W / Not Rated / DVD: Warner Home Video (with *Boys Town*); VHS: MGM/UA

The Messenger: The Story of Joan of Arc (1999, Gaumont)
Director: Luc Besson
Screenplay: Andrew Birkin, Luc Besson

Cinematography: Thierry Arbogast; Music: Eric Serra
Cast: Milla Jovovich, Dustin Hoffman, Faye Dunaway, John Malkovich, Vincent Cassel
148 minutes / Color / Rated R / DVD and VHS: Sony Pictures

The Miracle of Our Lady of Fatima (1952, Warner Bros.)
Director: John Brahm
Screenplay: James O'Hanlon, Crane Wilbur
Cinematography: Edwin B. DuPar; Music: Max Steiner
Cast: Susan Whitney, Angela Clarke, Gilbert Roland, Sherry Jackson, Jay Novello
102 minutes / B&W / Not Rated / DVD and VHS: Warner Home Video

The Miracle of the Bells (1948, Jesse L. Lasky Productions)
Director: Irving Pichel
Screenplay: Ben Hecht, Quentin Reynolds, based on the novel by Russell Janney
Cinematography: Robert De Grasse; Music: Leigh Harline
Cast: Fred MacMurray, Alida Valli, Frank Sinatra, Lee J. Cobb, Charles Meredith
120 minutes / B&W / Not Rated / DVD: Not Available; VHS: Artisan Entertainment

Miracle on 34th Street (1947, 20th Century Fox)
Director: George Seaton
Screenplay: George Seaton, Valentine Davies
Cinematography: Lloyd Ahern, Charles G. Clarke; Music: Cyril J. Mockridge
Cast: Maureen O'Hara, Edmund Gwenn, John Payne, Natalie Wood, Gene Lockhart
96 minutes / B&W / Not Rated / DVD and VHS: 20th Century Fox

The Miracle Woman (1931, Columbia Pictures)
Director: Frank Capra
Screenplay: Jo Swerling, Dorothy Howell, based on the play *Bless You Sister* by Robert Riskin
    and John Meehan
Cinematography: Joseph Walker
Cast: Barbara Stanwyck, David Manners, Sam Hardy, Beryl Mercer, Russell Hopton
90 minutes / B&W / Not Rated / DVD: Not Available; VHS: Sony Pictures

Misery (1990, Castle Rock Entertainment)
Director: Rob Reiner
Screenplay: William Goldman, based on the novel by Stephen King
Cinematography: Barry Sonnenfeld; Music: Marc Shaiman
Cast: Kathy Bates, James Caan, Richard Farnsworth, Frances Sternhagen, Lauren Bacall
107 minutes / Color / Rated R / DVD and VHS: MGM

The Mission (1986, Warner Bros.)
Director: Roland Joffé
Screenplay: Robert Bolt
Cinematography: Chris Menges; Music: Ennio Morricone

Cast: Robert De Niro, Jeremy Irons, Ray McAnally, Aidan Quinn, Liam Neeson
126 minutes / Color / Rated PG / DVD and VHS: Warner Home Video

Monsieur Vincent (1947, E.D.I.C.)
Director: Maurice Cloche
Screenplay: Jean Bernard-Luc, Jean Anouilh
Cinematography: Claude Renoir; Music: Jean Jacques Grunenwald
Cast: Pierre Fresnay, Aimé Clariond, Lise Delamare, Yvonne Gaudeau
111 minutes / B&W / French / Not Rated / DVD: Lion's Gate; VHS: Hollywood Select
    Video

Monty Python's Life of Brian (1979, HandMade Films)
Director: Terry Jones
Screenplay: John Cleese, Graham Chapman, Terry Gilliam, Eric Idle, Terry Jones, Michael
    Palin
Cinematography: Peter Biziou; Music: Geoffrey Burgon
Cast: John Cleese, Graham Chapman, Terry Gilliam, Eric Idle, Terry Jones, Michael Palin
94 minutes / Color / Rated R / DVD: Sony Pictures; VHS: Starz / Anchor Bay

The Name of the Rose (1986, Neue Constantin Film)
Director: Jean-Jacques Annaud
Screenplay: Andrew Birkin, Gerard Brach, Howard Franklin, Alain Godard, based on the
    novel by Umberto Eco
Cinematography: Tonino Delli Colli; Music: James Horner
Cast: Sean Connery, Christian Slater, F. Murray Abraham, Michael Lonsdale
130 minutes / Color / Rated R / DVD: Warner Home Video; VHS: Embassy

The Nativity Story (2006, New Line Cinema)
Director: Catherine Hardwicke
Screenplay: Mike Rich
Cinematography: Elliot Davis; Music: Mychael Danna
Cast: Keisha Castle-Hughes, Ciarán Hinds, Oscar Isaac, Shohreh Aghdashloo
101 minutes / Color / Rated PG / DVD: New Line Home Video; VHS: Not Available

The Night of the Hunter (1955, Paul Gregory Productions)
Director: Charles Laughton
Screenplay: James Agee, based on the novel by Davis Grubb
Cinematography: Stanley Cortez; Music: Walter Schumann
Cast: Robert Mitchum, Shelley Winters, Lillian Gish, James Gleason, Peter Graves
93 minutes / B&W / Not Rated / DVD and VHS: MGM

The Ninth Day (2004, Video Press; Provobis Film, Bayerischer Rundfunk)
Director: Volker Schlöndorff
Screenplay: Eberhard Görner, Andreas Pflüger, based on the memoir, *Pfarrerblock 25487*
    (*Priestblock 25487*) by Jean Bernard

Cinematography: Tomas Erhart; Music: Alfred Schnittke
Cast: Ulrich Matthes, August Diehl, Germain Wagner, Bibiana Beglau
98 minutes / Color / German / Not Rated / DVD: Kino Video; VHS: Not Available

Nuns on the Run (1990, HandMade Films)
Director: Jonathan Lynn
Screenplay: Jonathan Lynn
Cinematography: Michael Garfath; Music: David Kitay
Cast: Eric Idle, Robbie Coltrane, Janet Suzman, Lila Kaye, Camille Coduri, Doris Hare
89 minutes / Color / Rated PG-13 / DVD: Starz / Anchor Bay; VHS: 20th Century Fox

The Nun's Story (1959, Warner Bros.)
Director: Fred Zinnemann
Screenplay: Robert Anderson, based on the book by Kathryn Hulme
Cinematography: Franz Planer; Music: Franz Waxman
Cast: Audrey Hepburn, Peter Finch, Dean Jagger, Dame Peggy Ashcroft
149 minutes / Color / Not Rated / DVD and VHS: Warner Home Video

On the Waterfront (1954, Horizon Pictures)
Director: Elia Kazan
Screenplay: Budd Schulberg
Cinematography: Boris Kaufman; Music: Leonard Bernstein
Cast: Marlon Brando, Karl Malden, Lee J. Cobb, Rod Steiger, Eva Marie Saint
108 minutes / B&W / Not Rated / DVD: Sony Pictures; VHS: Columbia Pictures

One Foot in Heaven (1941, Warner Bros.)
Director: Irving Rapper
Screenplay: Casey Robinson, based on the book by Hartzell Spence
Cinematography: Charles Rosher; Music: Max Steiner
Cast: Fredric March, Martha Scott, Beulah Bondi, Gene Lockhart, Frankie Thomas
108 minutes / B&W / Not Rated / DVD and VHS: Not Available

The Order (2003, 20th Century Fox)
Director: Brian Helgeland
Screenplay: Brian Helgeland
Cinematography: Nicola Pecorini; Music: David Tom
Cast: Heath Ledger, Mark Addy, Shannyn Sossamon, Peter Weller, Benno Fürmann
102 minutes / Color / Rated R / DVD and VHS: 20th Century Fox

The Passion of Joan of Arc (1928)
Director: Carl Theodor Dreyer
Screenplay: Joseph Delteil, Carl Theodor Dreyer
Cinematography: Rudolph Maté
Cast: Renee Maria Falconetti, Eugene Sylvain, André Berley, Michel Simon
110 minutes / B&W / Silent / Not Rated / DVD: Criterion Collection; VHS: Homevision

The Passion of the Christ (2004, 20th Century Fox)
Director: Mel Gibson
Screenplay: Benedict Fitzgerald, Mel Gibson
Cinematography: Caleb Deschanel; Music: John Debny
Cast: James Caviezel, Maia Morgenstern, Monica Bellucci, Hristo Shopov
127 minutes / Color / Aramaic, Latin, Hebrew, Assyrian Leo-Aramic / Rated R / DVD and
     VHS: 20th Century Fox

Places in the Heart (1984, Delphi II Productions)
Director: Robert Benton
Screenplay: Robert Benton
Cinematography: Néstor Almendros; Music: John Kander
Cast: Sally Field, John Malkovich, Danny Glover, Lindsay Crouse, Amy Madigan
112 minutes / Color / Rated PG / DVD: Sony Pictures; VHS: Fox Home Entertainment

The Pope Must Die (1991, British Screen Productions)
Director: Peter Richardson
Screenplay: Peter Richardson, Pete Richens
Cinematography: Frank Gell; Music: Anne Dudley, Jeff Beck
Cast: Robbie Coltrane, Alex Rocco, Paul Bartel, Annette Crosbie, Adrian Edmondson
97 minutes / Color / Rated R / DVD: Not Available; VHS: Media Home Video

The Preacher's Wife (1996, Mundy Lane Entertainment)
Director: Penny Marshall
Screenplay: Nat Mauldin, Allan Scott, based on the original screenplay by Robert E. Sher-
     wood and Leonardo Bercovici, based on the novel by Robert Nathan
Cinematography: Miroslav Ondricek; Music: Hans Zimmer
Cast: Denzel Washington, Whitney Houston, Courtney B. Vance, Gregory Hines
124 minutes / Color / Rated PG / DVD: Buena Vista Home Entertainment; VHS: Walt
     Disney Video

Priest (1994, BBC)
Director: Antonia Bird
Screenplay: Jimmy McGovern
Cinematography: Fred Tammes; Music: Andy Roberts
Cast: Linus Roache, Tom Wilkinson, Robert Carlyle, Cathy Tyson, Lesley Sharp
105 minutes / Color / Rated R / DVD: Miramax; VHS: Walt Disney Video

Primal Fear (1996, Paramount)
Director: Gregory Hoblit
Screenplay: Steve Shagan, Ann Biderman, based on the novel by William Diehl
Cinematography: Michael Chapman; Music: James Newton Howard
Cast: Richard Gere, Edward Norton, Laura Linney, John Mahoney, Frances McDormand
129 minutes / Color / Rated R / DVD: Turner Home Entertainment; VHS: Sony Pictures

FILMOGRAPHY

The Prisoner (1955, Facet Productions)
Director: Peter Glenville
Screenplay: Bridget Boland
Cinematography: Reginald H. Wyer; Music: Benjamin Frankel
Cast: Alec Guinness, Jack Hawkins, Wilfrid Lawson, Kenneth Griffith
91 minutes / B&W / Not Rated / DVD and VHS: Sony Pictures

Quo Vadis (1951, MGM)
Director: Mervyn LeRoy
Screenplay: S. N. Behrman, Sonya Levien, John Lee Mahin, based on the novel by Henryk
    Sienkiewicz
Cinematography: William V. Skall, Robert Surtees; Music: Miklós Rózsa
Cast: Robert Taylor, Deborah Kerr, Leo Genn, Peter Ustinov, Patricia Laffan
171 minutes / Color / Not Rated / DVD: Warner Home Video; VHS: MGM

The Rapture (1991, New Line Cinema)
Director: Michael Tolkin
Screenplay: Michael Tolkin
Cinematography: Bojan Bazelli; Music: Thomas Newman
Cast: Mimi Rogers, Patrick Bachau, David Duchovny, Kimberly Cullum, Will Patton
100 minutes / Color / Rated R / DVD and VHS: New Line Home Video

Road to Perdition (2002, DreamWorks SKG)
Director: Sam Mendes
Screenplay: David Self, based on the graphic novel by Max Allan Collins and Richard Piers
    Rayner
Cinematography: Conrad L. Hall; Music: Thomas Newman
Cast: Tom Hanks, Paul Newman, Daniel Craig, Ciarán Hinds, Tyler Hoechlin
117 minutes / Color / Rated R / DVD and VHS: Dreamworks Video

The Robe (1953, 20th Century Fox)
Director: Henry Koster
Screenplay: Philip Dunne, Gina Kaus, Albert Maltz, based on the novel by Lloyd C. Douglas
Cinematography: Leon Shamroy; Music: Alfred Newman
Cast: Richard Burton, Jean Simmons, Victor Mature, Michael Rennie, Dean Jagger
135 minutes / Color / Not Rated / DVD and VHS: 20th Century Fox

Romero (1989, Paulist Pictures)
Director: John Duigan
Screenplay: John Sacret Young
Cinematography: Geoff Burton; Music: Gabriel Yared
Cast: Raul Julia, Richard Jordan, Ana Alicia, Eddie Velez, Tony Plana, Harold Gould
102 minutes / Color / Rated PG-13 / DVD and VHS: Lion's Gate

Rudy (1993, TriStar Pictures)
Director: David Anspaugh
Screenplay: Angelo Pizzo
Cinematography: Oliver Wood; Music: Jerry Goldsmith
Cast: Sean Astin, Jon Favreau, Charles S. Dutton, Ned Beatty, Lili Taylor, Greta Lind
116 minutes / Color / Rated PG / DVD: Sony Pictures; VHS: Columbia TriStar

San Francisco (1936, MGM)
Director: W.S. Van Dyke
Screenplay: Anita Loos, Robert T. Hopkins (story)
Cinematography: Oliver T. Marsh; Music: Herbert Stothart, Edward Ward
Cast: Clark Gable, Jeanette MacDonald, Spencer Tracy, Jack Holt, Jessie Ralph
115 minutes / B&W / Not Rated / DVD: Warner Home Video; VHS: MGM/UA

The Sandpiper (1965, Filmways Pictures)
Director: Vincente Minnelli
Screenplay: Martin Ransohoff, Irene Kamp, Louis Kamp, Dalton Trumbo, Michael Wilson
Cinematography: Milton R. Krasner; Music: Johnny Mandel
Cast: Elizabeth Taylor, Richard Burton, Eva Marie Saint, Charles Bronson
117 minutes / Color / Not Rated / DVD: Warner Home Video; VHS: MGM

Satan Never Sleeps (1962, 20th Century Fox)
Director: Leo McCarey
Screenplay: Claude Binyon, Leo McCarey, based on the novel *The China Story* by Pearl S.
    Buck
Cinematography: Oswald Morris; Music: Richard Rodney Bennett
Cast: William Holden, Clifton Webb, France Nuyen, Athene Seyler
125 minutes / Color / Not Rated / DVD and VHS: 20th Century Fox

Saturday Night Fever (1977, RSO)
Director: John Badham
Screenplay: Norman Wexler, based on the article "The Tribal Rites of the New Saturday
    Night" by Nik Cohn
Cinematography: Ralf D. Bode; Music: Barry, Maurice, and Robin Gibb
Cast: John Travolta, Karen Lynn Gorney, Donna Pescow, Martin Shakar, Barry Miller
118 minutes / Color / Rated R / DVD and VHS: Paramount

Saved! (2004, United Artists)
Director: Brian Dannelly
Screenplay: Brian Dannelly, Michael Urban
Cinematography: Bobby Bukowski; Music: Christopher Beck
Cast: Jena Malone, Mandy Moore, Patrick Fugit, Macaulay Culkin, Heather Matarazzo
92 minutes / Color / Rated PG-13 / DVD and VHS: MGM

FILMOGRAPHY

The Scarlet and the Black (1983, ITC)
Director: Jerry London
Screenplay: David Butler, based on the book *The Scarlet Pimpernel of the Vatican* by
J. P. Gallagher
Cinematography: Giuseppe Rotunno; Music: Ennio Morricone
Cast: Gregory Peck, Christopher Plummer, Sir John Gielgud, Raf Vallone
143 minutes / Color / Not Rated (Television Mini-Series) / DVD: Lions Gate; VHS:
Artisan

Schindler's List (1993, Universal Pictures)
Director: Steven Spielberg
Screenplay: Steven Zaillian, based on the novel by Thomas Keneally
Cinematography: Janusz Kaminski; Music: John Williams
Cast: Liam Neeson, Ralph Fiennes, Ben Kingsley, Caroline Goodall, Embeth Davidtz
196 minutes / B&W / Rated R / DVD and VHS: Universal Studios

Sergeant York (1941, Warner Bros.)
Director: Howard Hawks
Screenplay: Abem Finkel, Harry Chandle, Howard Koch, John Huston, based on the diary
of Alvin York (edited by Tom Skeyhill)
Cinematography: Sol Polito; Music: Max Steiner
Cast: Gary Cooper, Joan Leslie, Walter Brennan, Margaret Wycherley, June Lockhart
134 minutes / B&W / Not Rated / DVD: Warner Home Video; VHS: MGM/UA

The Seventh Seal (1957, Svensk Filmindustri)
Director: Ingmar Bergman
Screenplay: Ingmar Bergman
Cinematography: Gunnar Fischer; Music: Erik Nordgren
Cast: Max von Sydow, Bengt Ekerot, Nils Poppe, Bibi Andersson, Inga Landgré
96 minutes / B&W / Swedish / Not Rated / DVD: Criterion Collection; VHS: Home-
vision

Shadowlands (1993, Price Entertainment)
Director: Richard Attenborough
Screenplay: William Nicholson, based on his play
Cinematography: Roger Pratt; Music: George Fenton
Cast: Anthony Hopkins, Debra Winger, Edward Hardwicke, Joseph Mazzello
131 minutes / Color / Rated PG / DVD and VHS: HBO Home Video

The Shawshank Redemption (1994, Castle Rock Entertainment)
Director: Frank Darabont
Screenplay: Frank Darabont, based on the story, "Rita Hayworth and the Shawshank Re-
demption" by Stephen King
Cinematography: Roger Deakins; Music: Thomas Newman

Cast: Tim Robbins, Morgan Freeman, Bob Gunton, James Whitmore, Clancy Brown
142 minutes / Color / Rated R / DVD: Castle Rock; VHS: Turner Home Entertainment

The Shoes of the Fisherman (1968, MGM)
Director: Michael Anderson
Screenplay: James Kennaway, John Patrick, based on the novel by Morris L. West
Cinematography: Erwin Hillier; Music: Alex North
Cast: Anthony Quinn, Oskar Werner, David Janssen, Sir Laurence Olivier, Leo McKern
162 minutes / Color / Rated G / DVD: Warner Home Video; VHS: MGM

The Sign of the Cross (1932, Paramount)
Director: Cecil B. DeMille
Screenplay: Sidney Buchman, Waldemar Young, based on the play by Wilson Barrett
Cinematography: Karl Struss; Music: Rudolph G. Kopp
Cast: Fredric March, Claudette Colbert, Charles Laughton, Elissa Landi, Ian Keith
122 minutes / B&W / Not Rated / DVD: Universal Studios (The Cecil B. DeMille Collec-
    tion); VHS: Universal Studios

The Silver Chalice (1954, Victor Saville Productions)
Director: Victor Saville
Screenplay: Lesser Samuels, based on the novel by Thomas B. Costain
Cinematography: William V. Skall; Music: Franz Waxman
Cast: Paul Newman, Virginia Mayo, Jack Palance, Joseph Wiseman, Alexander Scourby
142 minutes / Color / Not Rated / DVD and VHS: Warner Home Video

The Singing Nun (1966, MGM)
Director: Henry Koster
Screenplay: John Furia, Sally Benson
Cinematography: Milton R. Krasner
Cast: Debbie Reynolds, Ricardo Montalban, Greer Garson, Agnes Moorehead
98 minutes / Color / Not Rated / DVD: Warner Home Video; VHS: MGM

Sister Act (1992, Touchstone Pictures)
Director: Emile Ardolino
Screenplay: Joseph Howard
Cinematography: Adam Greenberg; Music: Marc Shaiman
Cast: Whoopi Goldberg, Maggie Smith, Kathy Najimy, Mary Wickes, Harvey Keitel
100 minutes / Color / Rated PG / DVD and VHS: Touchstone

Sister Mary Explains It All (2001, Viacom)
Director: Marshall Brickman
Screenplay: Christopher Durang, based on his play, *Sister Mary Ignatius Explains It All
    for You*
Cinematography: Anthony B. Richmond; Music: Philippe Sarde

Cast: Diane Keaton, Brian Benben, Laura San Giacomo, Jennifer Tilly
77 minutes / Color / Not Rated / DVD: Not Available; VHS: Not Available

Sleepers (1996, Baltimore Pictures)
Director: Barry Levinson
Screenplay: Barry Levinson, based on the book by Lorenzo Carcaterra
Cinematography: Michael Ballhaus; Music: John Williams
Cast: Kevin Bacon, Robert De Niro, Dustin Hoffman, Jason Patric, Brad Pitt
147 minutes / Color / Rated R / DVD and VHS: Warner Home Video

The Song of Bernadette (1943, 20th Century Fox)
Director: Henry King
Screenplay: George Seaton, based on the novel by Franz Werfel
Cinematography: Arthur C. Miller; Music: Alfred Newman
Cast: Jennifer Jones, Lee J. Cobb, Charles Bickford, Anne Revere, Gladys Cooper
156 minutes / B&W / Not Rated / DVD and VHS: 20th Century Fox

The Sound of Music (1965, Robert Wise Productions)
Director: Robert Wise
Screenplay: Ernest Lehman, based on the stage musical by Howard Lindsay and Russel
    Crouse
Cinematography: Ted D. McCord; Music (Songs): Richard Rodgers, Oscar Hammerstein II
Cast: Julie Andrews, Christopher Plummer, Eleanor Parker, Peggy Wood, Richard Haydn
174 minutes / Color / Rated: G / DVD and VHS: 20th Century Fox

The Spitfire Grill (1996, Castle Rock Entertainment)
Director: Lee David Zlotoff
Screenplay: Lee David Zlotoff
Cinematography: Robert Draper; Music: James Horner
Cast: Alison Elliott, Ellen Burstyn, Marcia Gay Harden, Will Patton, Kieran Mulroney
117 minutes / Color / Rated PG-13 / DVD and VHS: Turner Home Entertainment

Stars in My Crown (1950, MGM)
Director: Jacques Tourneur
Screenplay: Joe David Brown, Margaret Fitts, based on Brown's novel
Cinematography: Charles Edgar Schoenbaum; Music: Adolph Deutsch
Cast: Joel McCrea, Ellen Drew, Dean Stockwell, Alan Hale, Ed Begley
89 minutes / B&W / Not Rated / DVD: Not Available; VHS: MGM (Warner)

Stigmata (1999, FGM Entertainment)
Director: Rupert Wainwright
Screenplay: Tom Lazarus
Cinematography: Jeffrey L. Kimball; Music: Elia Cmiral, Billy Corgan
Cast: Patricia Arquette, Gabriel Byrne, Jonathan Pryce, Nia Long, Enrico Colantoni
103 minutes / Color / Rated R / DVD and VHS: MGM

A Tale of Two Cities (1935, MGM)
Director: Jack Conway
Screenplay: W. P. Lipscomb, S. N. Behrman, based on the novel by Charles Dickens
Cinematography: Oliver T. Marsh; Music: Herbert Stothart
Cast: Ronald Colman, Elizabeth Allan, Reginald Owen, Basil Rathbone
128 minutes / B&W / Not Rated / DVD: Warner Home Video; VHS: MGM

The Ten Commandments (1923, Paramount)
Director: Cecil B. DeMille
Screenplay: Jeanie MacPherson
Cinematography: Bert Glennon, Peverell Marley, Archie Stout, Fred Westerberg
Cast: Theodore Roberts, Charles de Rochefort, James Neill, Rod la Rocque, Edythe Chapman, Leatrice Joy, Richard Dix, Nita Naldi
136 minutes / B&W, Technicolor (Two Strip) / Silent / Not Rated / DVD and VHS: Paramount

The Ten Commandments (1956, Motion Picture Associates)
Director: Cecil B. DeMille
Screenplay: Aeneas MacKenzie, Jesse Lasky, Jr., Jack Gariss, Fredric M. Frank, based on the novels *Pillars of Fire* by J. H. Ingraham, *On Eagle's Wing* by A. E. Southon, and *Prince of Egypt* by Dorothy Clarke Wilson
Cinematography: Loyal Griggs; Music: Elmer Bernstein
Cast: Charlton Heston, Yul Brynner, Anne Baxter, Edward G. Robinson
220 minutes / Color / Not Rated / DVD and VHS: Paramount

Tender Mercies (1983, Antron Media Production)
Director: Bruce Beresford
Screenplay: Horton Foote
Cinematography: Russell Boyd
Cast: Robert Duvall, Tess Harper, Betty Buckley, Wilford Brimley, Ellen Barkin
100 minutes / Color / Rated PG / DVD: Starz / Anchor Bay; VHS: Republic Pictures

There's No Business like Show Business (1954, 20th Century Fox)
Director: Walter Lang
Screenplay: Phoebe Ephron, Henry Ephron, Lamar Trotti
Cinematography: Leon Shamroy; Music: Irving Berlin
Cast: Ethel Merman, Donald O'Connor, Marilyn Monroe, Dan Dailey, Johnnie Ray
117 minutes / Color/ Not Rated / DVD and VHS: 20th Century Fox

Thérèse (1986, AFC)
Director: Alain Cavalier
Screenplay: Camille de Casabianca, Alain Cavalier
Cinematography: Philippe Rousselot

FILMOGRAPHY

Cast: Catherine Mouchet, Hélène Alexandridis, Aurore Prieto, Clémence Massart
94 minutes / Color / French / Not Rated / DVD and VHS: Fox Lorber

Thérèse: The Story of Saint Thérèse of Lisieux (2006, St. Luke Productions)
Director: Leonardo Defilippis
Screenplay: Patti Defillipis, based on the writings of Saint Thérèse of Lisieux
Cinematography: Lourdes Ambrose; Music: Sister Marie Terese Sokol
Cast: Lindsay Younce, Melissa Sumpter, Leonardo Defilippis, Maggie Rose Fleck
96 minutes / Color / Rated: PG / DVD: Xenon; VHS: Not Available

The Third Miracle (1999, American Zoetrope)
Director: Agnieszka Holland
Screenplay: John Romano, Richard Vetere, based on the novel by Vetere
Cinematography: Jerzy Zielinski; Music: Jan A. P. Kaczmarek
Cast: Ed Harris, Anne Heche, Armin Mueller-Stahl, Charles Haid, Michael Rispoli
119 minutes / Color / Rated R / DVD and VHS: Sony Pictures

3 Godfathers (1948, Argosy Pictures)
Director: John Ford
Screenplay: Laurence Stallings, Frank S. Nugent, Peter B. Kyne
Cinematography: Winton C. Hoch; Music: Richard Hageman
Cast: John Wayne, Pedro Armendáriz, Harry Carey, Jr., Ward Bond, Mildred Natwick
106 minutes / Color / Not Rated / DVD: Warner Home Video; VHS: MGM (Warner)

The Trouble with Angels (1966, Columbia Pictures)
Director: Ida Lupino
Screenplay: Blanche Hanalis, based on the novel by Jane Trahey
Cinematography: Lionel Lin; Music: Jerry Goldsmith
Cast: Rosalind Russell, Hayley Mills, Camilla Sparv, Mary Wickes, June Harding
112 minutes / Color / Rated PG / DVD and VHS: Sony Pictures

True Confessions (1981, Chartoff-Winkler Productions)
Director: Ulu Grosbard
Screenplay: John Gregory Dunne, Joan Didion, based on the novel by Dunne
Cinematography: Owen Roizman; Music: Georges Delerue
Cast: Robert De Niro, Robert Duvall, Charles Durning, Kenneth McMillan, Ed Flanders
108 minutes / Color / Rated R / DVD and VHS: MGM

Viridiana (1961, Films 59)
Director: Luis Buñuel
Screenplay: Julio Alejandro, Luis Buñuel, based on the novel *Halma* by Benito Pérez Galdós
Cinematography: José F. Aguayo; Music: Gustavo Pittaluga
Cast: Silvia Pinal, Francisco Rabal, Fernando Rey, José Calvo
90 minutes / B&W / Spanish / Not Rated / DVD: Criterion Collection; VHS: Hen's Tooth
  Video

We Were Soldiers (2002, Icon Entertainment International)
Director: Randall Wallace
Screenplay: Randall Wallace, based on the book *We Were Soldiers Once…and Young* by Harold
    G. Moore and Joseph L. Galloway
Cinematography: Dean Semler; Music: Nick Glennie-Smith
Cast: Mel Gibson, Greg Kinnear, Sam Elliott, Chris Klein
138 minutes / Color / Rated PG R / DVD and VHS: Paramount

When in Rome (1952, MGM)
Director: Clarence Brown
Screenplay: Robert Buckner, Dorothy Kingsley, Charles Schnee
Cinematography: William H. Daniels; Music: Carmen Dragon
Cast: Van Johnson, Paul Douglas, Joseph Calleia, Carlo Rizzo, Tudor Owen
78 minutes / B&W / Not Rated / DVD and VHS: Not Available

Wise Blood (1979, Anthea)
Director: John Huston
Screenplay: Benedict Fitzgerald, Michael Fitzgerald, based on the novel by Flannery
    O'Connor
Cinematography: Gerry Fisher; Music: Alex North
Cast: Brad Dourif, John Huston, Harry Dean Stanton, Dan Shor, Ned Beatty
108 minutes / Color / Rated PG / DVD: Not Available; VHS: Universal Studios

Witness (1985, Paramount)
Director: Peter Weir
Screenplay: William Kelley, Pamela Wallace, Earl W. Wallace
Cinematography: John Seale; Music: Maurice Jarre
Cast: Harrison Ford, Kelly McGillis, Lukas Haas, Jan Rubes, Alexander Godunov
112 minutes / Color / Rated R / DVD and VHS: Paramount

SELECTED BIBLIOGRAPHY

Books

Barsotti, Catherine M., and Robert K. Johnston. *Finding God in the Movies: 33 Films of Reel Faith*. Grand Rapids, MI: Baker Books, 2004.

Barzun, Jacques. *From Dawn to Decadence: 500 Years of Western Cultural Life, 1500 to the Present*. New York: HarperCollins, 2000.

Baugh, Lloyd. *Imaging the Divine: Jesus and Christ-Figures in Film* (Communication, Culture & Theology series). Kansas City: Sheed and Ward, 1993.

Bergeson, Albert, and Andrew Greeley. *God in the Movies*. Edison, NJ: Transaction Publishers, 2003.

Bernard, Jean. *Priestblock 25487: A Memory of Dachau*. Bethesda, MD: Zaccheus Press, 2007.

Black, Gregory D. *The Catholic Crusade against the Movies, 1940–1975*. London: Cambridge University Press, 1998.

Blake, Richard A. *Afterimage: The Indelible Catholic Imagination of Six American Filmmakers*. Chicago: Loyola Press, 2000.

Birchard, Robert S. *Cecil B DeMille's Hollywood*. Lexington: University Press of Kentucky, 2004.

Bosco, Antoinette. *Mother Benedict: Foundress of the Abbey of Regina Laudis*. San Francisco: Ignatius Press, 2007.

Butler, Ivan. *Religion in the Cinema*. New York: A. S. Barnes & Co., 1969.

Capra, Frank. *Frank Capra: The Name Above the Title*. New York: MacMillan, 1971.

Carroll, Andrew. *Grace Under Fire: Letters of Faith in Time of War*. Colorado Springs: Waterbrook Press, 2007.

Carter, Stephen L. *The Culture of Disbelief: How American Law and Politics Trivialize Religious Devotion*. New York: Anchor Books, 1994.

Clark, Eleanor. *Rome and a Villa*. Cambridge, MA: Zoland Books, 2000.

Corey, Melinda, and George Ochoa. *The American Film Institute Desk Reference*. London: DK, 2002.

Cornwell, John. *A Thief in the Night: The Mysterious Death of Pope John Paul I*. New York: Simon & Schuster, 1989.

Couvares, Francis G., ed. *Movie Censorship and American Culture*. Washington, DC: Smithsonian Institution Press, 1996.

Craughwell, Thomas J. *Saints Behaving Badly: The Cutthroats, Crooks, Trollops, Con Men, and Devil Worshippers Who Became Saints*. New York: Doubleday, 2006.

Cunneen, Joseph. *Robert Bresson: A Spiritual Style in Film*. New York: Continuum, 2003.

Dalin, David G. *How Pope Pius XII Rescued Jews from the Nazis*. Washington, DC: Regnery, 2005.

Dans, Peter E. *Doctors in the Movies: Boil the Water and Just Say Aah*. Lansing, MI: Medi-Ed Press, 2000.

Dawkins, Richard. *The God Delusion*. New York: Houghton Mifflin, 2006.

Doherty, Thomas. *Pre-Code Hollywood: Sex, Immorality and Insurrection in American Cinema, 1930–1934*. New York: Columbia University Press, 1999.

———. *Hollywood's Censor: Joseph I. Breen and the Production Code Administration*. New York: Columbia University Press, 2007.

Donnelley, Paul. *Fade to Black: A Book of Movie Obituaries*. London: Omnibus Press, 2000.

Ebert, Roger. *Roger Ebert's Video Companion*, 1995 Edition. Kansas City: Andrews and Mc-Meel, 1994.

———. *The Great Movies II*. New York: Broadway Books, 2005.

Ehrman, Bart D. *Truth and Fiction in* The Da Vinci Code*: A Historian Reveals What We Really Know about Jesus, Mary Magdalene, and Constantine*. New York: Oxford University Press, 2004.

Eilers, Franz-Joseph. *Church and Social Communication, Basic Documents*. Manila: Logos Publications Inc., 1993.

Epstein, Edward Jay. *The Big Picture: Money and Power in Hollywood*. New York: Random House, 2005.

Fogelman, E. *Conscience and Courage: Rescuers of Jews During the Holocaust*. New York: Anchor Books. 1994.

Fraser, Peter, and Vernon Edwin Neal. *ReViewing the Movies: A Christian Response to Contemporary Film*. Wheaton, IL: Crossway Books, 2000.

Gardner, Gerald C. *The Censorship Papers: Movie Censorship Letters from the Hays Office, 1934–1968*. New York: Dodd, Mead, 1987.

George, Robert P. *Clash of Orthodoxies: Law, Religion, and Morality in Crisis*. Wilmington, DE: Intercollegiate Studies Institute, 2002.

Ghezzi, Bert. *Voices of the Saints: A Year of Readings*. New York: Doubleday, 2000.

Godden, Rumer. *A House with Four Rooms*. Whitby, North Yorkshire: Quill Publishers, 1991.

Goldberg, Bernard. *Bias: A CBS Insider Exposes How the Media Distort the News*. Washington, DC: Regnery Publishing, 2001.

Giles, Paul. "The Cinema of Catholicism: John Ford and Robert Altman." In *Unspeakable Images: Ethnicity and the American Cinema*, ed. Lester D. Friedman, (140–66. Urbana: University of Illinois Press, 1991.

Hanson, Victor Davis. *Ripples of Battle*. New York: Doubleday, 2003.

Harris, Mark. *Pictures at a Revolution: Five Movies and the Birth of the New Hollywood*. New York: Penguin Press, 2008.

Hirsen, James. *Hollywood Nation: Left Coast Lies, Old Media Spin, and the New Media Revolution*. New York: Crown Forum, 2005.

Jenkins, Philip. *The New Anti-Catholicism: The Last Acceptable Prejudice*. New York: Oxford University Press, 2003.

Johnston, Robert K. *Reel Spirituality: Theology and Film in Dialogue, Second Edition (Engaging Culture)*. Grand Rapids, MI: Baker Academic, 2006.

Kael, Pauline. *5001 Nights at the Movies*. New York: Henry Holt, 1991.

Kamen, Henry. *The Spanish Inquisition: A Historical Revision*. New Haven, CT: Yale University Press, 1998.

Kane, Paula M. "Jews and Catholics Converge: *The Song of Bernadette*" in *Catholics in the Movies*. Ed. C. McDannell. New York: Oxford University Press, 2008.

Keller, James. *To Light a Candle: The Autobiography of James Keller, Founder of the Christophers*. New York: Doubleday, 1963.

Keyser, Les and Barbara. *Hollywood and the Catholic Church: The Image of Roman Catholicism in American Movies*. Chicago: Loyola University Press, 1984.

Kuhns, Elizabeth. *The Habit: A History of the Clothing of Catholic Nuns*. New York: Doubleday, 2003.

Lang, J. Stephen. *The Bible on the Big Screen: A Guide from Silent Films to Today's Movies*. Grand Rapids, MI: Baker Books, 2007.

Lapide, Pinchas E. *Three Popes and the Jews*. New York: Hawthorn Books, 1967.

Larson, Edward J. *Summer for the Gods: The Scopes Trial and America's Continuing Debate over Science and Religion*. New York: Basic Books, 2006.

Lawler, Philip F. *The Faithful Departed: The Collapse of Boston's Catholic Culture*. New York: Encounter Books, 2008.

Leff, Leonard J., and Jerold C. Simmons. *The Dame in the Kimono: Hollywood, Censorship, and the Production Code, Revised Edition*. Lexington: University of Kentucky Press, 2001.

Leonard, Richard. *Movies That Matter: Reading Film Through the Lens of Faith*. Chicago: Loyola Press, 2006.

Levi, Primo. *Survival in Auschwitz*. New York: Touchstone, 1996.

Lewerenz, Spencer, and Barbara Nicolosi, eds. *Behind the Screen: Hollywood Insiders on Faith, Film, and Culture*. Grand Rapids, MI: Baker Books, 2005.

Lewis, Clive Staples. *A Grief Observed*. New York: HarperOne, 2001.

——. *Letters to Malcolm Chiefly on Prayer*. New York: Harvest Books, 2002.

——. *Surprised by Joy*. New York: Houghton Mifflin Harcourt, 1993.

Lockwood, Robert P., ed. *Anti-Catholicism in American Culture*. Huntington, IN: Our Sunday Visitor, 2000.

Lopate, Phillip, ed. *American Movie Critics: An Anthology from the Silents Until Now*. New York: The Library of America, 2005.

Lourdeaux, Lee. *Italian and Irish Filmmakers in America: Ford, Capra, Coppola, and Scorsese*. Philadelphia: Temple University Press, 1993.

Madden, Thomas F. *The New Concise History of the Crusades (Critical Issues in History)*. Lanham, MD: Rowman & Littlefield, 2005.

Mahoney, Roger M. *Film Makers, Film Viewers, Their Challenges and Opportunities*. Boston: St. Paul Books and Media, 1992.

Malone, Peter. *Catholicism and Cinema in Companion to Religion and Film*. Ed. William Blizek. London: Continuum, 2009.

——. "The Roman Catholic Church and the Cinema (1967 to the Present)." In *The Routledge Companion to Religion and Film*, ed. John C. Lyden. New York: Routledge, 2009.

——. *Through a Catholic Lens: Religious Perspectives from 19 Directors from Around the World*. New York: Rowman & Littlefield, 2007.

Malone, Peter, with Rose Pacatte. *Lights, Camera . . . Faith! A Movie Lover's Guide to Scripture.* Boston: Pauline Books, 2001.

———. *Lights, Camera . . . Faith! A Movie Lectionary, Cycles A, B, C; The Ten Commandments; Beatitudes and Deadly Sins.* Boston: Pauline Media, (2001–2008).

Maltin, Leonard. *Leonard Maltin's 2005 Movie & Video Guide.* New York: New American Library, 2004.

Marius, Richard. "A Man For All Seasons," in *Past Imperfect: History According to the Movies.* Ed. M. C. Carnes. New York: Henry Holt, 1995.

Marlett, Jeffrey. "Life on the Frontier: *Lilies in the Field* (1963)," in *Catholics in the Movies.* Ed. C. McDannell. New York: Oxford University Press, 2008.

Marsh, Clive, and Gaye Ortiz, eds. *Explorations in Theology and Film.* Oxford: Blackwell, 1997.

May, John R. *New Image of Religious Film.* Kansas City, MO: Sheed and Ward, 1997.

Medved, Michael. *Hollywood vs. America: Popular Culture and the War on Traditional Values.* New York: Harper Collins, 1992.

Mezrich, Ben. *Bringing Down the House: The Inside Story of Six MIT Students Who Took Vegas.* New York: Free Press, 2002.

Morris, Charles R. *American Catholic: The Saints and Sinners Who Built America's Most Powerful Church.* New York: Random House, 1997.

Murphy, Francis J. *Père Jacques: Resplendent in Victory.* Washington, DC: ICS Publications, 1998.

Occhiogrosso, Peter. *Once a Catholic: Prominent Catholics and Ex-Catholics Discuss the Influence of the Church on Their Lives and Work.* Boston: Houghton Mifflin, 1987.

O'Donnell, Edward T. *Ship Ablaze: The Tragedy of the Steamboat General Slocum.* New York: Random House, 2003.

Olson, Carl E., and Sandra Miesel. *The Da Vinci Hoax: Exposing the Errors on* The Da Vinci Code. San Francisco: Ignatius Press, 2004.

O'Sullivan, John. *The President, the Pope, and the Prime Minister: Three Who Changed the World.* Washington, DC: Regnery, 2006.

Pacatte, Rose. "Shaping Morals, Shifting Views: Have the Ratings Systems Influenced How (Christian) America Sees Movies?" in *Reframing Religion and Film,* ed. Robert Johnston. Grand Rapids, MI: Baker Academic, 2007.

Poitier, Sidney. *The Measure of a Man: A Spiritual Autobiography.* New York: Harper San Francisco, 2000.

Reeves, T. C. *America's Bishop: The Life and Times of Fulton Sheen.* San Francisco: Encounter Books, 2001.

Reinhartz, Adele. *Jesus of Hollywood.* New York: Oxford University Press, 2007.

Riley-Smith, Jonathan. *What Were the Crusades?* San Francisco: Ignatius Press, 2002.

Rose, Michael S. *Goodbye, Good Men: How Liberals Brought Corruption into the Catholic Church.* Washington DC: Regnery, 2002.

Schumach, Murray. *The Face on the Cutting-Room Floor: The Story of Movie and Television Censorship.* New York: William Morrow, 1964.

Sennett, Ted. *Hollywood's Golden Year, 1939.* New York: Saint Martin's Press, 1989.

Shlaes, Amity. *The Forgotten Man.* New York: Harper Collins, 2007.

Spencer Robert. *The Politically Incorrect Guide to Islam (and the Crusades)*. Washington, DC: Regnery, 2005

Spoto, Donald. *Enchantment: The Life of Audrey Hepburn*. New York: Harmony Books, 2006.

Stahr, Walter. *John Jay: Founding Father*. London: Hambledon & London. 2005.

Stern, Richard C., Clayton N. Jefford, and Guerric Debona. *Savior on the Silver Screen*. Wahwah, NJ: Paulist Press, 1999.

Stone, Bryan P. *Faith and Film: Theological Themes at the Cinema*. Atlanta: Chalice Books, 2000.

Sykes, Charles J. *A Nation of Victims*. New York: St. Martin's Griffin, 1993.

Tatum, W. Barnes. *Jesus at the Movies: A Guide to the First Hundred Years*. Santa Rosa, CA: Polebridge Press, 2004.

Thompson, Francis. *The Hound of Heaven in Seven Centuries of Verse: English and American*, 2nd ed. Ed by A. J. M. Smith. New York: Charles Scribner's Sons, 1957.

Twain, Mark. "Personal Recollections of Joan of Arc." In *Mark Twain Historical Romances*. New York: Library of America, Penguin Putnam, 1994.

2005 Report on the Implementation of the Charter for the Protection of Children and Young People. Washington, DC: United States Conference of Bishops, March 2006.

Vieira, Mark. *Sin in Soft-Focus: Pre-Code Hollywood*. New York: Harry Abrams, 1999.

Walker, John. *Halliwell's Video & DVD Guide 2005*. London: Harper Collins, 2004.

Wallace, Lew. *Preface to The First Christmas*. New York: Harper and Brothers, 1902.

Walsh, Frank. *Sin and Censorship: The Catholic Church and the Motion Picture Industry*. New Haven, CT: Yale University Press, 1996.

Walsh, Richard. *Reading the Gospels in the Dark: Portrayals of Jesus in Film*. Philadelphia: Trinity Press, 2003.

Welborn, Amy. *De-Coding Da Vinci: The Facts behind the Fiction of* The Da Vinci Code. Huntington, IN: Our Sunday Visitor, 2004.

Wilk, Max. *The Making of* The Sound of Music. New York: Routledge, New York 2007.

Winchell, Mark Royden, *God, Man & Hollwood: Politically Incorrect Cinema from* The Birth of a Nation *to* The Passion of the Christ. Wilmington, DE: Intercollegiate Studies Institute (ISI) Books, 2008.

Yallop, David A. *In God's Name: An Investigation into the Murder of John Paul I*. New York: Bantam Books, 1984.

Articles

Allen, Charlotte. "Hollywood's 'Amazing' Glaze," *Wall Street Journal* (February 23, 2007), p. W11.

Alleva, Richard. "Dames at War: The Messenger and Dogma," *Commonweal* (December 17, 1999), pp. 17–18.

Baer, William. "Breach," *Crisis* (April 2007), pp. 58–59.

Bernstein, Adam. "Academy Award-Winning Actor Paul Newman Dies at 83," Washington post.com (September 27, 2008).

Bernstein, Richard. "The Hollywood Love Affair with Tibet: How One Fantasy Land Holds onto the Heart of Another," *New York Times* (March 19, 1997), p. B1.

Bottum, Joseph. "The Death of Protestant America: A Political Theory of the Protestant Mainline," *First Things* (August/September 2008), pp. 23–33.

———. "What Happened at Fatima," *The Weekly Standard*, (March 7, 2005), pp. 31–33.

———. "When the Swallows Come Back to Capistrano: Catholic Culture in America," *First Things* (October 2006), pp. 27–40.

Burris, Joe. "For 'Grace' director Apted, Politics were Paramount," *Baltimore Sun* (February 25, 2007), p. 3E.

Campbell, Colleen Carroll. "The Enduring Costs of John F. Kennedy's Compromise," *Catholic World Report* (February, 2007).

Catholic News Service. "Last Jesuit Involved in Exorcism That Inspired Movie Dies," *Catholic Review* (March 24, 2005).

Cider House Rules Production Notes.

Cloud, Barbara. "Dolores Hart: How a Movie Actress Left Hollywood for a Contract with God," *Post-Gazette* (April 08, 1998).

Colvert Colin. "Movie review: 'Elizabeth' a golden delight." October 12, 2007. www.startribune.com.

Conant Jennet. "Film; 'Chocolat' Is Only Icing on Her Cake," February 18, 2001, www.nytimes.com.

Dalin, David G. "History as Bigotry: Daniel Goldhagen Slanders the Catholic Church," *Weekly Standard* (February 10, 2003), pp. 38–41.

D'Andrea, Nicole. "Ex-Hollywood Starlet Recalls Icon 30 Years after His Death," *Register Citizen* (August 16, 2007).

Dans, Peter E. "Medical Students and Abortion. Reconciling Personal Beliefs and Professional Roles at One Medical School," *Academic Medicine*, (1992), 67: 207–11.

———. "Abortion in the Movies," *Pharos*, Spring 2008, 70: 32–36.

Davidson, Vicki McClure. "Caustic Critiques II: The Best and Worst Film Reviews," Demand Entertainment Inc., 2007.

Dead Man Walking Production Notes.

Denby, David. "Elizabeth," *New Yorker*, November 23, 1998, www.newyorker.com.

Dreher, Rod. "Lights, Camera, God II," *Weekly Standard* (May 1, 2000).

D'Souza, Dinesh. "The Decade of Greed that Wasn't," *Forbes Magazine*, November 3, 1997 www.dineshdsouza.com

Edwards, Bruce L. "*Shadowlands*: A Review," cslewis.drzeus.net.

Einstein, A. *Time* magazine (December 23, 1940).

Evans, Christopher G. "Jews Against Anti-Christian Defamation," *Human Events* (September 19, 2005), p. 26.

Forest, Jim. "Entertaining Angels: The Dorothy Day Story," *Catholic Worker* website.

Fund, J. "Freedom's Team: How Reagan, Thatcher, and John Paul II Won the Cold War." *Wall Street Journal* (June 7, 2004).

Gordon, Mary. "How Ireland Hid Its Own Dirty Laundry," *New York Times*, reprinted in *The Sun* (August 3, 2003), p. 9f.

Greydanus, Steven D. "The *Magdalene Sisters* Controversy," www.decentfilms.com, 2003.

———. "Off With Its Head: *Elizabeth* Sequel Pronounces Sentence on the Catholic Church," *National Catholic Register* (October 31, 2007), p. B3.

Harris, Aaron Keith. "*Amazing Grace* Leaves Out Hero's Grist of Faith," *Baltimore Examiner* (March 2, 2007), p. 19.

Hoberman, J. "Film: When the Spice of Choice was Sin," *New York Times* (August 15, 1999).

Hornaday, Ann. "Catching up with Kevin Smith: *Dogma* from a Devout Blasphemer," *Baltimore Sun* (November 14, 1999), p. 3F.

Hubbard, Rob. St. Thomas More Website, www.apostles.com/thomasmore.html.

James, Caryn. "Film Financed by a Religious Group," *New York Times* (February 3, 1996), pp. 15, 18.

Jeffers, D. "DeMille's Lost City and 'The Ten Commandments,'" January 2006, www.siffblog.com/reviews.

Johnson, Bridget. "Hollywood's Last Taboo," *Wall Street Journal* (July 13, 2005), p. D10.

Jones, Kenneth C. "The Incredible Shrinking Catholic Church," *Catholic World News* (May 2003), Trinity Communications, www.cwnews.com.

Karnick, S. T. "Leo Mc Carey: A Director to Remember," *Weekly Standard* (November, 8, 1999), pp. 36–39.

Kellow, Brian. "The Craftsman," *Opera News* (September 2008), pp. 38–41.

Klavan, Andrew. "Is Hollywood Too Timid for the War on Terror?" January 26, 2007. www.latimes.com.

Koehler, R. "Bella," www.variety.com/review/VE1117932633.html/category/id=31&CS=1, January 31, 2007.

Kroll, Jack, and Emily Yoffe. "The Godfather Part III," *Newsweek*, v. 116 (December 24, 1990), pp. 58–60.

Langfitt, Frank. "*Saved*: Fast Times at Christian High," *Baltimore Sun* (June 13, 2004), p. 2F.

Lapin, Rabbi Daniel. "Why Jews Should Pray for a Christian America," *American Enterprise* (March/April, 1999), pp. 70–72.

Last, Jonathan V. "Lost About *Saved!*" *Wall Street Journal* (June 18, 2004), p. W17.

Lorant, R. "'Schindler' Becomes a High School Lesson," *Baltimore Sun* (March 28, 1994), p. 6D.

Malkin, Michelle. "Protestant and Catholic Terrorists in PC School Drills," *Washington Times* National Weekly Edition (April 9, 2007), p. 30.

Maltby, Richard. "More Sinned Against than Sinning: The Fabrications of 'Pre-Code Cinema,'" *Senses of Cinema* (November 2003), www.sensesofcinema.com.

Manzi, Jim. "The Origin of the Species, and Everything Else," *National Review* (October 8, 2007), pp. 42–44, 46.

Marchioni, "Sister M. on the Church and the Holocaust: Excerpts from Books and Periodicals on the Subject in 'The Truth about Pope Pius XII,'" www.catholicleague.org.

Maslin, Janet. "Amour and High Dudgeon in a Castle of One's Own," *New York Times*, (November 6, 1998).

———. "Artificiality Vanquishes an Authenticity Issue," *New York Times* (October 18, 1996).

Mesiel, Sandra. "Dismantling *The Da Vinci Code*," *Crisis* (September 2003) pp. 18–21.

Middleton, Barbara. "From the Glitter of Hollywood to the Quiet of a Convent," *National Catholic Register* (July 10–16, 2005).

Morris, Wesley. "This 'Order' Will Put You to Sleep," September 9, 2003. www.boston.com.

Neuhaus, Richard John. "The Catholic Moment That Was," *First Things* (April 2003), pp. 79–81.

New York Times Editorials Praising Pope Pius XII (December 25, 1941, and December 25, 1942), www.catholicleague.org.

Niebuhr, Gustav. "Spiritual Values Are In, But, Please, No Sermonizing," *New York Times* (Sunday, September 1, 1996), pp. 7, 14.

Novecosky, Patrick. "Living La Vida *Bella* on OCT. 26." *National Catholic Register* (October 31, 2007).

Ollis, Todd. "The Passion of Renee Maria Falconetti," www.floyd.edu/webzine.

O'Malley, Sheila. "The Books: 'Sister Mary Ignatius Explains It All For You' (Christopher Durang)," June 29, 2005, www.sheilaomalley.com.

Pacepa, Ion Mihai. "Moscow's Assault on the Vatican," *National Review Online* (January 25, 2007).

Pelikan, Jaroslav. "Martin Luther" in *World Book Encyclopedia*, 1975.

Pew Forum on Religion & Public Life/ US Religious Landscape Survey, 2008.

Philips, Gene. "'C' is for Condemned," Letter to Editor, *New York Times Book Review* (December 19, 1999), p. 4.

———. "Jesuit Father Knows Movies and Directors Best," Interview in *Catholic New World* (April 16, 2001).

Playboy Interview: "Ingmar Bergman: A Candid Conversation with Sweden's One-Man New Wave of Cinematic Sorcery," *Playboy* 11:61–68. 1964.

Podheretz, Norman. "America the Ugly," *Wall Street Journal* (September 11, 2007), p. A19.

Ramsey, Nancy. "An Abuse Scandal with Nuns As Villains," *New York Times* (July 27, 2003), pp. E7, 12.

Randall, Beth. "Illuminating Lives: Dorothy Day, 1996," www.cs.drexel.edu.

Redzioch, W. "The Christian Rabbi," *Urbi et Orbi Communications*, New Hope, KY. June–July 2002, www.catholicculture.org.

Rich, Frank. "Mel Gibson's Martyrdom Complex," *New York Times* (August 3, 2003), Section 2, p. 1.

Ripley, Amanda. "In Plain Sight," *Time* magazine, April 22, 2002, www.time.com.

Rosenthal, A. M. "Questions from West 47th Street: Why So Much about Christians?" *New York Times* (June 10, 1997), p. A39.

Rothstein, M. "Ingmar Bergman, Master Filmmaker, Dies at 89," *New York Times* (July 30, 2007).

Rutler, George W. "The New Anti-Catholicism: The Last Acceptable Prejudice" book review, *National Review* (June 2, 2003).

Sjoerdsma, Ann G. "A Question of Truth: Lorenzo Carcaterra's Memoir of Violence, Abuse and Deceit in New York's Hell's Kitchen Inspires Disbelief," *Virginian-Pilot* (August 27, 1995).

Special Edition on Sexual Abuse in the Catholic Church. *Journal of Criminal Justice and Behavior*, 2008, 35: 545–678.

Sragow, Michael. "Making a Plea for Tolerance in the *Kingdom*; Ridley Scott Blasts Blind Faith in Epic Film about the Crusades," *Baltimore Sun* (May 1, 2005), p. 2F.

———. "Religious Disorder: Gripping, Searing *Magdalene Sisters*' Confronts the Hypocrisy of a Church that Victimized the 'Fallen' Women It Purported to Save," *Baltimore Sun* (February 22, 2003), p. D1.

Steinfels, Peter. "The Priest Who Helped Inspire *On the Waterfront*," *New York Times*, (May 3, 2003), p. A18.

Wamble, M. D. "Jesuit Father Knows Movies and Directors Best," www.catholicnewworld .com/archive/cnw/2000/0416/inter_0416.htm.

Weigel, George. "The Sixties, Again and Again," *First Things* (April 2008), pp. 32–38.

Weiskopf, Chris. "Cheering *The Code* after Punching *The Passion*," *The American Enterprise* (June 2006), p. 47.

Wellman, Sam. "Gladys Aylward," www.heroesofhistory.com.

Wilkinson, T. "Vatican Confronts Shortage of Exorcists." *Baltimore Sun*, February 18, 2005, p. 21A.

Wolfe, Tom. "The 'Me' Decade and the Third Great Awakening," *New York* (August 23, 1976), pp. 26–40.

Other Sources

Catholic Online

The Catholic Encyclopedia

Cecil B. DeMille: American Epic (TV Documentary), 2004

IMDb

Latin Mass

The Patron Saints Index

Rotten Tomatoes

Wikipedia

CDs

Cinemania 96 Microsoft CD

Ebert, R. Unless otherwise noted, all references to Roger Ebert are to his reviews collected in Cinemania 96 Microsoft CD and RogerEbert.com Great Movies.

Kael, P. All references to Pauline Kael are to her reviews collected in Cinemania 96 Microsoft CD.

Maltin, L. All references to Leonard Maltin are to his reviews collected in Cinemania 96 Microsoft CD.

INDEX

ABOUT THE AUTHOR

Peter E. Dans is an associate professor of Medicine at the Johns Hopkins University School of Medicine, with expertise in medical ethics, health policy, geriatrics, and infectious diseases. He is a graduate of Manhattan College and Columbia University College of Physicians and Surgeons. Since 1990, he has reviewed films as the Physician at the Movies for *Pharos*, the quarterly journal of the Alpha Omega Alpha Honor Medical Society.

Dans is the author of *Doctors in the Movies: Boil the Water and Just Say Aah!* about how doctors have been portrayed in films from 1931 to 2000; *Perry's Baltimore Adventure: A Birds-Eye View of Charm City*, a children's book about the peregrine falcons that nested on a Baltimore skyscraper; and *Life on the Lower East Side: Photographs by Rebecca Lepkoff 1937–1950*, a memoir/photography book about growing up on New York's Lower East Side in a now lost neighborhood.